Everyday Morality

AN INTRODUCTION TO APPLIED ETHICS

Second Edition

Mike W. Martin

CHAPMAN UNIVERSITY

Wadsworth Publishing Company

BELMONT, CALIFORNIA
A DIVISION OF WADSWORTH, INC.

PHILOSOPHY EDITOR: *Tammy Goldfeld*
EDITORIAL ASSISTANT: *Kelly Zavislak*
PRODUCTION EDITOR: *Michelle Filippini*
MANAGING DESIGNER: *Cloyce Wall*
PRINT BUYER: *Diana Spence*
TEXT DESIGNER: *Luba Yudovich*
COPY EDITOR: *Paul Green*
COVER: *William Reuter Design*
COMPOSITOR: *Margarite Reynolds, Wadsworth Digital Productions*
COVER ART: *"Embrace of Peace 1," by George Tooker*
PRINTER: *Malloy Lithographing, Inc.*

I(T)P ™

International Thomson Publishing
The trademark ITP is used under license.

Printed in the United States of America

1 2 3 4 5 6 7 8 9 10—99 98 97 96 95

Library of Congress Cataloging-in-Publication Data
Martin, Mike W.,
    Everyday morality : an introduction to applied ethics / Mike W. Martin.
    —2nd ed.
      p.   cm.
    Includes bibliographical references and index.
    ISBN 0-534-20178-4
    1. Applied ethics.   I. Title.
BJ1031M3156 1995
170—dc20   94-11022

Dedicated to Sonia Renée Martin and Nicole Marie Martin

Brief Contents

Detailed Contents

Preface

This book is an introduction to applied ethics, that is, to the philosophy of morality as it applies to practical moral needs. It focuses on the moral concerns of everyday life more than on general social issues (although many of these are explored as well). Moral character is explored in all its dimensions: virtues, vices, attitudes, emotions, commitments, and personal relationships, in addition to right and wrong conduct.

Applied moral philosophy, as approached here, seeks to clarify, organize, and enrich our grasp of practical moral interests. It seeks to sharpen the ideas that we use as tools in coping responsibly with our daily lives. And it explores contrasting moral perspectives that increase moral understanding.

I have tried to maintain contact with the wellspring of common moral experience, or at least overlapping moral understanding, that enables us to discuss moral issues with one another. I have also attempted to heed Molière's injunction to "humanize your talk, and speak to be understood" (the counsel he offers to writers in *The Critique of the School for Wives*). The aim of this book is to stimulate personal reflection and group dialogue rather than to offer solutions. This remains true even in places where I set forth my own views instead of merely summarizing those of others.

The book contains twenty-three chapters organized by unifying themes into six parts. Numerous discussion topics and suggested readings are provided at the end of each chapter. Some of the readings discussed and recommended are works of literature and social science, reflecting the interdisciplinary approach present in much of the book.

Second Edition

Well over a third of the material in the second edition is new. Six chapters have been added on the topics of drug abuse, suicide and euthanasia, abortion, interpersonal conflicts, the environment, and moral reasons. Several additional chapters have been extensively revised and reorganized. There are expanded discussions on many topics, including ethical relativism, egoism, self-respect, self-knowledge, authenticity, affirmative action, surrogate motherhood, and animals. All chapters contain some revisions, including fresh case studies, additional discussion topics, and updated bibliographies.

Acknowledgments

In writing the first edition of this book, I received financial support in 1984 and 1985 from an Arnold L. and Lois S. Graves Award from Pomona College, administered under the auspices of the American Council of Learned Societies. Chapman University gave me a sabbatical leave and a reduced teaching load to allow me to work on the manuscript.

Shannon Snow Martin shaped the book in many ways, suggesting topics and illustrations, discussing arguments and approaches, and providing insights. My students provided a valuable stimulus, as did my colleagues Virginia Warren and Joseph Runzo. Anita Storck displayed an array of virtues in helping with the typing and in contributing to a supportive work environment.

I received invaluable help from reviewers who provided comments that proved enormously helpful in improving the manuscript. For the first edition these reviewers were: Shane Andre, California State University, Long Beach; John Arthur, State University of New York at Binghamton; Joseph Des Jardins, College of St. Benedict; Ronald F. Duska, Rosemont College; Thomas K. Flint, North Idaho College; Ruth B. Heizer, Georgetown College; Craig Kei Ihara, California State University, Fullerton; Tom Moody, California State College, San Bernardino; Ellen K. Suckiel, University of California, Santa Cruz; and Joel Zimbelman, California State University, Chico.

For the second edition these reviewers were: Judith A. Boss, University of Rhode Island; Roger Ebertz, University of Dubuque; Michael S. Pritchard, Western Michigan University; Stephen Schwarz, University of Rhode Island; Hilquias Cavalcanti, University of Richmond.

I especially wish to thank my wife, Shannon Snow Martin, and my mother, Ruth Lochhead Martin, for their support and for their love.

Everyday Morality

AN INTRODUCTION TO APPLIED ETHICS

PART ONE

Character, Conduct, and Ethical Theories

How can we make ourselves morally better? Can we make ourselves morally better? These are questions the philosopher should try to answer.[1]

To do philosophy is to explore one's own temperament, and yet at the same time to attempt to discover the truth.[2]

Iris Murdoch

We are often more at ease discussing the global moral issues affecting society at large than we are exploring the moral texture of everyday life. Why is that? Larger social issues such as capital punishment, genetic engineering, and nuclear deterrence evoke our genuine concern, and sometimes they require our immediate action. Because we lack the authority to settle these issues, however, we can maintain a comfortable distance between us and them.

In contrast, personal responsibility for the moral aspects of day-to-day living is more direct, persistent, and urgent. Each day, fundamental moral considerations affect our lives in commonplace ways. Perhaps today we told or laughed at a joke expressing sexist attitudes we would eagerly disavow. Or maybe we were sufficiently angry at a friend to harbor sweet fantasies of revenge that, if implemented, would inflict extraordinarily cruel retribution. Possibly we were envious of a co-worker and expressed the envy in a way that undermined mutual respect. We may have failed to respond to an act of kindness with the gratitude dictated by common decency. Perhaps we abused alcohol, drugs, or food with a compulsiveness that made us wonder whether we respected ourselves anymore.

Social-political morality concerns global issues about the kinds of social policies and institutions that are desirable. *Everyday morality*, by contrast, concerns the kinds of persons we aspire to be in our daily relationships with others. Are we grateful and generous, or envious and filled with spite? Are we conscientious and concerned with helping others, or weak of will and readily self-deceived about the good we can do? Are we trying to become more sensitive to the suffering of other people and animals, or gradually hardening ourselves through indifference and vanity? Do we strive to be honest and open, or to avoid hurting others' feelings, and which do we choose when we cannot do both? Do we genuinely respect ourselves and other people?

Words like *generous, conscientious*, and *honest* refer to morally good character traits—*virtues*. Words like *envious, insensitive*, and *vain* refer to morally bad character traits—*vices*.* *Character* is the pattern of virtues and vices revealed in the life and relationships of an individual.

Some dictionaries define morality as entirely a matter of right and wrong actions, thereby emphasizing conduct over character. Until recently, philosophers also tended to focus on conduct in their attempts to define morality. This book seeks to give balanced attention to character and conduct, as well as to the relationships in which they are expressed. Accordingly, our first task is to understand the connections between good persons, right action, and meaningful relationships.

Chapter 1 introduces some of the complexities of moral reasoning about character and conduct. Morality is distinguished from ethics, which is the philosophical study of morality. Criticisms are raised against reducing moral reasons to matters of subjective feelings, self-interest, social customs, or religion. Chapter 2 explores the moral role of authenticity, which is being true to oneself in a way that implies self-fulfillment, creativity, and autonomy. Moral autonomy means reasoning and acting on the basis of moral concern, sometimes in creative ways. The study of ethics strengthens moral autonomy, if the student has a foundation of moral development. Chapter 3 introduces several major theories about virtue, and Chapter 4 sketches the main theories about right action. These key concepts and theories will be used throughout the book.

---

*In some contexts, the words *virtue* and *vice* have an old-fashioned ring, perhaps reminding us of a preoccupation with chastity or priggish forms of behavior. In other contexts, *vice* brings to mind vice squads fighting drug addiction and prostitution. We shall ignore these connotations.

CHAPTER 1

Moral Reasons

At 3:20 A.M. Kitty Genovese was returning from her work as a bar manager to her home in a middle-class neighborhood in Kew Gardens, Queens (New York). After parking within a hundred feet of her apartment, she noticed a man hiding in the shadows of the parking lot. Alarmed, she turned in the direction of a police call box, but before she reached it the man caught up with her and stabbed her with a knife. She screamed, "Oh, my God, he stabbed me! Please help me! Please help me!"[1]

Her screams awoke thirty-eight people living in a ten-story apartment house overlooking the well-lit scene. One man yelled, "Let that girl alone!" No one else did anything. The attacker, who was a complete stranger to Kitty Genovese, was scared away by the lights that went on, the windows that opened, and the excited talk that ensued. He walked toward his car but a few minutes later returned to find Kitty Genovese staggering toward her apartment. He then stabbed her again, and she again screamed, "I'm dying! I'm dying!" And again no one did anything. The man went to his car and drove away, only to return yet a third time. Kitty Genovese was still alive. This time he killed her.

Over half an hour passed from the first to the third, fatal stabbing. When the police were finally called, they arrived within two minutes. Any of the thirty-eight witnesses had plenty of time to prevent the murder by making a phone call. This event took place in 1964, but each day newspapers and television report additional horrors that cumulatively suggest a serious erosion of moral values in our society and which raise troubling questions about personal responsibility.

What Is Morality?

What are moral values, and what are the moral reasons for conduct and character which they generate? Each of us can offer a list of examples. The Kitty Genovese tragedy reminds us that morality implies not being cruel and also helping others in desperate need, at least when we can do so with no more inconvenience than making a phone call. We can also bring to mind familiar rules about honesty ("Don't lie"), fidelity ("Keep your promises"), fairness ("Do your share"), respect for property ("Don't steal"), and so on.

Providing a comprehensive definition of morality, however, turns out to be a complicated task. Morality concerns what we should become, how we should relate to others, and how we should act. This "should," however, means *morally* should; it is not concerned with other kinds of "shoulds," such as what should be done in order to, say, start a car or achieve some other definite end. This definition of morality is circular and somewhat empty, then, because we have essentially used the word we are trying to define.

The moment we invoke more focused concepts to characterize morality, we move toward theories that are controversial. Each of the following definitions, for example, suggests a particular theory which may be open to challenge: Morality is a matter of respecting human rights; morality is fulfilling our duties to others; morality concerns the most important values, which should override all others (such as the values of art); morality is obeying God's commandments; morality centers around the self-fulfillment of all persons.

For now, let us say that morality concerns the recognition of the inherent value of people (both others and ourselves), a value which is not reducible to how others benefit us. The stranger who attacked Kitty Genovese represents an extreme failure to value persons, as do sociopaths in general, that is, individuals who can murder or steal without any sense of wrongdoing or guilt. Morality also involves sensitivity to the suffering of animals.

Morality concerns how we should act, but also concerns the kinds of persons we should become, the kinds of relationships we should have, and the kinds of communities and institutions we should promote. It calls for *sensitivity* to people as morally significant creatures who sometimes deserve esteem, compassion, and support and who sometimes experience guilt, shame, vulnerability, and despair. It involves *appreciating* those aspects of situations which are relevant to valuing persons (and animals). It requires *understanding* our emotions and commitments in a way that reveals their moral significance and that is *responsive* to the worth of others. Appreciation, sensitivity, understanding, and responsiveness are not mere means to "doing the right thing." Instead, they constitute our *character*—the moral substance of who we are.

Morality is complex. It involves factual uncertainty, vagueness, conflicting reasons, and conflicting perspectives. *Factual uncertainty* means that we are often unsure of the facts relevant to applying moral values. Do the screams I hear indicate a serious assault which should concern me or a family squabble with which it is none of my business to get involved?

Vagueness surrounds many moral principles. Precisely what is cruelty? Exactly how much are we obligated to help others in desperate need? It is perfectly clear that we should not wantonly inflict suffering on others, as did the stranger who attacked Kitty Genovese. It seems clear enough, too, that we ought to be willing to phone the police to protect someone from being murdered. But how much more is required of us by way of not hurting or of helping others? Did the thirty-eight witnesses have a responsibility to undertake any personal risk in order to save Kitty Genovese?

Conflicting reasons arise because morality involves many different reasons. These reasons often come into conflict, creating *moral dilemmas*. Moral dilemmas are situations in which two or more moral reasons point to different courses of action. For example, should a student report a friend who cheats on an exam at a school with a strong honor code that requires reporting cheaters? Again, how should we balance our obligation to help others in desperate need against our responsibilities to our family and to ourselves? What if one of the thirty-eight witnesses had directly confronted the assailant and had been killed, leaving a spouse and three children? Often it is impossible to rank moral rules in priority as a means of resolving moral dilemmas.

Conflicting perspectives arise in part because it is often permissible to emphasize specific moral reasons differently in our conduct. In large measure, moral values center on our relationships with other people, and yet people may have contrasting understandings of moral values. For example, once we move beyond our agreement about the wrongness of wanton killing, torture, and rape, we may have very different outlooks on euthanasia, punishment, and sexual conduct. Let us acknowledge at the outset that morality leaves room for differences among reasonable persons who share overlapping, though not identical, ways of understanding moral reasons.

Applied Ethics

Ethics, as we shall use the term, is moral philosophy: the philosophical study of moral values. It embraces four main goals or interests: (1) *clarification* of important moral ideas and issues; (2) *critical assessment* of moral claims by testing their truth, justification, and adequacy through argument; (3) development of a *comprehensive vision* of moral ideas and principles by uncovering their interconnections and their roles in our lives; and (4) *moral guidance*, sometimes via simple principles, but more often through improved practical judgment about what we should aspire to be, what forms of relationships are desirable, and how we should seek those ends.

Philosophical ethics encompasses general and applied ethics. (See Figure 1.1.) *General ethics* deals with the more abstract theoretical issues, such as those touched on in the remainder of this chapter and in Chapters 3 and 4. *Applied ethics* (or *practical ethics*) focuses on more practical concerns. The distinction between general and applied ethics is rough. Wherever helpful, applied ethics integrates the comprehensive theories of general ethics, but its aim is practical clarity and guidance rather than the development and testing of general theories. Applied ethics is the activity of clarifying, organizing, and occasionally refining moral ideas with the goal of enriching moral experience and judgment.

Some issues in applied ethics pertain to public policy and the professions. For example, in recent decades entirely new specializations in applied ethics have arisen in such diverse fields as medicine, business, law, engineering, environmental policies, and the media and journalism. Other issues focus on the more mundane needs of individuals in shaping their characters, maintaining desirable forms of relationships, and exercising responsible conduct in everyday life. These everyday issues are emphasized in this book.

Before proceeding, we should take note of further meanings of the word *ethics*, other than the philosophical study of moral values. Sometimes the word is used to classify moral issues, experiences, judgments, and so on, as a category of human interest distinct from law, religion, art, science, economics, or sports. In this sense, for example, an ethical controversy is one involv-

FIGURE 1.1   *Branches of Philosophical Ethics*

ing moral reasons, and an ethical judgment is one using moral concepts or backed by moral reasons.

In another sense, *ethics* refers to the particular moral outlook of a group or an individual. Thus, we speak of the Protestant work ethic, the ethics of Albert Schweitzer, and the ethics of Victorian England. This usage relates to the Greek word *ethos*, which means customs or characteristic habits (just as the Latin root of the word *morals* is *mores*, meaning customs).

In yet another sense the word *ethical* has strongly positive connotations, referring to admirable character traits and morally correct judgments and acts. This honorific or praising meaning applies when we say that a friend acted ethically or when we call Abraham Lincoln an ethical person. The intended contrast is with unethical conduct or immoral character.

Finally, *ethics* can refer to the scientific study of moral values. When scientists study morality, they seek to describe the beliefs and conduct of individuals and cultures, and to explain why these beliefs and conduct arise. The tasks of describing and causally explaining are part of psychology, sociology, anthropology, and sociobiology (the study of genetic origins of social behavior and attitudes). Although we will distinguish between the philosophical and the scientific study of morality, note that these fields are interrelated and mutually enriching. In fact, from time to time we will draw upon psychology, as, for example, when we discuss moral development in Chapter 2.

We can now sharpen our understanding of moral values and moral reasons by responding to several forms of *reductionism*, that is, attempts to reduce moral reasons to something else. Examples of such theories are:

Emotivism—the view that morality is subjective, determined by the individual's feelings.

Ethical Egoism—the view that morality is what's good for oneself.

Ethical Relativism—the view that morals are relative; when in Rome do as the Romans do.

Divine Command Ethics—the view that morality is defined by God's commandments.

These views are familiar in everyday life and are also discussed in ethical theory. Each contains an element of truth which can give it an initial attractiveness.

Emotivism

According to emotivism, to say that an act is right, or a person is good, is merely to emote; that is, to show or express emotions. There are no moral truths; there are only feelings. Moreover, no one's feelings are more justified than another's, once the facts about a topic are made clear. Morality is entirely subjective.

The foundation for this view, although not the view itself, was articulated in the eighteenth century by David Hume (1711–1776).

> Take any action allow'd to be vicious: Willful murder, for instance. Examine it in all lights, and see if you can find that matter of fact, or real existence, which you call *vice*.... The vice entirely escapes you, as long as you consider the object. You never can find it, till you turn your reflexion into your own breast, and find a sentiment of disapprobation, which arises in you, towards this action. Here is a matter of fact; but 'tis the object of feeling, not of reason. It lies in yourself, not in the object.[2]

Thus, when we call the murder of Kitty Genovese vicious we are merely expressing our feelings of horror and outrage. Hume attempted to identify an objective aspect of morality based in widely shared human sentiments of caring for people. His successors, however, have been less optimistic about the extent of shared feelings.

Charles L. Stevenson (1908–1979) developed emotivism and helped make it an influential theory during the 1930s and 1940s. In his view, moral terms are used to express feelings and attitudes, but also to try to influence others to share our sentiments. Thus, my statement "This act is wrong" is used to express my negative attitude toward the act and tacitly to urge you to disapprove as well. Again, my assertion "This act is right" expresses my approval of the act and urges you to adopt a similar attitude.

Emotivism contains a half-truth: Moral judgments do involve expressions of feelings and attitudes. Furthermore, emotions and attitudes are crucial in motivating us. If we lacked the capacity to feel, we might be unable to respond to moral values. But morality also involves *reasons* that focus on the well-being of people, on character, and on relationships. When we condemn the murder of Kitty Genovese, the focus is on her, rather than on our emotions. In addition to expressing our disapproval, we are saying there are sound moral reasons for not taking her life. These reasons, which center on her value as a human being, prohibit taking her life.

In more abstract terms, we speak of violations of her right to life and of the failure to respect her as a human being. Additional reasons for our disapproval are based on the suffering caused to her family and friends, and the kinds of people we become if we fail to take a stand against what happened. The meaning of these moral reasons is not reducible to expressions of our feelings.

A further criticism of emotivism is that some feelings and attitudes are justified and others are not. Kitty Genovese's murderer may have had a strongly favorable attitude toward killing women, and found pleasure in doing so. We have other attitudes and feelings. Moral reasons are the basis for rationally determining which attitudes and emotions are morally appropriate. Once again, emotivism cannot adequately make sense of these moral reasons. Indeed, it constitutes a form of skepticism about the cogency of moral reasoning.

Ethical Egoism

According to ethical egoism, an act is right when it promotes one's own best interests, that is, what is good for oneself in the long run. Ethical egoism denies that we should ever promote the good of others out of consideration for them; we should help people only when doing so benefits us.

Like emotivism, ethical egoism makes primary reference to ourselves, rather than to objective reasons beyond ourselves. Unlike emotivism, however, it sets forth a standard for right and wrong, a standard by which to assess when our emotions and attitudes are justified. This standard, however, flies in the face of the most obvious feature of moral reasons—their reference to other people's interests as well as our own. Morality requires concern for others for the sake of their welfare as well as our own. Ethical egoism, by contrast, reduces all moral responsibilities to one: Look out for Number One—always and exclusively. As such, it is another form of skepticism about our ordinary conception of moral reasons.

Again like emotivism, ethical egoism also contains a partial truth, or rather two of them. For one thing, morality does recognize the importance of our own good, as well as the good of others. We have responsibilities to ourselves, such as to maintain our health and develop our talents. Ethical egoists remind us of the importance of these responsibilities, but unfortunately they try to reduce all morality to them. For another thing, heeding the ordinary dictates of morality does tend to promote our good. If we keep our commitments, people will respect us. If we help others in need, they are more likely to reciprocate when we need help. If we sustain ties of deep caring, we will benefit from friendship and love. By contrast, if we think only of ourselves we will probably be unable to maintain deep friendships or loves.

Because so many goods accrue from being moral, some philosophers have attempted to answer the question "Why be moral?" in terms of our self-interest. We should be wary of this attempt. Indeed, we should be wary of the question itself! Why be moral? The best answer is: Because morality matters; because people matter—morally. This answer is circular, but it draws attention to something very important: Moral values are valid in their own right, without the need for some further justification in terms of self-interest.

To develop this point, consider the Legend of Gyges, recounted by Plato (428–348 B.C.) in *The Republic*. Gyges was a shepherd who discovered a ring which, when he turned its bezel, made him invisible. Using his newly found powers, he entered the palace of the king, seduced the queen, murdered the king, took over the kingdom and gained great fame and fortune. Plato has us imagine by contrast a person who is a moral paragon but who suffers greatly and has an unjustifiably bad reputation. (Think of Job, in the Hebrew scripture, or Jesus.) The challenge is to present reasons why we should not do what Gyges did if we could get away with it, and why the virtuous sufferer is better off than Gyges.

Ethical egoism lacks the resources to meet this challenge. Why shouldn't we murder if we can get away with it and it makes us happy? Plato attempts to show that immorality wouldn't really make us happy, because it would destroy our inner harmony (as we will see in the next chapter). He was the first of many philosophers to try to answer the question "Why be moral?" by appeals to our own good. If we sustain our faith in the validity of moral reasons, however, we can refuse to be drawn into the attempt to justify morality entirely in terms of self-interest. The reason we, and Gyges, should not commit murder is that people have moral worth. Again, we are better off not to murder—*morally* better off. We can comment at length on how morality contributes to self-interest—indeed, we will begin to do that in Chapter 2—but we should resist the ethical egoist's insistence that moral values must always be justified solely in terms of self-interest.

Why would anyone embrace ethical egoism? Of course, the doctrine might appeal to selfish individuals who excessively and immorally pursue their interests at the expense of others or in callous disregard of them. Defenders of ethical egoism are not always selfish, however; sometimes they are confused.

Ayn Rand, both in her bestselling novels *Atlas Shrugged* and *The Fountainhead* and in her essays in *The Virtue of Selfishness*, argues that if everyone focused exclusively on his or her own self-interest, society would improve. If each of us concentrated on what we know best, namely, how to make ourselves happy, then all would prosper. I think this is false. It would leave seriously disabled people uncared for, and leave us oblivious to people like Kitty Genovese who fall into desperate circumstances. It would also undermine friendship, love, and community, all of which depend on a willingness to care for others, not merely for one's own sake, but for theirs.

Most telling, Rand's argument is based on a remarkable confusion. Her defense of ethical egoism appeals to our moral concern to achieve a better society and to have everyone prosper, even though ethical egoism asserts that the welfare of others is in itself irrelevant. Hence, her argument presupposes the validity of the moral reasons it is designed to reject! This inconsistency is revealing. It reminds us of how fundamental moral reasons are to our understanding of the world, and how difficult it is to reject them without falling into an inconsistency.

Psychological Egoism

Ethical egoism is perhaps most tempting for people who embrace *psychological egoism*; the view that all people are motivated only by what they believe to be good for themselves in some respect. This view was embraced by Thomas Hobbes (1588–1679), and also by many leading psychologists in this century, including the psychoanalyst Sigmund Freud and the behaviorist B. F. Skinner.

Psychological egoism is a theory about the facts concerning human motivation, rather than an ethical theory; hence its name, *psychological* egoism. Nevertheless, it renders ethical egoism more palatable. If we were able to care only about ourselves, then ethical egoism would gain plausibility as a call for us to focus on our long-term good in order to avoid foolishly self-destructive conduct. But is it true that we care only about ourselves? Psychological egoism flies in the face of our experience. We do sometimes care disinterestedly for others, at least in part. Why did Hobbes reject this commonsense perception? There are several reasons, but most philosophers have come to believe they are not good ones. Here are four arguments used by psychological egoists.[3]

(1) People always act on their own desires; therefore they always and only seek what they believe is good for themselves in some respect, namely the satisfaction of their desires. *Reply*: There are two kinds of desires, depending on the object of the desire (that is, the thing desired). Self-seeking desires are desires to get things for me, for my sake; altruistic desires are desires to promote the good of others, for the sake of others. Granted, we always act on our own desires, and in order to satisfy our desires. By definition, my acts are motivated by my desires! It does not follow that I desire only to get things for myself. Nor does it follow that I care only about the self-centered indulgence of my desires.

(2) People always and only seek pleasures for themselves; therefore, they seek only something good for themselves, namely their pleasures. *Reply*: The premise of this argument is false. Sometimes we act selflessly to promote others' interests. Even if the premise were true, however, psychological egoism would not follow. There are two sources of pleasure: One source is in obtaining things we see as good for ourselves, but another source is in obtaining things we see as good for other people (whom we care about, at least in part, for their sake). It is true that in helping our friends and people we love we derive pleasure, but that pleasure is not all we seek. We also want to help them, for their sake, and the pleasure comes from seeing them happy. Indeed, we are unselfish insofar as we obtain pleasure from helping others.

(3) For any type of action, we can always imagine a self-serving motive; therefore, psychological egoism is true. *Reply*: To imagine is one thing; to be correct is another. Letting my imagination run wild, I can imagine that soldiers who jump on enemy grenades to protect their comrades do it only to gain fame, or that Mother Teresa devoted her life to helping impoverished people in Calcutta, India, only to gain heavenly rewards. But only a cynic who held a thoroughly pessimistic view of human nature could conclude that these were in fact the only motives present in these cases.

(4) When we look closely we always find that an element of self-interest was a motive for helping others; therefore, psychological egoism is true. *Reply*: This premise is controversial, but I suspect it is true. It says that self-interest is *one* motive, not the only motive, or even the primary motive for

helping others. It suggests that helping is usually motivated by mixed motives: disinterested care for others plus some concern for ourselves (if only a concern for the pleasure we hope to receive in helping others).

To conclude, let us grant that self-interest is a powerful human motive, even the strongest motive most of the time. To grant that it is the predominant motive, however, is not to grant that it is the only motive. As long as we acknowledge some capacity for caring for others for their sake, psychological egoism is false. This rejection of psychological egoism removes most of the attraction of ethical egoism.

Moral reasons take into account the importance of our self-interest, and any moral theory must take account of the facts about human motivation. Yet moral reasons also place restrictions on the pursuit of self-interest. They prohibit killing, raping, stealing, and so on, even when these acts might promote our self-interest (assuming we could get away with them).

Ethical Relativism

The claim that values are relative takes many forms, depending on what the values are said to be relative to. Here we will discuss the view that moral values are relative and reducible to the conventions of societies; hence this view is also called *ethical conventionalism*. The conventions are specified by customs, laws, the beliefs of most people, or the ideology of those having the most power. Acts are right when a society approves of them, and only because a society approves of them; they are wrong when a society disapproves them.

This view regards the conventions of a given society as authoritative or self-certifying. The anthropologist Ruth Benedict said as much in her defense of ethical relativism: "We recognize that morality differs in every society, and is a convenient term for socially approved habits. Mankind has always preferred to say, 'It is morally good,' rather than 'It is habitual.' ... But historically the two phrases are synonymous."[4] So, according to this view, if a society approves of a habit or type of action by making it a convention, then that certifies that type of action as morally right.

Yet surely conventions are not self-certifying, and morality is not reducible to laws and customs. In fact, we use moral concepts to evaluate conventions both of our own society and of other societies. Some conventions are good, others are bad, and some are horrifying. Witness the Nazis' anti-Semitic beliefs about the inferiority of Jews, beliefs which were used to support the Holocaust. Witness, too, racist beliefs about black people that supported the practice of slavery, the purchase and sale and oppression of persons of color. Bigotry, slavery, and genocide are immoral, despite the fact that groups have believed otherwise.

Why did Ruth Benedict and many other social scientists embrace ethical relativism? One reason is the deep impression that cultural diversity made on them. The development of anthropology as a science brought with it documentation of the stunning variety in cultural norms. After citing a long list of exotic practices, such as cannibalism, head-hunting, and polygamy, Ruth Benedict immediately concludes that morality is just custom. That inference is mistaken, however; the mere fact of diversity of custom does not establish that customs are self-justifying. The jump from the facts about diversity to the claim about values needs further support. In short, the following argument is invalid (its conclusion does not follow from its premise).

1 Different societies have different moral beliefs.
2 Therefore, whatever a society believes to be right *is* right (for members of that society).

Although this argument is invalid, it may become seductive if we misconstrue several important truths. For one thing, it is true that we should value tolerance and respect for other cultures, as ethical relativists often insist. Respect for other cultures is vitally important in the increasingly multicultural, global environment in which we live today. Indeed, we can gain from understanding cultures which are better than ours in some respects. For example, the so-called primitive society of the !Kung, in Botswana, southern Africa, manages far better than we do in caring for all members of its population and in maintaining ties of community and mutual respect.[5] No members of that community, including the most severely disabled and diseased, are left homeless and uncared for.

Nevertheless, tolerance has its limits. There was nothing tolerant about the sanctioning of bigotry, racism, and genocide in Nazi Germany. Indeed, by equating moral values with customs, the ethical relativist tacitly draws us into complicity with intolerance and cruelty by telling us to respect whatever customs a group adopts, no matter how contrary they are to common decency.

Another truth that relativists misconstrue is that conventions are often morally *relevant* factors in deciding how we should act. For example, in England we ought to drive on the left side of the road in order not to kill people, and when entering a traditional Japanese home, we should take off our shoes as a sign of respect. Let us label this insight *contextualism*: In making specific moral judgments, we need to take account of particular contexts. As a general claim, contextualism is uncontroversial. It is simply a reminder that customs are morally relevant and need to be taken into account in deciding how to act. It does not, of course, tell us exactly which customs to respect and which to criticize. More importantly, however, it does not imply the extreme view of ethical conventionalism, which holds that customs are the final word.

Yet another truth that ethical relativists misconstrue is that there are alternative conceptions of good lives which different cultures (and individuals) may justifiably embrace. Morality, we noted, is complex. There are many virtues, ideals, and principles which it is permissible to emphasize, either in a given culture or an individual life (as we shall emphasize in the next chapter). For example, some individuals and groups give greater emphasis to truthfulness, not just in speech, but in the vigorous pursuit of the truth. Others emphasize love and friendship more. When these values conflict—for example when maintaining friendship requires less than full candor about a friend's shortcomings—different individuals and cultures may emphasize one value or the other.

This view is called *pluralism*. Pluralism accepts and tolerates multiple conceptions of the good life, and it acknowledges that those views are morally relevant in deciding how we should act toward other people. The spirit of pluralism is captured in the phrase, "Let a thousand flowers bloom." It allows, however, that we can "kill the weeds," that is, reject grossly immoral practices.[6] Pluralism does not imply that customs are automatically self-justifying. It acknowledges some objective values which we use in determining whether customs are good or meet the standards for justice.

Finally, we need to distinguish between two types of moral judgments: (1) judgments about right and wrong, and (2) judgments about responsibility and blame. We can condemn practices like head-hunting, cannibalism, and persecuting witches (who were usually nonconformist women). We can reasonably judge that engaging in these practices is typically immoral. That does not mean, however, we must always blame individuals in the past who engaged in such practices. They may have been "victims of their time," brought up in cultural beliefs that we now regard as discredited.

Divine Command Ethics

Let us now turn to an ethical theory that appeals not to social customs but instead to God's commandments. In the version discussed here, divine command ethics contends that the meaning and justification of moral values are reducible to God's commandments. For example, to say an act is morally obligatory means that God commands it, and to say an ideal of goodness is justified is to say that God approves it. Stated negatively, if there is no God, then there cannot be meaningful moral judgments. As Dostoevsky says in one of his novels, "If God is dead, anything goes." That is, if there is no God, then moral reasons would not be meaningful and cogent.

This view has things backwards. Let us assume for this discussion that God exists and issues commandments. *Why* does God issue certain commandments rather than others? Since God is morally good, indeed perfect, presumably the commandments are the ones that are morally justified, the ones for which there are the best moral reasons. The commandments are morally reasonable, not whimsical. Divine command ethics, however, cannot say this. According to it, moral reasons come into existence only after (or with) God's commandments, and hence they cannot be a basis for those commandments.

This point was made by Socrates (470–399 B.C.), as recorded by his student Plato (428–348 B.C.).[7] Socrates posed the question, Is what is holy holy because the gods approve it, or do they approve it because it is holy? Let us rephrase the question, replacing the allusion to many gods (polytheism) with a reference to one god (monotheism), and assume that God exists: What makes right acts right? Are they right simply because God commands them, and for no other reason? Or does God command them because God (as a morally perfect being) sees they are morally right? For example, is rape immoral only because God forbids it, so that rape would be unobjectionable in a universe without God? Or does God forbid rape precisely because it is immoral?

Most philosophers have agreed with Socrates that moral reasons are not created by God, but that instead a morally perfect God would use moral reasons as the basis for issuing commandments. Moral reasons, then, would not be reducible to religious beliefs. (Of course, God would have perfect recognition and appreciation of those moral reasons, unlike fallible humans.)

Having said this, let us take note of several important connections between morality and religion. One connection is historical. World religions have helped shape the moral outlooks we live by today. The moral perspectives in Western cultures, for example, have been enormously influenced by the Judeo-Christian tradition. We cannot, however, infer from this historical source of beliefs that their meaning and justification are reducible to religious terms. To do so would confuse causes of beliefs with reasons for them.

Another connection is psychological. For many people, religious beliefs provide not only comfort and moral guidance, but additional supportive motives for responding to moral reasons. Some of these motives are admirable, such as the love for and emulation of a morally perfect being in whom one has faith. Some religious motives are of more debatable quality, such as the belief that those who do not share one's religious outlook will be damned. The essential point here, however, is that moral reasons make their own distinctive appeal to us.

An especially intriguing connection is that religions sometimes affirm a higher moral standard than is commonly found. Christian scripture, for example, says that we should love our neighbor, and explains this precept using the parable of the good Samaritan. According to the story, the good Samaritan helped a man who had been beaten, robbed, and left half-dead by robbers. The Samaritan gave the man first aid, then carried him on his donkey into town, where he paid to have the man cared for at an inn. This story illustrates a higher standard of caring than is included in ordinary moral beliefs about helping others. Similarly, Judaism, Islam, Buddhism, and Hinduism also enrich moral dialogue by pressing for neglected values and higher standards.

SUMMARY

Morality concerns desirable forms of character, relationships, and conduct. Moral reasons derive from the worth of people (and other conscious beings), which makes them worthy of respect and consideration. These reasons are not reducible to matters (1) of mere feeling (in contrast to emotivism, which holds that moral terms serve only to express and evoke feelings); (2) of narrow self-interest (in contrast to ethical egoism, which holds that we ought only to promote our good); (3) of law and custom (in contrast to ethical relativism, which holds that social conventions dictate what is right); or (4) of religion (in contrast to divine command ethics, which holds that acts are right only because God approves them).

Moral reasons presuppose that we are capable of caring about the good of other people (and animals). While self-interest is certainly a potent motive for our actions, it is not the only motive, contrary to psychological egoism (which asserts that we only care about what we believe to be good for ourselves in some respect).

Applying moral reasoning to everyday living becomes complex because moral reasons (1) are numerous; (2) are sometimes vague; (3) can conflict, thereby creating moral dilemmas; (4) often cannot be placed in a simple hierarchy of relative importance; (5) can be understood from conflicting perspectives; (6) involve a plurality of permissible conceptions of goodness; and (7) are difficult to apply when we are unclear about the facts.

In studying morality, philosophical ethics has four aims: clarity, comprehensive perspective, critical assessment, and guidance. Philosophical ethics includes both general ethics and applied ethics.

DISCUSSION TOPICS

1   Is this an adequate definition of morality: Morality concerns what is right or wrong?

2   How much was required, as a moral responsibility, of the bystanders in the Kitty Genovese case? What general principle would you use to defend your view? What would be required by the Golden Rule, to do unto others as we would have them do unto us (a rule endorsed by virtually all world religions)? What would the good Samaritan standard have required?

3   Can moral reasons correctly be defined as those reasons that are always most important and that should override all other kinds of reasons, such as those concerning art, science, and self-interest? In answering this question, imagine several situations in which moral reasons conflict with other kinds of reasons. For example, consider a person at the scene of an accident who refuses to help in order to stand back and observe the "aesthetic" spectacle of movements, colors, and

sounds. Also consider the artist who decides that his art is more important than his responsibilities to his family. Such is the popular (though not entirely accurate) image of the Post-Impressionist painter Paul Gauguin (1848–1903), who left his family in Paris to devote himself to the study of art. Could Gauguin's very important contributions to art outweigh his neglect of his family?

4 According to the book of Genesis, Abraham was convinced that he heard God command him to kill his son Isaac as a sacrifice. Without asking any questions, Abraham proceeded to obey the command.

> God did tempt Abraham, and said unto him … Take now thy son, thine only son Isaac, whom thou lovest, and get thee into the land of Moriah; and offer him there for a burnt offering upon one of the mountains which I will tell thee of … And they came to the place which God had told him of; and Abraham built an altar there, and laid the wood in order and bound Isaac his son, and laid him on the altar upon the wood. And Abraham stretched forth his hand, and took the knife to slay his son.[8]

Hitchcock never set a more chilling scene. Fortunately, an angel intervenes, telling Abraham to replace Isaac with a sacrificial ram.

Jean-Paul Sartre (1905–1980) suggested that Abraham should have been more self-critical about interpreting the initial voice he believed was from God telling him to sacrifice Isaac.[9] We might also suggest that a morally perfect being would not command such a thing, not even to test Abraham's faith. But the philosopher Søren Kierkegaard (1813–1855) held a different view.[10] He thought that God might well override human morality for some higher, divine purpose. Kierkegaard called this the "teleological suspension of the ethical," that is, the subordination of morality to some higher *telos*, which in Greek means "purpose." How do you interpret and respond to the Abraham-Isaac story?

5 Religious people sometimes speak of God as the source of values, but scripture dealing with the world's creation does not usually speak of God as inventing values. For example, in the Genesis account of creation, after God creates the universe, he *sees* that it is good: "God saw everything that he had made, and behold it was very good."[11] Relate this quotation to Socrates' question, "Is what is holy holy because the gods approve it, or do they approve it because it is holy?"

6 Evaluate the following arguments:
  a Beliefs about morality differ from culture to culture. Therefore, what is right in one culture is wrong in another culture where beliefs differ. (Be sure to distinguish "what is right/wrong" from "what is believed to be right/wrong.")
  b Beliefs about morality differ from society to society. Therefore, what is right for one society may not be right for another society. (In your answer, distinguish between two senses of "right for a society," defined alternatively as "morally justified in the society" or "believed to be justified in the society.")
  c Some Eskimos and Native Americans once practiced the custom of leaving their elders to die when they could no longer travel with the tribe to fresh hunting grounds. Because this was the accepted custom, their conduct was morally permissible.

d Sometimes what is morally right (permissible or obligatory) in one society may be wrong in another society. This is not merely because customs differ, but because the customs may be morally justified in one situation and not in another. For example, economic conditions are sometimes relevant in evaluating the customs of a society. When the Eskimos and American Indians lived under conditions of extreme scarcity, they may have been justified in leaving their elderly to die if they became unable to travel with the tribe to find new hunting territories, even though comparable neglect of our elderly would be immoral in our society or in contemporary Eskimo and Indian societies.

7 Consider whether there might be circumstances in which some of the following practices would be morally permissible: (a) polygamy (perhaps in societies in which there are far more women than men, because so many men are regularly killed in wars); (b) cross-dressing; (c) a strict ban on premarital sex; (d) incest.

8 We have all heard, "Let your conscience be your guide." In this maxim, presumably *conscience* refers to an accurate sense of right and wrong, rather than one's mere beliefs about morality (which may be mistaken). Joseph Butler (1692–1752) developed an ethical theory whose standard of right conduct was obedience to conscience. Do you find such an approach promising?

SUGGESTED READINGS

Becker, Lawrence C. (ed.). *Encyclopedia of Ethics.* 2 vols. New York: Garland Publishing, 1992.

Frankena, William K. *Ethics.* 2nd ed. Englewood Cliffs, NJ: Prentice-Hall, 1973.

Helm, Paul (ed.). *Divine Commands and Morality.* Oxford: Oxford University Press, 1981.

Kavka, Gregory S. *Hobbesian Moral and Political Theory.* Princeton, NJ: Princeton University Press, 1986.

Kekes, John. *The Examined Life.* Lewisberg, PA: Bucknell University Press, 1988.

Krausz, Michael, and Jack W. Meiland (eds.). *Relativism, Cognitive and Moral.* Notre Dame, IN: University of Notre Dame, Press, 1982.

Ladd, John (ed.). *Ethical Relativism.* Belmont, CA: Wadsworth, 1973.

Martin, Mike W. "Applied and General Ethics." In Michael Bradie, Thomas W. Attig, and Nicholas Rescher (eds.), *The Applied Turn in Contemporary Philosophy.* Bowling Green, OH: Bowling Green State University, Department of Philosophy, 1983.

Nielsen, Kai. *Why Be Moral?* Buffalo, NY: Prometheus Books, 1989.

Olson, Robert G. *The Morality of Self-Interest.* New York: Harcourt Brace Jovanovich, 1965. (Defends ethical egoism.)

Outka, Gene, and John P. Reeder, Jr. (eds.). *Prospects for a Common Morality.* Princeton, NJ: Princeton University Press, 1993.

Rachels, James. *The Elements of Moral Philosophy.* 2nd ed. New York: Random House, 1993.

Sher, George (ed.). *Moral Philosophy: Selected Readings.* New York: Harcourt Brace Jovanovich, 1987.

Siegel, Harvey. *Relativism Refuted*. Dordrecht, The Netherlands: Reidel, 1987.

Singer, Peter (ed.). *A Companion to Ethics*. Cambridge, MA: Basil Blackwell, 1991.

Sommers, Christina Hoff, and Fred Sommers (eds.). *Vice and Virtue in Everyday Life: Introductory Readings in Ethics*. 2nd ed. New York: Harcourt Brace Jovanovich, 1989.

Stevenson, Charles L. *Ethics and Language*. New Haven, CT: Yale University Press, 1944.

Stout, Jeffrey. *Ethics After Babel: The Languages of Morals and Their Discontents*. Boston: Beacon Press, 1988.

Wallace, G., and A. D. M. Walker (eds.). *The Definition of Morality*. London: Methuen, 1970.

Wilson, James Q. *The Moral Sense*. New York: The Free Press, 1993.

CHAPTER 2

Authenticity

Authenticity has been a fundamental value in Western societies since at least the end of the eighteenth century.[1] In a wide sense, authenticity is genuineness or being oneself. In the normative (that is, value-laden) sense used here, authenticity is being true to one's best self and to one's own distinctive way of thinking and experiencing the world. Authenticity emerges as we assume responsibility for governing our lives in accordance with our vision of a life worth living. Psychologically, it implies identifying with and affirming the main aspects of our lives and experiencing them as expressions of ourselves. Morally, it implies three values explored in this chapter: self-fulfillment, moral creativity, and moral autonomy.

Self-fulfillment is the development of one's talents so as to achieve a happy and meaningful life. *Moral creativity* is living and reasoning in a morally innovative way. *Moral autonomy* is reasoning on the basis of moral concern. We will be especially interested in the process of moral development that culminates in adult moral autonomy. In examining psychological theories about this process, we will also consider the intriguing possibility that men and women tend to emphasize different ways of exercising moral autonomy.

Pluralism and Tolerance

Let us begin our discussion of authenticity with a brief comment on the social and political settings that foster authenticity by promoting liberty, pluralism, and tolerance of diversity. Democracy is the most important factor, but those social influences within democracies that encourage individuality are also important.

Recognition of democratic liberties in the eighteenth century was grounded in an appreciation of the diversity of conceptions of the good life.

Specifically, democratic liberties were institutionalized in order to minimize the conflicts caused by competing religious factions, which sometimes sought to impose their will on each other.[2] Often we bemoan the lack of moral consensus in our society, and certainly we have good reasons for seeking agreement on many social causes in order to avoid hurtful fragmentation. At the same time, we do have a strong consensus in our commitment to democratic freedoms. That consensus enables individuals to develop and pursue their personal visions of what is worthwhile.

To possess democratic freedoms is one thing; to exercise them so as to achieve individuality is another. In *On Liberty*, John Stuart Mill (1806–1873) warned that even in democratic societies there can be a "tyranny of the majority" that suppresses the development of individual tastes and talents. That warning may seem unnecessary in a post-1960s climate of personal freedom; yet today we face pressures toward uniformity arising from mass media and the dominance over our lives of large corporations and government bureaucracies. These forces often seem to narrow and flatten life, generating the kind of collective mediocrity that Mill warned against.

Mill urged that we should value "different experiments of living; that free scope should be given to varieties of character, short of injury to others; and the worth of different modes of life should be proved practically, when anyone thinks fit to try them."[3] Note that Mill says "short of injury to others." Our experiments of living must be conducted within the boundaries of moral responsibility. Nevertheless, these boundaries provide wide scope for creativity and for developing the best in ourselves.

Closer to our own time, Isaiah Berlin has defended the value of pluralism. Pluralism is the acceptance of multiple conceptions of the good life. As such it is central to democratic societies. Pluralism is not the same as ethical relativism, which endorses the outlooks of all groups as equally valid. Nor does it imply the subjectivism which reduces moral values to mere preferences unsupported by reasons. Instead, as Berlin wrote, pluralism is "the conception that there are many different ends that men [and women] may seek and still be fully rational, ... capable of understanding each other and sympathising and deriving light from each other."[4] Pluralism adds to democratic freedoms the attitude that we all benefit from a society that tolerates diversity. Our outlook is enriched insofar as we learn to see the world through the eyes of people with strikingly different views.

Self-Fulfillment

Today we worry that the pursuit of self-fulfillment has become so excessive as to overshadow commitments to other individuals and to communities. Few of us, however, would challenge the importance of self-fulfillment. Could it be that self-fulfillment requires enduring relationships, moral commitments, and community ties? Let us develop this idea, beginning with a conception of self-fulfillment as a process of self-development which leads to happiness and meaningful life.

Self-development is a normative (value-guided) process in which many valuable capacities and talents unfold. Of course, not all valuable potentials can be developed. Each of us has more talents than could be realized in a lifetime. Developing our interests in one profession, for example, demands forgoing other careers that would develop our talents in other directions.

Happiness follows from a life rich in enjoyable activities and relationships, but it is not reducible to pleasures. It implies an overall satisfaction with one's life as a whole. We are happy to the degree we can affirm the entire pattern of activities, relationships, and social practices in which we participate.[5]

Meaningful lives are intelligible in terms of the values that make life worthwhile. Meaningful lives cohere around worthwhile commitments. Subjectively, they are enlivened by a sense of the importance of one's life. Objectively, they embody and express justified values. There are many such values, including physical excellence, appreciation of beauty, scientific knowledge, and humanistic study. Here we focus on moral values that affirm the worth of persons.

According to an ancient paradox, self-fulfillment is achieved through caring for other people. The paradox takes several forms: In helping others we help ourselves; in giving we receive; self-sacrifice promotes self-development; freedom is won by surrendering it (in serving worthy causes); we find ourselves by losing ourselves (in caring for others); to get happiness, forget about it (while promoting the happiness of other people).

Consider the latter form of the paradox, often called the paradox of happiness, which John Stuart Mill expressed as follows.

> Those only are happy … who have their minds fixed on some object other than their own happiness; on the happiness of others, on the improvement of mankind, even on some art or pursuit, followed not as a means, but as itself an ideal end. Aiming thus at something else, they find happiness by the way.[6]

The idea is that our lives are most satisfying when we participate in activities and relationships that we find inherently valuable, rather than constantly thinking about our narrow self-interest. Self-preoccupation undermines our capacities to care about people and communities.

More generally, self-fulfillment usually demands that we respond to values that are not merely subjective preferences. We have wide discretion in choosing our friendships, loves, work, and community involvements; but we need to respond to them as valuable in themselves, rather than merely as contributions to our good. If I try to pursue them solely with an attitude of "what's in it for me," I will fail to be enriched by them. First I recognize their valid claims on me; then they can enrich my life.

Why is this? The answer concerns personal identity. We are what we care for. In particular, we are defined largely by the values and relationships to which we are committed. Who I am is a combination of my connections to my family, friends, work, and community. If I tried to justify my values solely by reference to obtaining things for myself, I would reduce my identity to a narrow and shallow set of self-seeking pleasures. By contrast, insofar as I understand myself in terms of ideals and relationships, my identity is enriched and my life becomes more meaningful.

Moral Creativity

Moral creativity consists of innovative autonomous reasoning and living. What specifically does that mean?

The existentialist Jean-Paul Sartre attempted to understand moral creativity as the invention of moral reasons. Voicing a form of moral skepticism, he denied there are objectively justified values: "Nothing, absolutely nothing, justifies me in adopting this or that particular value, this or that particular scale of values."[7] Moral values, in his view, are subjective and come into existence after we make choices, and hence they cannot guide our choices. Shaping our lives is like creating a work of art, as in painting a picture.[8] The aesthetic values of a painting, rather than guiding the artist in painting it, arise from the artist's creativity.

In illustrating this view, Sartre describes one of his students, who was faced with the choice between volunteering to go to war to defend his country or staying with his aging mother, who depended completely on him for support. Sartre says the student must invent the moral reasons applicable to his situation; but surely the student confronts a dilemma precisely because he is responding to two valid reasons that conflict in his situation, namely, love for his mother and commitment to his country. The challenge for the student is to find the best way to balance these reasons in his situation, not to jettison one of them altogether. Could the student, for example, find someone else to help his mother while he leaves to defend his country, or could he find a way to serve his country while staying with his mother?

Sartre is correct in asserting that values often have implications that are unclear, but that just means we must exercise discretion and judgment. It is also correct that our particular conception of goodness emerges as we live, and its decisive indicator is how we act rather than how we talk. As Sartre emphasized, we creatively shape our identities through our conduct. We do not, however, as Sartre suggests, invent values. We find ourselves confronted with values which are supported by good reasons and which in turn provide us with cogent reasons for conduct. Sometimes those values place responsibilities on us. Other times they offer options to us for achieving various forms of moral goodness through love, friendship, collegial relationships, and community involvements.

We need a conception of moral creativity which does not suggest a willy-nilly invention of values. Let us begin with the idea that creativity implies newness and ask, newness with respect to what? Newness can be identified by reference to one's past: It can consist of going beyond one's previously narrow or biased ways of thinking, or one's rigid and juvenile patterns of conduct, emotions, and attitude. Other reference points lie outside oneself: Newness can mean surmounting stifling views inherited from parents, peers, or culture; but it can also mean coming to appreciate the importance of inherited views and attitudes. All these forms of creative moral development play a significant role in our lives.

Newness alone is not creativity, however. Merely novel responses to moral problems may be as uncreative as doodling on paper—new patterns of lines may emerge, but not creative ones. If Sartre's student had decided to devote all his time to beachcombing in California, his decision would have been novel but not creative. Creativity implies that something *valuably new* is achieved. Moral creativity thus represents the discovery or accomplishment of something new and morally desirable. As such it both requires and exemplifies moral autonomy: reasoning for oneself in trying to live a morally good life.

Morally valuable newness can be revealed in several ways. Individuals who respond in new and morally valuable ways are creative in (1) identifying moral problems, issues, and needs, (2) identifying moral reasons and facts relevant to moral concerns, (3) imaginatively envisioning moral alternatives that could easily be overlooked, (4) effectively reasoning in resolving moral problems and guiding one's life, and (5) shaping one's life with a focus on particular ideals and virtues. All these areas of creativity, but especially the final one, are illustrated by moral leaders such as Socrates, Martin Luther King, Jr., and Elizabeth Cady Stanton.

Socrates: Intellectual Humility and Honesty

Socrates centered his life on a creative search for moral understanding. As the story is told in Plato's *Apology*, one of Socrates' friends asked the oracle of Apollo at Delphi whether anyone was wiser than Socrates. The priestess replied that no one was. This astonished Socrates, for he was certain he knew very little. To disprove the oracle's pronouncement, he began searching for someone wiser than himself by talking with politicians, poets, craftsmen, and anyone else having a reputation for wisdom. In each case he uncovered only ignorance, dogmatism, and intellectual complacency, which led him to conclude that what set him apart from others was his knowledge of his own ignorance. What is probable, he explained, is in fact that god is wise and that his oracular response meant that human wisdom is worth little or nothing, and that when he says this man, Socrates, he is using my name as an example, as if he said: "This man among you, mortals, is wisest who, like Socrates, understands that his wisdom is worthless." So even now I continue this investigation as the gods bade me—and I go around seeking out anyone, citizen or stranger, whom I think wise. Then if I do not think he is, I come to the assistance of the god and show him that he is not wise.[9]*

There is a positive goal in this Socratic enterprise of showing ignorant people that they lack the moral understanding they claim to have. Individuals who think they are wise see no reason to search for increased wisdom. By showing them that they are not wise, Socrates encouraged the intellectual humility and self-critical attitude with which moral inquiry must begin. And, according to Socrates, moral inquiry is the prerequisite for meaningful life: "It is the greatest good for a man to discuss virtue every day … for the unexamined life is not worth living."[10]† People do not attain either the capacity for moral inquiry or self-understanding once and for all, but rather must maintain an ongoing effort as part of everyday life.

Here is an example of the importance of self-understanding based on intellectual humility and honesty. According to Plato's dialogue *Euthyphro*, Socrates encounters a man (Euthyphro) who has just filed murder charges against his own father. Apparently one of Euthyphro's employees, in a drunken frenzy, had killed a family slave. Uncertain what to do, Euthyphro's father tied up the murderer and threw him in a ditch, then sent a messenger to the local priest for advice. While the father awaited the messenger's return, the bound man died from hunger and exposure, so Euthyphro prosecuted his father for murder—the same crime that the employee had committed.

Socrates is shocked by Euthyphro's assertion that the father is as guilty as the employee. He is even more astonished when Euthyphro argues that the virtue of justice requires him to prosecute his father despite their special relationship. In Socrates' view, the moral situation was murky, and Euthyphro's self-righteous pronouncements threatened to compound the harm already done. Socrates proceeds to deflate Euthyphro's conceit, showing that he really knows nothing about virtue.‡ We also sense that Euthyphro is motivated by hatred of and rivalry with his father, and that his lack of self-understanding distorts his sense of justice.

---

*Reprinted by permission of Hackett Publishing Company, Inc.

†Reprinted by permission of Hackett Publishing Company, Inc.

‡Upon questioning, Euthyphro defined virtue as that which the gods command. Recall, however, Socrates' assertion in Chapter 1 that virtue is not created by the gods, but rather that the gods would recognize valid moral reasons as worthy of their commandments.

Socrates' commitment to truth was uncompromising. During a lifetime of exposing and debunking ignorance he offended many people. That offensiveness was partly inevitable given the nature of his mission, but part of it also resulted from Socrates' lack of compassion in dealing with people, as suggested by his famous epigram, "The unexamined life is not worth living." If self-examination requires the kind of philosophical scrutiny he engaged in, then most lives lack worth! It would be more accurate, if less inspirational, to say that the morally examined life is *more* worth living.

Despite his excesses, and in part because of them, Socrates offers an inspiring paradigm of a life devoted to the virtues of honesty and intellectual humility. His death solemnized his commitment to truth and the virtues it demands of us. He was convicted and sentenced to death on the basis of false charges trumped up by some of the men he had offended. During his trial he was offered acquittal in return for abandoning his mission on behalf of truth, the mission that had made him an annoying "gadfly of Athens." He replied,

> As long as I draw breath and am able, I shall not cease to practise philosophy, to exhort you and to point out to anyone of you whom I happen to meet: Good Sir, you are an Athenian, a citizen of the greatest city with the greatest reputation for both wisdom and power; are you not ashamed of your eagerness to possess as much wealth, reputation and honours as possible, while you do not care for nor give thought to wisdom or truth, or the best possible state of your soul?[11]*

King: Love and Justice Through Nonviolence

The central moral commitment of Martin Luther King, Jr. (1929–1968) was to achieve social justice. In 1955, he was working in Montgomery, Alabama, as a Baptist minister, having that year completed a Ph.D. at Boston University. In part because he was too new to Montgomery to be compromised by political debts, he was asked to lead the Montgomery bus boycott in protest of the arrest of Mrs. Rosa Parks. Mrs. Parks, a black woman, had refused to give up her bus seat to a white man, thereby violating a Montgomery city ordinance (which also required blacks to sit at the back of the bus). King knew there were enormous risks in using this untried form of economic protest, yet he also saw the opportunity to draw national attention to the Jim Crow laws of segregation.

The boycott lasted one year, until the Supreme Court ruled that Mrs. Parks's rights had indeed been violated and that bus segregation laws were

---

*Reprinted by permission of Hackett Publishing Company, Inc.

unconstitutional. Beginning that year, King's life was repeatedly threatened in hate mail and phone calls. His home was bombed. He was arrested and harassed. And this pattern intensified throughout the next dozen years until he was assassinated.

While leading the Montgomery boycott, King articulated his philosophy of nonviolence based on agape, the Christian version of benevolence or love toward all humans. It enjoins, "Love your enemies, bless them that curse you, do good to them that hate you, and pray for them which despitefully use you, and persecute you."[12] According to King, agape is not an emotional form of love like romantic love and friendship; nevertheless, it requires more than mere respect for others. Agape is a positive attitude of goodwill toward all people as children of God who are capable of redemption.

Agape also requires us to forgive enemies who have wronged us. Forgiveness, however, is not simply a matter of overlooking harm done. Rather, it entails the free gift of releasing an enemy from having to pay for that wrong, the refusal to hate in response to hate, and the willingness to be reconciled to those who have wronged us.

Finally, in King's interpretation, agape requires us to confront unjust institutions and practices in a nonviolent way. He knew that verbal confrontation alone was ineffective in dealing with institutionalized racism. Even economic boycott was not enough. What was necessary was civil disobedience: nonviolent, public, conscientiously motivated violations of the law with a willingness to accept legal penalties. This form of protest was consistent with agape and could appeal to the consciences of the masses of Americans so as to bring about change.

King did not invent civil disobedience as a tactic of social protest. He was directly influenced by Henry David Thoreau (1817–1862), who had refused to pay his Massachusetts taxes as a protest against both the Mexican-American War and slavery. He was also influenced by Mohandas Gandhi (1869–1948), who had led the successful fight against British control of India by encouraging civil disobedience on a mass scale. King's moral creativity was not in inventing the tactic, but in Christianizing it and adapting it to the American civil rights movement. King's genius lay in part in his belief that, in the face of violent opposition, nonviolent civil disobedience could bring an end to a century of segregation. It was also his continuing dream that people "no longer be judged by the color of their skin but by the content of their character."[13]

Stanton: Women's Dignity and Self-Development

Elizabeth Cady Stanton (1815–1902) is widely regarded as the foremost intellectual of the early American feminist movement. She conceived and helped organize the first convention on women's rights in 1848 at Seneca Falls, New York. That convention, together with its statement of grievances, ignited the organized struggle for women's rights in the United States.

Stanton was the primary author of the statement of grievances entitled the "Declaration of Sentiments," modeled on the language of the *Declaration of Independence*. In an early paragraph she states:

> We hold these truths to be self-evident: that all men and women are created equal; that they are endowed by their Creator with certain inalienable rights; that among these are life, liberty, and the pursuit of happiness.... The history of mankind is a history of repeated injuries and usurpations on the part of man toward woman, having in direct object the establishment of an absolute tyranny over her. To prove this, let facts be submitted to a candid world.[14]

The document asserted that fundamental rights were being denied to women, including the right to vote, to own property (including their earned wages), to initiate divorce, to retain custody of their children when a husband initiated a divorce, to guide business activities without supervision by their husbands, and to attend college. (Except for Oberlin College, which had become coeducational, all American colleges and universities refused to admit women students.)

Defining these actions as rights, and demanding their exercise, was an explosive act. Even the right to vote was regarded by many convention members as too radical to assert at that time. Indeed, it was another seventy-two years before women's voting rights were recognized in the Nineteenth Amendment to the Constitution in 1920. Pursuing marriage and divorce rights was viewed as even more unrealistic and harmful. Only Stanton's enormous persistence, energy, and forceful arguments finally won endorsement of the Declaration at the convention.

Like King, Stanton did not invent the moral concepts and ideals she pressed to the center of public debate. She drew not only upon the *Declaration of Independence* but also upon earlier feminist writing such as *A Vindication of the Rights of Woman* by Mary Wollstonecraft (1759–1797). Stanton's creative moral leadership stemmed from her insight that the concept of human rights could serve as the rallying point against men who avowed principles of equality for all humans while denying equality to women.

Stanton knew from her own experience, which included raising seven children, how women were suppressed and exploited. Her husband, an activist in the antislavery movement, was largely indifferent to her efforts. And her father disowned her because of her activities (even though on his deathbed he sought a reconciliation with her).

Stanton also knew that the roots of patriarchy—that is, male dominance—ran even deeper than the roots of racial oppression. She traced them in part to religious thought. In the 1890s she published *The Woman's Bible*, in which she and others commented on scriptures concerning the relationship between men and women. For example, she cited Mark 12:43–44, in which Jesus praises a poor widow for giving her last farthing to the church. Although Stanton agreed with Jesus that the widow's gift showed greater generosity than did the much larger gifts of the rich, she also pointed out that praise of women's self-sacrifices had been used by organized religion throughout history to perpetuate women's second-class status.

> This woman, belonging to an impoverished class, was trained to self-abnegation; but when women learn the higher duty of self-development, they will not so readily expend all their forces in serving others. Paul says that a husband who does not provide for his own household is worse than an infidel. So a woman, who spends all her time in churches, with priests, in charities, neglects to cultivate her own natural gifts, to make the most of herself as an individual in the scale of being, a responsible soul whose place no other can fill, is worse than an infidel. "Self-development is a higher duty than self-sacrifice," should be woman's motto henceforward.[15]

Stanton called into question the conventional expectation that women should be more self-sacrificing, helpful, and caring than men. How far this expectation is generated by society's stereotypes of women, and whether it has any biological basis, is a "nurture-nature" dispute of considerable importance. Of more immediate interest here, however, is the question of whether women and men do tend to emphasize different virtues, whatever the origin of those differences may be.

Gilligan and Kohlberg: Caring Versus Justice

Do men and women, as groups, differ in the kinds of virtues they emphasize? Studies by some contemporary experimental psychologists suggest they do. We will look in particular at the works of Carol Gilligan and of Lawrence Kohlberg (1927–1987).

Gilligan distinguishes between two general outlooks on morality: the justice perspective and the care perspective. According to the results of her experiments, these views are roughly linked to gender. That is, men and women adopt both perspectives, but on average men emphasize justice and women emphasize care.*

The *justice perspective* stresses abstract rules, which deal primarily with the right to be left alone and free from the interference of others. Within this perspective, moral dilemmas are questions of conflicting rights that are resolved by identifying which right has the highest priority in general. Morality, in short, is viewed as a set of rules about rights, ordered hierarchically by relative importance. The moral identity of people is defined primarily in terms of their rights: It is the assertion of the right to pursue their lives freely while respecting the freedom of others. The aim of autonomous moral reasoning is to determine how to balance rights fairly or justly.

"Heinz's Dilemma" illustrates the kind of reasoning used within the justice perspective. This story, which poses a moral dilemma, was written by Kohlberg but is used by Gilligan as well.

> In Europe, a woman was near death from a very bad disease, a special kind of cancer. There was one drug that the doctors thought might save her. It was a form of radium that a druggist in the same town had recently discovered. The drug was expensive to make, but the druggist was charging ten times what the drug cost him to make. He paid $200 for the radium and charged $2,000 for a small dose of the drug. The sick woman's husband, Heinz, went to everyone he knew to borrow the money, but he could get together only about $1,000, which was half of what it cost. He told the druggist that his wife was dying and asked him to sell it cheaper or let him pay later. But the druggist said, "No, I discovered the drug and I'm going to make money from it." Heinz got desperate and broke into the man's store to steal the drug for his wife.[17]

The question is, Was the husband's act justified (permissible, obligatory)?

According to Kohlberg, morally mature individuals resolve this dilemma by contrasting the pharmacist's property rights with the wife's right to life and then deciding which right should have priority. Typically, they argue

---

* In the essay "Moral Orientation and Development," Gilligan summarizes the results of one study as follows: When asked to describe a moral conflict they had faced, 55 out of 80 (69 percent) educationally advantaged North American adolescents and adults raised considerations of both justice and care. Two-thirds (54 out of 80), however, focused their attention on one set of concerns, with focus defined as 75 percent or more of the considerations raised pertaining either to justice or to care. Thus, the person who presented, say, two care considerations in discussing a moral conflict was more likely to give a third, fourth, and fifth than to balance care and justice concerns—a finding consonant with the assumption that justice and care constitute organizing frameworks for moral decision. The men and women involved in this study (high school students, college students, medical students, and adult professionals) were equally likely to demonstrate the focus phenomenon (two-thirds of both sexes fell into the focus categories). There were, however, sex differences in the direction of focus. With one exception, all of the men who focused, focused on justice. The women divided, with roughly one third focusing on justice and one third on care. [16]

that the right to life is more important than the right to property, and hence that the husband should steal the drug. They might also reason that the general principle of respect for life has priority over the principle of respect for property.

Gilligan contrasts this justice-oriented approach with the *care perspective* in which priority is placed on kindness, giving, and caring about the needs of others. The aim is to avoid hurting others and to maintain relationships without hurting oneself. Moral dilemmas thus revolve around competing needs and incompatible ways of caring. They are resolved through communication and sensitivity to particular circumstances rather than through imposition of general rules and priorities among rules. Moral reasons are defined through a web of caring relationships rather than through the interplay of rights to be left alone. In this view, autonomous moral reasoning seeks a proper balance between the others' needs and one's own.

"Heinz's Dilemma" also illustrates the use of reasoning within the care perspective. Perhaps surprisingly, Kohlberg's studies suggested that fewer females than males endorsed Heinz's theft of the drug. Kohlberg interpreted this as a sign of moral immaturity, contending that women were bound by social conventions about respecting property and obeying laws. In applying the care perspective, however, Gilligan offered a very different interpretation. Gilligan suggests that the reluctance to steal the drug reveals sensitivity to the personal relationships at stake. Not only will Heinz probably end up in jail, where he can no longer help his wife, but also the relationship with the pharmacist will be severed altogether. In Gilligan's studies women frequently recommended further discussions with the pharmacist in hopes of changing his mind, or proposed innovative ways of raising money to pay for the drug.

In sum, according to Gilligan, women more than men use a care-oriented moral perspective. They seek innovative ways to sustain all relationships and to meet all needs. They are more context-focused than men and less preoccupied with abstract rules ranked in order of importance.

Development of Moral Autonomy

Kohlberg's emphasis on the justice perspective and Gilligan's emphasis on the care perspective underlie their differing theories about the stages of development toward moral autonomy. In his highly influential schema of moral development, Kohlberg lists three levels, each with a characteristic view of right action:

1 Preconventional Level: Right action is defined in terms of what brings pleasure or reward to oneself.

2 Conventional Level: Right action is interpreted as loyalty to others and respect for law and custom.

3 Postconventional Level: Right action is identified in terms of general principles discerned with one's autonomous judgment.

Each level is further divided into two stages, as summarized in Table 2.1.

Kohlberg claimed that these stages represent the appropriate steps of moral growth for all people in all cultures. People reach advanced stages only after progressing through earlier ones, and only a few rare individuals such as Socrates reach the highest stage. In addition, Kohlberg asserted that fewer women than men move beyond the conventional level to the postconventional level.

Gilligan charges that these conclusions, and indeed Kohlberg's schema of moral development, are biased. She points out that Kohlberg studied only males in creating his schema and then simply assumed that it was equally valid for both sexes. Moreover, in structuring the stages of moral progression, Kohlberg also assumed that reasoning that is based on abstract rules reflects greater moral maturity. As a result, caring-based reasoning focused on specific circumstances is condemned in advance as "conventional" in a pejorative sense. Thus, Kohlberg's emphasis on general rules about justice and rights may express his own bias as a male.

Gilligan offers an alternative schema, based on several studies, of the levels of development:

1 Preconventional Level: Rightness is viewed exclusively as what is good for oneself.

TABLE 2.1   *Kohlberg's Schema of Moral Devlopment*

Level of Moral Development	Stage or Orientation	View of Right Action
1. Preconventional	1. Punishment and obedience	Avoid punishment and submit to power
	2. Egoistic	Satisfy one's own needs
2. Conventional	3. Good-boy, nice-girl	Please and help others
	4. Society-maintaining	Respect authority and social rules
3. Postconventional	5. Social contract or legalistic	Obey useful, albeit arbitrary, social rules
	6. Conscience and universal principles	Autonomously recognize universal rules such as the Golden Rule

2 Conventional Level: Right action is viewed as self-sacrifice in always placing the interests of others before one's own—the socially favored view of how women in particular should behave.

3 Postconventional Level: The ethic of caring in which both one's own interests and those of others are valued and balanced with the aim of maintaining attachments to all people involved in specific situations.

Gilligan's study of women faced with abortion decisions was especially valuable in her redefinition of levels of moral development. That study examined how women actually reason about an important moral issue they are forced to act on, whereas Kohlberg's study of Heinz's Dilemma concerned hypothetical problems. Gilligan's subjects were women referred to her by a counseling service, which indicated they had experienced conflict in making the abortion decision. They were interviewed first while they were making their decisions and again a year later. Gilligan identified their reasoning levels in terms of their patterns of reasoning rather than the conclusions they reached.

The women who were solely or primarily concerned about what was best for themselves were at the preconventional (self-centered) level. Some in this group had an abortion in order to avoid harm or social stigma, without considering anyone else involved; others decided to have a baby to bring them social recognition. The women at the conventional (self-sacrificing) level were preoccupied with what was socially expected or with what helped others without regard to their own well-being. For some women this meant having a baby, even at enormous self-sacrifice, out of a concern for the developing fetus; for others it meant having an abortion in order to please a spouse or lover. Finally, those women who struggled to balance their own needs with the needs of others involved in order to sustain relationships, including in some cases the relationship with the fetus, were at the postconventional (mature, caring) level. For these women, the decision to have an abortion was motivated, for example, by the impossibility of properly caring for a baby while maintaining a relationship with a lover or pursuing a college education. Likewise, the decision to have a baby was perhaps prompted by the desire to develop a new relationship with the child that would complement other relationships.

The women in Gilligan's study frequently used the concepts of selfishness, self-sacrifice, caring, needs, and relationships. They seldom mentioned, however, the concepts used in public debates over abortion: the rights of women (to control their bodies, to make their own decisions) versus the (possible) right to life attributed to fetuses. Moreover, when Gilligan interviewed the women a second time, she frequently saw patterns of growth in terms of her schema of development: Many of the women had moved from preconventional and conventional levels to the postconventional level. Evidently, making the decision about abortion had encouraged maturation. By choosing autonomously between the lesser of two evils, the women were forced to move beyond the conventional self-sacrificing level that emphasized never harming others.

Gilligan's criticisms of Kohlberg led him to modify his claims about the universal applicability of the six stages of development. He came to acknowledge that they merely represent growth within a justice perspective and that a care-oriented perspective may be equally valid. For her part, Gilligan has emphasized that both the care and the justice perspectives express important aspects of most moral situations. As an analogy, she cites the alternative ways of perceiving visual data: Just as the image in Figure 2.1 can be seen as a duck or a rabbit, many moral situations can be viewed in terms of either rights or caring.

According to Gilligan, the richest and most acceptable moral outlook would integrate both moral perspectives. Men can benefit from integrating elements of the care perspective more fully into their moral outlook, and women can benefit from appreciating the justice perspective. In fact, the justice perspective can aid women in advancing from the conventional self-sacrificing level to the postconventional level, which balances the needs of others and oneself. (Table 2.2 summarizes the similarities and differences between Kohlberg's and Gilligan's views.)

As an example of ways in which women might adopt the justice perspective, Gilligan refers to Elizabeth Cady Stanton's appeal to rights as a way of raising women's awareness of their needs and their legitimate self-development. Gilligan might thus rephrase Stanton's slogan, "Self-development is a higher duty than self-sacrifice," to read, "Self-development is as high a duty as caring for others." At the same time, Gilligan is aware that on some occasions there are good reasons to emphasize one's own rights and needs. This is consistent with the sensitivity to context—rather than the reliance on abstract rules—that is integral to her ethic of caring. It is also compatible with the theme of this chapter that morality allows us to emphasize selected virtues and values.

FIGURE 2.1 *Duck-Rabbit*

Why Study Ethics?

Moral autonomy sometimes leads creative thinkers to emphasize certain commitments and virtues over others, as we saw with Socrates, King, and Stanton. Similar emphasis of selected virtues might be roughly linked with gender. Both Gilligan and Kohlberg agree that the capacity for moral autonomy and creative decision making develops gradually, although they trace different paths of development. Do liberal education and ethics courses contribute to this moral growth? Should they try or be expected to make people more morally responsible?

Let us approach these questions by bearing in mind that the study of morality is an aspect of liberal education, not just ethics courses. Liberal education is the study of the humanities, arts, and sciences with the overall aim of deepening our understanding and broadening our appreciation of values. It has three practical goals as well.

First, liberal education prepares one for significant work by strengthening the abilities to reason, research, and communicate. Significant work contributes to self-fulfillment and to the social good in such areas as public health (the goal of the health professions), justice (the goal of law), and education (the goal of teaching).

Second, liberal education encompasses an array of inherently worthwhile activities. These diverse pursuits include understanding cultures and computers, appreciating art and astronomy, and mastering theories of ethics and economics.

TABLE 2.2 *Kohlberg's and Gilligan's Schemas of Moral Development*

Levels of Moral Development	Kohlberg's Justice Perspective	Gilligan's Care Perspective
1. Preconventional	Self-centered, with concern for (1) avoiding punishment and (2) satisfying one's own needs	Self-centered: viewing one's own needs as all that matters
2. Conventional	Expectation-meeting, with concern for (3) pleasing others and (4) meeting society's expectations	Self-sacrificing: viewing others' needs as more important
3. Postconventional	Autonomous recognition of (5) social agreements and (6) universal rules	Mature care ethic: able to reason toward a balance of one's own and others' needs

Third, liberal education seeks to liberate us from ignorance and prejudice by fostering certain skills, attitudes, emotions, and virtues. Which skills? Those that enable clear thinking, cogent reasoning, and effective communication—the same skills that contribute to significant work. Which attitudes? Respect for truth and evidence, commitment to consistency and nonarbitrariness, and appreciation of beauty and understanding. Which emotions? Enjoyment of significant ideas, delight in creative endeavors, respect for honest reflection, and contempt for shoddy thinking. Which virtues? The ones that combine the preceding skills, attitudes, and emotions into settled patterns. Most central are the virtues of intellectual honesty, integrity, and courage; truthful communication; wisdom and passionate concern for truth; sensitivity to beauty and discernment in taste; and moral sensitivity, understanding, responsibility, and tolerance.

Studies in ethics form an essential part of liberal education and contribute to all of the goals cited above. They contribute to preparation for significant work, that is, work in some sense devoted to the public good and guided by moral norms (as well as based on advanced education). Ethics courses enrich moral understanding in inherently valuable ways. And ethics courses contribute more directly to moral development by strengthening our capacities for moral autonomy.

Moral autonomy requires many specific skills: the ability to identify moral problems and reasons; creative vision in imagining moral possibilities; skill in reasonably weighing conflicting moral reasons; adeptness in clarifying concepts that otherwise might be vague or ambiguous. It also requires a knowledge of people and the world that is relevant to making wise decisions. All these capacities mature through liberal learning and studies in ethics.

But should colleges seek to make people more responsible morally? On the one hand, ethics courses in college ought to continue the development of moral understanding already underway when students enter college. On the other hand, it is inappropriate to expect college professors to make their students more responsible morally. That would require professors to invade their students' personal lives to ensure that they practice the discipline and sensitivity necessary for moral responsibility. Not only do professors lack the right to invade students' privacy, they also lack certification as moral counselors and trainers.

These views can be reconciled by distinguishing between the direct aims of college courses and the underlying hopes concerning them. Certainly one direct aim of studies in ethics and the liberal arts is very practical: to strengthen the ability to reason autonomously about morality. By strengthening their students' moral autonomy, educators can hope to contribute indirectly to the development of morally responsible conduct and character. College courses cannot be expected to shape character directly. The direct increase of virtue cannot be a gradable classroom exercise, because it involves aspects of character development beyond autonomous reasoning. Moral responsibility remains a personal achievement, whether for students or teachers.

One qualification must be added. Moral responsibility and classroom goals in studying ethics are at some points more closely connected. Some character traits and patterns of conduct enter as prerequisites for effective education. Tolerance, for example, is a prerequisite for conducting any class, for without it dialogue based on mutual respect is impossible. Honesty is equally essential, because cheating erodes the trust among students and professors that helps facilitate learning.

SUMMARY

Authenticity involves self-fulfillment, moral creativity, and exercising moral autonomy. Self-fulfillment is self-development that leads to happiness and a meaningful life. Moral creativity entails discovering or achieving new and valuable solutions to moral dilemmas and ways of living. Moral creativity involves responding to the objective claims of values already present in human culture rather than inventing new values.

Psychologists who study moral development are exploring the possibility that there may be gender-linked differences in how virtues are emphasized. Lawrence Kohlberg identified patterns of moral development that he thought were universal, although he later accepted Carol Gilligan's criticisms that these patterns represented only the development of a sense of justice. Kohlberg defined morally mature reasoning as the autonomous recognition of universal moral rules—especially rules about rights to be free from the interference of others—and their order of priority. Gilligan argued that this justice perspective is favored by males and that females often emphasize a care perspective based on sensitivity to needs and personal relationships within particular contexts.

Kohlberg and Gilligan agree that moral autonomy, in the sense of the ability to reason for oneself without passive adherence to social conventions, emerges from earlier stages of moral development. Both of them also distinguish three basic levels of moral development—preconventional, conventional, and postconventional—and agree that the preconventional level is characterized by a self-centered preoccupation with satisfying one's own needs. Kohlberg describes reasoning at the conventional level as primarily based on a concern to please others or to meet society's expectations, whereas the postconventional level reflects autonomous recognition of social conventions as morally justified or (at the highest stage) autonomous acceptance of universal moral rules. Gilligan, in contrast, describes the conventional level as reasoning that is based on the self-sacrificing attitude that other people's needs are more important than one's own, and the postconventional level as autonomous reasoning in balancing one's own needs with the needs of others.

Moral autonomy is strengthened through studies in ethics and the liberal arts. It is also linked to all three practical goals of these studies: to prepare for significant work, to engage in inherently valuable activities, and to liberate the student from ignorance and prejudice.

DISCUSSION TOPICS

1   Euthyphro and Socrates disagreed about whether one's relationship with parents is relevant to how one pursues general principles of justice. Do you agree with what Euthyphro says in the following passage? Compare this issue with the controversy over whether children should report their parents to the police for using drugs (and vice versa). Also, relate the disagreement between Socrates and Euthyphro to the differences between Kohlberg's and Gilligan's views of moral autonomy.

> SOCRATES: Is then the man your father killed one of your relatives? Or is that obvious, for you would not prosecute your father for the murder of a stranger.
> EUTHYPHRO: It is ridiculous, Socrates, for you to think that it makes any difference whether the victim is a stranger or a relative. One should only watch whether the killer acted justly or not; if he acted justly, let him go, but if not, one should prosecute, even if the killer shares your hearth and table. The pollution is the same if you knowingly keep company with such a man and do not cleanse yourself and him by bringing him to justice.[18]*

2   Carol Gilligan believes that the justice and care perspectives are complementary and ideally should be integrated. Do you see such an integration in the life and thought of Martin Luther King, Jr.?

3   Gilligan suggests that most moral situations can be interpreted in terms of both the justice and care perspectives. Yet, is the justice perspective perhaps better suited to social and political contexts and the care perspective better suited to more personal relationships among people (and perhaps animals)? In answering this question, compare and contrast public debates over abortion laws with personal decisions about abortions. Are different moral concepts emphasized in these two contexts? Should they be?

4   Interpret the dilemma faced by Sartre's student in terms of the justice and the care perspectives. Does one of the perspectives seem more helpful? Do they point in similar directions for resolving the dilemma?

5   Return to the biblical story of Abraham and Isaac cited as a discussion topic in Chapter 1. In her book *In a Different Voice*, Gilligan links Abraham's willingness

---

*Reprinted by permission of Hackett Publishing Company, Inc.

to sacrifice his son to a male, justice-oriented way of thinking. Do you agree? Is it less likely that a woman would do what Abraham did, as Gilligan also suggests?

6 Apply both Kohlberg's and Gilligan's schemas of moral development to classroom cheating, both plagiarism and cribbing during tests. Describe the kinds of reasoning that would be used at the preconventional, conventional, and postconventional levels of development within each schema.

7 Compare and contrast moral creativity with creativity in science and in art. In each case, is creativity best thought of as making a discovery or as inventing something?

8 We suggested that moral creativity consists of emphasizing particular virtues or sensitively applying them to situations, but not of inventing values, as Sartre had suggested. Does anyone ever invent an entirely new virtue? In answering this question, consider the following passage written by philosopher Mary Midgley:

> If there had been no such thing as mercy before, the first merciful man would have been an innovator of a quite dramatic kind.... But in fact ... mercy is, and has to be, an extremely ancient and gradual development, something *evolved* as a precondition of social life by any social species, not a sudden invention to transform it. And the same is true of the other virtues. Slow, painful evolution, not sudden cleverness nor divine fiat, puts them in our repertoire.[19]

9 The self-fulfillment paradoxes are often used to encourage self-sacrificing conduct. How might they be abused in this regard? Think of an example in which the cause that one is urged to sacrifice for is unjust. Also, is there a special danger that the paradoxes could be used to encourage stereotypes of women as the self-sacrificing sex? Consider in this connection Elizabeth Cady Stanton's comment on the parable of the widow who gives her last farthing to charity. Could Gilligan's work also be used to reinforce limiting stereotypes of women as the caring sex?

SUGGESTED READINGS

Berlin, Isaiah. *The Crooked Timber of Humanity*. New York: Vintage, 1992.

Blanshard, Brand. *The Uses of a Liberal Education*. La Salle, IL: Open Court, 1973.

Cole, Eve Browning, and Susan Coultrap-McQuin (eds.). *Explorations in Feminist Ethics*. Bloomington: Indiana University Press, 1992.

Cua, A. S. *Dimensions of Moral Creativity*. University Park, PA: Pennsylvania State University, 1978.

Flanagan, Owen. *Varieties of Moral Personality*. Cambridge, MA: Harvard University Press, 1991.

Garrow, David J. *Bearing the Cross: Martin Luther King, Jr., and the Southern Christian Leadership Conference*. New York: Vintage, 1986.

Gilligan, Carol. *In a Different Voice: Psychological Theory and Women's Development*. Cambridge, MA: Harvard University Press, 1982.

Held, Virginia. *Feminist Morality*. Chicago: University of Chicago Press, 1993.

Jaspers, Karl. *Socrates, Buddha, Confucius, Jesus: The Paradigmatic Individuals*. Trans. Ralph Mannheim. New York: Harcourt Brace Jovanovich, 1962.

Kekes, John. *Moral Tradition and Individuality*. Princeton, NJ: Princeton University Press, 1989.

King, Martin Luther, Jr. *Strength to Love*. Philadelphia, PA: Fortress Press, 1981.

Kittay, Eva Feder, and Diana T. Meyers (eds.). *Women and Moral Theory*. Totowa, NJ: Rowman & Littlefield, 1987.

Kohlberg, Lawrence. *The Philosophy of Moral Development*. San Francisco: Harper & Row, 1981.

Larrabee, Mary Jeanne (ed.). *An Ethic of Care: Feminist and Interdisciplinary Perspectives*. New York: Routledge, 1993.

Manning, Rita C. *Speaking from the Heart: A Feminist Perspective On Ethics*. Lanham, MD: Rowman & Littlefield, 1992.

Midgley, Mary. "Creation and Originality." In *Heart and Mind: The Varieties of Moral Experience*. New York: St. Martin's Press, 1981.

Mill, John Stuart. *On Liberty*. Indianapolis, IN: Hackett, 1978.

Minas, Anne (ed.). *Gender Basics: Feminist Perspectives on Women and Men*. Belmont, CA: Wadsworth, 1993.

Noddings, Nel. *Caring: A Feminine Approach to Ethics and Moral Education*. Berkeley: University of California Press, 1984.

Norton, David L. *Personal Destinies: A Philosophy of Ethical Individualism*. Princeton, NJ: Princeton University Press, 1976.

Perry, William G., Jr. *Forms of Intellectual and Ethical Development in the College Years*. New York: Holt, Rinehart & Winston, 1970.

Peters, R. S. (ed.). *The Philosophy of Education*. New York: Oxford University Press, 1973.

Plato. *Apology* and *Euthyphro* in *The Trial and Death of Socrates*, trans. G. M. A. Grube. Indianapolis, IN: Hackett, 1975.

Pritchard, Michael S. *On Becoming Responsible*. Lawrence, KS: University Press of Kansas, 1991.

Stanton, Elizabeth Cady, and Susan B. Anthony, *Correspondence, Writings, Speeches*. Ellen Carol Du Bois (ed.). New York: Shocken Books, 1981.

Taylor, Charles. *The Ethics of Authenticity*. Cambridge, MA: Harvard University Press, 1992.

Tong, Rosemarie. *Feminine and Feminist Ethics*. Belmont, CA: Wadsworth, 1993.

Trilling, Lionel. *Sincerity and Authenticity*. Cambridge: Harvard University Press, 1971.

CHAPTER 3

Theories of Virtue

Everyday patterns of living both manifest and mold character. In exploring these everyday patterns in subsequent chapters, we will often draw upon insights from philosophical theories about good character and right conduct. This chapter introduces key ideas of some influential *virtue ethicists*: Plato, Aristotle, Aquinas, Hume, MacIntyre, and Pincoffs. According to these philosophers, the moral aim of life is to be a good person—to have a virtuous character and to relate to other people in desirable ways. Right conduct is important, but its role is to express and to support good character.

Virtues as Desirable Character Traits

What is a virtue? It is a trait of character that is desirable because it contributes to the good of humans (and sometimes of animals). Usually the human good includes both the good of the person who has the trait and the good effected by that person. In contrast, a vice is an undesirable trait of character that causes unjustified harm to people (or animals).

What is a trait of character? It is a general feature of a person that is manifested in patterns of actions, intentions, emotions, desires, attitudes, and reasoning. Virtues thus involve, but are not reducible to, actions. Virtues involve tendencies to act *in the right spirit*—that is, for the right reasons, with the right intentions, motivated by appropriate emotions, desires, and attitudes. Moreover, character traits can be revealed not only through actions, but also in feelings, wants, intentions, hopes, interests, attitudes, thoughts, reasoning, and speech.

As an illustration of how character traits involve more than acts, consider the difference between beneficent acts and the virtue of benevolence. Imagine a wealthy person making a very large donation to a charity that distributes food and shelter to the needy. Considered by itself, the act can be called a beneficent one. Does it necessarily follow that the person is benevolent, at least on this occasion? Clearly not. Suppose the government had just passed a law allowing large tax deductions for contributions to this charity. Suppose also that the sole reason the individual made the donation was to gain the deduction, based on the strong recommendation of a financial advisor. In fact, suppose that the donor felt revulsion for the needy people helped by the contribution, regarding them as weak failures. Perhaps the person even feels some regret about the donation and wishes that a better tax deduction had been available, yet takes some consolation from the public recognition he or she receives after making sure that others learn about the donation. Considered by itself, perhaps the *act* can still be called beneficent; but the *person* is not benevolent in making the donation!

Benevolent people are kindhearted. Their actions often spring from concern for the well-being of others. They experience satisfaction in seeing someone helped and in being the one who helps. It is their hope, wish, desire, and intention to benefit others, and they act with the aim of doing so.

In general, virtues require that we act with appropriate attitudes and commitments. They require our actions to be motivated by a perception of the moral good to be achieved rather than by ulterior self-seeking motives alone. Virtues involve our inner life, which defines us just as much as do our actions.

Human Nature and Virtue Theories

Traditional theories of virtue are grounded in theories about human nature, that is, theories about what it means to be a human being. Human nature is described in terms of the capacities, possibilities, limitations, and aspirations of people. Virtues are then defined as character traits that enable people to achieve the good that is possible for them. Virtue theories also offer systematic frameworks revealing the connections among the various virtues and explaining which are most fundamental.

Traditional theories of virtue, then, seek to do three things: (1) provide a theory of human nature that identifies morally relevant facts about human possibilities; (2) use that theory of human nature to define those character traits, or virtues, that enable people to achieve the good made possible by their nature; and (3) present a schema for understanding the relationships among the virtues.

Plato and Aristotle, the two great Greek ethicists inspired by Socrates, base their theories of human nature on a key assumption: that reasoning is the primary purpose or function that sets humans apart from other creatures. In their view, virtues are the excellences that enable humans to exercise their powers of reasoning and live accordingly. Hence, to be virtuous is to live effectively the distinctive form of life for humans.

Plato: Moral Health

According to Plato, the function of something is the task that it is best or uniquely suited to perform. As an example he noted that many objects can be used to trim vines: a carving knife, a chisel, fingernails, or a sharp rock. Only a pruning knife, however, is perfectly suited to the task. Hence, pruning is the function of pruning knives but not of the other objects.

As another example Plato noted that parts of the body have functions to which they are especially well suited: eyes for seeing, ears for hearing, and lungs for breathing. And workers also have professional functions defined by their social roles: for physicians, promoting health; for soldiers, defending the country; for teachers, teaching. By analogy he concluded that humans have a distinctive function to which their lives as a whole are best suited: to exercise, and live by, reason.

Division of the Mind into Three Parts

Plato developed this thesis by distinguishing three main parts of the mind (or soul): Reason, the Spirited Element, and the Appetites. Each has a characteristic function to perform. Reason coordinates and directs the diverse activities of the individual. The Spirited Element, which we might call a sense of honor or pride, has the task of supporting reason in controlling the Appetites. Even though Reason has its own motives for self-control, the Spirited Element is needed to strengthen Reason's ability to maintain control and to avoid shameful conduct. The Appetites maintain the body by satisfying physical cravings for food, drink, exercise, and sex; but they also include undesirable urges.

Why did Plato divide the mind into three parts? These divisions seemed to him to explain psychological conflict. For example, a person has a desire to eat too much and also a directly opposed desire not to overeat. These conflicting desires suggest that one part of the person, Reason, is at war with another part, the Appetites.

Wrongdoing occurs when Reason and the Spirited Element are unable to control the Appetites. Immoral action is thus a symptom of a disordered personality whose proper functions are out of balance. In contrast, morally right action is a sign of inner harmony, in which each part of the mind performs its function well. Virtues make this harmony possible.

Each mental part has its own distinctive virtue that enables it to perform its function with excellence. (The Greek word for "excellence," *aretē*, also translates as "virtue.") *Wisdom* is the virtue that enables Reason to effectively guide both the Appetites and the Spirited Element. *Courage* makes it possible for the Spirited Element to support Reason in controlling troublesome Appetites. *Temperance* or moderation enables the Appetites to be satisfied to a healthy degree and without overindulgence. *Justice* is simply a summary label indicating the presence of the other three virtues: The just (or moral) person is someone whose Reason wisely supervises the Appetites in a temperate manner with the help of a courageous Spirited Element. The four classical Greek virtues, then, are wisdom, courage, temperance, and justice.*

Just as Reason is the most important faculty of humans, wisdom is the most important virtue. In fact, wisdom makes possible all the other virtues. The insight it provides guides the Spirited Element and determines how far the Appetites should be restrained or indulged. Thus, genuine courage and temperance are expressions of wisdom. Plato also believed that complete wisdom would automatically lead to courage and temperance and hence to justice. This belief is called the Doctrine of the Unity of the Virtues: to fully have any one of the main virtues is to have them all.

Plato also applied the idea of virtue as inner harmony in defending another controversial doctrine: that the life of virtue is the happy life. Today we do not think of virtue and happiness as necessarily connected; a good person might be unhappy, and a very bad person might be happy. By happiness, however, Plato did not mean emotional contentment or satisfaction with life. Instead he meant self-fulfillment. He was convinced that the fulfilling life was guided by the virtues, which bring inner harmony. Moreover, he argued, because wisdom makes inner harmony possible and because people gain wisdom through philosophical reflection, the most happy life was that of the philosopher!

Plato and Freud

Plato's ideas bear some interesting similarities to the theories of Sigmund Freud (1856–1939), similarities that are especially striking in view of the fact that their lives were separated by 2,200 years.[1] Like Plato, Freud divided the mind into three main parts: the ego, the id, and the superego, each with its special function. The *ego*, which corresponds roughly with Plato's Reason, integrates activities and deals with problems. The *id* is something like the unconscious parts of the Appetites, especially the sexual and aggressive desires. The *superego* is composed of the values instilled by parents and society. Al-

---

*In the *Republic*, Plato develops an elaborate analogy between good character (inner harmony) in individuals and moral justice in countries (or city-states). He divides countries into three main parts—Rulers, Guardians (police and military), and Producers (farmers and businesspeople)—each with a corresponding virtue: wisdom, courage, and temperance.

though the superego involves more than the Spirited Element (the sense of honor), both can be viewed as aspects of conscience (the sense of right and wrong). To carry the analogy one step further, note that Freud's superego pressures the ego to control the id, much as the Spirited Element helps Reason control the Appetites.

Furthermore, both Freud and Plato hypothesized that this three-part framework could be used to explain mental conflicts and to understand mental health. Freud regarded human life as best when the ego is in full control in dealing with the pressures from the id, the superego, and everyday reality. Neuroses and other forms of mental illness arise when the ego is overwhelmed by an out-of-control id, an overdemanding superego, or a traumatic experience. Mental health involves inner harmony, or at least a healthy balance of tensions, which we achieve when we are able to confront internal and external dangers courageously as a result of self-understanding. According to Freud, self-understanding makes a meaningful life possible through healthy forms of pleasure and work, even though it does not guarantee self-fulfillment as Plato thought.

These similarities are remarkable, but one major difference between Plato and Freud, concerning the nature of wisdom, needs to be stressed. Plato viewed wisdom as insight into what he called the Form of the Good—a purely rational vision of a divine exemplar of goodness, albeit not a personal God. That insight was essential in order to fully acquire all other virtues. Freud, however, would entirely reject Plato's Form of the Good. From the perspective of Freud's secular and scientific outlook, Plato's attempt to ground the virtues in a vision of the Form of the Good was an illusion. In this respect Freud is closer to Aristotle than to Plato. Although Aristotle believed in God, he also believed the virtues are acquired through practical experience, rather than from a grand vision of the Form of the Good.

Aristotle: Rational Emotions and Desires

Even if there existed a supernatural Form of the Good inaccessible to the senses, Aristotle asserted, it would have no relevance to morality. Morality is concerned with practical understanding within this world of experience. Goodness is known through practical endeavors and relationships rather than through semi-mystical encounters with supernatural entities.

Nevertheless, Aristotle accepted virtually all of Plato's other main ethical doctrines. He agreed that the distinctive function of humans is to exercise reason. Good character entails reasoning in accord with wisdom. In turn, wisdom brings with it happiness, understood as well-being and self-fulfillment. And the highest form of happiness is a life based upon philosophical reflection.

The Doctrine of the Mean

Aristotle developed these themes in rich detail, the intricacies of which defy brief summarization. Here we will focus on his central doctrine concerning the virtues: the Doctrine of the Mean, or the Doctrine of the Golden Mean, as it has since been called. The Doctrine of the Mean is intended to apply only to moral virtues such as courage, temperance, justice, and generosity, which Aristotle distinguished from intellectual virtues such as wisdom, intelligence, and prudence. The two groups of virtues are intimately connected in that intellectual virtues are necessary for complete moral virtue (just as Plato believed that wisdom makes the other virtues possible). However, the moral and intellectual virtues differ in two respects.

First, intellectual virtues represent excellences in reasoning skills that can be taught through inquiry and study. Moral virtues, by contrast, are products of habits that begin in childhood and are strengthened in adult life. For example, intellectual understanding of the virtues can be taught in an ethics course, but prudence and courage in confronting danger must evolve from habitual acts of facing risks with discipline and self-control.

Second, there are no limits on the skills and desires involved in exercising intellectual virtues; when it comes to insight and careful reasoning, more is indeed better. By contrast, the moral virtues are defined precisely by limits. That is, moral virtues are tendencies to seek and to identify an intermediate point, or mean, between two extreme desires, emotions, or actions. At one extreme is excess (too much), while at the other extreme is deficiency or defect (too little): "Moral virtue is … a mean between two vices, one of excess and the other of deficiency, and … it aims at hitting the mean point in feelings and actions."[2] That is, moral virtues involve our ability to regularly discern and act on the appropriate middle ground between extremes (of feeling and action), assuming we are not prevented by external obstacles. In this sense, moral virtues are dispositions or habits.

Each moral virtue is directed toward a specific range or spectrum of emotions, desires, and actions. For example, courage consists of excellence in responding to danger and in experiencing fear and confidence. Cowards feel fear on inappropriate occasions or respond to fear and danger without confidence and self-control (that is, they are deficient in self-confidence or self-control). At the other end of the spectrum are foolhardy or rash people, who increase their chances of harm by being excessively confident. Because courage involves *appropriate* confidence and self-control in confronting dangers—which serves to minimize the likelihood of harm—it represents the mean between too little daring and confidence (the defect of cowardice) and too much (the excess of foolhardiness).

Temperance, proper pride, and friendliness are other virtues that were especially important for Aristotle and classical Greek society. Temperance is the tendency to hit the mean between unrestrained indulgence of the appetites (the excess of gluttony) and too little enthusiasm for the pleasures of the appetites (the defect of lacking lively tastes and being inhibited). Proper pride is the mean between self-glorification (the excess of vanity) and insufficient self-confidence (the defect of "poor-spiritedness," which today we might call an inferiority complex). Friendliness is the mean between disingenuous flattery of others (the excess of obsequiousness) and aloofness or surliness (the defect of rudeness). Table 3.1 summarizes these and other virtues that Aristotle discussed (the terminology is updated in a few places).[3]

It may come as a surprise to see wittiness included in the table, since we do not generally think of wit and a sense of humor as moral virtues. For Aristotle, however, *all* desirable qualities of persons were virtues, either moral or intellectual; thus, wit, friendliness, good manners, and social decorum all counted as moral excellences.[4]

Aristotle intended his Doctrine of the Mean to apply to emotions and desires as well as to the actions they motivate. The Doctrine of the Mean is a theory about rational desires and morally desirable emotions. This may seem problematic: We tend to think of morality as concerned with what is under

TABLE 3.1 *Summary of the Virtues as Discussed by Aristotle*

Sphere of Action: Kind of Situation	Type of Emotion, Desire, Attitude	Vice of Too Much (Excess)	Virtue (Mean)	Vice of Too Little (Deficiency or Defect)
Responses to danger	Fear, confidence	Foolhardiness	Courage	Cowardice
Satisfaction of appetites	Physical pleasure	Overindulgence	Temperance	Inhibition
Giving gifts	Desire to help	Extravagance	Generosity	Miserliness
Pursuit of accomplishments	Desire to succeed	Vaulting ambition	Proper ambition	Unambitiousness
Appraisal of oneself	Self-confidence	Vanity	Proper pride	Sense of inferiority
Self-expression	Desire to be recognized	Boastfulness	Truthfulness	False modesty
Response to insults	Anger	Irascibility	Patience	Apathy
Social conduct	Attitudes to others	Obsequiousness	Friendliness	Rudeness
Awareness of one's flaws	Shame	Shyness	Modesty	Shamelessness
Conversation, humor	Amusement	Buffoonery	Wittiness	Boorishness

our immediate control, which appears to rule out emotions from a discussion of morality. Recall, however, that Aristotle regarded moral virtues as the product of years of training in proper habits and modes of response that shape emotions and desires.

Moral Prudence

Virtue consists in "hitting the mean" of emotions and desires as well as of the actions they motivate; but how is this mean determined? Is it simply moderation in the sense that our feelings and desires should always be "lukewarm," never very strong or very weak? Definitely not! Very strong emotions—even distressing emotions such as anger or very exciting emotions such as joy, love, and political enthusiasm—often are precisely the mean in the sense that they are morally reasonable. Hence, the maxim "moderation in all things" does not accurately express Aristotle's view. Furthermore, if mere emotional calm were the goal, virtue would be relatively easy to identify. As Aristotle emphasizes, this is not the case.

> It is a difficult business to be good; because in any given case it is difficult to find the midpoint—for instance, not everyone can find the center of a circle; only the man who knows how. So too it is easy to get angry—anyone can do that—or to give and spend money; but to feel or act towards the right person to the right extent at the right time for the right reason in the right way—that is not easy, and it is not everyone that can do it. Hence to do these things well is a rare, laudable, and fine achievement.[5]

The mean, as Aristotle defines it, is not the lukewarm, but instead the morally reasonable. Reasonable emotions and desires are those directed toward the appropriate person or object, on the suitable occasion, for the correct reason, and with fitting intensity. Unfortunately, this is not very informative: Aristotle seems to move in a circle that does not advance understanding. Having explained morally reasonable conduct in terms of finding the mean, he then explains the mean in terms of morally reasonable conduct. Virtue may indeed be the mean between extremes, and the mean may indeed be the virtuous middle ground between two nonvirtuous extremes. But how is the virtuous middle ground determined?

Aristotle offers two ways out of the circle. First, for each virtue he analyzes in detail the many occasions and motives appropriate to it and its characteristic sphere of action, emotion, and desire. Many of these analyses remain helpful starting points for more precise contemporary discussions of the virtues. Second, Aristotle insists there is a limit to how far such analyses can go. Morality is too complex and too imprecise to be captured in simple rules. It requires the finely tuned sensitivity of wise and prudent individuals. Indeed, Aristotle completes his definition of virtue by alluding to such individuals: "So virtue is a purposive disposition, lying in a mean that is relative to us and determined by a rational principle, and by that which a prudent man would use to determine it."[6] By "rational principle" Aristotle does not mean an abstract rule, but instead the exercise of sound practical judgment.

Critics of Aristotle charge that this ultimate appeal to moral prudence is as much a dead-end as Plato's fruitless appeal to the Form of the Good. Lawrence Kohlberg, for example, dismissed Aristotle's ethics as the "bag of virtues" approach to morality. Most of the act-oriented ethicists discussed in Chapter 4 also criticize Aristotle for failing to look further for general rules about right action.

Yet perhaps Aristotle is simply being true to the moral facts! Even though rational emotions and desires are an essential aspect of the moral life, they defy precise formulation in abstract rules, which cannot express the intricacies of the actual circumstances. Moreover, the subtleties of moral insight and sensitivity that develop through years of experience, study, and habit formation cannot be reduced to simple generalizations. Carol Gilligan would find this emphasis on context-oriented moral reasoning to be on the right track, as do many contemporary virtue ethicists.

Difficulties with Greek Ethics

Much of classical Greek ethics has contemporary relevance, such as Plato's idea of virtue as moral health and Aristotle's insights into practical reasoning. Yet Greek ethics rests on three questionable claims: (1) Human beings have one distinctive function; (2) that function is reasoning; and (3) because this function is distinctively human, it defines human good (as life in accord with reason). Many contemporary ethicists would reject all these claims.

To begin with the third questionable claim, is it obvious that the distinctiveness of a function should define goodness? How do we move from "is distinctive of" to "is the basis of goodness"? It is also distinctive of humans that they display more cruelty than any other earthly creature, but obviously that capacity does not define the good. Perhaps human good lies instead in developing capacities that are shared with other mammals; for example, the capacity to care for members of one's species, or even for members of other species. (Here we think of Koko, the gorilla who lovingly raised a kitten.)

Concerning the second questionable claim, is it true that reasoning is distinctive of human beings? Today we know that some mammals, such as gorillas, chimpanzees, and dolphins, have remarkable reasoning capacities. Admittedly there are great differences of degree between their reasoning capacities and ours. That is also true, however, of many other shared capacities, such as caring for others, forming social ties, or even enjoying sophisticated physical pleasures—capacities that Plato and Aristotle refused to regard as distinctively human.

Turning to the first questionable claim, is it true that humans have just one distinctive function? Humans do many things better than members of other species. Perhaps most of those things involve reasoning in the very wide sense of making inferences and thinking cogently; however, this wide sense of "reason" is too broad to define what is good for humans. Such reasoning is also used in pursuing ingenious forms of evil, as well as sophisticated forms of play, work, and inquiry. Moreover, what about capacities that are not reducible to reason, such as living by religious faith or being altruistic?

Aquinas: Religious Virtues

Emphasis on human capacities other than reason has formed the basis for alternative theories about human nature and virtue. Let us briefly consider two of these theories, one stressing religious faith and the other stressing altruism.

In discussing the Reverend Martin Luther King, Jr., we alluded to the Christian tradition of virtue ethics. Like other religious traditions, it defines human nature by reference to faith in God. Saint Thomas Aquinas (1224–1274) is of special interest because he developed his virtue ethics as a synthesis of the Greeks' four cardinal virtues—wisdom, courage, temperance, and justice—and the key Christian virtues—faith, hope, and charity (love).

Aquinas agreed with Plato and Aristotle that the one purpose of human beings is to live by reason and that pursuing this purpose results in well-being or happiness. Aquinas, however, saw the primary role of reason was to prove that God exists and to discern the "natural law" that God built into our very nature. Hence, for Aquinas, the natural purpose in living by reason became a supernatural purpose: supreme happiness through communion with God, a happiness imperfectly realizable in this world and perfected only in life after death.

Aquinas thought that wisdom (the paramount Greek virtue) implies the theological virtues of faith, hope, and love. He also thought he could use wise reasoning to give several proofs that God exists. Then, from the premise that God is loving and commands that we love, Aquinas derived the virtue of love for God and for humanity. Faith became fidelity to God's commandments with the hope of salvation. The other Greek virtues were also reinterpreted along Christian lines. Courage became the virtue that enables us to endure the dangers of this world, in particular the temptations of sin on the journey toward salvation. Temperance was expanded to include patience and humility, fasting and chastity.

Aquinas's approach to the virtues differs greatly from Aristotle's. For example, Aristotle would view the Christian virtue of humility as more like the vice of failing to have proper pride. Christian discipline of the body through chastity and fasting hardly jibe with the Greek exuberance in the physical. And the idea of charity as the virtue of loving all humankind would be alien to Aristotle, who valued only those exceptional people who achieved high degrees of virtue.

Even more foreign to Aristotle and Plato would be the Christian idea of sin as betrayal of God. For Aquinas and other orthodox Christians, pride, in the sense of setting oneself above God by refusing to live by God's commandments, is the worst sin. By contrast, Aristotle did not view pride in this sense as a vice at all. Earlier than Aquinas, the monastic movement had stressed seven deadly sins: pride, envy (covetousness), anger, sloth, avarice, gluttony, and lust. Aristotle would not have regarded at least two of these— anger and lust—as vices; nor would he have singled out the others as the worst failures of virtue.

Hume: Benevolence and Sympathy

Now consider a very different kind of virtue ethics, the one offered by David Hume (1711–1776). Hume was a skeptic who incisively criticized Aquinas's attempts to offer proofs of God's existence. His view of human nature was based neither on religious faith nor on praise of reason, but rather on the psychology of his day combined with his own attempts to explain the origin of virtue. Yet there is an important overlap between Hume and Aquinas: Both view benevolence as a central virtue. Hume makes it the supreme virtue, and hence of all virtue ethicists Hume most deserves to be called the philosopher of benevolence.[7]

Hume divided the human mind into the domains of reason and sentiment. Unlike Plato, Aristotle, and Aquinas, Hume argued that reason does not provide the moral ends of human life. It merely identifies facts and logical relationships among ideas. Moral purposes in human life derive from sentiment, that is, from our emotional capacities and attitudes. One sentiment in particular is crucial: sympathy, which is the capacity and tendency to feel distress when we see others in distress, and to be pleased when we see them happy. Sympathy, for Hume, is not a virtue, but it enables us to identify and appreciate virtues. It makes us naturally inclined to approve of benevolence in all its forms.

> It may be esteemed, perhaps, a superfluous task to prove, that the benevolent or softer affections are estimable; and wherever they appear, engage the approbation and good-will of mankind. The epithets *sociable, good-natured, humane, merciful, grateful, friendly, generous, beneficent,* or their equivalents, are known in all languages, and universally express the highest merit, which *human nature* is capable of attaining.[8]

Accordingly, for Hume the worst vice is cruelty, not ignorance (as Plato and Aristotle thought) or pride (as Aquinas thought).

In Hume's view, reason does play an important role in morality by providing information about how to act virtuously and by enabling us to adopt an impartial point of view that counteracts bias and ensures consistency. Reason also aids in the development of useful social conventions about how best to distribute property. Because societies differ so greatly, Hume recognizes as legitimate variations in the social conventions that define justice. He also refers to justice as an "artificial virtue," that is, one defined by social conventions, in contrast with the "natural virtue" of benevolence, which recommends certain responses independently of laws and customs.

From Theory to Practice

Our four classical theories of virtue all attempt to identify distinctive human capacities and use them to show the direction of human good and self-fulfillment. Yet these theories are founded on ideas of human nature that differ greatly, some stressing reason, others faith, and still others sympathy. Which theory of human nature is correct or best?

Whereas theoretical ethics has the luxury of engaging in subtle disputes over these theories—as it has done for many centuries—applied ethics must proceed with the urgent task of addressing practical moral needs. Because applied ethicists cannot hope to resolve all theoretical disputes before proceeding, it may seem that the theories are irrelevant for our purposes. Alternatively, should each of us simply choose a theory we find personally appealing and apply it to practical issues?

The view advanced in this book is that the applied ethicists—you and I—are justified in bypassing abstract disputes about human nature and the ultimate theoretical foundations for the virtues. We are free to borrow from any and all theories that offer insights into practical concerns. Notice that we have begun to do that already by emphasizing Plato's notion of inner harmony, an idea of contemporary relevance. We have also focused on Aristotle's Doctrine of the Mean independently of his theoretical contentions about the function of humans. To continue in this eclectic way does not lead to methodological chaos. It simply indicates a desire to benefit from the practical wisdom of great thinkers, a wisdom that can be disentangled from their more debatable speculations.

MacIntyre: Self-Knowledge and Social Goods

This approach to the rich legacy of philosophical theory is in tune with the works of two recent virtue ethicists: Alasdair MacIntyre in *After Virtue* and

Edmund L. Pincoffs in *Quandaries and Virtues*. Both MacIntyre and Pincoffs retrieve and develop central concepts from the tradition of virtue ethics while freeing them from any narrow view of human nature.

MacIntyre retains the hope of grounding the virtues in a theory of human nature, perhaps one emerging from contemporary social science. In this and other respects he can lay claim to an Aristotelian perspective. Yet, unlike Aristotle, he stresses that individuals find their good in an enormous variety of ways. He is sensitive to the great range of settings and legitimate emphases on particular virtues that we referred to in our discussions of Socrates, King, and Stanton. Above all, he emphasizes that the good for an individual cannot be spelled out all at once in advance on the basis of abstract notions such as "reason." Instead, it must be uncovered piecemeal by each of us through a continuing search for self-knowledge.

Life as a Narrative Quest

MacIntyre views each human life as a "narrative quest": a search through time, with intricate threads connecting past, present, and hoped-for future. The quest is a search for self-fulfillment that also allows us to maintain unity among our activities and relationships. At every step there is uncertainty, unpredictability, conflict, and confusion. Hence, we have a recurring need to reexamine our purposes and our grasp of the good. In this sense a human life "is always an [ongoing] education both as to the character of that which is sought and in self-knowledge."[9]

Virtues in this view represent qualities that support us in this pursuit of our good; they do not represent a complete vision of what that good is. MacIntyre writes: "The good life for man is the life spent in seeking for the good life for man, and the virtues necessary for the seeking are those which will enable us to understand what more and what else the good life for man is."[10] This aspect of MacIntyre's theory reminds us more of Socrates' ongoing search for a meaningful life, with the virtues as aids in that search, than of Plato's and Aristotle's belief that the virtues fully define the good and happy life.

Yet the quest for our good and its supporting virtues is not conducted in a vacuum. Many of its key ingredients derive from social *practices*—complex forms of cooperative human activity, such as professions, academic disciplines in science and the humanities, the fine arts, political institutions, families, and even games like chess. Each such practice is directed toward its distinctive "internal goods," that is, toward desirable ends that partially define the practice itself. For example, the profession of medicine aims at health, law aims at social justice, and family life aims at intimate relationships. Achieving these internal goods is largely made possible by the practice itself. In contrast, "external goods" like money, power, and fame do not define the nature of a social practice; they can be achieved in many other ways besides engaging in a particular practice.

Virtues are traits that enable individuals effectively to pursue these internal goods and thereby to enrich their lives. As it pertains to practices, MacIntyre defines a virtue as "*an acquired human quality the possession and exercise of which tends to enable us to achieve those goods which are internal to practices and the lack of which effectively prevents us from achieving any such goods.*"[11] For example, conscientiousness, trustworthiness, loyalty, benevolent concern for the public good, and respect for colleagues are virtues that contribute to the successful pursuit of the internal goods of most professions.

Virtues also help make social practices prosper. Without displays of virtue by many individuals, the practices could not survive or advance. For example, courage in undertaking risks and challenges makes possible the advancement of medicine. Honesty in being careful about facts is essential to all professional practices. And justice plays a role in the recognition of proper authority and respect for others' contributions to a profession.

Each of us participates in many practices, and those forms of participation can come into conflict. Familiar examples might include professional versus private life, college studies versus parental demands, one friendship versus another. The virtues, especially practical wisdom, enable us to integrate the numerous roles we play in various practices and keep them in proper perspective. MacIntyre's most complete characterization of the virtues as aids to our achievement of unity and self-fulfillment is in the following passage:

> The virtues ... are to be understood as those dispositions which will not only sustain practices and enable us to achieve the goods internal to practices, but which will also sustain us in the relevant kind of quest for the good, by enabling us to overcome the harms, dangers, temptations and situations which we encounter, and which will furnish us with increasing self-knowledge and increasing knowledge of the good.[12]

In addition to their role in relation to practices, the virtues are exercised within particular moral traditions that individuals inherit. The good for members of particular families, religions, nations, and cultures is not altogether the same as for others.[13] We are free to modify, but not altogether remove, the influence of the traditions within which we conduct our personal quest for the good. Sometimes, in fact, to deny their influence and relevance is immoral, as in the case of those Americans who deny any responsibility for dealing with contemporary racism on the grounds that they never owned slaves or shot Indians.

Pincoffs: Choices Among Persons

Edmund L. Pincoffs is another contemporary theorist who frees virtue ethics from any narrow theory of human nature. Pincoffs, however, criticizes MacIntyre for focusing so much on practices. In Pincoffs's view, the primary focus in understanding the virtues should be choices among persons rather than social practices: "The natural home of the language of virtue and vice is in that region of our lives in which we must choose between, not acts, lines of acting, or policies, but persons."[14] Choosing among persons has many dimensions: choosing to pursue personal relationships with individuals such as friends, lovers, or a spouse; deciding how to raise children; picking people for a job or public office; and choosing a lawyer, physician, or other professional for some service. It also includes making nuanced adjustments in relationships.

Instrumental and Noninstrumental Virtues

Although Pincoffs is critical of all attempts to confine the virtues within a theory of human nature, he sees it as a legitimate task to organize and clarify connections among the virtues. His classification scheme is depicted in Figure 3.1.[15] As the figure indicates, Pincoffs, like Aristotle, includes as virtues (which are special instances of personality traits) all excellences of the personality, not just moral excellences. Unlike Aristotle, however, he tries to distinguish between moral virtues and nonmoral good traits like wit, social decorum, and noble bearing. Let us briefly explain the terms he uses as headings in the figure.

Instrumental virtues are traits that enable people to pursue their goals effectively or to perform tasks well, whether as individuals (*agent instrumental virtues* such as persistence) or as part of a group (*group instrumental virtues* such as cooperativeness). *Noninstrumental virtues* are traits that are inherently desirable, whether or not they serve as means to further ends. Some noninstrumental virtues, such as nobility and charm, are *aesthetic*, that is, aspects of beauty. Others are *meliorating*; they make life with other people more tolerable. Meliorating virtues include those of tolerance, tact, and other qualities of peacemakers and negotiators (mediating virtues); virtues such as gentleness and cheerfulness, which make individuals more pleasant to live with (temperamental virtues); and traits such as politeness and decency, which make interactions more pleasant (formal virtues).

Finally we arrive at the specifically *moral virtues*. According to Pincoffs, moral

> virtues and vices have the common characteristic that they are forms of regard or lack of regard for the interests of others. They are, roughly, of two closely related classes: those that have to do with direct concern or lack of concern for the interests of other persons, on the one hand, and those that have to do with the unfair advantage that one accords to one's own interests over the interests of others.[16]

FIGURE 3.1   *Pincoffs's Classification of Virtues*

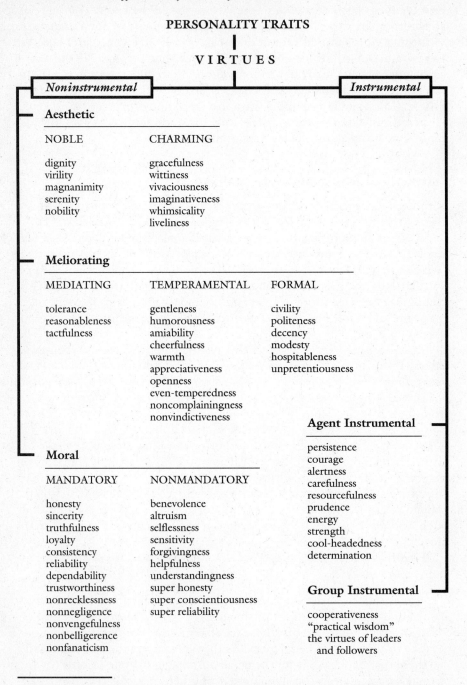

PERSONALITY TRAITS

VIRTUES

Noninstrumental   *Instrumental*

Aesthetic

NOBLE	CHARMING
dignity	gracefulness
virility	wittiness
magnanimity	vivaciousness
serenity	imaginativeness
nobility	whimsicality
	liveliness

Meliorating

MEDIATING	TEMPERAMENTAL	FORMAL
tolerance	gentleness	civility
reasonableness	humorousness	politeness
tactfulness	amiability	decency
	cheerfulness	modesty
	warmth	hospitableness
	appreciativeness	unpretentiousness
	openness	
	even-temperedness	
	noncomplainingness	
	nonvindictiveness	

Agent Instrumental

persistence
courage
alertness
carefulness
resourcefulness
prudence
energy
strength
cool-headedness
determination

Moral

MANDATORY	NONMANDATORY
honesty	benevolence
sincerity	altruism
truthfulness	selflessness
loyalty	sensitivity
consistency	forgivingness
reliability	helpfulness
dependability	understandingness
trustworthiness	super honesty
nonrecklessness	super conscientiousness
nonnegligence	super reliability
nonvengefulness	
nonbelligerence	
nonfanaticism	

Group Instrumental

cooperativeness
"practical wisdom"
the virtues of leaders
    and followers

Source: Edmund L. Pincoffs, *Quandaries and Virtues: Against Relativism in Ethics*. Lawrence, KS: University Press of Kansas, 1986. p 85. © 1986 University Press of Kansas. Reprinted by permission of the publisher.

For Pincoffs, forgoing unfair advantages to ourselves is the minimal requirement of morality, and it is a firm requirement. The *mandatory virtues* pertain to this area of morality. Honesty, truthfulness, and nonrecklessness, for example, are always required. The *nonmandatory virtues*, by contrast, indicate desirable, though not obligatory, traits. Their presence in a person is good, but their absence need not indicate a vice. This is true of benevolence, altruism, forgivingness, and exceptional ("super") degrees of honesty and conscientiousness.

It is possible to accept Pincoffs's main distinctions while objecting to his classification of specific virtues. For example, some of the virtues he lists as nonmoral, such as tolerance, appreciativeness, and decency, might better be regarded as moral virtues, at least insofar as they are forms of direct regard for the interests of other people.

Another objection concerns his characterization of the "natural home" of the virtues as those matters in which we must choose among persons, which oddly centers virtue ethics on acts (acts of choosing among people). It might be closer to the truth to say that virtues guide our *evaluations* of and *attitudes* toward persons, as well as our *relationships* with them. Moreover, choosing among persons, even in Pincoffs's wide sense of "choosing," represents only one dimension of evaluating them. Other dimensions include understanding, encouraging, being inspired by, pitying, and criticizing them.

To say that the virtues guide only our evaluations of other persons, however, is still too restrictive. The virtues are just as important in shaping and fulfilling our own lives and, as MacIntyre argued, in evaluating practices. Moreover, the virtues serve as guides for all our actions, not just those of choosing among persons. Very often moral reasoning and guidance arise from asking what is the honest, decent, considerate, or courageous thing to do. Admittedly, this guidance is rough, as Aristotle emphasized; but the point is that virtues play multiple "natural" roles in our lives, guiding actions, habits, participation in practices, and relationships, as well as guiding choices among persons.

Beyond noting these criticisms, we need not choose between MacIntyre's and Pincoffs's theories. Each offers enriching theoretical frameworks for doing applied ethics without entering into disputes over theories of human nature.

SUMMARY

Virtues are desirable character traits consisting of patterns of emotions, desires, attitudes, intentions, and reasoning as well as actions. Classical virtue theories sought to link the virtues to particular theories about human nature, that is, about the distinctive or most significant human capacities and possibilities. Virtues were then defined as excellences that enable

Theorist	View of Human Nature	Main Concepts	Paramount Virtue	Worst Vice
Plato	Exercise reason to achieve happiness	Moral health as inner harmony	Wisdom, courage, temperance, justice	Ignorance
Aristotle	Exercise reason to achieve happiness	Golden Mean	Wisdom, courage, temperance, justice	Ignorance
Aquinas	God's plan leading to happiness after death	Faith; sin	Faith, hope, charity	Pride
Hume	Sentiment vs. reason	Sympathy	Benevolence	Cruelty

TABLE 3.2   *Four Classical Theories of Virtue*

people to achieve their good by fulfilling their human nature. Virtue theories also identified the virtues most important for self-fulfillment. Table 3.2 summarizes some key concepts discussed in four classical theories of virtue.

Applied ethics bypasses theoretical disputes over which aspects of human nature are most significant for understanding morality and which virtues are paramount. Applied ethicists are free to draw on insights from all virtue theories whenever they are helpful in dealing with practical concerns. MacIntyre and Pincoffs have provided theories of virtue that offer frameworks for doing applied ethics of this sort. MacIntyre defines the virtues as desirable traits that bring unity to the lives of people whose specific good is constantly being reshaped through participation in practices, moral traditions, and personal relationships. Pincoffs defines the virtues as excellences used in choosing among persons. For our purposes, the virtues are best viewed as desirable traits that guide our attitudes toward other people and provide ideals for shaping our own lives and relationships. Pincoffs also offers a classification of the virtues and distinguishes the moral virtues as forms of regard for others' interests.

DISCUSSION TOPICS

1   Discuss Plato's Doctrine of the Unity of the Virtues, which says that to have any one of the main virtues is to have them all. This doctrine contradicts common sense, which tells us that people can be courageous but not benevolent, or honest but not temperate. Is Plato's doctrine plausible only as applied to the four

main virtues he discusses, indeed, only if those virtues are perfectly achieved? In particular, do complete temperance and courage require wisdom?

2   Both Plato and Freud divided the mind into three parts in order to explain inner conflict and to understand mental health. Discuss whether their distinctions are plausible and helpful. Compare and contrast them with Hume's distinction between the sentiments and reason.

3   Plato described the relationship between good character and right conduct in the following passage.

> Justice [i.e., morality]... is not a matter of external behavior, but of the inward self and of attending to all that is, in the fullest sense, a man's proper concern. The just man does not allow the several elements in his soul to usurp one another's functions; he is indeed one who sets his house in order, by self-mastery and discipline coming to be at peace with himself.... When he speaks of just and honorable conduct, he will mean the behavior that helps to produce and to preserve this habit of mind; and by wisdom he will mean the knowledge which presides over such conduct. Any action which tends to break down this habit will be for him unjust; and the notions governing it he will call ignorance and folly.[17]

This passage seems to suggest that right conduct is determined by looking within our personalities and characters. Do you agree? What would Aristotle say about this, given his Doctrine of the Mean?

4   Discuss the similarities and differences between Carol Gilligan's ethics of care (discussed in Chapter 2) and the theories of virtue of Hume and Aristotle.

5   In this chapter we focused on virtues while alluding to vices. Based on what was said, compare and contrast the views of Plato, Aristotle, Aquinas, and Hume about which vices are worst. In doing so, explain their views by reference to their theories of human nature. Which view do you find most insightful?

6   On the basis of Pincoffs's definition of a moral virtue, is faith in God a moral virtue? How about faith in the prospects for sustaining human community and for avoiding nuclear holocaust?

7   Apply to education MacIntyre's distinction between the internal and the external goods of practices, from both a student's and a teacher's viewpoint. Relate this distinction to what was said in Chapter 2 about the aims of liberal education.

8   Select four of the moral virtues listed in Figure 3.1, two mandatory ones and two nonmandatory ones. For each, try to identify what Aristotle would call their corresponding vices (excess and deficiency), their characteristic spheres of action, and their types of emotions and desires.

SUGGESTED READINGS

Aquinas, Saint Thomas. *Introduction to St. Thomas Aquinas.* Anton C. Pegis (ed.). New York: Modern Library, 1948.

Aristotle. *Ethics*. Trans. J. A. K. Thomson and Hugh Tredennick. New York: Penguin, 1976.

Baier, Annette C. "Hume, the Women's Moral Theorist?" In Eva Feder Kittay and Diana T. Meyers (eds.), *Women and Moral Theory*. Totowa, NJ: Rowman & Littlefield, 1987.

Brandt, Richard B. "Traits of Character: A Conceptual Analysis," and "The Structure of Virtue," in *Morality, Utilitarianism, and Rights*. Cambridge: Cambridge University Press, 1992.

Deigh, John (ed.). *Ethics and Personality: Essays in Moral Psychology*. Chicago: University of Chicago Press, 1992.

Fairlie, Henry. *The Seven Deadly Sins Today*. Notre Dame, IN: University of Notre Dame Press, 1979.

Flanagan, Owen, and Amelie Oksenberg Rorty (eds.). *Identity, Character, and Morality: Essays in Moral Psychology*. Cambridge, MA: MIT Press, 1990.

Foot, Philippa. *Virtues and Vices*. Berkeley, CA: University of California Press, 1978.

French, Peter A., Theodore E. Uehling, Jr., and Howard K. Wettstein (eds.). *Midwest Studies in Philosophy, Volume XIII. Ethical Theory: Character and Virtue*. Notre Dame, IN: University of Notre Dame Press, 1988.

Hudson, Stephen D. *Human Character and Morality*. Boston: Routledge & Kegan Paul, 1986.

Hume, David. *Hume's Ethical Writings*. Alasdair MacIntyre (ed.). New York: Macmillan, 1965.

Kruschwitz, Robert B., and Robert C. Roberts (eds.). *The Virtues: Contemporary Essays on Moral Character*. Belmont, CA: Wadsworth, 1987.

MacIntyre, Alasdair. *After Virtue*. Notre Dame, IN: University of Notre Dame Press, 1981.

Meilaender, Gilbert C. *The Theory and Practice of Virtue*. Notre Dame, IN: University of Notre Dame Press, 1984.

Norman, Richard. *The Moral Philosophers*. New York: Clarendon Press, 1983.

Paul, Ellen Frankel, Fred D. Miller, Jr., and Jeffrey Paul (eds.). *The Good Life and the Human Good*. Cambridge: Cambridge University Press, 1992.

Pence, Gregory E. "Recent Work on the Virtues." *American Philosophical Quarterly*, vol. 21 (1984): 281–97.

Pieper, Josef. *The Four Cardinal Virtues*. Notre Dame, IN: University of Notre Dame Press, 1966.

Pincoffs, Edmund L. *Quandaries and Virtues*. Lawrence, KS: University Press of Kansas, 1986.

Plato. *The Republic of Plato*. Trans. Francis MacDonald Cornford. New York: Oxford University Press, 1945.

Stevenson, Leslie. *Seven Theories of Human Nature*. 2nd ed. New York: Oxford University Press, 1987.

Thomas, Laurence. *Living Morally: A Psychology of Moral Character*. Philadelphia, PA: Temple University Press, 1989.

Wallace, James D. *Virtues and Vices*. Ithaca, NY: Cornell University Press, 1978.

CHAPTER 4

Theories of Right Action

Character and conduct are distinguishable but inseparable. Character is displayed largely through patterns of conduct, and conduct shapes character. Up to this point we have emphasized character. Now we focus on philosophical theories about what makes acts right or wrong.

These theories fall into three major categories: duty ethics, rights ethics, and utilitarianism. *Duty ethics* regards duty as the fundamental moral concept, *rights ethics* sees human rights as basic, and *utilitarianism* views overall good consequences as the ultimate moral standard. For each type of theory we will discuss an early classical thinker and a more recent defender.

Lying

Although we will also use other illustrations, we will return throughout this discussion to one common example: the moral status of lying. Lying is a useful point for comparing and contrasting the various theories of right action because it is a simple and familiar act in which all of us have engaged. A lie is an act of stating something believed to be false with the intention of deceiving.

Keep in mind that lying is an instance of trying to deceive, but it is not synonymous with deception. For one thing, to deceive is to succeed in misleading someone, whereas to lie is merely to attempt to do so. Lies sometimes fail to achieve their intended purpose of deceiving, such as when the hearer knows the truth or has reason to suspect that a lie is being told. Furthermore, deception takes forms other than lying, including pretense, withholding information, and purposefully giving so much information that a hearer is overwhelmed and thereby misled. For the sake of simplicity we shall focus on lies, even though most of what we will say applies to other forms of deception as well.

Duty Ethics: Kant and Respect for Persons

Most of us believe that some lies are morally justified—whether permissible or obligatory—but that most lies are not. Philosophers have generally shared this commonsense view, with one dramatic exception. Immanuel Kant (1724–1804) argued that lying is never morally permissible. Kant was a duty ethicist, that is, someone who defines right acts as those required by duty. Unlike most of his followers, he believed there is an *absolute* (exceptionless) duty never to lie. His reasons for this belief will become clear as we discuss other, more influential elements of his moral theory.

Kant endorsed as valid a long list of duties, such as to be honest, to keep promises, to be fair, to help others, to show gratitude for favors, to develop our talents, and to refrain from hurting others or ourselves. For Kant, morality consisted of always trying to do our duty—because we see it is our duty. His importance as a moral philosopher rests in his account of what makes something our duty. He suggested that three abstract duties underlie all others: (1) act so as to respect persons, (2) act on universal principles, and (3) act autonomously. Let us consider each of these duties.

First, to respect persons is to recognize them as being rational or autonomous in ways that should restrict our own actions. Rationality or autonomy is the capacity to make decisions for oneself in the pursuit of reasonable purposes, such as seeking happiness, developing talents, and obeying universal principles of duty that apply to all rational beings. Kant expressed this idea of respect by saying that people are "ends-in-themselves," as opposed to mere means to be used for our own purposes or ends. To put it another way, people have their own rational purposes, which place moral constraints on how we may treat them. Their rationality or autonomy gives them a worth and dignity beyond any price.

For example, to murder, rape, or torture other people is to flagrantly treat them as objects to be used for our purposes, in disregard of their own rational desires not to be treated in these ways. Kant also thought that by lying to and deceiving other people we are using them as objects. To deceive is to manipulate people's beliefs, as well as their actions based on those beliefs, thus striking disrespectfully at the heart of their rationality as they attempt to live truthful lives. Lying represents a kind of coercion by which we seek to distort other people's minds.*

Second, all duties have in common that they are universal; that is, they apply to all rational beings, both human beings and divine beings (if they exist). To determine how we ought to act, we must formulate principles that we can envision and affirm everyone acting on. For example, we can easily imagine everyone acting on the principle "Do not lie," but we cannot imagine

---

*Kant also thought that in lying to ourselves we undermine our own purposes as rational beings. In Chapter 6 we will take up the topic of self-deception and self-directed lies.

everyone acting on the principle "Lie when it suits your own purposes." If everyone followed the latter principle, communication would break down. People would no longer take one another's statements seriously, so both sincere and deceitful statements would become impossible. In trying to conceive of everyone acting on the principle "Lie when it suits your own purposes," a contradiction arises: Everyone does tell lies (which is the hypothesis we begin with) and no one can tell lies, in the sense that it would be impossible to attempt seriously to deceive anyone (which is the implication of the hypothesis).

In other cases we can conceive of everyone acting on a principle, but the principle conflicts with what we will (or choose) as rational beings. For example, we can imagine everyone acting on the rule, "Do not help others who are in desperate need." Yet, as rational agents—by definition of "rational"—we would want people to help us when we are in desperate need. The no-help rule conflicts with our own rational purposes. Thus, the attempt to will the no-help rule as a universal principle results in a conflict within our own will. By contrast, there is no conflict when we universalize a principle of mutual aid: "Help others in desperate need, at least when no great personal sacrifice is required."

Third, the duty to respect persons entails the duty to respect oneself. That duty involves appreciation of our own autonomy as we recognize and respond to specific duties. It is not enough to do only what is required by universal duties; we must also act out of a sense of duty. This is the *good will*: the good intentions to act on principles that respect all rational beings. This sense of duty is the only thing Kant praises as intrinsically good—good in and of itself, independently of its consequences.

Our real nobility lies in this capacity to do what is right because we see it is right, and not solely from ulterior motives such as to make our parents or peers or ourselves happy, advance in careers, or gain religious rewards. Because this good will is a personal expression of our own rational nature, we can be said to "give ourselves the moral law" we live by. And because the moral law consists of universal principles applicable to everyone, we can also regard our own rational nature as the source of moral principles.

To sum up, Kant thought there were three principles underlying all the more specific principles of duty or, as he called them, "maxims" and "moral laws." In his words, these principles are as follows:

1 *Respect persons*: "Act so that you treat humanity, whether in your own person or in that of another, always as an end and never as a means only."[1]

2 *Universalize principles*: "Act only according to that maxim by which you can at the same time will that it should become a universal law."[2]

3 *Be autonomous*: "Act only so that the will through its maxims could regard itself at the same time as universally lawgiving."[3]

Kant spoke of his three fundamental duties as three versions of *the categorical imperative*. He also referred to specific duties like "Don't lie" as categorical imperatives. An imperative is simply a command, and a categorical command is one without conditions or qualifications attached. This is Kant's way of emphasizing that morality requires us to fulfill our duties simply because those duties make valid claims on us, and not solely because we have self-seeking desires. For example, a slogan such as "Honesty pays" says, in effect, that *if* (on the condition that) you want to be successful in business, then you ought to be honest. Such "iffy" commands are *hypothetical imperatives*, to which a condition or hypothesis is attached. Categorical moral commands, by contrast, prescribe such behavior as "Be honest" and "Don't lie"—period.

Duty Ethics: Ross and Prima Facie Duties

More recent ethicists who share Kant's basic orientation reject his belief that everyday principles such as "Don't lie" are absolute. To take an extreme case, suppose that the only way to protect a friend is to lie to her violent spouse who comes looking for her. Here two duties come into conflict: the duty to protect innocent life versus the duty not to lie. One duty has to give way in order that the other duty can be met. Virtually all duty ethicists agree that the duty to protect innocent life should have priority. In fact, even Kant's own fundamental principle to respect persons supports this judgment. Respecting the autonomy of the friend implies protecting her against her violent spouse.

David Ross (1877–1971) was a duty ethicist who was especially sensitive to conflicts among duties. To underscore the frequency of these conflicts, he introduced a technical term widely used today. He said that duties which have justified exceptions when they conflict with other more pressing duties are *prima facie duties*. Most familiar moral maxims, such as "Tell the truth" and "Keep your promises," express prima facie duties in that they all have the potential to conflict with and be overridden by other duties. Even the duty "Do not kill" may be overridden by the duty to defend innocent life, as in a war, or to defend oneself or others against a murderer. Our *actual duty* is what we should do in a specific situation, all things considered, and after we have weighed all applicable prima facie duties reasonably.

What is involved in weighing prima facie duties reasonably so as to determine our actual duty? How should we decide which duty has priority on a particular occasion? There is no infallible test. Kant's guidelines of respecting other persons, universalizing the principle we act on, and being autonomous are too general to resolve all practical dilemmas. Ross argues that we must simply think through all relevant aspects of the situation and exercise our most careful judgment.

When I am in a situation, as perhaps I always am, in which more than one of these *prima facie* duties is incumbent on me, what I have to do is to study the situation as fully as I can until I form the considered opinion (it is never more) that in the circumstances one of them is more incumbent than any other.[4]

This context-bound reasoning is reminiscent of both Carol Gilligan and Aristotle.

When are we allowed to make exceptions, say, to the duty not to lie? Sometimes we may do so to conform to the duty of benevolence, as when we lie to protect the friend from a violent spouse. Should we lie, however, out of benevolence to a close relative who is dying from cancer and does not know it? It depends perhaps on whether the person would want to know the truth in order to make final decisions about his or her affairs or whether the person would want a few peaceful final hours. As Kant would say, the final touchstone is respect for persons' autonomy.

Unlike Kant, Ross saw no need to search beneath the numerous prima facie duties for underlying fundamental moral principles. He does, however, organize prima facie duties into clusters that highlight certain connections among them, yielding the following organizational scheme.[5]

1 Duties deriving from my previous acts
   a Duties of fidelity: those arising from my promises and commitments
   b Duties of reparation: those arising from my previous harm to others
2 Duties deriving from other people's acts
   a Duties of gratitude: duties to return favors or unearned services
3 Duties of justice: to support fair distribution, and oppose unfair distribution, of benefits and burdens in accord with merit
4 Duties of beneficence: duties to help other people
5 Duties of self-improvement: duties to improve our own virtue, intelligence, and talents
6 Duties of non-maleficence: duties not to injure others

Ross contended that it is intuitively obvious, at least to morally mature adults, that each of these is our (prima facie) duty, and they need not be based on more fundamental duties. This intuitive obviousness vanishes, however, when duties come into conflict with each other, creating moral dilemmas. Then we must simply exercise our best moral judgment, realizing, we might add, that others can sometimes aid our reflections.

Rights Ethics: Locke and Liberty Rights

Duty ethicists regard duties as basic, but for most duties they acknowledge a corresponding and derivative right. For example, if I have a duty to you to tell the truth, then you have a right to be told the truth; if I have a duty not to kill you, then you have a right not to be killed by me. Rights ethicists contend that this is backwards. Rights and duties are correlated, but rights are morally fundamental; duties arise because people have moral rights.

The most basic rights of people are *human rights*—rights that exist because we are human beings. We are familiar with this idea from the American *Declaration of Independence:** "We hold these truths to be self-evident; that all men are created equal; that they are endowed by their creator with inherent and inalienable rights; that among these are life, liberty, and the pursuit of happiness." John Locke (1632–1704), who was a major influence on Thomas Jefferson as he drafted the *Declaration of Independence*, listed the three fundamental rights as life, liberty, and property. Other rights ethicists offer different lists, but the key idea remains constant: All people have rights, simply because they are people.

Human rights are "inalienable"; they cannot be given or taken away (made "alien" to us). We may, of course, decide not to exercise them on certain occasions or to allow someone else to exercise them on our behalf. For example, we may sign a "living will" that authorizes our selected guardian to exercise our rights in deciding how we should be treated by physicians if our capacity to think is irreversibly damaged by accident or disease. Even in a coma, however, we retain rights; we merely transfer their exercise to our guardian.

The rights mentioned in the *Declaration of Independence* are human rights; as such they are recognized but not created by that document. Note that human rights and political rights are distinct, even when their content is the same. Political rights are simply those accepted by governments, whereas human rights exist even when governments do not recognize them. Black South Africans, for example, have human rights that their government violates. Similarly, the human rights of women and minorities, especially black people and Indians, have been widely violated in the United States.†

In addition to human rights, there are *special moral rights* which are created by commitments and relationships. Thus, children have a special right to care from their parents, and students have special rights to attend classes at the colleges and universities they enroll in. Again, when a promise is made, the recipient of the promise acquires a special right to have the promise kept.

Locke was especially interested in *liberty rights*, that is, the rights to be left alone by governments and by citizen majorities, which sometimes persecute individuals. Because liberty rights are rights *not* to be interfered with,

---

*We also mentioned human rights in Chapter 2 while discussing Elizabeth Cady Stanton.

†How are such violations possible, given the statement endorsing human rights in the *Declaration of Independence?* Clearly, blacks and women were not regarded by the "founding fathers" as being full and complete people who therefore had human rights. They were treated, in varying dgrees, as property rather than persons.

they are also called *negative rights*. This emphasis on liberty (or negative) rights is represented in contemporary politics by libertarians, who emphasize the rights to property and to privacy, that is, the general right to live as we choose without interference from others.

One need not be a libertarian, of course, to recognize the important role of privacy rights in everyday life. These rights justify some lies; for example, lies to strangers who ask prying questions. Intrusive callers have no right to know certain information, and if a lie is the only way to protect our privacy, so be it. Parents may prudently exercise rights to security when they teach their children to tell certain lies to strangers who call when the children are at home alone.

People have a right, however, to be told the truth in certain situations. Citizens within a democracy have a right to be informed of important governmental actions (except when national security requires secrecy—a much-abused exception). Consumers have the right to be warned of the risks in using products and services, a right that derives from the fundamental right to life. And spouses or close friends may have the right to be told many things that a stranger has no right to know.

Rights Ethics: Melden and Welfare Rights

Just as duty ethicists try to identify a hierarchy of importance among the various duties, so rights ethicists try to distinguish between more and less fundamental rights. Unlike Locke and Jefferson, who singled out three rights as basic, A. I. Melden (1910–1991) suggests there is just one ultimate right from which others can be derived and justified: the right to pursue one's legitimate interests. Legitimate interests are those interests that do not violate other people's similar and equal rights.

This basic right to pursue one's interests can be applied to show why lying is usually wrong. Lies give misleading information that interferes with the pursuit of our interests in large or small ways. Lying subverts, or at least shows a willingness to subvert, the agency (i.e., ability to act) of the person lied to, thereby infringing on that person's right to pursue her or his interests. Justified lies involve situations in which more pressing considerations enter, such as the right to life (as in the violent spouse example) or the rights to privacy and security (as in the example of telephone lies).

Going well beyond Locke, Melden suggests that the basic right to pursue our interests entails rights to be helped in some situations. These are *welfare rights* or *positive rights* to receive certain goods, by contrast with liberty or negative rights to be free from interference. Melden argues that contemporary societies ought to institutionalize welfare systems (contrary to the libertarian political ideology) to support the disadvantaged—who, under certain circumstances, could be any of us. The basic right to pursue our affairs entails a right to the minimal necessities for a decent existence within societies that can readily provide them. This right is limited, however. We have no right, for example, to bankrupt society by demanding millions of dollars of medical care each year.

What are the precise limits of welfare rights to be helped and of liberty rights to pursue our interests? At what point do others' rights restrict our own? No answer is both general and specific enough to resolve all practical disagreements. The extent of rights, and the reasonable exercise of rights, must be understood within given communities of people who live together, make certain claims on one another, and are in a position to help one another. Melden's view of the interplay of rights within communities of shared moral concern is as complex as Ross's account of how duties are interrelated.

Utilitarianism: Mill and Act-Utilitarianism

Utilitarianism is the view that there is a single moral requirement: to produce the most good for the most people, giving equal consideration to each person potentially affected. All duties and all rights arise because of this requirement.

Notice first that utilitarianism is entirely forward-looking—it defines right conduct strictly in terms of future consequences. This contrasts sharply with both duty ethics and rights ethics. As an illustration, consider the question of why promises should be kept. Both duty ethicists and rights ethicists would look first to the past: to the promise itself. The promise is an act of committing oneself to do something, and that commitment, according to the duty ethicist, generates a duty. The promise can also be viewed as an act that gives someone else the right to have something done by the promiser, and that right, according to the rights ethicist, provides the reason to keep the promise. By contrast, according to the utilitarian, promises should be kept only because of the good effects of keeping them and the bad effects of not keeping them.

What about lies? According to John Stuart Mill (1806–1873), lies are usually wrong because they lead to more bad than good effects. Yet there are exceptions to the rule against lying,

> the chief of which is when the withholding of some fact (as of information from a malefactor, or of bad news from a person dangerously ill) would save an individual (especially an individual other than oneself) from great and unmerited evil, and when the withholding can only be effected by denial.... It is not the fault of any creed, but of the complicated nature of human affairs, that rules of conduct cannot be so framed as to require no exceptions, and that hardly any kind of action can safely be laid down as either always obligatory or always condemnable.[6]

With the exception of Kant, all the philosophers we have discussed would agree that some lies are justified. Mill, however, offers a different account of what is usually wrong but occasionally right about telling lies. Instead of referring to duties of veracity (duties to tell the truth) or respect for persons, and instead of appealing to rights to privacy or to pursue our interests, he appeals solely to the good and bad effects of telling lies. Mill says that we should examine each individual action to assess its consequences compared with other options in the given situation. That option which produces the greatest balance of good over bad is the right action. This view is called *act-utilitarianism* (to distinguish it from rule-utilitarianism, which we shall examine later).*

What is the status of everyday rules such as "Do not lie" and "Keep your promises"? Mill believed they are important, but only as rules of thumb that express what should usually be done. They accurately summarize the shared human experience that, usually, more bad than good results from lies and broken promises. The rules do, however, have valid exceptions in situations where to break them is likely to produce more good than bad.

For all utilitarians, rightness is defined in terms of goodness; but what is goodness? Although utilitarians do not agree on the answer to that question, Mill's answer has been influential. Only happiness, according to Mill, is intrinsically good, that is, good in and of itself, independent of any further good effects it may have. All other good things are either components of happiness or means to attaining it ("instrumental goods"). Likewise, unhappiness is intrinsically bad.

What is happiness? Mill often confused it with pleasure. In his more careful moments, however, he distinguished between pleasures, which are short-term emotions, and happiness, which is a long-term state that involves many pleasures, in great variety, mixed with some inevitable pains.† Moreover, Mill stated that the happy life is rich in "higher pleasures," which are better in kind than lower pleasures. The higher pleasures are those of the mind: pleasures of the intellect, of friendship, of love, of art and beauty. The lower pleasures are those of the body: pleasures of eating, drinking, sex, and napping on a sunny afternoon.

Utilitarianism is attractive in part because it seems to provide a way to avoid the reliance on intuitive judgments about how to weigh conflicting duties or competing rights. One simply tallies up the happiness and unhappiness likely to be produced by various options (considering everyone affected) and picks the option that maximizes overall happiness or minimizes overall unhappiness. Unfortunately, Mill's distinction between higher and lower pleasures, as well as between kinds of happiness, greatly

---

*In some passages, however, Mill seems closer to the rule-utilitarian view we will discuss later.

†Perhaps happiness is better viewed as a positive attitude toward our lives when they consist of a satisfying mixture of pleasures, pains, activities, and relationships.

complicates matters. Instead of considering quantities of pleasures and pains, as measured by their intensity and duration, one must factor in elusive *quality* as well. How, in any case, can we make reliable judgments about quality?

Mill proposes to measure quality by taking a poll of qualified judges, that is, people who have experienced and appreciated both of the pleasures being compared. A large majority is decisive.

> Of two pleasures, if there be one to which all or almost all who have experience of both give a decided preference, irrespective of a feeling of moral obligation to prefer it, that is the more desirable pleasure.... Now it is an unquestionable fact that those who are equally acquainted with and equally capable of appreciating and enjoying both, do give a marked preference to the manner of existence which employs their higher faculties. Few human creatures would consent to be changed into any of the lower animals for a promise of the fullest allowance of a beast's pleasures.[7]

In a famous sentence he adds, "It is better to be a human being dissatisfied than a pig satisfied; better to be Socrates dissatisfied than a fool satisfied."[8]

Something puzzling occurs in the passage quoted. Mill begins by comparing the qualities of kinds of pleasures, but ends up talking about "manners of existence" or ways of life involving various kinds of pleasures. It is true that few humans would choose to change places with pigs, but how does that fact prove that physical pleasures are inferior in quality to mental pleasures? Even if philosophers and artists did the voting, would the pleasures of eating and sex (at their best) be voted inferior to those of philosophy and art? The happy life does not banish or minimize physical pleasures; it integrates both physical and mental pleasures.

Nevertheless, Mill's attempt to distinguish among qualities of pleasures is instructive. Without some such distinctions the utilitarian would be forced to sympathetically take into account the pleasures that rapists, sadists, and murderers derive from their grisly deeds. Common sense, however, sees no value or intrinsic goodness in the pleasures of cruelty. How can such pleasures be ruled out without assuming we already know what is right or wrong independently of the utilitarian standard?

Utilitarianism: Brandt and Rule-Utilitarianism

Richard B. Brandt, a contemporary utilitarian, places restrictions on which pleasures are intrinsically good. He suggests that only rational desires, rational preferences based on those desires, and rational pleasures derived from satisfying those desires should be counted in calculating good and bad consequences. Intrinsic good thus becomes the satisfaction of rational desires.

Rational desires are those that survive after intensive and persistent scrutiny in light of all facts relevant to them and on the basis of clear and logical thinking. Desires to overeat, to smoke, to use harmful drugs, or to hurt ourselves in other ways would not survive this scrutiny. Nor, Brandt hopes, would cruel desires such as those of the rapist and the sadist. This process of making ourselves vividly aware of the full implications of our desires is "cognitive psychotherapy" in that it involves the same kind of dramatic transformations brought about by therapeutic psychology.

An act-utilitarian who accepted this view of intrinsic goodness would define right acts as those that maximize satisfaction of the rational desires of all people affected. Brandt, however, does not proceed in this direction. Like all the ethicists discussed in this chapter except for Mill, Brandt thinks that morality must give more weight to principles or rules than to individual actions. He suggests that calculation of the consequences of each act individually encourages biased reasoning rather than impartial concern for all people's interests. It also means we are less able to count on how others will behave. For example, it is more impartial, as well as more publicly reliable, to have all people obey the rule "Pay your taxes as required by law" than to encourage each person to calculate the good and bad effects of reporting all their taxable income. Similarly, it is better for people simply to obey the rule "Don't lie" except in certain exceptional instances (such as to protect innocent life) than to encourage people to calculate the good and bad effects of each contemplated lie.

Brandt also argues that act-utilitarianism requires far too much of us. It would have us constantly striving to be benevolent so that each of our actions would bring about maximum good. Such moral pressure is better suited to saints than to humans. A realistic morality would require only limited benevolence, such as helping other people in desperate need. Nevertheless, Brandt agrees with Mill that good consequences are all that matter in deciding what is right and wrong. This, together with his emphasis on rules rather than individual acts, led him to develop rule-utilitarianism.

Rule-utilitarianism is the view that an act is right when it falls under a set of rules which, if accepted by the society in which one lives, would produce the most good for the most people. The set of rules is called a moral code. Acts are right, then, when they conform to that moral code that would produce more overall good than would alternative moral codes.

Justifiable moral codes must be workable within a given society. They are not ideal principles for angels, but rules that the vast majority of people in a given society can grasp and use to guide their conduct. A satisfactory moral code must also be comprehensive and specific enough to apply to most of the moral decisions we confront. Brandt objects, for example, that some of Ross's rules are too abstract. He prefers rules like "Tell the truth except when great harm would result."

Which Theory Is Best?

Each of the theories we have examined has many defenders, and philosophical debates over them are subtle and centuries-old. What does this controversy imply for applied ethics? Does it mean that we should disregard all theories until disputes about them are resolved? Or should the applied ethicist simply pick the one that seems most reasonable?

Let us first ask what it means to say that one theory is more reasonable than another. Several criteria are widely used in evaluating theories about right action. The theory must be clear, coherent (rather than contradictory), comprehensive (widely applicable to moral problems), and not contradicted by any facts. The most important criterion, however, is that the theory be consistent with our most carefully considered moral convictions about what ought to be done in practical situations. If, for example, a theory implied that it is all right to torture babies or lie just to hurt others for fun, we would know something was wrong with the theory!

Most debates over the theories turn on whether the theories do have unacceptable implications in specific instances. One problem is that tracing the precise implications of an abstract theory for a specific example can be an intricate procedure. Another problem is that different people have different judgments about what is right or wrong in given examples! For example, people have different opinions about whether early fetuses are persons, and that hampers the testing of theories with respect to abortion questions.

So should we then just pick a theory, somewhat arbitrarily or on the basis of debatable intuitions? Or should we jettison all the theories while doing applied ethics? I suggest that we are free to employ all the theories (as was suggested in connection with theories about virtues).

There are three reasons for allowing ourselves this freedom. First, for the most part all the theories are compatible; they usually agree with each other in their practical implications (with the possible exception of act-utilitarianism). For example, duty ethics, rights ethics, and rule-utilitarianism all condemn lies that wantonly hurt people. They all justify the principle "Do not lie except in special circumstances where a more pressing moral principle justifies the lie." With the exception of Kant's absolutistic versions of duty ethics, all the theories also agree that lies to protect innocent life—as in the case of the violent spouse—are justified.

Such a wide agreement in applications should not be surprising. All the theories are designed to express the common or overlapping moral experiences of people, and all are roughly consistent with it. These wide areas of overlap suffice for many purposes of the applied ethicist. Examined in this light, the theories are alternative ways of systematizing our view of morality, rather than competing foundational principles that attempt to provide more basic and certain principles. Indeed, do we need any more fundamental principles to establish our convictions that rape and torture are wrong?

Second, besides being largely compatible, the theories are also complementary. Each points to important moral considerations but highlights them in different ways. Suppose, for example, we ask whether it is permissible to lie to our parents to protect a friend whom the parents unfairly condemn because of her or his ethnic identity. The duty ethicist emphasizes the relationships of trust with both the parents and the friend, as well as the duties to maintain trust in those relationships. The rights ethicist emphasizes the rights of parents to know certain things about their children, and also the rights of children to lead their own lives. The utilitarian points to the effects of lying on both relationships. Although the three theories have different emphases, each appreciates the importance of the relationships involved, and each tries to balance conflicting moral reasons.

Third, and perhaps most important, relatively little of import turns on whether one is a duty ethicist, a rights ethicist, or a rule-utilitarian. Theories are best viewed as general frameworks for organizing moral reflection and for developing moral arguments. The precise practical implications of those arguments depend on the specific version of the theory employed. Notice the remarkable differences between the two versions of each theory that we mentioned. Kant's absolute (exceptionless) duties are dramatically different from Ross's prima facie duties that must be weighed against one another on the basis of contextual judgments. Locke's emphasis on liberty rights has vastly different practical implications from Melden's acceptance of welfare rights. Mill's act-utilitarianism, which also stresses certain kinds of pleasures, is considerably different from Brandt's rule-utilitarianism, which stresses rules and rational desires.

In fact, for practical purposes it seems that Brandt's rule-utilitarianism has more in common with Ross's duty ethics than it does with Mill's act-utilitarianism. Act-utilitarianism might allow occasional cheating on taxes when good effects for oneself outweigh minimal good effects to others. Brandt is as stern as Ross, however, in urging obedience to rules that sustain social trust.

Again, a libertarian who, like Locke, emphasizes liberty rights (rights to be free from interference by others) would find many taxes immoral because they are used to support welfare systems. Hence, he or she may feel justified in not reporting some taxable income. In contrast, a rights ethicist who shares Melden's appreciation of welfare rights would stress the importance of paying taxes to benefit those in need.

In short, the applied ethicist should feel free to employ all three types of ethical theories when they aid practical reflection. The concepts of duties, rights, and utility are all of practical use in doing applied ethics; it is unnecessary to decide which is most fundamental.

SUMMARY

There are three main types of ethical theories about right action, each of which can be further subdivided based on the viewpoints of individual philosophers. Duty ethicists define right acts as those required by duties. Kant views duties as absolute (having no exceptions); however, Ross believes that duties are typically prima facie (i.e., they may have exceptions when they conflict with other duties). One's actual duty is determined by context-bound reasoning about which prima facie duty is most important on a specific occasion.

Rights ethicists define right acts as those that respect rights. Locke sees the basic human right as liberty, or the negative right not to be interfered with by others. Melden theorizes that the basic human right is to pursue one's legitimate interests, and he argues that we have welfare or positive rights to be helped by other members of a community.

Utilitarians reduce all obligations to one moral requirement: to produce the most good for the most people, giving equal consideration to each person affected. Mill defends act-utilitarianism, which requires each act to produce the most good, and he understands goodness to be happiness. Brandt favors rule-utilitarianism, which classifies right acts as those falling under a moral code which, if adopted in a specific society, would produce the most good. He construes goodness as the satisfaction of rational desires (those desires that survive scrutiny in light of all relevant facts).

DISCUSSION TOPICS

1 In each of the instances a–e below, decide whether it is permissible (all right), obligatory (required), or impermissible (wrong) to deceive. If you cannot answer, what more information do you need to know? Which moral considerations are relevant to each case according to duty ethics, rights ethics, act-utilitarianism, and rule-utilitarianism?

   a You are invited to a party that you do not wish to attend. So as not to hurt the host's feelings, you lie, saying you have to go somewhere else that night.

   b Persistent insomnia and nervousness send you to your doctor seeking tranquilizers. Your doctor discerns that the problem is psychosomatic, caused by temporary problems at home. When she cannot convince you of this, she says she will give you only one month's supply of tranquilizers. Unbeknownst to you, she writes a prescription for a placebo—a sugar pill—that actually calms you down because you believe it is a tranquilizer.

c You know your car needs major repairs, but you also need to sell it for more than it is worth in order to pay an overdue college tuition bill. When a potential buyer asks if anything is wrong with the car, you state emphatically that it is in great shape.

d Like 20 million other Americans, you have genital herpes, a viral disease, usually transmitted through sexual contact, whose symptoms range from painless blisters to extremely painful sores, shooting muscle pains, and fever. You have been celibate for fifteen months when the partner you are dating offers to change that. You very much desire to consent and do not think that the affair would be immoral. At the time, you have good reason to believe that the herpes is not contagious, because you have no open sores or incipient sores. In a half-joking tone your partner asks, "You don't have any medical problems, do you?" With similar playfulness you shake your head no.

e In a situation similar to the previous one, your potential partner this time lies to you to conceal the fact that he or she has AIDS, the deadly, sexually transmitted Acquired Immune Deficiency Syndrome.

2 In an essay entitled "On a Supposed Right to Lie from Altruistic Motives," Kant argued that if we lie in an attempt to prevent a murder, we are legally and morally blameworthy for any ill effects of the lie:

> If by telling a lie you have prevented murder, you have made yourself legally responsible for all the consequences; but if you have held rigorously to the truth, public justice can lay no hand on you, whatever the unforeseen consequences may be. After you have honestly answered the murderer's question as to whether this intended victim is at home, it may be that he has slipped out so that he does not come in the way of the murderer, and thus that the murder may not be committed. But if you had lied and said he was not at home when he had really gone out without your knowing it, and if the murderer had then met him as he went away and murdered him, you might justly be accused as the cause of his death. For if you had told the truth as far as you knew it, perhaps the murderer might have been apprehended by the neighbors while he searched the house and thus the deed might have been prevented. Therefore, whoever tells a lie, however well intentioned it might be, must answer for the consequences, however unforeseeable they were.[9]

Do you agree with Kant? In your answer, distinguish between the question of right and wrong conduct and the question of blameworthiness and guilt for wrongdoing.

Also, in commenting on Kant's view, consider a lie told in Sartre's short story, "The Wall." A soldier tries to deceive enemy interrogators by saying his compatriot is hidden at a cemetery. The soldier believes he is lying because he is confident that his compatriot is staying at a cousin's house, not at the cemetery. Unbeknownst to the soldier, the compatriot sneaks to the cemetery, where he is captured and shot by the enemy soldiers. Is the soldier guilty for the death of the compatriot?

3 List all the absolute moral principles you can think of; that is, all the moral principles for which you believe there are no permissible exceptions under any circumstances. Is it a long list?

4   The protagonist in Dostoevsky's novel *Crime and Punishment* plans and carries out the murder of a very wealthy pawnbroker. He does so with the intention of stealing her money and distributing it to poor people who desperately need it. The idea was inspired by the following remarks about the pawnbroker he overheard in a restaurant.

> On one side we have a stupid, senseless, worthless, spiteful, ailing, horrid old woman, not simply useless but doing actual mischief, who has not an idea what she is living for herself, and who will die in a day or two in any case.... On the other side, fresh young lives thrown away for want of help and by thousands, on every side! A hundred thousand good deeds could be done and helped, on that old woman's money.... Hundreds, thousands perhaps, might be set on the right path; dozens of families saved from destitution, from ruin, from vice.... Kill her, take her money and with the help of it devote oneself to the service of humanity and the good of all. What do you think, would not one tiny crime be wiped out by thousands of good deeds?[10]

How would a duty ethicist, a rights ethicist, an act-utilitarian, and a rule-utilitarian respond to this question?

5   In discussing Locke and Melden we drew a distinction between liberty (negative) and welfare (positive) rights. Apply that distinction to Carol Gilligan's conception of rights (Chapter 2): Which of the two kinds of rights did she have in mind in her "ethics of justice"? How might her "ethics of care" accommodate what Melden says about positive rights?

6   Lawrence Kohlberg, discussed in Chapter 2, was directly inspired by the work of Kant. What connections do you see between the ideas of Kant and Kohlberg?

SUGGESTED READINGS

Bok, Sissela. *Lying*. New York: Vintage Books, 1979.

Bok, Sissela. *Secrets*. New York: Pantheon Books, 1982.

Brandt, Richard B. *A Theory of the Good and the Right*. Oxford: Clarendon Press, 1979.

Gowans, Christopher W. (ed.). *Moral Dilemmas*. New York: Oxford University Press, 1987.

Hill, Thomas E. *Dignity and Practical Reason in Kant's Moral Theory*. Ithaca, NY: Cornell University Press, 1992.

Kant, Immanuel. *Foundations of the Metaphysics of Morals*. Trans. L. W. Beck. New York: Liberal Arts Press, 1959.

Kant, Immanuel. "On a Supposed Right to Lie from Altruistic Motives." In L. W. Beck (trans. and ed.), *Critique of Practical Reason and Other Writings in Moral Philosophy*. Chicago: University of Chicago Press, 1949.

Locke, John. *Two Treatises of Government*. Cambridge: Cambridge University Press, 1960.

Melden, A. I. "Are There Welfare Rights?" In Peter G. Brown, Conrad Johnson, and Paul Vernier (eds.), *Income Support: Conceptual Policy Issues*. Totowa, NJ: Rowman & Littlefield, 1981.

Melden, A. I. (ed.). *Ethical Theories: A Book of Readings*. 2nd ed. Englewood Cliffs, NJ: Prentice-Hall, 1967.

Melden, A. I. *Rights and Persons*. Berkeley, CA: University of California Press, 1977.

Mill, John Stuart. *Utilitarianism*. Indianapolis, IN: Hackett, 1979.

Narveson, Jan. *The Libertarian Idea*. Philadelphia, PA: Temple University Press, 1988.

Norman, Richard. *The Moral Philosophers: An Introduction to Ethics*. Oxford: Clarendon Press, 1983.

Rachels, James. *The Elements of Moral Philosophy*. 2nd ed. New York: McGraw-Hill, 1993.

Rawls, John. *A Theory of Justice*. Cambridge, MA: Harvard University Press, 1971. (A very influential Kantian)

Ross, David. *The Right and the Good*. Oxford: Clarendon Press, 1930.

Sartre, Jean-Paul. "The Wall." In Walter Kaufmann (ed.), *Existentialism from Dostoevsky to Sartre*. New York: New American Library, 1975.

Smart, J. J. C., and Bernard Williams. *Utilitarianism: For and Against*. Cambridge: Cambridge University Press, 1973.

PART TWO

Self-Respect and Integrity

Humility, on the one hand, and true, noble pride on the other, are elements of proper self-respect.... In the light of the law of morality, which is holy and perfect, our defects stand out with glaring distinctness and on comparing ourselves with this standard of perfection we have sufficient cause to feel humble. But if we compare ourselves with others, there is no reason to have a low opinion of ourselves; we have a right to consider ourselves as valuable as another. This self-respect in comparison with others constitutes noble pride.[1]

Immanuel Kant

By "proper self-respect" Kant meant an appreciation of our own moral worth, which appreciation we demonstrate by acting in ways appropriate to our dignity. To treat ourselves with respect requires acting in ways that express our self-worth as moral agents, that is, as persons having moral capacities and concerns. In turn, to act so as to express our moral self-worth requires striving to be moral by treating ourselves and other people as having moral worth. This connection between self-respect and moral striving makes sense of the above quotation: Self-respect entails moral humility, which is the awareness of our moral flaws; yet self-respect also entails having a sense of our moral worth and dignity—"noble pride"—as beings who strive to be moral. Because it has its basis in moral striving, self-respect is closely tied to moral integrity—the coherence of a life based on moral concern. In Kant's terms, integrity requires that we (1) commit ourselves to live by correct moral principles and (2) struggle to live up to those commitments in our actions and relationships. This effort to live a morally unified life is the basis for proper self-respect.

We will use the term *self-respect* in the sense of what Kant called *proper self-respect*, as we defined it above: the appreciation of one's moral worth based on moral integrity and demonstration of that appreciation by treating oneself with respect. Part Two explores some of the ways in which self-respect is undermined or supported.

At the very least, treating ourselves with respect requires that we care about ourselves, value our talents and aspirations, and seek our self-fulfill ment. In Chapter 5 it is argued that self-destructiveness violates our moral duty to treat ourselves with respect.

Self-understanding is needed in order to appreciate our moral worth and to assess our character in light of moral standards. We can become aware of our character flaws and wrongdoing only by being honest with ourselves, which requires that we avoid self-deception about immorality, as Chapter 6 discusses.

Self-respect, as mentioned above, is based on moral integrity, which requires a genuine effort to live up to our moral convictions and commitments. Moral weakness is the failure to make such an effort. Chapter 7 shows how moral weakness undermines integrity and erodes self-respect. Chapter 7 also discusses courage in confronting risks and dangers so as to meet our moral and personal aspirations—the kinds of moral effort and courage which enable us to maintain integrity.

Voluntary death raises poignant questions about self-respect, integrity, and dignity. Chapter 8 discusses why there is a strong presumption against suicide but also presents the cases for and against viewing suicide and voluntary euthanasia as sometimes justified.

CHAPTER 5

Valuing Oneself

Self-respect is valuing oneself in morally desirable ways. As such, it concerns the ethics of attitudes as well as the ethics of conduct. Recalling Aristotle's Doctrine of the Golden Mean, we can understand the virtue of self-respect as the appropriate middle ground between the undervaluaton of oneself and inflated self-evaluations. We will discuss masochism, self-depreciation, and irrational forms of guilt and shame as examples of undervaluing oneself. We will discuss snobbery as an example of inflated self-evaluations. First, however, we will consider the idea of responsibilities (to ourselves) to respect ourselves.

Responsibilities to Oneself

Those philosophers who draw a sharp distinction between morality and prudence have denied there are responsibilities to oneself. Prudence, they assert, involves promoting one's own good (self-interest), whereas morality is concerned with promoting the good of others. The only moral duties concerning self-interest are negative duties *not* to pursue self-interest when it hurts other people.

This separation of morality and prudence seems tempting if we are preoccupied with the human tendency toward selfishness, that is, toward excessive pursuit of self-interest at the expense of other people. Thinking along these lines, it is easy to assume that people are naturally inclined to seek their own good and that morality essentially represents a set of restrictions on that pursuit. Yet, as the examples in this chapter remind us, we do not always pursue our own good; sometimes we unjustifiably harm ourselves.

Another source of the separation between morality and prudence is a narrow conception of rights. If morality is regarded essentially as respect for others' rights, then harming oneself does not seem immoral. If we choose to harm ourselves, that is our business—and our right—as long as we do not infringe on other people's rights. Some human rights ethicists, however, have rejected this line of thought, and for good reason. They emphasize that we ought to appreciate our own moral rights and assert them responsibly so that we do not allow other people to enslave or degrade us. Implicit in this argument is the idea that we ought to have a sense of dignity because we possess human rights.

Other ethical theories embrace the idea of responsibilities to ourselves even more directly. Utilitarians stress that we ought to produce the most good for the most people, counting each person equally—including ourselves. To inflict harm on ourselves without justification is as wrong as wantonly harming other people, and for exactly the same reason. Moreover, utilitarians emphasize that many of our actions primarily affect ourselves. Because we have direct control over our own actions, we have more chances to affect our own good.

Virtue ethicists stress that good character traits are often as beneficial to ourselves as to others. This is certainly true of the virtues of courage and self-discipline, which enable us to pursue both our own good and the good of other people. Similarly, vices harm not only others but also ourselves. For example, cruelty is bad whether it is directed toward other people or toward oneself, and weakness of will damages our interests as well as those of other people.

Of all the ethicists, Kant placed the greatest emphasis on moral duties to ourselves. He insisted that these duties arise because we have the same moral worth as other people. Consider his fundamental principle to "act so that you treat humanity, whether in your own person or in that of another, always as an end and never as a means only."[1] The basic duty to treat ourselves with respect is not a mere "hypothetical imperative" that states, "*If* you want to be happy, then don't harm yourself." Instead, it is a categorical imperative that commands without conditions attached: "Respect yourself!"

Indeed, Kant thought that duties to ourselves were even more fundamental than duties to other people: "Far from ranking lowest in the scale of precedence, our duties towards ourselves are of primary importance and should have pride of place.... The prior condition of our duty to others is our duty to ourselves; we can fulfill the former only in so far as we first fulfill the latter."[2] In particular, failure to meet our duties to ourselves to maintain our rational capacities erodes our ability to meet our duties to other people. Some glaring examples, which are discussed in later chapters, are unjustified suicide and abuse of drugs and alcohol. In this chapter we will discuss instances of harming oneself through distorted emotional attitudes toward oneself.

Valuing oneself, then, is no less morally obligatory than valuing other people is. We have a responsibility to respect ourselves, just as we have responsibilities to respect other people. Let us next clarify self-respect by distinguishing it from self-esteem.

Self-Respect Versus Self-Esteem

Self-respect is often confused with self-esteem. *Self-esteem* refers to self-affirmation—feeling good about oneself, approving of and liking oneself. It is a subjective matter in that the self-affirmation may be excessive and unwarranted. Self-respect, by contrast, consists of valuing oneself for the right reasons and in morally appropriate ways, on the basis of moral integrity. It is a justified attitude. It is a virtue.

In the following passage, John Rawls, an influential contemporary Kantian philosopher, equates self-respect and self-esteem: "We may define self-respect (or self-esteem) as having two aspects. First of all ... it includes a person's sense of his own value, his secure conviction that his conception of his good, his plan of life, is worth carrying out. And second, self-respect implies a confidence in one's ability, so far as it is within one's power, to fulfill one's intentions."[3]

In equating self-respect and self-esteem, Rawls defines them interchangeably in terms of two positive attitudes about oneself: (1) self-affirmation, the attitude that one's life is worthwhile, and (2) self-confidence, the attitude that one has the ability to meet one's goals if given the opportunity. Note that these attitudes could be held by sadists or entirely selfish people. Such people might value their lives and be self-confident. They would then have self-esteem but not self-respect, in Kant's sense, for they would lack moral integrity, which requires one to strive to unify one's life around moral commitments. Our *description* of them as having self-esteem would not entail an *evaluation* of them as having the virtue of self-respect. Self-esteem is a purely psychological idea; self-respect is a moral concept.

Despite this difference, Kant might agree with Rawls's insight into the psychological importance of self-esteem and extend it to emphasize the importance of proper self-respect.

> When we feel that our plans are of little value, we cannot pursue them with pleasure or take delight in their execution. Nor plagued by failure and self-doubt can we continue in our endeavors. It is clear then why self-respect is a primary good [i.e., a good that every rational person desires]. Without it nothing may seem worth doing, or if some things have value for us, we lack the will to strive for them. All desire and activity becomes empty and vain, and we sink into apathy and cynicism.[4]

Thus, in Kant's view, both self-esteem and self-respect are essential in pursuing a life of moral integrity. Both bring a sense of significance to our endeavors and lead us to pursue them with vigor. Without them we easily become cynical about the moral contribution we have to offer, and cynicism can damage our relationships with other people. In this and other ways, self-respect and self-esteem are prerequisites for respecting other people. At the same time, the primary importance of self-respect remains centered on oneself: Self-respect is the recognition of one's moral worth and the accompanying disposition to act in morally appropriate ways with regard to oneself.

We can distinguish between two types of self-respect which differ according to the reasons for valuing oneself.[5] *Recognition self-respect* is valuing oneself because one has inherent moral worth, just as each and every person does. This was Kant's notion. *Appraisal self-respect* is accurately evaluating oneself according to how well one sets and meets moral standards. It concerns assessments of one's specific character. Hence, it can be possessed in varying degrees depending on how fully one meets one's standards, as well as on how high one sets those standards. By contrast, recognition self-respect is not a matter of degree, but instead a simple recognition of our moral worth. This distinction parallels two types of moral attitudes toward other people: recognition of their value as persons versus evaluation of their character as better or worse.

Recognition self-respect consists of valuing oneself as having inherent moral worth, but what is that? Each of the traditional ethical theories implies an answer. Kant's duty ethics locates the worth of persons in their capacities for rational action, and in particular in their capacities (or potentials) for responding to universal principles of conduct. Plato and Aristotle's virtue ethics also linked the worth of persons to their rational capacities, but stressed the role those capacities play in promoting self-fulfillment (rather than in discerning universal principles of conduct). Locke's rights ethics understands the worth of persons in terms of their possession of human rights. Mill's utilitarianism implies that persons have special worth because of their capacity for happiness, which is linked to friendship, love, and other caring relationships.

In the eyes of some philosophers, these traditional accounts of the basis for self-respect seem too narrow. Each attempts to pinpoint the inherent worth of persons in one abstract feature, whether rationality, the capacity for happiness, or the possession of rights. Alternatively, Robin Dillon suggests that an adequate conception of recognition self-respect would accent the individuality of persons and our responses to persons as individuals.[6] Writing from a feminist viewpoint and influenced by Carol Gilligan, Dillon seeks to enrich the idea of recognition self-respect with the idea of caring for oneself. Traditional conceptions of self-respect, especially Kant's, seem to her emotionally impoverished. Self-respect implies caring *about* and *for* oneself in an emotionally rich way. Thus, it implies paying attention to one's needs as they are perceived on the basis of self-understanding. It also implies valuing oneself as a specific individual, in awareness of one's particular features, as well as one's general human capacities. Because we view ourselves as individuals largely in terms of our social relationships, self-respect consists of valuing oneself in relation with other persons, rather than in the abstract.

Some philosophers would go further and expand the idea of self-caring to include self-love.[7] Just as parents should love their children unconditionally, or at least unconditionally within wide limits, so we should love ourselves. Self-love does not mean mushy sentimentality and self-indulgence. It means self-affirmation based on realistic self-understanding and self-control. It is unconditional in that it remains constant and does not waver according to our merits or faults at any given time.

Whether or not we expand traditional accounts of self-respect by introducing the emotionally rich ideas of self-caring and self-love, we can agree that self-respect requires certain minimum conditions. It requires due attention to our self-fulfillment and happiness and appreciation of our inherent moral worth as persons. Even more fundamentally, just as the most blatant way to undervalue other people is to inflict undeserved harm on them, the most obvious way to undervalue oneself is to inflict undeserved harm on oneself. Here we shall consider three examples of unjustified self-harm: masochism, self-depreciation, and excessive shame and guilt. These examples provide an interesting range: suffering intentionally inflicted on oneself, passive submission to degradation, and irrational emotional responses.

Masochism

Let us begin with a clear-cut example of self-destructiveness. Lise, in *The Brothers Karamazov*, breaks her engagement to Alyosha. She explains to him that he is too gentle and forgiving for her taste:

> I was just thinking for the thirtieth time what a good thing it is that I broke off our engagement and decided not to become your wife. You wouldn't be much of a husband, you know.... I want someone to marry me, tear me to pieces, betray me, and then desert me. I don't want to be happy.[8]

After Alyosha leaves, Lise

> unlocked the door, opened it a little, put her finger in the crack, and slammed the door as hard as she could. Ten seconds later she released her hand, went slowly to her chair, sat down, and looked intently at her blackened, swollen finger and the blood that was oozing out from under the nail. Her lips quivered.

> "I'm a vile, vile, vile, despicable creature," she whispered.[9]

As this example suggests, we should distinguish between pain and emotional responses to pain, and between suffering and the attitudes adopted toward suffering. Pain cannot be defined as something inherently unenjoyable, or suffering as something that a person dislikes. Lise both seeks and causes her pain and suffering. To that extent she enjoys it and has an affirmative attitude toward it. This partially explains why she inflicts it on herself; the deeper explanation no doubt lies in her upbringing and social conditioning, which instilled in her low self-esteem and self-respect.

Lise is a masochist. She causes and enjoys her own pain, without justification. Many a saint and marathon runner have inflicted worse harm to their bodies and found value in doing so. And whereas many of us may have enjoyed "toying" with a loose and slightly irritating tooth, this pain, although lacking justification, is very mild. In contrast, people are masochists when, like Lise, they enjoy or seek severe pain, subjugation, or degradation because of irrational motives. As with Lise, the suffering of masochists is not redeemed by some reasonable goal for which the masochistic act is the necessary means.

Why, however, cannot the enjoyment of suffering for its own sake be morally permissible, or at least not irrational? There are many acceptable diversions that need not serve some overarching reasonable goal. Why is enjoyed pain not just an entertaining, albeit bizarre, form of diversion? Occasionally it is (as with the toothache example), depending on what motivates it and on what role it plays in one's life. Most often, however, self-inflicted pain constitutes an attempt to damage oneself, if not to hurt others as well. The causes of masochism are a matter for psychology to explore, but whatever the explanation, masochists usually undermine their own capacities for enriching relationships as equals among other equals. They cut themselves off from the enjoyment of more fulfilling activities. And they are typically in conflict with themselves in ways that prevent a more meaningful life.

Lise's actions, for example, are compulsive, anxiety-ridden, and damaging to her relationships with other people. Many of us, however, perhaps even most of us on occasion, display masochistic tendencies that are not related to neuroses. In addition, we frequently fail to perceive (or deceive ourselves about) our self-destructive tendencies, which may be more vague and ambiguous than Lise's clear-cut self-hatred. Some of those self-hurtful tendencies involve self-depreciation.

Self-Depreciation

Self-criticism is sometimes justified, and mild self-effacement can be an endearing quality. *Self-depreciation* refers to more systematic and destructive ways of "putting oneself down." Servility, inferiority complexes, and excessive self-sacrifice are three (of many) varieties of self-depreciation.

Servility is the attitude that one lacks moral worth, or at least lacks moral worth equal to that of others. It is the failure to endorse oneself as being worthy of the same recognition respect due to every person. One form of servility is the excessively deferential or submissive attitude known as obsequiousness. Obsequiousness is illustrated by the sycophant who practices excessive flattery. Another example is the fawning attempt always to please others. Still another is the willingness to do whatever one is told by people in power, no matter what the circumstances.

What repels us in these examples is not just the groveling behavior itself, but the frame of mind the behavior expresses. Often it is the motive that is distressing, as in someone's attempt to gain money or power at the expense of his or her dignity, or in the attempt to create a basis for self-worth in the prestige of others. Yet we are also disturbed by the failure of the servile person to appreciate and honor his or her own worth.

A second form of self-depreciation is an anxiety-ridden sense of inferiority, or what Alfred Adler (1870–1937) called an inferiority complex. This consists of more than the occasional feelings of inadequacy we all experience; it involves experiencing these feelings in excess and on inappropriate occasions, typically accompanied by crippling anxiety and depression. The person with an inferiority complex is overwhelmed by these feelings and by being unable to cope with them. Sometimes the person develops irrational coping devices, such as the tendency toward self-deprecation and expectations of mistreatment, as if these help to maintain a stable self-identity as a failure.

A third form of self-depreciation is more ambiguous morally. This is the self-depreciation of the excessive altruist. Consider a woman who, pressured by cultural stereotypes, zealously devotes herself to her husband and children to the point where she betrays her own talents and interests. The psychiatrist Theodore Isaac Rubin captures the ambivalence we feel about such a person. Reflecting on his mother, who was overflowing with "love, esteem of me, devotion and care," he remarks:

> She was never exploitative and despite deep concern for me had never been manipulative, overprotective, or in any way stifling. So I describe the perfect mother? NO: she was exasperating in her compliance to my father.... I suppose she exasperated him, too, in her complete abandonment of herself in favor of him. This was certainly a form of glorious martyrdom for her.[10]

There is a fine line between (a) sacrifice for the good of others, which is admirable and leads to one's own fulfillment, and (b) destructive forms of self-depreciation. Rubin suggests that his mother displayed both, sometimes in inextricable combinations. And although he deeply admires her and is grateful for her sacrifices, he also sees her as falling into society's trap of glorifying the altruistic wife-mother, even when it leads to self-harm. Where we draw the line between admirable altruism and degrading self-depreciation may depend primarily on the motives of the person in question: a genuine care for others versus an ulterior desire for gain (such as social approval); or the need to protect oneself and one's children from a violent husband versus the fear of asserting oneself and taking risks in order to develop one's talents. In Rubin's case, he saw an element of timidity in his mother's relationship with her husband. Yet the line between altruism and self-depreciation can also be crossed when one habitually underappreciates one's worth.

In addition, there is a fine line between self-depreciation and genuine humility. Humility is the virtue of not being arrogant or, more positively, of maintaining perspective on one's accomplishments and possibilities. Truly humble people avoid the excess of arrogance (conceit or excessive self-regard) without falling into the defect of undervaluing themselves or failing to appreciate their achievements. Genuinely humble individuals do not "put themselves down"; instead, they put their lives into appropriate perspective, typically on the basis of a value perspective deeper than that which conventional society, with its preoccupation with prestige and reputation, has to offer. Their concern is for truth and accurate evaluation, not with self-disparagement and devaluation. Humility can be an honest recognition of one's lesser abilities and talents, and the moral virtue of humility reflects genuine acknowledgment of one's moral imperfections. Self-depreciation, by contrast, reflects an attitude of undervaluing the worth of one's genuine achievements, of one's worthwhile interests and activities, and of one's highest aspirations and capacities. Above all it reflects the undervaluation of one's inherent dignity as the equal in moral worth of others.

Irrational Shame and Guilt

Shame and guilt are painful, self-critical emotions that are responses to what we believe are our failures to live by our values.* As such they are inevitable aspects of being committed to values. Often they are fully appropriate and warranted aspects of maintaining appraisal self-respect. To never feel shame would imply a brazen—a "shameless"—apathy toward ideals and standards.

---

*The words *shame* and *guilt* are ambiguous. In the sense intended here they refer to emotions, to *feeling* guilty or ashamed. They can also refer, however, to actions and to the moral status of persons who commit the actions: *being* guilty for wrongdoing or *acting* in shameful ways. *Feeling* guilty or ashamed does not imply that we actually *are* guilty or shameful, because we may be entirely mistaken in believing we are at fault or have failed. Conversely, we are frequently guilty or deserving of shame for faults to which we are blind or indifferent and concerning which we do not feel guilt or shame.

To never feel guilt would imply that one holds a very low set of moral standards, or that one (psychotically?) believes oneself to be morally perfect, or even that one is a callous sociopath who, by definition, has no sense of moral right and wrong. We *ought* to experience shame and guilt insofar as we are blameworthy—"ought" in the sense that these emotions are appropriate reactions to many of our failures. Yet, as we know from personal experience, shame and guilt can be self-destructive when they are excessive or when we respond to them irrationally.

Shame and guilt can be felt simultaneously toward the same object, and even have similar physiological manifestations (such as tightened muscles, constricted breathing, and lowered energy level). Yet they are distinguishable. Whereas shame is focused on personal shortcomings and failures to meet standards, guilt is focused on harm done to people. Shame is the experience of feeling lowered self-esteem and self-respect because we believe we have betrayed our ideals, standards, or sense of propriety. *Nonmoral shame* pertains to nonmoral standards, as in feeling ashamed of one's social awkwardness, poor athletic ability, bowed legs, or crooked teeth. *Moral shame* is the feeling of lowered self-respect arising from failure to meet our moral ideals. By contrast, *moral guilt* is the pain we feel because we think we have morally wronged someone, whether by insulting them, physically hurting them, violating their rights to privacy, or breaking a promise to them.*

Irrational shame and guilt are usually based on unreasonable beliefs about one's wrongdoing or vices, beliefs that are false or unsupported by evidence. Such beliefs reflect unwarranted evaluations of our conduct or character traits. Shame and guilt can also be irrational because of their excessive intensity or because of our unreasonable reactions to them.

A vivid example of irrational shame is given by Virginia Woolf in her short story "The New Dress." Her main character, Mabel Waring, is a forty-year-old woman who displays the emotional flip-flops characteristic of adolescence. She has spent hours with her dressmaker helping to fashion a new yellow dress that will be perfect for a party, but upon arriving at the party she collapses in self-doubt:

> Mabel had her first serious suspicion that something was wrong as she took her cloak off.... No! It was not *right*. And at once the misery which she always tried to hide, the profound dissatisfaction—the sense she had had, ever since she was a child, of being inferior to other people—set upon her, relentlessly, remorselessly, with an intensity which she could not beat off... for oh these men, oh these women, all were thinking—"What's Mabel wearing? What a fright she looks! What a hideous new dress!"[11]

---

*In addition to moral guilt, there is *religious* guilt, in which a theist feels guilt for violating what are believed to be God's standards. The theist presumably harms him- or herself, not God.

Mabel's spiraling shame quickly extends to include her own cowardice in being so ashamed about such a trivial matter and her pettiness in devoting so much time to the dress in the first place. Her shame revives a long-standing sense of failure for having chosen a safe, dull marriage, for being a mediocre mother and wife, and for leading a "creeping, crawling life" in which she feels like a fly struggling to escape a saucer while its wings are stuck together by milk. The story ends with her fantasies about becoming a nun to escape worries about clothes and about discovering an astonishing book at the library that will radically transform her life.

As this example suggests, intense experiences of inappropriate shame (as well as guilt) provide clues to understanding what most matters to us. Shame and guilt, like most emotions, are largely involuntary and spontaneous responses. As such, they have singular importance in revealing our values, because by definition they are painful experiences of having failed to live by those values.

Thus, for example, when parents and children catch themselves being ashamed of each other's appearance or clothing, they may be shocked into awareness of how self-centered their concern for each other has become. Similarly, writers who feel deep shame over negative reviews of their work may be forced to admit how dependent they have grown on praise from critics. And the guilt that some young adults continue to feel about their sexual desires may help them to see that they are not free from the inhibitions of a puritanical upbringing.

Irrational guilt can be as self-destructive as irrational shame, but with added complications arising from the sense of having wronged another person. When feelings of guilt are warranted, it is appropriate to make amends (where possible) for the wrong done. Perhaps all that is required is a sincere apology; other times one must try to compensate for the damage done. When guilt is irrational, however, matters can become painfully complex.

Let us consider an example of guilt that initially represents a rational or warranted emotion and later moves in an irrational direction. In *The Scarlet Letter*, Nathaniel Hawthorne tells the story of the adultery of Reverend Dimmesdale and Hester Prynne that leads to Hester's pregnancy. From their perspective, a serious moral wrong has occurred, and, given that perspective, their feelings of guilt are fully warranted. Although from our perspective their judgments may seem unduly harsh, we nevertheless see a deep moral wrong in Dimmesdale's cowardly refusal to assume responsibility for his adultery. He does not marry Hester, but instead conceals his role and allows her to bear the public shame by herself.

After Dimmesdale fails in his responsibility to make amends for his wrongdoing, his guilt quickly takes an irrational turn. He tortures himself with self-loathing and self-flagellation. By the end of his life he is left without self-respect or even a clear sense of his own identity. Hawthorne, summarizing the self-destructive effect of Dimmesdale's guilt and hypocrisy, writes that it is the unspeakable misery of a life so false as his, that it steals the pith and substance out of whatever realities there are around us, and which were meant by Heaven to be the spirit's joy and nutriment. To the untrue man, the whole universe is false—it is impalpable—it shrinks to nothing within his grasp. And he himself, in so far as he shows himself in a false light, becomes a shadow, or, indeed ceases to exist.[12]

Only near death does Dimmesdale attain a moment of peace when he seeks Hester's forgiveness.

Hester's guilt and responses to her guilt stand in sharp contrast with Dimmesdale's. In caring for their daughter under the cruel gaze of a Puritan society, she finds a way to make amends for any wrongdoing and thereby release her feelings of guilt. Whereas Dimmesdale's suffering is pathetic and tragic, Hester's is noble. Dimmesdale cowardly refuses to admit his guilt openly; Hester courageously refuses to betray her love by revealing Dimmesdale as her lover. Dimmesdale spurns responsibility for his daughter; Hester lovingly raises her. Dimmesdale shows how the self-condemnation inherent in guilt becomes unhealthy when indulged in masochistically; Hester reminds us of the creative growth that comes with acting responsibly concerning our feelings of guilt.

Snobbery

So far we have discussed undervaluing the self, but self-evaluations can also go astray in the direction of overvaluation. Snobbery is a notable illustration. Snobbery is the attitude that one is superior in worth to people who are not members of a select group to which one belongs. One can, of course, truthfully and humbly recognize that one is superior in certain talents or achievements without being a snob. Snobbery results when one withholds recognition respect from others, when one refuses to treat them with the dignity they deserve as persons. The snob regards others as inferiors to be treated with contempt and disdain, or at best with pity and condescension. In addition, often the snob wants others to suffer—to feel inferior—on the basis of one's alleged superiority.

The grounds for snobbery can be almost anything: wealth, intellectual capacity, skill in sports or chess, or taste in clothing or fine china. Sometimes it has nothing to do with abilities or achievements but instead is based on inherited name, social standing, or club membership. Whatever its basis, snobbery is usually accompanied by arrogance. Arrogance can take one of two forms: (1) making unwarranted claims to superiority or (2) flaunting one's genuine superiority in offensive ways. The first form is objectionable because it claims an unfair basis for social esteem, the second because it threatens the self-esteem of others.

Snobbery is also frequently accompanied by hypocrisy, as when one pretends to be better than one is. Snobs thus make ready-made targets for satire aimed at ridiculing and deflating their pomposity. Even when their accomplishments are genuine, snobs exaggerate them beyond any reasonable perspective, making themselves vulnerable to the satirist's way of providing perspective. In his nineteenth-century classic, *Book of Snobs*, William Thackeray satirizes most major varieties of snobbism, including academic varieties. Here, for example, is his portrayal of college president Crump:

> Crump thinks Saint Boniface [College] the centre of the world, and his position as President, the highest in England. He expects the fellows and tutors to pay him the same sort of service that Cardinals pay to the Pope. I am sure Crawley would have no objection to carry his trencher [i.e., academic cap], or Page to hold up the skirts of his gown as he stalks into chapel.[13]

Allegations of snobbery can themselves be expressions of snobbery and hypocrisy! Vice President Spiro Agnew became something of a professional debunker of snobs. With bitter wit he defended President Nixon's Vietnam policies against liberal journalists, whom he derided as pretentious and hypocritical snobs. Of all his targets, however, student radicals were dealt with most viciously. The leaders of the student protest movement were, according to his famous phrase, "an effete corps of impudent snobs who characterize themselves as intellectuals."[14] As he explained, "I call them snobs for most of them disdain to mingle with the masses who work for a living. They mock the common man's pride in his work, his family and his country."[15] In retrospect, however, Agnew can be seen as a snob who set himself above honest critics of the war. Beneath his eagerness to debunk anyone who disagreed with him was hypocrisy about his own pettiness. On October 10, 1973, he was forced to resign as vice president because of charges of bribery and tax evasion during his earlier career as county executive of Baltimore County in Maryland. In that role he had awarded county engineering contracts on the basis of lucrative kickbacks. As the example of Agnew suggests, both snobs and people who are eager to call others snobs can be hypocrites.

Snobbery can involve other vices in addition to cruelty, arrogance, and hypocrisy. It may be accompanied by cowardice and disloyalty; for example, one may fear to be seen in the company of certain relatives and friends lest they lower one's social status among the "in-group" to which one belongs. It can express a lack of collegiality, as when one snubs colleagues and co-workers in order to be accepted by a small group of "superior" people. It can lead one to ignore the needs of entire groups of people from whom one turns away as part of a preoccupation with a selected social group.

SUMMARY

Morality has to do with our relationship to ourselves as well as to others. As morally concerned persons, we have the same moral worth as other people and we owe ourselves self-respect. Recognition self-respect consists of valuing ourselves for our inherent moral worth and caring about ourselves as unique individuals. Appraisal self-respect consists of accurately valuing one's character because one sets and meets high moral standards. Both forms of self-respect differ from self-esteem: Self-esteem simply entails feeling good about oneself (for whatever reason), whereas self-respect entails appreciating one's moral worth. This appreciation is shown by one's attempts to live up to duties to oneself, such as the duty not to harm oneself without justification.

Masochism, self-depreciation, and irrational guilt and shame are examples of harm to oneself that arises from inappropriate attitudes toward oneself. Masochism involves infliction of suffering on oneself for irrational motives. Self-depreciation is the attitude that one lacks full moral worth. The attitude is manifested in many ways, such as through servility (subservience to others at the expense of one's own rights and talents), inferiority complexes, or excessive altruism. Irrational guilt is the feeling that one has wronged another person when one has not done so, and irrational shame is the unjustified feeling that one has failed to live up to appropriate standards of personal excellence.

Snobs value themselves in inappropriate ways. They feel superior to people outside their select group, whether that group is defined by intellect, tastes, wealth, social status, or any number of other things. Often, snobs are cruel in making others feel inferior. Usually, they are arrogant hypocrites who fail to have a reasonable perspective on their own achievements. Frequently, they betray relatives and former friends as they aspire to be seen only with their "in-group."

DISCUSSION TOPICS

1   Masochism is not simply a matter of causing or enjoying one's pain; there must also be an irrational motive in doing so. Often, however, there are disagreements about which motives are irrational. Decide whether any of the following may reflect—at least in some cases— examples of masochistic behavior: (1) enjoyment of pain during sex; (2) injuries to oneself sustained in dangerous sports such as hang-gliding or auto racing; (3) risks to one's health incurred through excessive amounts of work.

2   Review the examples of Lise (in *The Brothers Karamazov*), Mabel Waring (in "The New Dress"), and Theodore Isaac Rubin's mother. These examples were used to illustrate the absence of the virtue of self-respect. Do the author's remarks about

these women amount to "blaming the victims" for their lack of self-respect, especially in light of traditional society's pressure on women to be self-sacrificing? In your answer, distinguish between the assertion that a virtue is absent and assignment of blame (where blame is a negative attitude).

3   What responses to our feelings of guilt are morally appropriate? Discuss this general question in connection with the following examples and more focused questions.

   a   In *The Scarlet Letter*, Dimmesdale was able to find peace from the guilt that tortured him only when he sought Hester's forgiveness. Seeking forgiveness is an act of humbling oneself by placing oneself at the mercy of another person. Why is seeking forgiveness, as in Dimmesdale's case, often a morally appropriate response to guilt? Why is a resolution not to commit similar wrongs in the future insufficient? How does guilt differ in this respect from shame, and why?

   b   We saw that, before seeking Hester's forgiveness, Dimmesdale punished himself in ways that were masochistic. Is self-punishment always an unhealthy response to guilt, or can you think of instances in which some kinds of self-punishment are appropriate?

   c   Sometimes we seek to relieve guilt for hurting one person by engaging in a project to help other people, perhaps at some sacrifice to ourselves. Describe situations in which this compensation is not an appropriate response to guilt. (Examples might include Dimmesdale, who ministers to others while disregarding Hester, or a thief, who tries to make amends by giving a token donation to charity but does not return the rest of the money to its owner.) Describe other situations in which helping others *is* an appropriate response to guilt (as might be the case for a drunk driver who killed someone and cannot seek forgiveness from the victim). What is the moral difference between the two cases?

4   Is snobbery often inevitable, as the following passage from Judith N. Shklar suggests?

> Our most genuine experiences of equality, of intimacy, and of fraternity occur only within a "clique"—that is, in an excluding group of like-minded people, modeled on that most irreducible and necessary of all societies, the family. Many groups do not have exclusion as their main object, and some are hardly aware of it; but whatever their real ends may be, they exclude by including selectively. Snobbery is the by-product of this multiplicity, and it is a personal price that must occasionally be paid for the sake of freedom. Not all doors are or can be open.[16]

5   Thomas E. Hill suggests that "snobs, in a sense, undervalue themselves as well as others" by basing their "self-respect on an unstable ground."[17] By "unstable ground" he refers to things that may not be lasting, such as achievements, talents, reputation, or social class, rather than what we have called recognition self-respect. Is he right? Can inflated self-esteem be a sign of too little self-respect?

6   Moral snobbery—that is, snobbery in moral matters—is the devaluation of others because they are not as morally admirable as oneself. It is shown in the arrogant self-righteousness of persons who are excessively preoccupied with their

own characters. Do you see a special danger of moral snobbery in the adoption of a virtue ethics perspective? Or is moral snobbery a potential risk in all moral self-appraisal? In your answer, discuss the difference between (a) concern to do a virtuous (honest, kind, generous) act, (b) concern to become a virtuous person, and (c) preoccupation with embellishing one's character so as to gain praise.

7   To betray another person is to violate a trust that is based on one's commitments or responsibilities to that person. What does it mean to betray oneself? Connect this idea with the idea of responsibilities to oneself to maintain one's integrity and self-respect.

8   In *Hamlet* (act 1, scene 3), Polonius gives the following advice to his son Laertes. What do you think Polonius meant, and is he right?

> *This above all: to thine own self be true;*
> *And it must follow, as the night the day,*
> *Thou canst not then be false to any man.*

9   Depression has been called one of the worst afflictions of our century. It is the emotional state in which we experience a sweeping loss of our responsiveness to values, and also a loss of self-confidence, self-esteem, and self-respect, so that our lives seem dull, boring, and hopeless. Is depression an emotional form of masochism? Consider both the tendency to frequent depression and individual episodes of depression. In doing so, respond to Robert Solomon's apparently positive view of (at least some) episodes of depression as expressed in the following passage:

> Our depression is our way of wrenching ourselves from the established values of our world, the tasks in which we have been unquestioningly immersed, the opinions we have uncritically nursed, the relationships we have accepted without challenge and often without meaning. A depression is a self-imposed purge. It is the beginning of self-realization, unless it is simply ignored, or drugged away, or allows itself to give in to the demands for its own avoidance—the most extreme of which is suicide.[18]

SUGGESTED READINGS

Adler, Alfred. *The Individual Psychology of Alfred Adler.* Heinz L. Ansbacher and Rowena R. Ansbacher (eds.). New York: Harper Torchbooks, 1964.

Benson, Jann, and Dan Lyons. *Strutting and Fretting: Standards for Self-Esteem.* Niwot, Colorado: University Press of Colorado, 1991.

Darwall, Stephen L. "Two Kinds of Respect." *Ethics,* vol. 88 (1977).

Deigh, John. "Shame and Self-Esteem: A Critique." *Ethics,* vol. 93 (1983).

Dillon, Robin. "How To Lose Your Self-Respect." *American Philosophical Quarterly,* vol. 29 (1992).

Dillon, Robin. "Toward a Feminist Conception of Self-Respect." *Hypatia,* vol. 7 (1992).

Goldstein, Irwin. "Pain and Masochism." *Journal of Value Inquiry,* vol. 17 (1983).

Hill, Thomas. "Servility and Self-Respect," "Self-Respect Reconsidered," and "Social Snobbery and Human Dignity." In *Autonomy and Self-Respect*. New York: Cambridge University Press, 1991.

Horney, Karen. *Neurosis and Human Growth*. New York: Norton, 1950.

Jones, Hardy. "Treating Oneself Wrongly." *Journal of Value Inquiry*, vol. 17 (1983).

Kant, Immanuel. "Proper Self-Respect" and "Duties to Oneself." In *Lectures on Ethics*. Trans. Louis Infield. New York: Harper & Row, 1963.

Lynd, Helen Merrill. *On Shame and the Search for Identity*. New York: Harcourt, Brace & World, 1958.

Massey, Stephen J. "Is Self-Respect a Moral or a Psychological Concept?" *Ethics*, vol. 93 (1983).

Morris, Herbert (ed.). *Guilt and Shame*. Belmont, CA: Wadsworth, 1971.

Rawls, John. *A Theory of Justice*. Cambridge, MA: Harvard University Press, 1971.

Shklar, Judith N. "What Is Wrong with Snobbery?" In *Ordinary Vices*. Cambridge, MA: Harvard University Press, 1984. Pp. 87–137.

Solomon, Robert. *The Passions*. Notre Dame, IN: University of Notre Dame Press, 1983.

Taylor, Gabriele. *Pride, Shame, and Guilt: Emotions of Self-Assessment*. Oxford: Clarendon Press, 1985.

Taylor, Richard. "The Virtue of Pride." In *Ethics, Faith, and Reason*. Englewood Cliffs, NJ: Prentice-Hall, 1985. Pp. 98–106.

Thackeray, William M. *The Book of Snobs*. In W. P. Trent and J. B. Henneman (eds.), *The Complete Works of William M. Thackeray*. Vol. XIV. New York: Thomas Y. Crowell [undated]. Pp. 1–240.

Warren, Virginia. "Explaining Masochism." *Journal for the Theory of Social Behavior* (1985).

CHAPTER 6

Self-Knowledge and Self-Deception

The virtue of self-respect consists of valuing oneself as a moral self, that is, as someone who has inherent moral worth and as someone who is responsive to moral reasons and ideals. Recall that self-respect is not reducible to self-esteem (in the sense of feeling good about oneself), because that feeling can be based on illusions about oneself. Self-respect demands of us a high degree of honesty with ourselves, which in turn requires that we avoid or overcome self-deception about our wrongdoing and character faults.

Self-deception about wrongdoing can undermine the basis for our self-respect by corrupting our integrity. At the same time, an interest in preserving self-esteem sometimes motivates self-deception: The desire for a high estimate of ourselves can prompt us to deceive ourselves. These connections among self-respect, self-esteem, and self-deception about immorality will be explored in this chapter.

Self-Knowledge

"Know Thyself!" This injunction, which was inscribed in stone at the Temple of Apollo at Delphi, was central to Socrates' quest for self-understanding. Socrates viewed self-understanding as the core of wisdom—the highest virtue, which makes possible the other cardinal virtues of courage, temperance, and justice. What is self-knowledge?

Self-knowledge involves both specific information about ourselves as individuals and more general information about human nature. Let us say that having this information consists of *knowing that* certain facts are true. But which facts? Surely we do not need to know the number of hairs on our heads or the latest predictions for our lives from the newspaper's astrology column. The kind of knowledge sought by Socrates had vital significance for living a good life. That means that the knowledge must be relevant and important to how we live; it also means that the knowledge must be active in motivating our conduct. Let us say this practical knowledge consists of *knowing how* to live in a manner that both leads to self-fulfillment and enables us to meet our responsibilities and contribute to the lives of others.

What does this practical knowledge involve? To begin with, it implies that we know what we want. What are our strongest desires, how can they fit together so as to be expressed coherently, and what is the relative importance of each? As the last question suggests, self-knowledge is not a mere grasp of fact; it requires interpretation of facts in light of values that specify the relative importance of our desires. Self-knowledge, then, requires knowledge of the values and ideals that give life meaning. Self-knowledge is *value-laden*: It is permeated by the values we use to interpret our lives.

Self-knowledge involves value-laden understanding of many other aspects of our lives besides our desires. It implies an understanding of our emotions, habits, personal relationships, and the wider ties to communities that add meaning to our lives. It implies an imaginative grasp of the possibilities that are open to us, as well as a realistic sense of our limitations. And it implies an understanding of our strengths, weaknesses, and faults. Self-deception arises in all these areas, but especially in connection with our faults.

Self-Deceiving Tactics

To deceive others is to purposefully mislead them, usually by concealing some truth from them. This can be accomplished by keeping them ignorant about a topic, leading them to believe something false, diverting their attention from an important matter, or distorting their attitudes and emotions. Similarly, to *deceive oneself* is purposefully to mislead oneself, usually by avoiding an unpleasant truth or a painful topic. It can be accomplished by keeping oneself ignorant about a topic, persuading oneself to believe something false, refusing to pay attention to an important matter, or distorting one's attitudes and emotions.

An example will help clarify what self-deception is and how we engage in it. In *The Death of Ivan Ilych*, Leo Tolstoy describes a man who is forced to become aware that he has a terminal illness. In the days before his death, Ivan Ilych reflects honestly for the first time on the meaning of his life. He concludes that he had been living a lie. His life had been pleasant enough, but it was based entirely on a desire for his own comfort, social acceptance, and power. This selfishness had corrupted his relationships with his family and colleagues, and, as he painfully admits to himself, it was accompanied by self-deception concerning the deeper values of love, friendship, and community that should have guided him. He now feels alienated from his past—as if he had lived someone else's life, not his own authentic life.

How did he deceive himself? Consider these familiar psychological tactics. He *refused to reflect* on his deeper responsibilities, often stifling his impulses to stand up for values that were being trampled on at his job. No doubt he also *rationalized*—that is, reasoned in a biased way—that, since most people were comfortable with their failures to pursue higher values, it was acceptable for him to do so as well. He succeeded in *compartmentalizing* his life into separate channels, ignoring the moral implications each of these aspects of his life had for the others. Thus, he managed to neglect his family in the midst of his preoccupation with social climbing. He also managed to keep himself ignorant—*willfully ignorant*— of much detailed information about his family's needs that might provoke him into doing something he would rather not do, such as pay greater attention to them.

Equally important in self-deception is our manipulation of our attention and emotions concerning what we already do know. For example, Ilych knew he would someday die, just like everyone else, but he refused to think about death and what it meant for how a life should be lived. He *selectively ignored* unpleasant facts and engaged in *emotional detachment* from unpleasant realities, such as occasional doubts, depression, and guilt feelings, that signaled something was amiss. Finally, in addition to all these tactics he undoubtedly *accepted social reinforcement* from his circle of friends and acquaintances, who were doing the same thing. A peer group in which most others act like oneself serves as a hall of distorting mirrors that reinforce self-deception.

These self-deceiving tactics are quite familiar. All of us have sometimes avoided acknowledging information that we suspected would be unpleasant to confront head-on. We are all aware of the various evasion tactics: We willfully ignore, selectively attend, become detached emotionally, manipulate our emotions so as to avoid acting, compartmentalize our lives, allow our biases to shape rationalized belief and attitudes, and acquiesce to peers who mold our opinions and self-images in comforting ways. No one of these tactics by itself constitutes self-deception, but they often serve as ways to evade painful realities.

Paradoxes

Even though these ways of deceiving ourselves are familiar, the idea of deceiving oneself has proven puzzling to some philosophers. They have argued that the idea is paradoxical—not just in the literary sense of paradoxes as mere seeming absurdities (which upon deeper understanding are perfectly coherent), but in the sense of paradoxes as contradictions. To actually deceive oneself, they argue, is an impossibility, especially in the sense of telling oneself a lie and coming to believe it.

In a situation in which one person deceives another, there is a deceiver, who is aware of a truth, and a deceived, who is not aware of it (and who is prevented from becoming aware of it by the lie). For example, consider an employee who lies to his employer about his alcoholism, and suppose that the employer is in fact deceived by the lie. The employee is fully aware that he is an alcoholic: He believes it, he knows it, and he is fully conscious of it (that is, he can and does attend to the fact that he is an alcoholic). The employer, by contrast, is not aware that the employee is an alcoholic: She does not believe it, she does not know it, and she is not conscious of it.

When we try to imagine the alcoholic lying to himself, we must, it seems, imagine him functioning simultaneously as the deceiver and as the victim of the deception. That seems impossible for three reasons. First, he would have to believe and not believe the same thing at the same time. Second, he would have to know and not know the truth at the same time. Third—and most puzzling—he would have to *use* his awareness of the truth as part of the process of hiding the truth from another person. In lying to the employer, both the content of the lie ("I am not abusing alcohol") and the way the lie is told (with apparent conviction) are guided by awareness of the truth. How, by contrast, could the alcoholic use his awareness of the truth in pursuing his intention to deceive himself? It seems he would have to maintain an awareness of the truth even as he tried to block that awareness, thereby making the attempted deception self-defeating.

These three paradoxes all stem from the attempt to interpret self-deception on the model of a lie; but why should that model be accepted? After all, "deceiving" and "lying" are not synonymous terms, as we noted in Chapter 4. A lie is a false statement told with the intention to deceive. If, however, the lie is not believed, no deception occurs. Hence, there can be lies without deception. Conversely, there can be deception without lies. To deceive is to intentionally mislead someone into holding a false belief or into being ignorant. Such deception can be achieved without lying, perhaps by saying nothing in a situation in which the truth should be spoken or by engaging in pretense (using "body language").

The expression "lying to oneself" is a metaphor that, if taken too literally, leads to the three paradoxes. The concept of "deceiving oneself," however, is meaningful and nonparadoxical even when taken literally to mean purposefully misleading oneself. It need not involve full awareness of the truth at any time. Most often, the self-deceiver has only a suspicion that something might be true, or perhaps an intimation that an entire topic might prove deeply troubling if examined closely. This is illustrated by Ivan Ilych, who refused to reflect about death because he suspected it might lead him to make unwanted changes in how he was living. Similarly, an alcoholic might deceive himself by refusing to reflect fully and honestly (without bias) about his pattern of drinking and its effects on his life.

These suspicions may involve fleeting moments of consciousness of the truth or just a vague, peripheral awareness that something may be amiss in certain areas of our lives. Moreover, if we engaged in honest reflection, we could in many cases obtain a clearer and fuller awareness. As self-deceivers, we avoid precisely this kind of honest self-scrutiny, for it threatens to reveal disturbing truths or topics that we are deliberately avoiding.

If Sigmund Freud was correct, there are additional forms of self-deception in which self-scrutiny by itself may be insufficient to bring truths to consciousness.[1] He postulated that there are psychological "defense mechanisms" that block truths from our awareness and that themselves operate (in the unconscious part of the ego) without our consciousness of them. We cannot become conscious of the mechanisms or the truths they conceal without (in most cases) the special help of psychoanalysts or other types of psychotherapists. One such defense mechanism, for example, is *repression*, the process by which ideas are blocked from being accessible to our attention. Repression operates unconsciously, unlike the act of *suppression*, in which we consciously avoid attending to something ("I must stop worrying about that exam and get my mind back on my work"). Another example is *projection*, in which people unconsciously ascribe their problems, hostility, or other attitudes to other people (often in modified forms). Thus, paranoid people who irrationally think everyone is out to get them are unconsciously ascribing both their own fears and their feelings of aggression to other people they come in contact with. Other defense mechanisms include *denial* (refusing to recognize an unpleasant reality by engaging in wish-fulfilling fantasies or conduct), *regression* (reverting to an infantile mode of behavior), and *reaction formations* (transforming an attitude into an excessive version of its opposite; for example, transforming hatred into effusive affection or resentment into servility).

Responsibility

Self-deception proceeds without our full awareness of either what we are deceived about or the act of deceiving ourselves. We ignore things, for example, without attending to the fact that we are ignoring them, or rationalize without admitting that we are rationalizing. Self-deception may also involve the unconscious process Freud described. Does this absence of full awareness mean that we are not responsible for any harm that may be attributable to our deception? Is self-deception an excuse, or partial excuse, for immorality?

Herbert Fingarette, in his book *Self-Deception*, suggests that self-deceivers' moral responsibilities are at best ambiguous. Usually, people are deemed responsible for their conduct on the basis of two conditions: First, they were aware or able to become aware of what they were doing; second, they acted voluntarily, that is, without coercion and without uncontrollable inner compulsions. Self-deceivers, by contrast, because they lose full awareness of what they are doing, are less able to fully control their actions.

Fingarette writes:

> There is thus in self-deception a genuine subversion of personal agency and, for this reason in turn, a subversion of moral capacity. The sensitive and thoughtful observer, when viewing the matter this way, is inclined not to hold the self-deceiver responsible but to view him as a "victim."[2]

In Fingarette's view, self-deception is a morally puzzling state about which it is impossible to make our usual moral judgments. Self-deceivers are not clearly acting voluntarily, because they are not fully aware of what they are doing. Nor are they clearly acting involuntarily—they are, after all, the source of their own deception. Should we accept Fingarette's view?

Fingarette was especially interested in neurotic forms of self-deception in which mental illness is involved. Neurotic persons are often handicapped in the attempt to gain full awareness of their self-deception and then to use their self-understanding to help control their actions. They may need the help of a psychotherapist, or sometimes just a supportive friend, in order to confront the truths they are avoiding. Fingarette's perspective on self-deception is not convincing, however, with respect to the many individuals who *are* able to become conscious of their self-deceiving activities and the truths they are evading. Certainly mere ignorance and lack of consciousness are not automatically excuses for immorality. We are each responsible for knowing what our obligations are and for obtaining information relevant to meeting them. Our blindness to those obligations and facts does not automatically cancel or diminish moral accountability.

In fact, when the obligations involved are especially important, self-deception in the sense of willful ignorance about those obligations is itself immoral. In such cases, persons may be at fault for two reasons: (1) because of the wrongdoing they engage in and (2) because they deceive themselves about the wrongdoing in order to proceed without a troubled conscience. Joseph Butler (1692–1752) made this point. Self-deception about wrongdoing and character faults, he wrote,

> is essentially in its own nature vicious [that is, a vice] and immoral. It is unfairness; it is dishonesty; it is falseness of heart: and is therefore so far from extenuating guilt, that it is itself the greatest of all guilt in proportion to the degree it prevails; for it is a corruption of the whole moral character in its principle.[3]

Butler's expression "moral character in its principle" refers to conscience, to our sense of right and wrong. Self-deception about immorality corrupts conscience by preventing it from properly guiding conduct and character development.

Furthermore, Butler said that self-deception about immorality represents unfairness and hypocrisy. It is unfairness in that it involves cheating on our own moral standards. We gain undeserved advantages through wrongdoing and through an unwarranted view of our own character. Self-deception about immorality is "inner hypocrisy"—hypocrisy before ourselves—in that we appear better in our own eyes than we really are. Our unjustified self-esteem is bolstered by false beliefs about our conduct and character.

Self-Respect, Self-Esteem, and Immorality

Now that we have clarified the nature of and responsibility for self-deception, let us draw together the connections between self-respect, self-esteem, and self-deception about immorality. First, self-respect is based on self-understanding and on an appreciation of our true character and moral worth. Whereas mere self-esteem (a favorable view of ourselves) is often based on illusions or self-deceptions, self-respect requires that we value ourselves as morally concerned persons whose characters are based on moral commitments. Accordingly, self-respect is eroded when self-deception grossly distorts our understanding of our character. Thus, whatever positive feelings of self-esteem may accrue from self-deception about our wrongdoing, that self-esteem is not the same as genuine self-respect based on moral self-understanding.

Second, the desire to retain a sense of self-respect and self-esteem is a major motive for self-deception. We deceive ourselves about our wrongdoing and character flaws in order to avoid the pain that results from acknowledging those faults to ourselves, as well as to avoid the burden of having to alter them. We would have little reason to deceive ourselves if we were sociopaths who lacked all moral concern.

Third, a desire to maintain a sense of self-respect also motivates us to avoid acknowledging our own self-deceptions. We like to think of ourselves as having the courage to willingly face the truth, not as having the cowardice and hypocrisy implied in evading it. Of course, many other motives generate or support self-deception, including fear, laziness, envy, a desire for self-esteem, and so on. Perhaps no motive is stronger or more common, however, than the desire to sustain an attitude of self-respect. Thus, in everyday life we employ an array of devices for bolstering an unjustifiably high estimate of our own characters and the sense of self-respect based on it. Two centuries ago Samuel Johnson (1709–1784) identified several of these devices:

1   We selectively emphasize our occasional good deeds, eagerly treating one isolated act as if it were a habit constituting a virtuous character trait: "A miser who once relieved a friend from the danger of a prison, suffers his imagination to dwell for ever upon his own heroic generosity; he yields his heart up to indignation at those who are blind to merit, or insensible

to misery ... and though his whole life is a course of rapacity and avarice, he concludes himself to be tender and liberal, because he has once performed an act of liberality and tenderness."[4]

2   We dismiss our wrongdoing as uncharacteristic lapses or else as flaws belonging to everyone. Nights of debauchery, Johnson notes, are easily excused by noting that even great people have similar lapses. Such lapses, we tell ourselves, do not detract from our essential goodness.

3   We confuse "lip service" to virtue with the real thing: "There are men who always confound the praise of goodness with the practice, and who believe themselves mild and moderate, charitable and faithful, because they have exerted their eloquence in commendation of mildness, fidelity, and other virtues."[5]

4   We tend to focus our attention on the worst deeds of other people as a way to downplay our faults. To dwell on the worst faults of our acquaintances, or attend to the vicious deeds of criminals reported in the daily newspaper, brings a comforting sense of our superior virtue.

5   We choose friends who share our vices, and we eagerly listen to the words of flatterers. This reinforces our vices and enables us to avoid that serious self-reflection that Johnson calls "communion with our own hearts."

A fourth connection between self-respect and self-deception concerns overcoming self-deception about our faults. We must honestly acknowledge our lack of moral commitment before we can reclaim our self-respect. Initially, this acknowledgment diminishes our feelings of self-respect, assuming we are morally concerned. Within limits, this is as it should be, for at such times we feel guilt both for the wrongdoing concealed by the self-deception and for having deceived ourselves about it. There may sometimes be a sense of self-disillusionment, as with Ivan Ilych, who eventually sees through his own lies. Yet remorse and diminished feelings of self-respect can prepare the way for a renewed and stronger basis for self-respect. Genuine remorse should prompt a resolve to try to make some form of amends and to avoid similar self-deceptions in the future.

Fifth, even if we persist in self-deception about our faults, we may still experience diminished self-respect because of a haunting sense of our "inner dishonesty." Just as we can have a suspicion of the truths we are evading, we can have a sense that we are evading the truth—that we are not being fully honest with ourselves in acknowledging truths important to our lives. In severe cases of habitual self-deception, the consequences can be worse than mere anxiety, as Fyodor Dostoevsky (1821–1881) suggested in his novel *The Brothers Karamazov*:

> Above all, don't lie to yourself. The man who lies to himself and listens to his own lie comes to such a point that he cannot distinguish the truth within him, or around him, and so loses all respect for himself and for

others. And having no respect he ceases to love. And in order to distract himself without love he gives way to passions and coarse pleasures and sinks to bestiality in his vices—all this from continual lying to other men and to himself.[6]

Sixth, some self-deception is damaging to our own talents, happiness, and self-development in ways that undermine self-esteem and sometimes self-respect. For example, self-deception can be used to conceal the motives and significance of tendencies to belittle ourselves—to "put ourselves down" with irrational condemnations. Painful feelings of inferiority can be generated in part by applying self-deceivingly unrealistic standards to ourselves. Many of the examples of masochism and servility discussed in the previous chapter involved self-deception of this sort. In such cases, self-deception conceals our capacities for goodness.

Here is a further example of how, through self-deception, we can hurt ourselves more than anyone else by weakening our appreciation of our own talents and possibilities. In her autobiography *From Housewife to Heretic*, Sonia Johnson describes her struggle to escape submissiveness to a male-dominated culture and servility toward a patriarchal religion. She writes, "I was a person who had unconsciously known for a very long time that something was wrong with patriarchy, but because my entire culture, to say nothing of my church, was based upon it almost as given, I hadn't had the courage to face what I knew."[7]

For the most part, she made innumerable accommodations and sacrifices that undermined her own opportunities and talents. These included the familiar one-sided burden of household chores and responsibility for her four children; the assumption that she was responsible for caring for her husband without comparable reciprocity; an automatic and largely uncritical dependence on the views of her husband and the male leadership of her church; indulgence not only of her husband's childish habit of emotional withdrawal when problems arose, but also of his frequent absences from home for work related reasons (especially when he had the option not to go on business trips); and a blind trust in her husband of twenty years to the point where she was an easy dupe when he connived a plot to divorce her in a way that minimized his legal responsibilities—the act that finally shocked her into sustained self-reflection.

In retrospect Johnson was able to see that her primary tactic of evading the truth about her submissiveness was a systematic suppression of her emotions:

> I was living a sort of half life, in half light, a grayish, half-awake limbo of neither clouds nor sunlight, a gray same numbness.... I accomplished this great reductionist feat by lowering the threshold of my awareness, allowing very little stimuli into my consciousness for fear of inadvertently letting in the scary things. At the same time, I unconsciously

dulled my perception of the stimuli I did choose so that I would not see clearly what I did not want to see, would not feel what I did not want to feel, would not have to face what I feared to face.[8]

Suppression of so many of her own emotions, ideas, attitudes, and needs prevented her from emerging as fully authentic through fidelity to her own talents and aspirations.

Seventh, and finally, it should be pointed out that self-deception may in some situations be beneficial and supportive of self-esteem and self-respect. It sometimes can actually aid our personal growth and the development of our talents without harmful side effects. A familiar example is overcoming the fear of public speaking. Even without self-deception, if one ignores such stage fright by pretending not to be afraid, one can cultivate self-confidence and thereby strengthen one's speaking ability. Deceiving oneself into believing one is a better speaker than in fact one is may yield similar results. Likewise, an athlete might "psych up" for a race by engaging in a bit of innocent self-deception about her or his abilities to win.

Indeed, we frequently approach difficult tasks by self-deceivingly magnifying our abilities to succeed or minimizing the difficulties ahead. Such self-deception enables us at least to try things we otherwise might turn away from in discouragement. Undoubtedly, some distinctively moral commitments can be strengthened in this way as well. Many parents engage in some useful self-deception to help sustain their efforts in caring for their children—self-deception about the difficulties involved in raising children, for example.

Perhaps such forms of self-deception are not entirely rational in the sense of showing a full devotion to truth. Perhaps it would be more rational to proceed on the basis of hope and faith that did not involve self-deception. Certainly, habitual self-deception threatens to undermine the standards of rationality that are essential to living up to moral and other values—standards such as respect for evidence, concern for consistency, impartiality, clarity of thought, rigor of argument, and so on. Nevertheless, when isolated instances of self-deception do not contribute to general habits of irrationality, and when they are beneficial rather than harmful, it seems the element of irrationality (evasion of the truth) may be outweighed by other values.

SUMMARY

Self-deception is the evasion of painful truths or topics, whether specific or general. It is typically a refusal to acknowledge truths to ourselves, whether through ignoring something we suspect is true, avoiding inquiry into disturbing topics, engaging in rationalization (biased reasoning), emotionally detaching ourselves from difficult situations, conveniently acquiescing to social pressures, or using other tactics. These tactics are employed without attending to them with full consciousness. Understood in this way, self-deception does not involve paradox or self-contradiction.

Some self-deception may be beneficial, as it may contribute to personal development without having bad side effects. Self-deception is immoral, as Joseph Butler suggested, when it conceals wrongdoing, character faults, or facts we need to meet our obligations. In that context, our self-deception prohibits us from honestly confronting the morally harmful aspects of our lives. As such, the self-deception is a kind of derivative wrong; its badness derives from its support of other wrongdoing. In addition, apart from being a form of dishonesty about the truth, it reflects an "inner hypocrisy," that is, a propensity to think better of ourselves than is warranted by our character.

Insofar as we can refrain from or overcome self-deception about immorality, we are responsible for both the immorality of our actions and the self-deception. The extent to which we are blameworthy depends on the answers to several questions: How serious is the immorality about which we deceive ourselves? Are we aware of being in a situation where self-deception threatens to do harm? How much control do we have over the self-deception, and are we capable of facing the truth? Is there mental illness involved that weakens our capacity to confront the truth, and if so, is there help available that we can be expected to take advantage of? As these questions suggest, responsibility for self-deception mirrors the complexity of morality in general.

Self-deception is related to self-respect (proper appreciation of our moral worth) and self-esteem (a favorable view of ourselves) in a number of ways. First, because self-respect consists of an accurate appreciation of our moral worth, based on self-understanding, self-deception about our faults undermines self-respect. Second, one major motive for self-deception is the desire to maintain a high opinion of our own characters. Third, the desire to sustain self-esteem and a sense of self-respect motivates us to avoid acknowledging that we are self-deceivers, because the recognition of our cowardly evasions of truth is not flattering. Fourth, overcoming self-deception can bring a temporary deflation of self-esteem and self-respect, even as subsequent remorse and efforts to make amends can strengthen them. Fifth, habitual self-respect sometimes creates a nagging sense that we are not being honest with ourselves—a sense that weakens self-respect. Sixth, some self-deception damages self-development and the basis for self-esteem. Finally, some self-deception (as in the public speaking example) can contribute to self-development and can strengthen self-esteem.

DISCUSSION TOPICS

1 Suppose someone argued that the idea of "teaching oneself" is confused and self-contradictory because a person would have to know (as teacher) what he or

she does not know (as learner). Respond to this argument, and in doing so compare and contrast what is involved in teaching oneself and in deceiving oneself.

2 Discuss the role played by self-deception in avoiding complete honesty regarding plagiarism and cheating in tests. In addition to rationalization, discuss the possible roles of other self-deceiving tactics such as refusal to reflect, selective attention, compartmentalization, willful ignorance (about the harm to other students), emotional detachment, acquiescence to social pressure, and so on.

3 Kant believed that all self-deceptions, or what he called "inner lies," are immoral because they violate our duty to be truthful with ourselves: "By a lie a man makes himself contemptible—by an outer lie, in the eyes of others; by an inner lie, in his own eyes, which is still worse—and violates the dignity of humanity in his own person."[9] In addition to finding it inherently objectionable, Kant believed that "the evil of deceitfulness spreads into man's relations with other men, when once the principle of truthfulness has been violated." How might an act-utilitarian and a rule-utilitarian reply to Kant's unqualified condemnation of self-deception?

Focus your answer by discussing whether you think self-deception is wrong or morally permissible in the following cases. If you are unsure, what further information would you need in order to make a decision about the case?

Case 1. A friend of yours is having trouble with her courses. It is clear to you that the reason is a deep lack of interest in the major selected by the student, and that, indeed, the "selection" was made primarily by the student's parents. The student has deceived herself into thinking that the problem is with the poor professors who fail to make the subject matter exciting.

Case 2. A player on the varsity basketball team is good, but not sufficiently talented to become a professional player after college. The player has deceived himself into thinking otherwise: that a lucrative profession is ahead if only he does his personal best. In fact, the self-deception actually improves the student's performance on the court, evoking the student's best efforts, and serving as a (partially) self-fulfilling prophesy that he will succeed. The deception also leads the student to focus his energies on his basketball practice and to minimize the time spent on classwork.

Case 3. A parent is diagnosed with a form of cancer for which physicians can offer little hope for a cure. The parent and the rest of the family deceive themselves into thinking the chances of a cure are high.

4 We suggested that self-deception can be permissible, benign, and even beneficial; but could it ever be morally obligatory? Jack Meiland offers the following two examples of when he thinks self-deception is obligatory. Do you agree with his view?

Case 1. Suppose that Jones and Smith have been business partners and exceptionally close friends for more than thirty-five years. One day Jones discovers a discrepancy in the business's accounts. Upon investigation he comes into the possession of evidence which is sufficient (in anyone's eyes) to justify the belief that Smith has been secretly siphoning off money from the business. Now Jones is in the following predicament. He is, and knows he is, the type of person who is unable to conceal his feelings and beliefs from others. He thus knows that if he decides that Smith has indeed been stealing money from the firm it will definitely affect his behavior toward Smith. Even if Jones tries to conceal his belief, he knows that he will inevitably act in a remote, cold, censorious and captious manner toward Smith and that eventually both the friendship and the business partnership will break up. Jones decides that this price is too high and therefore decides not to believe that Smith stole money from the firm. In fact, he goes farther: he decides that Smith did not steal money from the firm.

Case 2. Take the classical case in which a wife finds a blonde hair on her husband's coat, a handkerchief with lipstick on it in his pocket, a scrap of paper with a phone number scrawled on it, and so on until everyone would agree that the evidence is sufficient that the husband has been seeing another woman. However, the wife believes that their marriage is basically sound and can weather this storm. Like Jones, she knows that she cannot conceal her suspicions and hence decides to believe that her husband is not being unfaithful to her.[10]

In defending your agreement or disagreement with Meiland, consider two possibilities: (1) Things turn out as hoped for—that is, Smith stops stealing and the friendship remains intact; and the husband stops having affairs and the marriage grows stronger than ever. (This is the situation Meiland had in mind.) (2) It is not known what consequences are likely to result from the self-deception.

5   When we accuse someone of self-deception we usually mean they (1) hold a false belief or are ignorant of something they should have known (given the evidence available) and (2) purposefully avoid the truth. What should be said about the use of the concept of self-deception to criticize people's religious beliefs, which are based on faith?

In *The Future of an Illusion*, for example, Freud criticized theists (people who believe in God) for engaging in self-deceptive forms of wishful thinking (that is, believing what makes them happy). Jean-Paul Sartre made similar sweeping criticisms of theists, as did Karl Marx when he portrayed religion as "the opiate of the people."

Many theologians and ministers have made the opposite charge: Atheists are guilty of evading the recognition of God's existence. For example, the Protestant theologian Reinhold Niebuhr stated that rejection of belief in God is a sin of pride that bases human concerns above God. He traced this "sin" to willful dishonesty and self-deception: "Man loves himself inordinately. Since his determinate existence does not deserve the devotion lavished upon it, it is obviously necessary to practice some deception in order to justify such excessive devotion."[11]

In such charges and counter-charges, is the concept of self-deception being properly used or misused?

SUGGESTED READINGS

Butler, Bishop Joseph. "Upon Self-Deceit." In W. E. Gladstone (ed.), *The Works of Joseph Butler*. Oxford: Clarendon Press, 1896.

Dilman, Ilham, and D. Z. Phillips. *Sense and Delusion*. New York: Humanities Press, 1971.

Elster, John (ed.). *The Multiple Self.* Cambridge: Cambridge University Press, 1986.

Fingarette, Herbert. *Self-Deception*. Atlantic Highlands, NJ: Humanities Press, 1969.

Freud, Sigmund. *The Future of an Illusion*. New York: Norton, 1960.

Goleman, Daniel. *Vital Lies, Simple Truths: The Psychology of Self-Deception*. New York: Simon & Schuster, 1985.

Haight, M. R. *A Study of Self-Deception*. Atlantic Highlands, NJ: Humanities Press, 1980.

Kekes, John. "Self-Knowledge." In *The Examined Life*. Lewisburg, PA: Bucknell University Press, 1988.

King-Farlow, John, and Sean O'Connell. *Self-Conflict and Self-Healing*. Lanham, MD: University Press of America, 1988.

Lockard, Joan S., and Delroy L. Paulhus (eds.). *Self-Deception: An Adaptive Mechanism?* Englewood Cliffs, NJ: PrenticeHall, 1988.

Martin, Mike W. *Self-Deception and Morality*. Lawrence, KS: University Press of Kansas, 1986.

Martin, Mike W. (ed.). *Self-Deception and Self-Understanding: New Essays In Philosophy and Psychology*. Lawrence, KS: University Press of Kansas, 1985.

McLaughlin, Brian P., and Amelie Rorty (eds.). *Perspectives on Self-Deception*. Berkeley, CA: University of California Press, 1988.

Mele, Alfred R. *Irrationality: An Essay on Akrasia, Self-Deception and Self-Control*. New York: Oxford University Press, 1987.

Sartre, Jean-Paul. "Bad Faith." In *Being and Nothingness*. New York: Washington Square Press, 1966.

Sloan, Tod S. *Deciding: Self-Deception in Life Choices*. New York: Methuen, 1987.

Steffen, Lloyd H. *Self-Deception and the Common Life*. New York: Peter Lang, 1986.

Taylor, Shelley E. *Positive Illusions: Creative Self-Deception and the Healthy Mind*. New York: Basic Books, 1989.

Tolstoy, Leo. *The Death of Ivan Ilych*. Trans. Aylmer Maude. In *Great Short Works of Leo Tolstoy*. New York: Harper and Row, 1967.

CHAPTER 7

Self-Control and Courage

Knowing what is right is one thing. Doing it is something else. No aspect of morality is more poignant than the struggle to live up to our moral convictions. Judging that we should perform some act or engage in some activity, all things considered, we may nevertheless fail to do so, even though we have the power to do so. This is *weakness of will*, and when the judgment is specifically moral it is *moral weakness*.

By contrast, *self-control* is the virtue of living according to one's values and standards of rationality insofar as one has the capacity to do so. In this chapter we discuss two important aspects of self-control that enable us to surmount weakness of will: moral effort and courage. We also discuss the related topics of inner conflict and the way we use excuses to protect self-esteem and self-respect.

Loss of Self-Control

Weakness of will can be occasional or habitual. Occasional weakness of will is one or a few periodic acts (or omitted acts). Habitual weakness of will involves a longer-term pattern of actions. As the following example suggests, habitual weakness of will takes various forms.[1]

A student begins the year with the firm resolve to study as hard as possible. Within a few weeks, however, the student *backslides*, forgetting on many nights to keep the resolution to study. The initially firm resolutions to do homework are transformed into *weak-resolves*, *wavering-commitments*, and increasingly *vague commitments* that lack clear implications for how many hours are to be spent studying. Only *half-hearted efforts* are made in which only a small part of the requisite time and effort are invested. On some days a greater struggle is made to attend class and do homework, but too quickly the student *surrenders the struggle, giving in to temptations* to watch television or go to parties. On other days the student *succumbs to strong emotions,* perhaps anger or love, in ways that *distort judgment* about how time should be spent. When essays are assigned, days pass in *procrastinating* until the last moment.

Weakness of will, as it is usually understood, involves four elements: (1) judging that an act or pattern of activity ought to be avoided; (2) desiring to perform the act or engage in the activity anyway; (3) intentionally acting on that desire;* (4) doing so voluntarily, without external coercion or irresistible inner compulsions. (Sometimes the last condition is omitted, thereby widening the idea of weakness of will to include irresistible compulsions.)

Most of us are familiar with instances in our own lives when we could have exercised self-control but failed to do so because we did not try hard enough. Familiar examples include neglecting to write thank-you letters for gifts received, failing to keep promises, overeating, abusing alcohol, and missing important deadlines.

Paradoxes

Despite the familiarity of these examples of acting against our better judgment, some philosophers find weakness of will paradoxical. They question whether one can sincerely judge an act as right and then voluntarily fail to do it. This skepticism about weakness of will takes several forms, depending on whether judgments are understood as: (1) knowledge or beliefs, (2) commitments, or (3) decisions that entail wants. We consider each of these grounds for skepticism in turn.

Socrates and Aristotle were skeptical about weakness of will because of their view that genuine moral knowledge must produce good conduct. Socrates held that "knowledge *is* virtue": To know what is morally right is to do it, when the opportunity arises, and unless outside forces prevent one.[2] As he also stated, "Knowledge is a fine thing quite capable of ruling a man, and ... if he can distinguish good from evil, nothing will force him to act otherwise than as knowledge dictates, since wisdom is all the reinforcement he needs."[3]

Aristotle's view was more complex, but he agreed with Socrates that knowledge about how we ought to act, together with awareness of relevant information about our situation, leads us to act accordingly unless external

---

* That is, knowingly and purposefully acting to satisfy the desire, although usually not specifically intending (or seeking) to be weak of will.

obstacles interfere. He suggested that "incontinent [i.e., weak-willed] people must be said to be in a similar condition to men asleep, mad, or drunk."[4] Either they are momentarily blinded to the reality of what they are doing or they temporarily lose awareness of its wrongness.

Socrates and Aristotle remind us of how an intense pleasure close at hand can momentarily distort judgment or deflect attention from what we otherwise know is right. Yet their perspective obscures the important distinction between (a) knowing, believing, or judging something to be right and (b) being motivated to do it. Sometimes we are insufficiently motivated to do what we know is right, perhaps because we do not try hard enough or care deeply enough about our responsibilities.

In *Freedom and Reason*, R. M. Hare regards value judgments—in contrast to Socrates and Aristotle—as more closely resembling commitments than beliefs or knowledge. In Hare's view, to judge an act obligatory is to commit oneself to doing it when the occasion arises. Moreover, this commitment entails that one will perform the act unless prevented by external forces, by an absence of any opportunity to act, or by a psychological inability to so act (perhaps due to a powerful addiction). The idea of weakness of will, which requires that one could have acted differently but failed to do so because of a lack of effort, is a self-contradictory notion.

Hare's view has more plausibility than Socrates' and Aristotle's view when applied to simple cases such as failing to write letters to one's parents. Hare forces us to ask, "Are persons sincerely committed to writing the letters if they repeatedly fail to write them when the opportunity arises?" The familiar adage "Actions speak louder than words" is relevant here in determining where a person's commitments really lie.

Yet is Hare correct in equating moral judgments with fully sincere commitments? A judgment that something is wrong is not the same as a full commitment to avoid it. Moreover, even when we are fully committed, we may have momentary lapses of effort and caring. Guilt feelings and efforts to make amends following the failures may confirm the sincerity of our commitments.

The third type of skepticism about weakness of will holds that value judgments entail wants or desires (rather than commitments). According to this view, our judgment that an act is right entails that we will most want to do it, which in turn entails that we will act when the opportunity arises. Thus, if we judge that it is right to keep a promise, all things considered, then we will most want to keep it. Since we always do what we most want to do, how could we fail to keep the promise (assuming we are able to do so)? In general, it seems impossible to act contrary to our evaluations about what ought to be done.

This view is based on the confusion of two senses of "wants most." In one sense this phrase means "values most highly." This concerns evaluations, and the relative value of things. Although we may value promise keeping more than promise breaking, it does not necessarily follow that we always make the effort to keep our promises.

In a second sense, "wants most" means "is most strongly motivated by." This is a psychological notion pertaining to the strength of a want or desire. In this sense people do indeed—by definition—always do what they want most to do (when they are able).* They may nevertheless, however, be subject to weakness of will. We judge that we ought to keep a promise, but our strongest motivating desire may be to do something else. Again, people may want most (in the sense of judging it most desirable, all things considered) to preserve their marriages by avoiding adultery. In a moment of weakness of will, however, they may want most (in the sense of being most strongly motivated) to have an affair.

Inner Conflict and Self-Respect

The most perplexing aspect of weakness of will is inner conflict, or the self divided against itself. By definition, weakness of will involves a split between our judgments and the desire that most strongly motivates us to act. Typically, it also entails conflicts among our desires. Usually we have at least some desire to do what we judge is right, a desire that conflicts with a second desire to act otherwise.

These inner conflicts are distressing. Unless they are successfully resolved, we suffer feelings of shame for being unable or unwilling to live up to our own standards, as well as feelings of guilt when our failures harm other people. If continued long enough, habitual weakness of will can cause self-alienation—a sense of being out of touch with who we are—because our sense of identity depends largely on our central commitments. Habitual weakness of will can erode our confidence in the genuineness of those commitments.

There are several ways to avoid these negative responses to weakness of will, which we now discuss; we can (1) try harder in the future, (2) honestly rethink our values, (3) accept our flaws, or (4) make excuses.

First, we can try harder in the future to live up to our moral convictions and other standards of conduct. "Trying harder" implies forming habits that minimize the temptations we feel. To overcome habitual weakness of will we must make long-term adjustments of conduct and attitudes, as anyone knows who has successfully gone on a diet. Certain kinds of food can no longer be brought home, and other foods must be available in abundance; hunger can be deflated by drinking water before meals; eating in front of a

---

*It is important not to confuse this sense of "wants most"—most motivated by—with a third sense. A want can "feel" strongest (carry more psychological agitation with it) and yet not necessarily motivate most strongly.

television, which invites casual munching, should be avoided; taking smaller bites and chewing longer helps; emotionally based attitudes, inherited from childhood, about food as a reward need to be rethought; and so on.

When we are faced with temptations, "trying harder" means making greater efforts of the sort summarized by Alfred Mele:

> An agent can, for example, keep clearly in mind, at the time of action, the reasons for doing the action that he judged best; he can refuse to focus his attention on the attractiveness of what might be achieved by performing a competing action, and concentrate instead on what is to be accomplished by acting as he judges best; he can refuse to entertain second thoughts concerning matters about which he has just very carefully made up his mind; he can seek to add to his motivation for performing the action judged best by promising himself a reward ... for successfully resisting temptation. Such exercises of self-control can have a desirable effect upon the balance of his motivation at the time of action.[5]

Mele refers to these tactics as *skilled resistance* to impulses that threaten to prevent us from doing what we judge best. They constitute rational attempts to strengthen our motives, in addition to the sheer *brute resistance* of exerting willpower so as not to give in to a temptation. Most weakness of will results from failures to exercise a combination of skilled and brute resistance to impulses contrary to our best judgment.

The second way we might contend with weakness of will is to reflect on and modify our value judgments and attitudes. Perhaps the struggling student is embarked on a self-defeating course of study in which she or he has little genuine interest. A change of major or career plans may be the best way to surmount the weakness of will.

Third, on some occasions and with respect to some habits, it may not be worth the effort necessary to avoid weakness of will altogether; or it may be worth only a moderate effort that only partially succeeds. At these times an informal cost-benefit analysis of effort may be warranted. When the degree of effort required to achieve complete self-control would use up energies needed for more important endeavors, the best compromise might be to accept a particular shortcoming in order to channel effort where it can do the most good. Ironically, there can be strength in accepting some weakness of will, as Friedrich Nietzsche (1844–1900) suggested:

> To "give style" to one's character—a great and rare art! It is practiced by those who survey all the strengths and weaknesses of their nature and then fit them into an artistic plan until every one of them appears as art and reason and even weaknesses delight the eye.... For one thing is needful: that a human being should *attain* satisfaction with himself....[6]

Each of these first three responses—rethinking our values, trying harder, and accepting ourselves—is subject to abuse. They can be made dishonestly, in self-deception rather than with genuine moral concern. The belief that we are trying hard may be only self-deception masking idle handwringing and token gestures.* Again, rethinking our values may amount to little more than rationalization. As in Aesop's fable of the fox and the grapes, when we cannot reach the grapes (the good to which we aspire), we may persuade ourselves that the grapes are too sour to be worth seeking. Similarly, self-acceptance may be sheer complacency rather than creative resignation based on a reasonable apportionment of energies.

Excuses

Our tendency to make excuses, which is the fourth response to weakness of will, deserves a fuller discussion because of its importance in protecting our self-esteem and self-respect.[7] An excuse is a convenient explanation of a failure (or seeming failure) to live up to our standards. Some excuses are made primarily to protect us from criticisms by other people. Most are designed to maintain our own self-image, our own sense of self-esteem and self-respect. They may represent reasonable explanations, or may be the dishonest product of hypocrisy or self-deception.

Justification strategies arise when the excuse is intended to justify the act. For example, recall (from Chapter 1) that any of the thirty-eight witnesses to the murder of Kitty Genovese had plenty of time to prevent the murder by making a telephone call. Most of the witnesses, when interviewed later, attempted to justify their inaction with excuses to the effect that "It wasn't my responsibility to get involved" or "I thought someone else would call." One witness went further, saying that he had thought it was a lovers' quarrel with which it would be wrong to interfere.

By contrast, *blame-lessening strategies* occur when one admits one's wrongdoing but tries to lessen the resulting blame by appealing to extenuating circumstances. In the Kitty Genovese case, a few witnesses admitted that they should have called the police; but their excuses for failing to do so reflected blame-lessening strategies such as "Frankly, we were afraid." Some also indicated that it had been the middle of the night and they had been too tired and upset to think clearly.

Blame-lessening strategies take two forms. *Consensus-raising strategies* appeal to the notion that most people act similarly in similar situations. The idea is to lessen blame by arguing that one's actions conform with what can be expected from others. This would be illustrated by witnesses who comforted themselves by saying, "Everyone else did what I did, too." Many everyday excuses fall into this category: "I know the joke was racist, but

---

*Self-deception, we might add, is at times itself a form of weakness of will. Self-deception most often involves some degree of awareness of or suspicion about the truth or the painful topic we are avoiding. If we fail to make an effort to confront the truth more directly, to struggle against our biases in reasoning, and to "open up" to other viewpoints that might help us arrive at the truth, then we are being weak of will in the actions that self-deceivingly shape our beliefs.

everyone else laughed at it too." "Sure, adultery is wrong, but the majority of married people do it sometime, so don't come down hard on me."

In contrast, *consistency-lowering strategies* portray one's failure as a rare lapse that is inconsistent with one's general good character (in light of which one should be judged). This strategy is illustrated by the witnesses who claimed that fear or fatigue prevented them from acting with their normal degree of involvement and concern. This appeal to one's overall integrity and good character is also common in everyday excuses: "I know I didn't try very hard to resist the temptation to have the affair, but I've never done it before and I'll never do it again."

Excuses, understood as explanations of failures or apparent failures, sometimes succeed and are justified: Our act was in fact not bad, contrary to appearances, or we are in fact not as blameworthy as it first seemed. These are *valid excuses*. Other excuses, however, are not justified. How do we know which are valid and which are not? We draw upon our understanding of what we can reasonably require of people—both people in general and the individual in question in particular—in the given circumstances. Hence, our assessment of excuses is as complex as our moral sensitivity itself.

To complicate matters further, we assess excuses by using pragmatic criteria, as well as criteria of validity. The struggle to maintain self-esteem is often difficult and sometimes demands any kind of excuse—valid or not—especially in light of the increasing complexity of contemporary life. Without excuses we would take fewer risks, knowing they might result in inexcusable errors. Preservation of self-esteem would become impossible without drastically lowering our value standards. Thus, giving and accepting excuses is a necessary way of coping with our imperfections.

In addition, our encouragement of excuse making helps us to maintain personal ties and support each other in matters of self-esteem. Consider a teenager who tells his parents he failed to show up for an exam because he did not feel like taking it and because he hates the class. Not only is he defying his parents, he may be threatening to drop out of the educational system. Friends or parents might ease tensions, however, by offering excuses as a kind of social lubricant that will help bring the student back into the school community ("I know it's tough staying with that class given all your other worries right now ..."). In short, without excuses life might be unbearable. Within limits, excuse making is justifiable as a part of self-acceptance and tolerance of others' weakness of will.

Forms of Courage

Thus far, our discussion has centered around weakness rather than strength. Let us turn to a form of strength which is crucial in avoiding weakness of will in confronting dangers: courage. Courage comes in many forms, depending in part on the type of danger in question. *Physical courage* is a response to dangers to life or limb; *social courage* is a response to social dangers; and *intellectual courage* (or courage of one's convictions) is a response to threats to one's commitments. All these types of courage are exemplified by Elizabeth and Paul Glaser in their struggle against AIDS (Acquired Immune Deficiency Syndrome).

When the Glasers were married in 1980, they had every hope of a happy life together. Paul Glaser was quickly becoming a television star in his role as Starsky in the detective show "Starsky and Hutch." Elizabeth had their first child Ariel a year later. Complications in the cesarean delivery required transfusions with blood which, as the Glasers learned five years later, was contaminated with the AIDS virus. The virus was passed to Ariel during breast feeding, and later to their second child Jake while he was in utero.

Ariel was diagnosed with AIDS in 1986 when she was five. This was the height of public panic over AIDS, and the Glasers immediately found themselves socially and emotionally isolated. Friends turned away, afraid to have their children play with Ariel, and schools blocked her admission. The family drew strength each from the courage of the others, especially from the courage of Ariel in undergoing repeated medical procedures. Ariel's courage continued to the end, according to Elizabeth's account of her death.

> Doctors were in and out, in and out, but we paid no attention to them.
>
> She [Ariel] looked at me. Paul was on the other side of her.
>
> I said, "You know it's going to be okay. Are you scared?"
>
> She said, "No."
>
> And then very quietly, but very quickly, she died as Paul and I lay beside her in her bed.[8]

The tragedy almost wrecked the Glasers' marriage, but somehow they coped. They continued with a campaign they had begun while Ariel was alive to gain funding for pediatric AIDS research. They met with President Reagan, who, while sympathetic, did not help them, because of conservative political pressures. Next they established a private foundation which raised research money from the Hollywood community and nationally. They pursued their activities despite knowing that if the press learned of their involvement Paul's career could be ended, even though Paul had not himself contracted AIDS, because of the AIDS hysteria at the time. Eventually, intrusive reporters from the *National Enquirer* forced them to make their situation public, but that merely intensified their efforts, leading them to testify in congressional hearings about the need for increased AIDS research and therapy. Elizabeth spoke for both of them when she said, "I identify with the oppressed, but not as a victim.... Becoming active in the fight against AIDS made me realize I'm not a victim. I have power and I can work for change."[9]

The Glasers manifest long-term patterns of physical, social, and intellectual courage in their actions. Courage can also be shown on a single occasion, however, as in the next example of physical courage.

In a wilderness area near the city where I live, a woman was hiking with her five-year-old daughter in 1986. A mountain lion attacked the girl and dragged her into some bushes. The mother's frantic screams were heard by Gregory Ysais, a thirty-six-year-old electronics technician who happened to be hiking in the same area. Without any hesitation Ysais ran to the scene to find the cougar gripping the bloody and squirming child by the back of her neck. Ysais grabbed a branch and repeatedly swung it over the cougar's head. The full-grown cougar responded with threatening roars and quick strikes with his huge paws. After a few minutes the cougar dropped the child long enough for her to be pulled away.

Ysais later reported that he had never been in a life-and-death situation before and had never thought of himself as a hero: "I didn't give it much thought. I just heard people crying for help, and I just ran as fast as I could. I was just doing what I had to do. I couldn't think of anything else."[10]

Courage, Cowardice, and Fear

Aristotle defined courage as the tendency to do good in situations where fear is involved. The courageous person tends to "hit the mean," that is, to find the reasonable middle ground between excess (too much) and deficiency (too little). Aristotle writes: "In the field of Fear and Confidence the mean is Courage; ... the one who exceeds [the mean] in confidence [i.e., risk-taking] is called Rash, and the one who shows an excess of fear and a deficiency of confidence is called Cowardly."[11]

Aristotle's definition differs somewhat from the courage outlined in our examples, for two reasons. First, we called Ysais courageous even though he performed only one good deed in the face of danger, without knowing whether he had a habit or tendency of acting courageously. If in a later situation he acted cowardly, we would describe him, more cautiously, as a person who sometimes acts courageously and sometimes does not. As long as he is not a coward later, however, we are perfectly justified in calling him a courageous person because of his one extraordinary act. Thus, people are courageous if they either (1) show a tendency to do admirable acts in situations they see as dangerous or (2) act admirably to an extraordinary degree on one occasion, without acting cowardly on other occasions.

Second, Aristotle defines courage in terms of fear, but we have not done so. We have referred instead to behavior in situations regarded as dangerous, whether or not one actually feels fear in response to the danger. Ysais was courageous because he acted effectively in an emergency involving danger, whether or not he felt a fear that he had to overcome.

Cowardice, by contrast, is logically connected with fear. By definition, cowardice is a moral failing due to fear—fear that motivates one to flee, causes one's responses to freeze, or otherwise prevents one from confronting the danger in a responsible manner. People who fail to meet their obligations in dangerous situations because of sheer laziness are not cowards—they are just lazy. Cowardice arises when fear is the specific motive for the failure.

A Definition of Courageous Actions

We have defined courageous people as those who perform courageous acts (either as a pattern of behavior or as an extraordinary instance in the absence of later cowardice); but what is a courageous act? In *Virtues and Vices*, James Wallace offers the following defining criteria for courageous acts. Each criterion is set forth as a necessary condition (that is, one that must be met for an act to be courageous), and taken together the six criteria are intended to be sufficient (that is, enough to distinguish an act as courageous).

(a) A [a person] believes that it is dangerous for him to do Y [an action].

(b) A believes that his doing Y is worth the risks it involves.

(c) A believes that it is possible for him not to do Y.

(d) The danger A sees in doing Y must be sufficiently formidable that most people would find it difficult in the circumstances to do Y.

(e) A is not coerced into doing Y by threats of punishment, which he fears more than he fears the dangers of doing Y.

(f) A is under self-control, at least in the sense of not being in a frenzy, stupor, or intoxication.[12]

Focus on condition (b), which requires only that the person *believe* the act to be worth doing despite the risks, not that the act actually be good. Aristotle would require that courageous acts actually be good. Who is correct?

Wallace's definition seems preferable when we think of soldiers who fight with valor on an immoral side during a war. For example, Field Marshal Rommel was a highly distinguished and intrepid soldier for Hitler's side during World War II. Rommel repeatedly won battles by using daring tactics, frequently risking his own life. The Allied officers both feared and respected him. Because Rommel's acts were for an immoral cause, Aristotle's definition would not allow us to call him courageous, whereas Wallace's definition more plausibly does allow this conclusion.

Consider alternatively, however, someone who plays deadly games of "chicken." In a movie role made famous by James Dean, a teenager races at breakneck speed toward a high cliff, competing with a teenager in another car to see who "chickens out" first. Such acts are foolhardy, tragically stupid, or cruel. Here Aristotle's definition of courage seems preferable because it sees nothing courageous in such acts of daring, whereas Wallace's definition requires us to call such acts courageous when the individuals believe their acts are worth the risks involved.

Our hesitation or refusal to ascribe courage in the case of the "chicken" games reflects an important linguistic fact: The word "courage" carries strongly positive connotations. To ascribe courage to a person expresses some approval—at least with respect to the risk taking involved. There is, however, nothing worth approving in, say, the game of chicken. One way to refine our definition of courageous acts at this point would be to add a further condition to Wallace's list of criteria:

> (g) We admire [person] A for [act] Υ, at least for the risk taking involved in Υ.

This would allow us to ascribe courage to Field Marshal Rommel (if we admire his risk taking) but not to the players of chicken games.

A complementary approach would be to insist that, to qualify as courageous, a person must have good reasons for his or her actions. Following a suggestion of Douglas Walton in his book *Courage*, we could modify Wallace's condition (b) as follows:

> (b') A believes that doing Υ is worth the risks it involves and A has at least one good reason for believing Υ is worthwhile. Acting on these intentions, he intends Υ to be good.

Field Marshal Rommel was mistaken in believing his acts were good, but no doubt he believed that it was his duty as a soldier to act as he did. If we see any value in this conscientiousness we will see his conduct as courageous, unlike the conduct of the players in the chicken games.

The Good of Courage

Based on our revised version of Wallace's definition, courage always involves some good, for it entails an *intention* to do something good or right. Risk taking on behalf of such intentions is good, even though the act may be bad in other respects.

Courage is especially good when it contributes to the good of other people, as in the Glasers' campaign for AIDS research and in Ysais's rescue of the child. Douglas Walton makes some insightful comments about how risk taking on behalf of altruistic aims is especially admirable. He asks us to consider two men who perform acts with equally good intentions and consequences. In one case, all that is required is for the man to pull a child from a shallow pond into which the child has fallen. In the second case, the man saves a small child trapped in a burning auto following a crash. When he arrives at the scene of the accident, he sees a group of people shouting and waiting for a rescue team. Fearing that the gas tank is about to explode, he rushes into the flames and, at considerable risk to himself, pries the child free from the burning wreckage. In doing so he is seriously burned and cut. Commenting on why we admire the second man even more than the first one, Walton writes:

> What is of moral import in evaluating actions over and above the goodness of an intention in itself is the commitment of the agent to carrying out that intention. The depth of that commitment is indicated by the time, effort, ingenuity, and sacrifice the agent is willing to put into the carrying out of his good intention.... The greater the sacrifice, risk, and danger of carrying out a good objective, the more meritorious is the course of action directed to that end.[13]

Courage, however, does not always involve altruism, that is, a desire to promote the good of other people out of concern for their welfare. It is also courageous to take risks in fulfilling our duties to ourselves and in pursuing self-fulfillment, rather than always taking the prudent course. As W. D. Falk pointed out:

> Prudence is only one way of looking after oneself. To act prudently is to play safe, for near-certain gains at small risks. But some good things one cannot get in this way. To get them at all one has to gamble, taking the risk of not getting them even so, or of coming to harm in the process. If one values them enough, one will do better by oneself to throw prudence to the winds, to play for high stakes, knowing full well the risk and the price of failure. Explorers, artists, scientists, mountaineers are types who may serve themselves better by this course. So will most people at some juncture.[14]

SUMMARY

Weakness of will is a failure to live up to our value standards and has four elements: (1) judging that an act or pattern of activity ought to be avoided; (2) desiring to engage in it anyway; (3) intentionally acting on that desire; and (4) doing so voluntarily, without external coercion or irresistible inner compulsions.

By definition, weakness of will involves a loss of self-control in the sense that we fail to guide our acts in light of our values; but it does not entail a loss of self-control in the sense that we are unable to act otherwise. Perhaps most weakness of will can be avoided if we make a greater effort to resist impulses contrary to our value standards, whether by exerting our energies (brute resistance) or by strengthening our motivation by concentrating our attention on what we ought to do and on why it is important (skilled resistance).

Weakness of will and the inner conflict it involves threatens self-esteem and self-respect. Its harmful effects can be lessened in four ways: We can (1) try harder in the future, (2) honestly rethink our values, (3) accept our flaws, and (4) make excuses. Justification excuses portray an act as not really wrong, contrary to first appearances. Blame-lessening excuses are appeals to extenuating circumstances, made with the hope of reducing the blame incurred. They include consensus-raising strategies, which portray one's failure as comparable to similar failures by most other people, and consistency-lowering strategies, which portray the failure as a rare lapse in one's otherwise admirable character.

Courageous acts are performed in the face of danger in pursuit of what one believes, with some good reason, to be a good end. When the reason is insufficient to justify the act, the courage is misguided and not entirely good (as with Field Marshal Rommel). Courageous people either show a tendency to perform courageous acts or perform one extraordinary act of heroism not followed by cowardly acts. Courage is especially valuable when it promotes the good of other people or one's moral integrity and self-fulfillment, and also when it is prompted by good intentions and motives, or reveals skill and judgment in the face of great danger.

DISCUSSION TOPICS

1   Suppose half of the students in a class are cheating on an exam. How might they attempt to excuse their cheating using each of the following excuse strategies: (1) justification strategies and (2) blame-lessening strategies, including (a) consensus-raising strategies and (b) consistency-lowering strategies. Are any of the excuses valid?

2   Are the following people courageous? Explain, using your definition of courage. (1) A man who invests all his family's earnings in high-risk stocks with the aim of making his family wealthy. (2) A mountain climber who risks her life for the sake of the joys and challenges of the hike. (3) A man who commits suicide by igniting his gasoline-soaked clothes to protest his government's immoral policies.

3   Is it more admirable to display courage without feeling any fear ("fearlessness") or to feel fear and act courageously despite it? Or is there no moral difference between the two? Consider, for example, two variations on the Ysais example: Ysais felt terror and struggled to overcome it before rushing to the aid of the child; or Ysais felt no fear whatsoever.

4   The first of Wallace's six criteria for courageous acts was that "A [a person] believes that it is dangerous for him to do Y [an action]." Consider situations in which this belief is irrational, as in the case of acts motivated by phobias. For ex-

ample, a person with a spider phobia irrationally believes it is dangerous for him to be within yards of a perfectly harmless garden spider. Is the person showing courage by approaching the spider despite the fear? Or should we modify Wallace's criterion to require that the belief about the danger must be reasonable?

5   We noted that it is best to rethink one's moral views when one's conscience is mistaken, and not to exert an effort in obeying conscience. When a person's conscience is seriously distorted, is it perhaps obligatory not to live up to it? Would it be positively immoral to obey one's conscience?

Consider Huck Finn's decision not to return his friend, the slave Jim, to his master. As Huck was helping Jim escape on a raft down the Mississippi River, his conscience began to disturb him:

> Jim said it made him all over trembly and feverish to be so close to freedom. Well I can tell you it made me all over trembly and feverish, too, to hear him, because I begun to get it through my head that he *was* most free—and who was to blame for it? Why, *me*. I couldn't get that out of my conscience, no how nor no way.... I tried to make out to myself that *I* warn't to blame, because *I* didn't run Jim off from his rightful owner; but it warn't no use, conscience up an says, every time: "But you knowed he was running for his freedom, and you coulda paddled ashore and told somebody."[15]

Huck's conscience tells him that he ought to return Jim—that is what he takes to be morally obligatory. Nevertheless, he refuses to live up to his conscience, instead accepting himself as a sinner. Should we say that he was weak of will but his weakness is virtuous? Would he have displayed a vice by exercising greater strength of will in following his conscience?

6   Are self-control, self-discipline, perseverance, and strength of will always virtues? Clearly, deeply immoral people sometimes have great self-control and strength of will: witness Hitler, Stalin, and the Ayatollah Khomeini. The strength of will of these people gave them the power to accomplish their horrors. If we condemn their conduct, should we not also condemn the traits that enabled them to succeed?

The same question arises with respect to other words commonly used to refer to virtues, because many of them allude to self-control and strength of will. Courage, for example, entails the exercise of self-control in situations involving danger; temperance is the exercise of self-control when the appetites urge otherwise; and prudence involves self-control over one's thoughts and conduct in situations where one might "lose one's head." Villains can show self-control in pursuing evil ends; when they do so, are they displaying virtues, and are they in that respect admirable?

There are several options in answering this question. (1) We might admit that evil people can be virtuous in the limited respects these traits identify, thus, embracing the irony that virtues (admirable traits) can promote vice. (2) We might refuse to call something a virtue when it directly serves evil ends, and interpret the traits as good only when they serve good ends. In a sense they are "dependent virtues": Their qualification as virtues depends on their connection with a restricted range of goals and intentions.[16] (3) We might refuse to call them virtues at all, even dependent ones, and think of them instead as "powers" that, like all power, can serve either virtuous or immoral ends.

Which of these options is preferable? Is there a still better option?

SUGGESTED READINGS

Davidson, Donald. "How Is Weakness of the Will Possible?" In Joel Feinberg (ed.), *Moral Concepts.* New York: Oxford University Press, 1970. Reprinted in Donald Davidson, *Essays on Actions and Events.* Oxford: Clarendon Press, 1980.

Foot, Phillipa. *Virtues and Vices and Other Essays in Moral Philosophy.* Berkeley, CA: University of California Press, 1978.

Hare, R. M. *Freedom and Reason.* New York: Oxford University Press, 1970. Pp. 67–85.

Hill, Thomas E., Jr. "Weakness of Will and Character." In *Autonomy and Self-Respect.* Cambridge: Cambridge University Press, 1991.

Mele, Alfred R. *Irrationality: An Essay on Akrasia, Self-Deception, and Self-Control.* New York: Oxford University Press, 1987.

Milo, Ronald D. *Immorality.* Princeton, NJ: Princeton University Press, 1984. Pp. 115–139.

Mortimer, G. W. (ed.). *Weakness of Will.* New York: St. Martin's Press, 1971.

Rachman, S. J. *Fear and Courage.* San Francisco, CA: Freeman, 1978.

Snyder, C. R., Raymond L. Higgins, and Rita J. Stucky. *Excuses.* New York: Wiley, 1983.

Tillich, Paul. *The Courage to Be.* New Haven, CT: Yale University Press, 1952.

Wallace, James D. "Courage, Cowardice, and Self-Indulgence." In *Virtues and Vices.* Ithaca, NY: Cornell University Press, 1978.

Walton, Douglas N. *Courage: A Philosophical Investigation.* Berkeley, CA: University of California Press, 1986.

Watson, Gary. "Skepticism about Weakness of Will." *Philosophical Review,* vol. 86 (1977).

CHAPTER 8

Suicide and Euthanasia

Albert Camus (1913–1960) remarked, "There is but one truly serious philosophical problem, and that is suicide. Judging whether life is or is not worth living amounts to answering the fundamental question of philosophy."[1] Notwithstanding his literary use of hyperbole, Camus insightfully draws attention to how suicide raises fundamental issues about morality, the meaning of life, and the responsibilities of communities. Suicide is an issue for old and young alike, and it is especially alarming with regard to teenagers, for whom suicide is the second leading cause of death (next to car accidents).

Euthanasia—"mercy killing"—also raises basic issues about the conditions under which life is worth living. It has emerged as a pressing issue as medicine extends life beyond the point that many people find desirable. After discussing suicide we will turn to the question of whether euthanasia is justified.

What Is Suicide?

Defining suicide seems easy enough. Unlike accidental death or being killed by someone else, suicide is the act of killing oneself voluntarily (without extreme coercion) and intentionally (acting knowingly with the purpose of killing oneself). Our actions can be voluntary, however, to greater or lesser degrees, and some degrees of coercion may be compatible with suicide. Also, suicide often occurs when persons are severely depressed, which raises questions about whether they are acting freely. Finally, can it be considered suicide if one's ultimate intention is to defend someone else or to preserve one's integrity, rather than to secure death per se?

Consider first the situation in which a suicide occurs during severe depression or emotional distress. In such cases, do individuals genuinely choose to kill themselves, or are their acts symptoms of a psychological (if not physiological) illness beyond their control? For centuries coroners tended to view self-killing as strong evidence of insanity, and hence technically not suicide, unless there was explicit evidence to the contrary, such as a carefully written suicide note.[2] This trend reversed with the development of insurance policies that refuse benefits in cases of self-killing. Perhaps for the purposes of business and law, a wider definition of suicide is needed, but should severe depression lead us to question whether persons are acting voluntarily in killing themselves?

Furthermore, what should be concluded when persons kill themselves because of duress or coercion (from outside) rather than compulsions (from within)? Did Socrates, for example, commit suicide?[3] On the basis of trumped-up charges, he was found guilty of corrupting the young and inventing false gods and was given the choice between exile from Athens or death by drinking hemlock. He "chose" to drink the hemlock, but did he commit suicide?

Finally, consider heroic persons whose intentions are to serve a worthy cause and at the same time preserve their own integrity as someone committed to that cause. A soldier, for example, takes a cyanide pill rather than be subjected to torture that could force revelation of secrets to the enemy. Again, Buddhist monks burned themselves to death to protest the Vietnam War. Are they martyrs or suicides or both? And Captain Oates, who was too sick to continue with Captain Scott in an expedition to the South Pole, left camp to walk into a blizzard so that the group could continue unhampered by him. In all these cases, the primary intention was not to die, but instead to achieve some larger noble purpose. Are the individuals martyrs, suicides, or both?

For the purposes of moral inquiry, it seems preferable to adopt a wide interpretation of suicide, and then inquire into the reasons for and against suicide in a particular case. Unless there is clear evidence of insanity beyond the act of self-killing, we will count depression-motivated self-killing as suicide. We will count Socrates' death as suicide since he had at least one option, exile. And we will also count as suicide cases where the self-killing has a strategic intent to serve some additional noble purpose.[4] The following discussion, however, will focus on clear-cut instances of suicide.

Is Suicide Ever Justified?

Saint Thomas Aquinas argued that all suicide is immoral. Most of his reasons were religious. In his view, suicide violates the natural laws created by God, usurps God's power over life and death, and destroys bodies which are the property of the God who created them. Not all theists share Aquinas's interpretation of scripture, but it is clear that one's religious views will influence one's understanding of whether suicide is ever justified.

Without invoking religious beliefs, can we find distinct moral reasons against suicide? Aquinas mentioned one moral reason that provides a useful starting point: Suicide is contrary "to charity whereby every man should love himself."[5] Let us develop the idea that the virtue of self-respect (or self-love) poses a strong presumption against suicide. Then we will ask whether that presumption can ever be overridden by other moral considerations.

Thomas E. Hill, Jr., distinguishes four cases of suicide that reveal conduct that is less than morally ideal or virtuous. (1) *Impulsive suicide*: A person commits suicide as a result of a brief but intense emotion, such as grief in losing a spouse or lover, despair in losing one's job, or fear upon learning one has a serious illness. (2) *Apathetic suicide*: A person commits suicide because of a temporary or ongoing depression in which life seems empty and meaningless. (3) *Self-abasing suicide*: A person is filled with self-hatred and commits suicide as a form of self-contempt and self-punishment. (4) *Hedonistic calculated suicide*: A person commits suicide because he or she calculates that the future will probably bring more pain than pleasure.

In each case, the individuals fail to value themselves in appropriate ways and degrees. Self-respect requires us to resist suicide in these cases. Blame is not at issue here; often we should respond with compassion for individuals who were tragic victims of situations beyond their control. Even then, however, we can reasonably believe that no one who commits suicide for any of Hill's reasons has met our ideal of a morally good life. Inspired by Kant, Hill states the ideal this way: "A morally ideal person will value life as a rational, autonomous agent for its own sake, at least provided that the life does not fall below a certain threshold of gross, irremediable, and uncompensated pain and suffering."[6] (We might further attribute to this ideal person the virtues of faith, hope, courage, and caring, displayed in the search for meaningful life through personal relationships and through community.)

Hill acknowledges that sometimes suicide is justified in the following circumstances. (1) *Suicide to prevent subhuman life*: A person has good reason to believe that he or she will survive an illness physically alive but mentally destroyed with life reduced to the level of a lower animal or vegetable. (2) *Suicide to end severe irremediable suffering*: A person is in intense pain that can no longer be controlled by medication, short of constant unconsciousness. (3) *Morally principled suicide*: A person acts on justified commitments central to her or his moral integrity in order to help others and preserve that integrity. In each of these three cases, self-respect is no longer an argument against suicide. Indeed, self-respect provides a reason favoring suicide as a way to secure death with dignity.

So far, we have focused on self-respect, primarily within the framework of virtue ethics. How do the other ethical theories apply to suicide?

A human-rights ethics that emphasizes the right to liberty would recognize a right to make decisions about taking one's life. Nevertheless, a rights ethicist might add two qualifications. First, rights ethics implies that we should have a respect for ourselves as persons who have rights. That respect is lost in throwing away our lives without a compelling justification. Second, rights ethics requires us to take into account the rights of others. While other persons do not have a right to demand that I live, people close to me do have rights not to be harmed wantonly. When suicide causes enormous suffering to family and friends, as it often does, there is a presumption against it.

Duty ethics balances duties to oneself and to others. Duties to others, especially duties not to inflict suffering on them, often provide strong reasons against suicide. In addition, Kant believed there is an absolute (exceptionless) duty to oneself not to take one's life. That belief seems too strong, however, since it disregards the equally significant responsibility to maintain one's integrity and a minimally decent human life—considerations that may justify some suicides.

Utilitarianism, which focuses exclusively on good consequences, justifies those suicides which are reasonably intended to prevent irremediable suffering or the loss of humanly significant life or to heroically promote the good of others. At the same time, utilitarianism forbids many suicides by which meaningful life is prematurely cut short or needless suffering is inflicted on others.

Preventing Suicide

What are our responsibilities when we can prevent other persons from committing suicide? At first glance it seems the answer depends entirely on whether the suicide is justified: If the suicide is not justified then we should intervene to prevent it (when we can do so without great risk or cost), and if the suicide is justified we should refrain from intervening. Matters are not that simple, however; often we cannot tell whether an attempted suicide is justified, at least at the time the attempt is made.

Rights ethics, duty ethics, and rule-utilitarianism all justify a strong principle of autonomy (self-determination): People should be left alone to make their own decisions as long as those decisions do not harm others. John Stuart Mill articulated this principle in *On Liberty*: "[T]he only purpose for which power can be rightfully exercised over any member of a civilized community, against his will, is to prevent harm to others. His own good, either physical or moral, is not a sufficient warrant."[7]

This principle may seem to suggest that we should leave alone those adults who decide to commit suicide; but in fact the principle of autonomy justifies suicide interventions when we have reasons to think the person is not acting autonomously or when we can reasonably presume they are not.

Suicide is irreversible; it permanently ends the ability to exercise further autonomy. Thus, in order to support others' autonomy, we are often justified in intervening, especially with positive support intended to preserve their future agency.

The principle of autonomy, however, justifies only temporary intervention, as Glanville Williams argued:

> If one suddenly comes upon another person attempting suicide, the natural and humane thing to do is to try to stop him, for the purpose of ascertaining the cause of his distress and attempting to remedy it, or else of attempting moral dissuasion if it seems that the act of suicide shows lack of consideration for others, or else again from the purpose of trying to persuade him to accept psychiatric help if this seems to be called for. ... But nothing longer than a temporary restraint could be defended. [8]

Those who oppose Mill's heavy emphasis on autonomy embrace *paternalism*. According to a strong version of paternalism, we are sometimes justified in promoting the positive well-being of others against their will, indeed forcing them to seek their own good. According to a weaker (but still potent) version of paternalism, we are sometimes justified in forcing people not to harm themselves or in preventing themselves from voluntarily harming themselves. Paternalists favor more insistent and thoroughgoing interventions to prevent suicide, including forced hospitalization if necessary. They tend to interpret suicide attempts as cries for help, and they also stress the value of human life.

Whether we agree with Mill or with paternalists, we can agree that a caring society will make positive resources available for suicidal individuals. For example, suicide "hot lines," staffed primarily by volunteers, provide immediate support for individuals who need to talk with someone.

Assisting Suicide

Are we ever justified in actually helping someone commit suicide? In particular, suppose that a person who is mentally competent voluntarily chooses to commit suicide in circumstances where death is a reasonable option and where the person needs or requests help in committing suicide. Does respect for the person's autonomy permit (or even require) us to assist a suicide?

For several years, beginning in 1990, Dr. Jack Kevorkian assisted a number of persons in committing suicide. In most cases he provided them with a simple "suicide machine" that they could operate by pushing a lever with one finger, so as to inject a lethal dose of potassium chloride through an intravenous needle he attached to them. Other times he made available a mask through which they breathed carbon monoxide. The people he assisted were not terminally ill, but they suffered from severe disabilities that in their view warranted suicide. For example, his first three patients in Michigan suffered variously from one of the following conditions: Alzheimer's disease, multiple sclerosis, and a painful pelvic disease. At the time, there was no law in Michigan forbidding physician-assisted suicide, although by 1993 Michigan had passed such a law. Were Kevorkian's acts permissible? The courts and many members of the medical community were outraged and revoked his medical license. Members of the public were uneasy, but far from unanimously hostile to Kevorkian.

Dr. Kevorkian acted in part to help particular individuals and in part to draw national attention to what he believed was a justified case for legalizing physician-assisted suicide. He was not alone in this belief. During these years several states placed on ballots proposals to legalize physician-assisted suicide in cases where a person is diagnosed with a terminal illness and has less than six months to live. In 1992, for example, a California ballot proposal won 43 percent of the general vote. In fact, before the election the polls showed a majority of Californians would vote for the proposal, but during the debate many voters became concerned about possible abuses if the law passed. In particular, there were not adequate safeguards to ensure that informed and voluntary consent was secured.

Dr. Kevorkian's cases are not the only nationally debated examples of persons who, although they do not have terminal illnesses, have disabilities that they believe make their lives not worth living. Consider Elizabeth Bouvia, who in 1983 entered a hospital in Riverside, California, complaining of depression. After being admitted, she asked to be allowed to starve herself to death while receiving pain medication and sanitary care. At the time Ms. Bouvia was twenty-six years old. As a quadriplegic who was almost completely paralyzed, she was physically unable to kill herself without help. She also suffered palsy and severe arthritic pain which could not be entirely controlled by medication. Yet she could speak, was highly intelligent, and had earned a college degree. In defending her decision to die, she appealed to self-respect and personal dignity: "I hate to have someone care for every personal need ... it's humiliating. It's disgusting, and I choose to no longer do that, no longer to be dependent on someone to take care of me in that manner."[9] Despite her initial complaint about depression, she was evaluated as fully competent to make her own decisions.

Almost no one would argue that her nurses and physicians were morally *required* to help her commit suicide, since that might violate their personal moral convictions, but were they morally *permitted* to assist Ms. Bouvia if they chose to do so?

Here is what actually happened. Ms. Bouvia's lawyer sought a court order forbidding the hospital from either force-feeding her or discharging her from the hospital against her will. The court refused to grant such an order. Ms. Bouvia soon checked out of the hospital, but in 1986 entered another hospital to try again. This time she won court approval not to be fed against her will, but then she changed her mind. A year later, however, she tried yet again to starve to death with the assistance of hospital personnel. The constant vomiting from pain-killing medication (taken on an empty stomach) was too exhausting an ordeal, and she abandoned her attempt. Since that time she has lived in a small hospital room in Los Angeles County.

As this example illustrates, the medical community, courts, and even patients like Ms. Bouvia are not altogether clear about the desirability of suicide when issues about quality of life are at stake. Nevertheless, the courts have increasingly come to recognize the legal and moral rights of mentally competent individuals to decide what happens to their bodies. Long ago the Supreme Court ruled that adult Jehovah's Witnesses have the right to refuse life-essential blood transfusions, not only because of their religious freedom to act on their belief that such transfusions were prohibited by the Bible, but because of their right to privacy—their right to autonomy or self-determination. More recently, the Supreme Court has ruled that a competent person has the right to refuse even food and water.[10]

Euthanasia

Death by starvation takes many days and can be unpleasant. Would it not be far more humane and merciful, once a mentally competent person voluntarily chooses to die, to end life instantaneously, perhaps with a simple injection of morphine? The taking of someone's life for humane reasons is called *euthanasia* or mercy killing. Is it morally permissible? Currently it is illegal, but let us consider the moral issues independently of that important fact. These moral issues will decide whether the law should remain the same or be changed in the future.

Precisely what is euthanasia? It implies an intention to bring about the death of someone and to do so from beneficent motives (concern for the person). Usually it is also understood to pertain to situations in which a person has a terminal illness or suffers from extreme disabilities such as those of Elizabeth Bouvia. *Passive euthanasia* is the omission of actions which would prolong life; examples include the withholding of medicine, medical technology, or food and water with the intention of letting a person die. *Active euthanasia* is the performance of actions which bring about death, such as the administration of lethal injections of morphine. The distinction between passive and active euthanasia is not crystal clear. For example, "pulling the plug" is the act of turning off a patient's respirator or removing a feeding tube, but it is usually viewed as passive euthanasia because it is the withholding of a technology that prolongs life.

We can also distinguish between voluntary, involuntary, and nonvoluntary euthanasia. *Nonvoluntary* euthanasia occurs without a person's consent, usually when the person is in a coma or otherwise mentally incapacitated. *Involuntary* euthanasia would be the special case of euthanasia that is performed against a person's wishes. *Voluntary* euthanasia occurs when a mentally competent individual requests euthanasia on the basis of free and informed consent—that is, without coercion and in possession of relevant information that a reasonable person would want to know. That consent may be given (as a precaution against the possibility one might enter a coma or lose mental capacities) by a "living will" or an "advanced directive" to physicians and courts. It can also be given by a surrogate, such as a close relative or someone one appoints (in a "Durable Power of Attorney" document) to make such decisions should one become incapacitated.

We will focus on voluntary active euthanasia, since it is the only type of legalization which is currently being debated. It has been permitted in the Netherlands for over two decades under the following conditions: (a) A competent patient (b) who is suffering intolerably and without possible relief (whether or not a terminal illness is involved) (c) requests euthanasia voluntarily and consistently over a reasonable time and (d) secures the approval of both the attending physician and a second physician not involved in the case.[11] Despite polls which show the majority of Americans favor legalization of active euthanasia if adequate safeguards can be secured, the American Medical Association (AMA) continues to oppose active euthanasia while condoning passive euthanasia (in cases where a person is terminally ill and continued therapy holds no promise). Is this firm dichotomy between passive and active euthanasia justified?

James Rachels criticized the AMA's position. Contrary to the AMA, he argued that letting someone die is not in principle more acceptable than actively killing the person. He offers several arguments. First, compare Smith and Jones, each of whom will inherit a large amount of money if his six-year-old cousin dies. Smith drowns his cousin while the child is bathing and carefully makes the death look accidental. Jones is about to do the same thing when by chance he sees the child slip, strike his head, and fall unconscious into the water. He watches to make sure the child dies before sneaking away. Smith killed his cousin; Jones let his cousin die. Both, however, are equally blameworthy. Therefore, "the bare difference between killing and letting die does not, in itself, make a moral difference. If a doctor lets a patient die, for humane reasons, he is in the same moral position as if he had given the patient a lethal injection for humane reasons."[12]

No doubt the law would distinguish between the cases of Smith and Jones: Smith is guilty of first-degree murder, while Jones is not (and perhaps could not be convicted unless he had been in charge of the child's care at the time of the accident). Morally, however, the cases are equally immoral and horrifying. Rachels's example, then, does establish that *sometimes* the mere difference between killing and letting someone die is morally insignificant; but does the example show that the difference is *always* insignificant? Rachels's example involves malicious motives and the intention to kill. In medicine the motives and intentions are typically quite different. The intention is usually to respect a patient's right to refuse further medical treatment, or to acknowledge the desirability of withholding therapy in some cases where there is no reasonable hope of improving the patient's condition.[13]

Is it inconsistent to respect the right to refuse treatment and yet not condone active killing? Apparently not. The right of autonomy (self-determination) gives us a right to prevent health professionals from performing unwanted procedures on our bodies, but it does not imply a right to be killed. Thus, the intuitive distinction between killing and letting someone die does sometimes have moral significance, contrary to Rachels. However, there are other arguments favoring active euthanasia.

Active Euthanasia, Mercy, and Autonomy

Rachels's main argument appeals to mercy. To allow a person to die slowly rather than quickly seems patently cruel. In Rachels's view, once a decision has been made not to prolong life—indeed to bring it to a rapid close by withholding life-essential medicine or food—the compassionate thing is to bring about that result quickly and without suffering, if a person so requests. (Notice that this argument actually distinguishes between the moral status of killing and letting someone die, and favors the former as more humane in this case.)

It might seem that the argument for mercy is not so important, given the techniques of modern medicine which enable physicians to control pain. In fact, however, there are instances in which pain cannot be controlled without simply making a person unconscious. As Margaret Pabst Battin, another defender of active euthanasia, points out, "Some people still die in unspeakable agony ... [and] complete, universal, fully reliable pain control is a myth."[14] Indeed, suffering includes more than physical pain. It also involves the great discomfort of lying helplessly in bed in an utterly dependent state that one regards with abhorrence, or would so regard if one's consciousness were not blurred by medication.

Rachels's and Battin's appeal to mercy is compelling, but is it decisive? According to the AMA, mercy matters greatly but it cannot override the fundamental duty not to kill (innocent) persons. Mercy justifies administration of whatever medication is necessary to control pain, even if the medication might well lead to death, but it does not warrant intentional killing.

The AMA's position is supported by the *principle of double effect*, which was developed over hundreds of years in the Catholic Church. A potentially lethal dose of morphine may have two possible effects: control of pain and death. According to the principle of double effect, the moral act is to intend only the control of pain while knowing, but not intending, that death will occur. More generally, the principle of double effect says that it is morally permissible to perform an act which will have an unintended bad side-effect when one's motive and intention are to achieve the good result only, when the side-effect does not directly produce the intended result, and when the good effect is at least as valuable as the bad effect. Since administering active euthanasia involves intentional killing (a bad effect) as a means to the good effect, the principle of double effect does not allow it.

It is understandable that the Catholic Church and the AMA might emphasize not killing over other moral considerations regarding euthanasia; but what about the wider public (including many Catholics and physicians who disagree with their religious and professional organizations)? Should not individuals be free to make their own decisions in this matter? This returns us to the issue of autonomy and self-respect. It also returns us to the issue of assisted suicide, insofar as assisted suicide is sometimes preferable to active euthanasia.

Earlier we noted that the right to autonomy does not imply a right to be killed. Advocates of euthanasia, however, argue that it does sometimes imply a (positive) right to assistance in dying. Margaret Pabst Battin writes, "Although we usually recognize only that the principle of autonomy generates rights to noninterference, in some circumstances a right of self-determination does generate [justified] claims to assistance or to the provision of goods. We typically acknowledge this in cases of handicap or disability."[15] Is it not reasonable to extend this right to aid to a person who has become physically unable to carry out her or his intention to die? Or would doing so cross a taboo of active killing that is inherently unacceptable (because it devalues life) and possibly open to abuses?

SUMMARY

Suicide is intentional and voluntary self-killing, but questions arise about whether suicide occurs in cases of severe depression and coercion (where voluntariness is questioned) and altruism (where the primary intention is a noble goal rather than death per se). Thomas Hill argued for a strong presumption against suicide, especially in cases where it reveals a lack of self-respect. Whereas Aquinas and Kant viewed all suicide as immoral, however, Hill thinks suicide is justifiable to prevent conditions of subhuman life and severe irremediable suffering, and in some instances to achieve morally principled goals (such as helping others or preserving one's dignity).

Intervention to prevent suicide can be justified if one accepts the principle of paternalism: It is permissible to interfere with the freedom of others in order to promote their great good (strong paternalism) or to prevent great harms to them (weak paternalism). For Mill, by contrast, only temporary interventions are permissible in order to make sure persons are acting voluntarily; otherwise we fail to respect individual autonomy (self-determination). Assisted suicide is defended by Dr. Jack Kevorkian and much of the public on the grounds of one's autonomy to decide the kinds of suffering one wishes to prevent. Critics fear that legalization of physician-assisted suicide will generate too many abuses and mistakes.

Euthanasia can be active (killing someone) or passive (letting someone die), and voluntary (informed consent is obtained) or nonvoluntary. Passive voluntary euthanasia is legal, including the withholding of food and water in some circumstances, but active euthanasia is illegal. Arguments for legalizing active euthanasia include appeals to mercy and patient autonomy. Arguments against legalization emphasize respect for life and concern over possible abuses. Opponents of active euthanasia sometimes invoke the principle of double effect to justify some acts which bring about death although death is unintended. That principle says that it is morally permissible to perform an act which will have an unintended bad side-effect when one's motive and intention are to achieve the good result only, when the side-effect does not directly produce the intended result, and when the good effect is at least as valuable as the bad effect.

DISCUSSION TOPICS

1   Do the following examples qualify as cases of suicide? (a) A soldier goes on a "suicide mission," as did Japanese kamikaze pilots who flew their airplanes into enemy ships. (b) A pilot dies because she decided not to parachute, in order to crash her plane away from a populated area. (c) A man jumps off a life raft after losing in a lottery to see who would die in order that the others could survive with the limited supply of food and water.[16]

2   Is suicide ever morally justified? In which cases? Comment on why you agree or disagree with Thomas Hill's analysis of the examples he provides. In particular, do you agree with Hill that hedonistic calculated suicide is objectionable because it reveals a lack of self-respect?

3   Present and defend your view concerning the circumstances under which we are permitted and required to intervene to prevent someone from committing suicide. Would you emphasize the principle of autonomy or the principle of paternalism?

4   In 1975, twenty-one-year-old Karen Quinlan was brought to the hospital unconscious and seriously brain-damaged from an unknown cause (although it was known she had been drinking some alcohol at a birthday party and had some

traces of aspirin and Valium in her blood). Over several months her condition deteriorated. Her weight went from 120 to 70 pounds, and she shriveled into a rigid fetal position. She retained some brain function and hence was not "legally dead" (the state in which no electrical activity takes place in the brain), but she was in a permanent and irreversible vegetative state. Her parents went to court and, by proving to the court that Karen would not wish to continue life in a vegetative state, won the right to have a respirator removed. When the respirator was removed, however, Karen's anticipated death did not occur. At the time, laws required that she be given food and water. She remained alive in a comatose state for ten years before she died in 1985. Would active euthanasia have been justified in her case? More generally, is active voluntary euthanasia ever morally permissible? Defend your view by reference to one or more ethical theories.

5   Explain whether you agree with the principle of double effect. In particular, consider this: The principle of double effect is often used to justify giving a terminal-cancer patient a dose of morphine which the physician knows might be lethal but which is intended only to alleviate pain. Is there any genuine moral difference in such cases between acting on the principle of double effect and acting with the intention to bring about a quick and painless death to a patient (thereby engaging in active euthanasia)?

6   Some people believe that particular acts of voluntary active euthanasia are morally justified, but they join with groups opposed to euthanasia to fight laws legalizing its practice. They are concerned about the possible abuses and mistakes that might occur if active euthanasia became widely practiced. They cite the following facts.[17] (a) Physicians sometimes make mistakes when they diagnose an illness as terminal or beyond hope. (b) There is always the possibility that medical research may discover new cures if persons just stay alive to wait for them. (c) Greedy relatives might pressure parents into requesting euthanasia. (d) To allow physicians to engage in euthanasia might cause them inner turmoil in their primary role as healers and undermine their patients' trust in them. (e) Laws permitting active euthanasia might make the public more callous about killing and open the door (of Pandora's Box) to legalization of euthanasia in further contexts. Do these facts constitute decisive reasons against legalizing euthanasia?

7   In the past, questions about money were often dismissed as irrelevant to debates over euthanasia and assisted suicide, because human life is precious and beyond any dollar figure. Due to skyrocketing costs of medical care, however, paid for largely by the public through government programs, the question of money increasingly enters into the euthanasia debate. A huge percentage of medical costs goes to care of terminal patients who require high-tech medical attention. In a time of dwindling resources for medical care, that means that fewer resources are available for preventative medical care, including prenatal and early child care. This raises questions about justice and fairness in the distribution of medical resources. Present and defend your view concerning whether and how questions about money should influence decisions about legalizing physician-assisted suicide and active euthanasia.

8   This chapter focused on voluntary euthanasia, but consider instances of nonvoluntary euthanasia. Do you think euthanasia (either passive or active) is justified

in either of the following two cases? (a) A bedridden and irreversibly senile eighty-year-old man, who can no longer communicate or be socially involved, never indicated his views on suicide. (b) A child is born with a severe case of spina bifida, a genetic disability that greatly restricts possibilities of movement, so that many operations would be required to make possible a life of even very limited social interaction.

SUGGESTED READINGS

Alvarez, A. *The Savage God: A Study of Suicide*. New York: Bantam Books, 1973.

Battin, M. Pabst. *Ethical Issues in Suicide*. Englewood Cliffs, NJ: Prentice-Hall, 1982.

Battin, M. Pabst, and David J. Mayo (eds.). *Suicide: The Philosophical Issues*. New York: St. Martin's Press, 1980.

Becker, Ernest. *The Denial of Death*. New York: The Free Press, 1975.

Campbell, Robert, and Diane Collinson. *Ending Lives*. New York: Basil Blackwell, 1988.

Donnelly, John (ed.). *Suicide: Right or Wrong?* Buffalo, NY: Prometheus Books, 1990.

Downing, A. B., and Barbara Smoker (eds.). *Voluntary Euthanasia*. London: Peter Owen, 1986.

Glover, Jonathan. *Causing Death and Saving Lives*. New York: Penguin Books, 1977.

Hill, Thomas E., Jr. "Self-Regarding Suicide: A Modified Kantian View." In *Autonomy and Self-Respect*. Cambridge: Cambridge University Press, 1991. Pp. 85–103.

Kohl, Marvin (ed.). *Beneficent Euthanasia*. Buffalo, NY: Prometheus, 1975.

Kushner, Howard I. *American Suicide: A Psychocultural Exploration*. New Brunswick, NJ: Rutgers University Press, 1991.

Rachels, James. *The End of Life: Euthanasia and Morality*. Oxford: Oxford University Press, 1986.

Regan, Tom (ed.). *Matters of Life and Death*, 3rd ed. New York: Random House, 1993.

Sartorius, Rolf (ed.). *Paternalism*. Minneapolis, MN: University of Minnesota Press, 1983.

Weir, Robert (ed.). *Ethical Issues in Death and Dying*. New York: Columbia University Press, 1986.

Respect for Others

*Our self-respect normally depends upon the respect of others. Unless
we feel that our endeavors are honored by them, it is difficult if
not impossible for us to maintain the conviction that our ends are
worth advancing.*

*[There is a] duty of mutual respect.... This is the duty to show a
person the respect which is due to him as a moral being, that is, as
a being with a sense of justice and a conception of the good.[1]*

John Rawls

Respect for other people can mean two things. First, it might mean
appraisal respect: We value or admire others for their achievements, status,
or character (either in its entirety or for some specific virtues). Second, it
might mean *recognition respect:* We recognize the worth of people as (in
Rawls's words) "moral beings," that is, beings who have either a sense of
moral values *or* (to add to Rawls) the potential to acquire it. This recognition respect, which is the minimum owed to other people, is the topic of
Part Three.

   Appraisal respect and recognition respect differ in two important ways.
First, appraisal respect is highly selective. It is directed toward specific persons whose virtues, moral accomplishments, or endeavors evoke our admiration and perhaps inspire us to emulate them. In this sense we might respect
Martin Luther King, Jr., because of his extraordinary courage in leading the
Civil Rights Movement, and we might respect Mother Teresa for her compassion and self-sacrifice in helping the desperately poor people in Calcutta,
India. In contrast, recognition respect is highly inclusive: It is owed to everyone who has a sense of morality or a potential for acquiring one.

Second, appraisal respect can come in varying degrees. The respect felt for Martin Luther King, Jr., and for Mother Teresa is usually greater than the respect felt for persons who, say, take care of their families but are indifferent to wider moral issues. In contrast, recognition respect has a set (minimal) degree; it is the least we owe to all people who have any sense of moral values. Recognition respect is based on the concept of equality of moral worth. In Kantian terms, recognition respect implies a duty to treat all moral beings with dignity and decency; in terms of human rights ethics, it implies that all moral beings have equal rights; in utilitarian terms, it implies that all people ought to be taken into account equally in deciding how to produce the most good.

Part Three explores an array of issues centering on recognition respect. Chapter 9 discusses drug abuse, a topic which provides a natural transition from self-respect to respect for others. Chapter 10 deals with mutual respect amidst hostile conflicts. This also constitutes a transition topic because many of the attitudes underlying hostility bear on attempts to assert self-esteem at the expense of others. Chapters 11 and 12 deal (respectively) with prejudice and abortion, two conflict-generating topics that have special contemporary importance. Chapter 13 discusses rape and sexual harassment.

CHAPTER 9

Drug Abuse

Responsibilities to oneself interweave with responsibilities to others. Nowhere is this clearer than in regard to responsibilities concerning drug abuse. Driving under the influence of drugs risks both one's own life and the lives of others, and becoming addicted to a dangerous drug threatens our well-being and the well-being of people who care about us.

What attitudes should we adopt concerning our own or others' use of drugs for nonmedical purposes? What responsibilities do we have in responding to the drug problems that afflict our society? These are troubling and difficult questions about which there is little consensus. Hardliners condemn all nonmedical uses of drugs. Softliners point to the positive aspects of some drugs and the rights of individuals to make their own decisions. Moderates offer complex assessments of drug use that are often morally ambiguous.

Problem Drugs

We speak of *the* drug problem, but of course different problems are associated with different drugs. *Drug abuse* refers to any nonmedical use of a drug that causes or has a substantial risk of causing harm, whether to oneself or to others. The expression is pejorative; it is a label for drug uses that are objectionable in some way. Thus, if we consider it objectionable to break the law, we will view all illegal uses of drugs—as well as morally objectionable though legal uses—as drug abuse.

For our purposes, a *drug* can be defined as any psychoactive chemical, that is, any chemical which directly and significantly influences consciousness.[1] Drugs are classified according to what kind of influence they have on the central nervous system. Since a given drug can have a variety of effects, classification schemas vary. The following is only one possible schema, illustrated with a small sampling of frequently abused drugs.

Stimulants ("uppers") arouse the central nervous system, producing alertness or excitation. They include *amphetamines* such as Benzedrine and Dexedrine, which operate much like natural bodily substances that prepare us to deal with stress. They also include nonamphetamines such as cocaine, crack (a crystalline form of cocaine), nicotine, and caffeine. *Depressants* ("downers") slow down the impulses transmitted within the central nervous system. Some depressants are *analgesics* (pain killers), in particular narcotics such as opium and its derivatives (morphine, heroin, codeine)—all of which are addictive. *General depressants*, which have a wider effect than killing pain, include *alcohol, sedatives* such as barbiturates and Quaalude, *tranquilizers* such as Valium and Librium, and many *inhalants* such as aerosols, benzene, and glue. *Hallucinogens*, such as LSD, mescaline, and many "designer drugs" (synthetically manufactured chemicals), alter the mind so as to produce visual, auditory, or other kinds of perceptual illusions. *PCP* ("angel dust") is a depressant capable of producing extreme violence, bizarre hallucinations, and permanent alterations in the personality, making it one of the most dangerous illicit drugs. *Marijuana* is usually placed in a category by itself because it produces a combination of sedation, mood change, and mild hallucination.

Why Use Drugs?

Drugs serve many purposes. *Medical* purposes include pain relief and healing. *Recreational* use has as its object an enjoyable experience sought for its own sake. *Creative* uses are intended to produce an interesting imaginative experience, perhaps affording insights (as celebrated by Aldous Huxley in *The Doors of Perception*). *Instrumental* purposes consist of the enhancement of work performance or some other practical activity. An example is the use of caffeine (in coffee, tea, or colas) while studying for an exam. *Religious* purposes include not only personal quests but also ceremonial uses. For example, some groups have believed that peyote, which contains the hallucinogen mescaline, is a messenger from the gods. Such groups have used peyote in religious ceremonies for centuries. The ceremonies began with the Aztecs and are continued today by members of the Native American Church.

Whatever their intended purpose, drugs produce experiences that go beyond the chemical effects of the drug. A particular drug experience is shaped by the mind-set of the user (including mood, expectations, and imagination), the user's physiological and psychological tolerance for the drug, the immediate social setting in which the drug is taken, and the wider social and cultural setting which attaches meanings to specific drugs. Similarly, the amount of use depends on the dynamics between social setting and personal choice. For example, over 70 percent of the American soldiers who became dependent on heroin in Vietnam, where heroin was plentiful and inexpensive, voluntarily gave up its use when they returned to the United States.

Peer pressure, a desire for social interaction, curiosity, and a desire to experiment are frequent motives for nonmedical drug use. In addition, many drugs are charged with symbolic meanings that enhance their attraction. For example, marijuana may convey a sense of rebellion against parents and conventional society. Cigarettes are for some teenagers a sign of growing up. Cocaine seems to add glamour to life, if not a charming element of danger. And alcohol is widely touted as a social lubricant and vehicle of holiday cheer.

Not everyone gets hurt by using dangerous drugs. Most people do not, and it is impossible to know exactly who will. We are familiar with how all forms of drug abuse can have devastating effects: ruined health, destroyed education, loss of job, child abuse, and fatal car crashes. Yet none of these consequences usually occur, which makes it easy for risk-takers to believe they will be exempt from harm in using drugs.

Much of the appeal of drugs has to do with control over our lives. We have a curious double-mindedness here. On the one hand, drugs promise greater control over our immediate consciousness and hence over our lives. They charm us with a sense of power by stimulating our energies, reducing stress, or inducing euphoria. On the other hand, if they do not satisfy our expectations, they offer ready-made excuses for the problems they cause. Irresponsible conduct is readily dismissed as the fault of the drug, rather than the person using the drug. Drugs, then, have a double allure. They promise greater self-control and simultaneously offer excuses for our failures to exercise control when we are under their influence.

This double-mindedness about the power of drugs is reflected in two general perspectives about drug abuse. From a medical perspective, drug abusers are regarded as sick and unfortunate victims who need medical attention. Witness the proliferation of "rehabilitation programs" at drug "clinics" for "treating" drug abuse. Also, the medical profession has taught us to speak of the "disease of alcoholism." From moral and legal perspectives, by contrast, drug abusers are chastised as immoral lawbreakers who ought to be punished.

These two perspectives are often mixed and conflated in confusing ways, but in fact they can be appropriate with respect to different aspects of drug use. Perhaps someone's initial decision to use a dangerous drug was fully voluntary, but subsequent addiction removed or seriously impaired control, turning the drug use into a sickness. Conversely, perhaps the original use was partially excusable as a product of intense peer pressure, but at present it is within the user's power to stop abusing the drug. Even when full-blown addiction has developed, individuals have the power to ask for help. We respect and admire people who seek help, and this presupposes that we do not view them as completely helpless invalids, although their immediate and direct control over the drug may be seriously impaired in dependency and addiction.

Dependency and Addiction

Drug abuse takes many forms. *Periodic abuse* is the occasional misuse of a drug in a manner that generates problems, such as disrupting a party or driving a car while intoxicated. *Drug dependency* occurs when drug use becomes more frequent and is relied upon more heavily. Health professionals have yet to agree on a more precise definition of dependency. One often-cited defining criterion is the physiological withdrawal syndrome, that is, bodily changes that occur when the drug is withdrawn, such as chills, sweating, nausea, aches and pains. Another criterion is drug tolerance, in which an increasingly higher quantity of the drug must be taken to achieve the same effect. *Physical dependence* occurs when either of these criteria is met.

A different criterion for drug dependency is *psychological dependence*, which is shown by strong cravings for the drug when it is withdrawn or by behavioral patterns of compulsive drug use. Cravings may or may not be resistible without help from others, but (by definition) they entail a strong desire that can be resisted only with great effort. Compulsive drug use is indicated by the extent to which a person's life is oriented toward obtaining and using the drug and by how much a person is willing to sacrifice to use the drug.

Addiction is an overwhelming involvement with a drug—the kinds of preoccupation with a drug produced by high degrees of physical or psychological dependence. It is manifested in one's extreme difficulty in giving up drugs. Addictions may seem utterly irrational, but they serve various psychological purposes. For example, all the anxiety-producing complexity of life may become focused on obtaining and using a substance.

> A heroin addict may be trying to reduce all the problems of life to a single one, so that it will no longer be necessary to make fundamental choices or be subject to ordinary emotional vicissitudes. A life is given structure of repetitive acts that produce an artificial stability. Addicts can be devoted as much to hustling—the daily routine of getting the next fix—as they are to the drug itself. It becomes a way of life.[2]

Addictions usually produce only an illusion of control over one's life, not genuine control. Even setting aside the damage done to one's health, to relationships with others, and to innocent bystanders, there are moral objections to becoming addicted that are linked to the virtues. Addictions diminish rational self-control and threaten self-respect. Often they dramatically restrict our capacity to choose from the full range of human goods in pursuing a fulfilling life.

In extreme cases, addicts lose not only self-respect, but even the sense of who they are. Eugene O'Neill explores this loss of identity in *Long Day's Journey Into Night,* an autobiographical play about his mother, who was addicted to morphine, and about himself, his father, and his brother, each of whom was an alcoholic. O'Neill viewed the addictions as interwoven with self-deception about the addiction and about underlying problems which led to the addiction. The fictional version of his mother says at one point, "I've become such a liar. I never lied about anything once upon a time. Now I have to lie, especially to myself.... I've never understood anything about it, except that one day long ago I found I could no longer call my soul my own."[3]

Problem Drinkers

Alcohol is the most widely used drug; over 100 million Americans drink. Alcohol may cause more harm than all illegal drugs put together. One in ten drinkers—some 10 million Americans—becomes an alcoholic. (By contrast, there are fewer than 500,000 heroin addicts.) In addition, about half of all fatal car collisions, accidental drownings, violent crimes (including rapes, spouse abuse, and child abuse) are alcohol-related. One of the most common severe birth defects, fetal alcohol syndrome, is caused by women who drink while pregnant. And alcohol costs our economy $120 billion yearly in work, property, and medical costs.

We would not legalize any currently illegal drug that caused even a fraction of these problems, yet we tolerate alcohol. Perhaps we do so with the misimpression that the attempt at prohibition during 1920–1933 was a ludicrous mistake. In fact, prohibition succeeded in dramatically lowering the use of alcohol and its attendant problems. More startling, adjusting for the relative scale of drug problems, "alcohol prohibition probably worked just about as well (or badly) as present drug prohibition laws work. Repeal came not because prohibition was totally ineffective, but because we decided—although we seldom express it this way—that we wanted the pleasure of convenient, legal alcohol more than we feared an increase in drunkenness and alcoholism."[4]

Laws can discourage abusive drinking in ways short of outright prohibition. For example, high taxes on alcohol are an effective way to lower usage. Again, thousands of lives have been saved as a result of campaigns by MADD (Mothers Against Drunk Driving) and SADD (Students Against Drunk Driving) that helped raise the legal drinking age to 21 and toughened laws against drunk drivers. Nevertheless, it is clear that America's alcohol problem will need to be addressed in additional ways that encourage responsible ways of drinking.

Earlier we emphasized that drug experiences are largely the result of the user's social setting and mental state rather than simply the chemical effects on the body. Nowhere is this more important than in regard to alcohol. It comes as a surprise to learn that many societies have few problems with alcohol. For example, Americans in the seventeenth and eighteenth centuries (including Puritans!) drank much more than Americans today, with relatively minor problems. Their drinking was integrated into structured social activities and controlled by strong social attitudes against abuses.

The fact that some societies have no major problems with alcohol is one reason why some researchers are uneasy with the idea that alcoholism is a disease that removes all ability to control drinking. "It's not your fault" has been the message. Scientific studies are confirming that alcohol abuse probably has some loose connection with genetic, physiological, and family influences; but these are merely influences, to which we can respond in a variety of ways, including seeking help.

Herbert Fingarette argues that problem drinkers are far more able to control their conduct than the disease model allows. In his view, heavy drinkers have made drinking a "central activity" or a deeply entrenched way of life adopted to deal with anxiety and problems. The way of life acquires a momentum: "When we speak of the momentum of a way of life, we are using a convenient label to refer to the cumulative impact of many long-cultivated and interrelated habits of mind, heart, soul, and body."[5] Changing this way of life can be enormously difficult, but not impossible when help is available. Most heavy drinkers need help that matches the drinker's particular personality to one of the many different types of supportive programs.

Fingarette's criticism of the dominant disease model is controversial. Nevertheless, it draws attention to the mixture of responsible conduct and supportive help from others that is usually required in order to break addictions. Consider Alcoholics Anonymous (AA), which embraces the ideology that alcoholism is a disease. Heavy drinkers are told they must admit their utter helplessness to solve their problem and seek the help of others, including other members of AA and a "Higher Power" whose precise identity is left for each drinker to decide. Simultaneously, they are told they must solve their problems through personal effort and by accepting help! Fingarette views this as a paradox: Drinkers who seek treatment "are told that they are the unwilling victims of a disease that destroys their ability to manage their drinking and yet that they must strive to exert absolute self-control, that only total abstinence can save them."[6] Alcoholics Anonymous does not work for everyone—indeed most of its participants drop out—so why does it work for some? Fingarette argues that it helps those individuals who find it an appealing alternative central activity—a new way of life—replete with numerous reinforcement meetings, social activities, and a new network of emotional bonds.

Of course, major problems can arise from periodic, rather than habitual, heavy drinking. Here we can note the same kind of double-mindedness mentioned earlier. One widespread attitude is that drinking relaxes moral requirements or even provides a moral "time-out." Thus the familiar excuse for misbehavior at a party: "I'm sorry, but I just wasn't myself last night after that second drink." Yet, most adults quickly learn their personal "limit," the point beyond which drinking threatens to lower their responsible conduct. They also learn the wisdom of finding ways to control drinking situations, such as the appointment of "designated drivers" when attending parties.

The Right to Smoke

Whereas moderate and responsible drinking is harmless, no use of cigarettes is safe. Cigarettes lead all drugs in death statistics, killing five times the number of people killed by alcohol. Each year, 350,000 people die from smoking-related causes that include an array of cancers (of the lungs, mouth, larynx, and esophagus), emphysema, and heart diseases. About one in four people who smoke a pack of cigarettes a day will die from that addiction.

So what? Do we not have a moral right to smoke if we freely choose to do so? Isn't smoking just a high-risk behavior, like hang-gliding, scaling mountains, and having sex with strangers? Whether these activities are foolish depends on one's risk-taking attitudes, and these attitudes are no one's business but one's own!

In reply, note first that smoking can cause serious harm to others, in four ways. (1) Smoking adds greatly to the social costs of medical care. While insurance companies now penalize smokers, all of us pay the government costs for smoking-related diseases. (2) Smoking during pregnancy harms the fetus, contributing to premature births, low birth weight, and higher infant mortality. (3) A quarter of all fire-related deaths in the United States—some 2,300 people (including nonsmokers)—are caused by smoldering cigarettes. (4) Most important, secondary or "passive" smoke causes several thousand deaths each year and adds to a variety of other health problems. This fact has led to increasingly restrictive laws against smoking on airplanes, in restaurants, and in government buildings. In addition, employers have had to ban smoking because of successful lawsuits by nonsmoking employees. The smoker's right to smoke is trumped by the nonsmoker's right to breathe clean air, a right implied by the right to life.

Furthermore, is the choice to smoke always completely voluntary? Consider the initial decision to smoke. The great majority of smokers are "hooked" before they reach adulthood, and about 60 percent of smokers began smoking by age fourteen. Granted, each pack of cigarettes now is labeled with a brief warning about the health hazards, but during adolescence such warnings have little effect. Again, while cigarette ads must carry the same warning, the message is easily lost amidst the sex appeal and glamour of the person shown smoking. Few smokers completely avoid knowing that cigarettes are dangerous, but do they genuinely understand, emotionally appreciate, and appropriately attend to the full risks?

Next consider people who have become addicted. Nicotine is as addictive as heroin or cocaine. To stop smoking usually causes strong withdrawal symptoms such as anxiety, headaches, irritability, dizziness, and sweating. In addition, there are innumerable symbolic connections that must be broken, as in the case of the emotionally resonant after-dinner or after-sex cigarette. Arguing in a vein opposed to Fingarette's approach to alcoholism, Robert E. Goodin argues that addicted smokers have impaired voluntary control and are not fully responsible for their habit. He contends that government action should aim at abolishing smoking: "People may bear responsibility for their own bad habits and for whatever follows from them. They bear responsibility for having become addicted to drugs. Once addicted, though, they ought no longer be considered responsible for their addiction-driven actions."[7]

Is Goodin's claim justified? Granted, nicotine addiction makes quitting very difficult, but does it make quitting impossible? Smoking is what Fingarette called a central activity, one that is intermingled with many other central activities. That psychological dependence, combined with physiological dependence, makes change difficult but usually not impossible. Many people manage to quit smoking through great effort and with the support of a caring community, as annual "smoke outs" have shown.

Illegal Drugs

Society has dealt with dangerous drugs other than alcohol and cigarettes primarily by making them illegal. Laws provide two additional reasons against the use of dangerous drugs. One reason is prudential: Avoid illicit drugs in order to avoid legal penalties. The other reason is moral: Avoid illicit drugs in order to heed the *prima facie* obligation to respect the legal system that makes civilized life possible.

At least twenty-six million Americans used illegal drugs in 1991. Marijuana, which is the most widely used illegal drug, has been tried by sixty million Americans and twenty million use it regularly. For years the government has blamed international drug dealers and waged "a war" against suppliers of drugs. At a cost $100 billion during the last decade, the war has been lost, at least if its goal was to end the easy availability of low-cost drugs. The enormous profits to be made in illicit drug trafficking continue to attract an ample number of people willing to run the risks of being caught.

Some critics of the government have abandoned all hope of reducing the supply of illegal drugs. They include conservatives such as the journalist William F. Buckley, Jr., and the Nobel-laureate economist Milton Friedman, who have recommended legalizing most abused drugs.[8] They acknowledge that to do so will dramatically increase drug use, at least doubling the number of addicts, but they point to overriding benefits. Legal drugs will be far less expensive, which would lower the incentive to commit crimes to support drug habits. This benefit is substantial: One study showed that an average heroin addict in Miami, Florida, commits 375 crimes each year![9] In addition, the huge amount of money required for law enforcement could be put to better use, as could taxes imposed on the newly legalized drugs.

Nevertheless, most drug experts reject wholesale legalization. They point to the success of laws in containing the scale of problems by discouraging millions of citizens from experimenting with drugs. Increasingly, however, they recommend a shift in priorities away from stopping international traffickers and toward addressing the ultimate problem that lies with users.

Some of these experts are pessimistic about seriously reducing usage but more hopeful about managing problems. Erich Goode, a sociologist, concludes that drug problems, like automobile and environmental problems, are here to stay for the foreseeable future: "To be plain about it, there will always be certain forms of behavior that will produce, or will be associated with, the use of drugs. The use of mind-altering drugs is linked to broader social forces and influences that are not going to change very much, at least during this century."[10] Although Goode is opposed to legalization of all drugs, he recommends reduction or removal of the penalties for the use of marijuana. He also recommends making free therapeutic (and methadone) programs available to heroin addicts.

Other researchers are more optimistic about programs currently being tested. They draw attention to the fact that greater health awareness and social attitudes against drug use have succeeded in lowering drug abuse since the end of the 1960s. Mathea Falco, who spent four years as Assistant Secretary of State for International Narcotics Matters, calls for massive support for programs designed to prevent drug use through education, advertising campaigns to change attitudes, and wide community involvement.[11] Educational programs, Falco emphasizes, must be realistic. By contrast with the bumper-sticker approach ("Just Say No"), programs must be tailored to the needs of each age group. For example, programs for early adolescents must provide detailed suggestions about how to refuse offered drugs without inviting rejection by peers. Other programs dealing with high-risk children must involve entire families and communities where drugs are widely used.

SUMMARY

Drugs are used for many purposes, including medical, recreational, instrumental, and religious purposes. "Drug abuse" refers to illegal or morally objectionable uses of drugs. Drug dependency is substantial reliance on drugs, whether manifested in physiological withdrawal symptoms, drug tolerance, or psychological difficulty in abandoning drug use. Addiction is the special case of overwhelming involvement with a drug.

Drugs are doubly seductive because they promise increased control over our lives and also provide ready-made excuses when that control is not achieved. Heavy dependency and addiction constitute an immediate loss of rational self-control, but researchers disagree over how many addicts can by themselves effect long-term change. Herbert Fingarette views alcoholism and other addictions as central activities that, like any strong habits, require great effort to alter. Robert Goodin, by contrast, emphasizes that smoking addiction decreases voluntary control and hence must be prevented from occurring in the first place.

Several questions are pertinent in assessing responsibility for particular drug uses. What direct or indirect harm to others might be caused? What is the threat to our own health, and what are the legal implications? Is it worth the risks, given the likely benefits? Are we becoming so preoccupied with the drug that our attention, energy, money, and time are diverted from worthwhile activities? Is the drug causing a dependency that lessens our sense of self-control, autonomy, and self-respect? Does the drug threaten to distort our capacity to process information rationally and to conduct a meaningful life?

DISCUSSION TOPICS

1   Sketch how a rule-utilitarian and an act-utilitarian might approach the question of whether to use illegal drugs. How might each respond to what Kant says in this passage: "A drunkard [sometimes] does no harm to another, and if he has a strong constitution he does no harm to himself, yet he is an object of contempt. We are not indifferent to cringing servility [to drugs]; man should not cringe and fawn; by so doing he degrades his person."[12]

2   Emotions and moods usually have strong correlation with our beliefs about events; indeed, beliefs partly define what emotions are. For example, when we are cheerful, it is usually because our lives seem to us to be going well, and when we are sad, it is because of a loss of something or someone we value. What would you say about a repeated use of drugs to alter the emotions appropriate to various situations, for example in order to feel cheerful at the funeral of a friend, or to feel exhilarated after failing exams?

3   Does peer pressure constitute coercion to use drugs, such that people are not able to make voluntary decisions based on their own wishes? Are "Just Say No"

clubs and other peer groups that influence people not to use drugs also coercive in a way that undermines the ability of people to make their own decisions, or do they support autonomy?

4 Compare two groups of drivers who cause serious accidents: (a) sober but reckless drivers, and (b) drivers who are so intoxicated that they are unable to prevent an accident. Are the second drivers less blameworthy for their actions and thus deserving of lighter penalties?

5 Many corporations have adopted random drug-testing programs as a condition of employment. These programs are relatively uncontroversial where safety is a major part of the job, as in the case of soldiers, police officers, pilots, and public transportation drivers. Some companies, however, such as Texas Instruments, require random drug-testing of all employees, including engineers and top management. Critics charge that this violates privacy rights.[13] They argue that drug use either harms work performance or it does not. If it does, then an employer can penalize an employee because of the bad performance itself; if it does not, then drug use is not the employer's business. Defenders of the programs argue that the widespread drug use in our society inevitably lowers overall work productivity. How would you balance employee and employer rights on this issue?

6 Attempts are being made to ban all drugs, including muscle-building and performance-enhancing drugs such as steroids, in both amateur and professional sports. Critics of these attempts argue that people have a right to make their own decisions about drug use and to undergo any risks the drugs involve. They point out that participation in sports is itself inherently risky. Defenders argue that drugs unjustifiably add to the risks incurred by athletes and pressure competitors into using steroids to compensate for their opponents' use of steroids. They also suggest that drugs change the nature of sports so that they are no longer expressions of natural talent combined with effort. Formulate and defend your view on this issue.

7 Several general responses to weakness of will were described in Chapter 7: One can revise one's values, try harder in the future, accept one's flaws, or make excuses. Illustrate how a chain-smoker might use each of these responses in (a) an honest way and (b) a self-deceiving and dishonest way.

8 Executives and professionals (including physicians) who work for tobacco companies often argue that they are not engaged in a harmful enterprise, since consumers are free to choose whether to use their product. Do you agree? What tactics (such as those discussed in Chapter 6) might employees of tobacco companies use to deceive themselves about their work?

9 David A. J. Richards advocates the legalization of most presently illegal drugs, using the following argument.

> It is initially important to distinguish two kinds of paternalism: interference on the basis of facts unknown to the agent, in order to save the agent from harms that he would wish to avoid, and interferences on the basis of values that the agent does not himself share. Paternalism of the first kind, as applied in such laws as those securing the purity of drugs, is unobjectionable. Paternalism of the second kind, which underlies many laws cur-

rently criminalizing drug use, is not only objectionable, it is a violation of human rights."[14]

Assess Richards's view, focusing your discussion on the issue of whether marijuana should be legalized.

SUGGESTED READINGS

Bach, Julie S. (ed.). *Drug Abuse: Opposing Viewpoints.* St. Paul, MN: Greenhaven, 1988.

Bakalar, James B., and Lester Grinspoon. *Drug Control in a Free Society.* New York: Cambridge University Press, 1984.

Douglas, Mary (ed.). *Constructive Drinking: Perspectives on Drink from Anthropology.* New York: Cambridge University Press, 1987.

Dworkin, Gerald. *The Theory and Practice of Autonomy.* New York: Cambridge University Press, 1988.

Falco, Mathea. *The Making of a Drug-Free America: Programs that Work.* New York: Times Books, 1992.

Feinberg, Joel. *Harm To Self.* Vol. 3 of *The Moral Limits of the Criminal Law.* New York: Oxford University Press, 1986.

Fingarette, Herbert. "Alcoholism and Self-Deception." In M. W. Martin (ed.), *Self-Deception and Self-Understanding.* Lawrence, KS: University Press of Kansas, 1985.

Fingarette, Herbert. *Heavy Drinking: The Myth of Alcoholism as a Disease.* Berkeley, CA: University of California Press, 1988.

Goode, Erich. *Drugs in American Society.* 3rd ed. New York: McGraw-Hill, 1989.

Goodin, Robert E. *No Smoking: The Ethical Issues.* Chicago: University of Chicago Press, 1989.

Huxley, Aldous. *The Doors of Perception* and *Heaven and Hell.* New York: Harper, 1963.

Krogh, David. *Smoking: The Artificial Passion.* New York: W. H. Freeman, 1991.

Liska, Ken. *Drugs and the Human Body, With Implications for Society.* 3rd ed. New York: Macmillan, 1990.

Murray, Thomas H., et al. (eds.). *Feeling Good and Doing Better: Ethics and Nontherapeutic Drug Use.* Clifton, NJ: Humana Press, 1984.

Nakken, Craig. *The Addictive Personality: Roots, Rituals and Recovery.* Centre City, MN: Hazelden, 1988.

Richards, David A. J. *Sex, Drugs, Death, and the Law: An Essay on Human Rights and Overcriminalization.* Totowa, NJ: Rowman & Littlefield, 1982.

CHAPTER 10

Interpersonal Conflicts

Conflicts between individuals or groups are ubiquitous in everyday life. Here we are interested in conflicts which generate hostilities and threaten mutual respect. We begin by distinguishing several forms of hostility: anger, envy, *ressentiment,* and other forms of hatred. Then we discuss several creative responses to hostile confrontations: forgiveness, compromise, and other forms of conflict resolution.

Anger

Anger is easily confused with hatred, but they are defined by different beliefs and desires. Hatred is based on the belief that someone or something is bad, together with the desire to hurt, destroy, or at least remove it from our presence. Anger is based on the belief that an offense has occurred, together with the desire to punish or in other ways have the offense set right.

The intensity of anger varies from mild annoyance (being peeved or piqued) to rage (being outraged or furious). The complexity of anger also varies according to the perceived offense. *Simple anger* is the reflex of getting mad when something frustrates our plans, as when we kick a flat tire in a frustrated furor. *Indignation* is anger over a (perceived) violation of a principle or value that we cherish, as in the case of someone's outrage over the government's treatment of AIDS victims during the 1980s. *Resentment* is an angry response to an insult or injustice to us or to people we identify with, such as our family or friends. Indignation and resentment are moral emotions in that they are based on a response to (perceived) moral violations and injuries. They, rather than simple anger, will be the focus in what follows.

Anger—including the occurrence, continuance, and expression of anger—can be justified or unjustified. The initial experience of anger is justified or not depending on the reasons for it. Indignation is justified if a genuine value has been violated by someone who should be held responsible for the violation. Resentment is appropriate when one has been wronged and someone is blameworthy for the wrong. I might understandably experience simple anger at some teenagers who play their radio too loud when I am trying to read, but (depending on the location) it might be inappropriate to react with indignation or resentment.

Justified anger is sometimes desirable, as well as permissible, in that it manifests moral concern and self-respect. The failure to feel indignation at gross injustice can be a fault, and a failure to feel resentment can be a sign that we lack self-respect. For example, persons who are sexually harassed should feel resentment. If they do not, we suspect they do not properly value themselves.

There is also a pragmatic justification for sustaining these emotions and acting on them. If we act on the anger (in a certain way), are we likely to correct an injustice, or will it make things worse for everyone involved? If an acquaintance insults us, perhaps an immediate and direct confrontation is appropriate. If a friend in an "off" moment insults us, perhaps we should let things cool down, and then forgive and forget. If an employer insults us, a controlled expression of resentment may damage the employee–employer relationship. The circumstances, as well as our personalities, determine whether anger is creative or harmful to relationships.

Envy

If anger is often fully justified, envy is not. Envy, in the special sense intended here, is *malicious envy*: hatred of others because of their possessions, achievements, or virtues. Suppose that someone wins an award. If we reasonably believe the award should have gone to us, we might feel justified resentment, but we would feel envy if we hated the person simply for winning an award he or she deserved. Envy is based on either a perception that one is inferior to someone else or a feeling that one's self-esteem is threatened by someone else's well-being. Envy is a form of unjustified hatred; as such, it is immoral, even when it is not expressed in outward attacks on others. Not surprisingly, medieval Christians included envy among the seven deadly sins.

Malicious envy differs from other kinds of envy not at issue here. *Admiration envy* is the admiration for and desire to emulate someone. When a person we respect wins a contest or receives an award, we might compliment them by saying, "I envy you." This remark conveys our admiration and makes the compliment more personal, as if we were saying, "What you have done is so superb I wish I had been able to do it." In contrast, *envy* in the more traditional sense used here is something we would be unlikely to acknowledge openly. Malicious envy is unjustified hatred of others because of their good fortune, as well as a desire to see that good fortune reversed because it makes us feel inferior.

Envy—by which we will now mean malicious envy—should also be distinguished from jealousy. When we feel envy, we perceive ourselves as inferior to others and want them brought down to our level or lower. When we feel jealousy, however, we feel hurt and afraid of losing something (or someone) dear to us. Unlike envy, jealousy is not always unjustified and bad, as we will suggest in Chapter 15.

Envy takes two forms, particular and general.[1] General envy entails the hatred of entire classes of people because they have some good thing that we want for ourselves, or at least do not want them to have. For example, we might hate all rich people or detest people with better athletic skills than ours. Particular envy, by contrast, is directed toward specific individuals with whom we compare ourselves or against whom we compete.

A vivid example of particular envy is found in Salieri, a character in Peter Shaffer's play and movie *Amadeus*. The character is based on a composer who was a contemporary of Wolfgang Amadeus Mozart during the late eighteenth century. Salieri rose to prominence and became the official court composer for Austria's emperor. From his youth he burned with the ambition to become the greatest composer of his day, but that ambition was shattered when he encountered Mozart, whose talents were vastly superior to his own.

It was a tribute to Salieri's genuine abilities that he, unlike most of his peers, could fully appreciate the majesty of Mozart's music. His appreciation was tainted, however, with intense bitterness. Not only did Mozart's arrival make him feel inferior, empty, and worthless; it also generated rage against Mozart and a desire to see Mozart's superiority overthrown. The rage was accompanied by a sense of powerlessness to do anything about his inferiority. These, then, are the primary ingredients of particular envy: feelings of inferiority, hatred, and impotence.

In Shaffer's play, Salieri, tortured by envy, sets out to destroy Mozart. In conversations with influential people he downplays Mozart's talents. Using his influence as court composer, he prevents Mozart from obtaining the work and public recognition he deserved. When he learns later that Mozart is suffering from guilt and hallucinations following the death of his father, he proceeds to push him over the edge of sanity. Discovering that Mozart's hallucinations contain a father figure wearing a black mask and cape, he mimics the figure and appears at Mozart's apartment to commission a "death mass." Then he forces Mozart to complete the work at a frantic pace, periodically appearing outside the window of the apartment. A combination of alcoholism, overwork, poverty, and tortured guilt causes Mozart to die at the young age of thirty-five, but even Mozart's death does not end Salieri's self-imposed suffering. Rather, his envy continues as Mozart's reputation grows following his death.

Amadeus, we might add, explores envy within a religious context. When Salieri devoted his life to music at age sixteen, he promised God he would be morally conscientious if only God would grant him sufficient fame to enjoy his work as a composer. When he realized that Mozart's accomplishments would undermine his fame, he swore vengeance against God. God, he reasoned, had chosen to make Mozart rather than himself his musical agent; hence, God could be attacked by destroying Mozart. Recast in secular terms, the play suggests that, in envy, we feel we are outraged over a fate that made us inferior. In retaliation we assault the person who received the superiority we want for ourselves.

Envy can be overcome if we eliminate our feelings of hate and inferiority. Occasionally, rational reflection by itself enables us to purge these feelings by allowing us to see their unreasonableness. Usually, however, deeper emotional adjustments are required. Hating other people for their good fortune is best tackled with a combination of efforts to: (1) increase one's own self-confidence, (2) strengthen the basis of one's self-esteem so it becomes more durable and less prone to collapse when confronted by others' well-being, and (3) increase one's capacity to appreciate, rather than hate, the achievements of others. These avenues for dissipating envy can be blocked when we avoid admitting our envy—admitting it to others or to ourselves.

Ressentiment

To acknowledge envy forces us to confront several unflattering truths: that we hate without justification, that we feel painfully inferior, and that our self-esteem is so flimsy as to depend on the misfortune of others. In avoiding these painful truths, we tend to deceive ourselves about envy, and when we do, the envy often finds devious ways of expressing itself. Nietzsche used the French word *ressentiment* to refer to unconscious envy, as well as to other forms of repressed hatred.

In one of his applications of this concept, Nietzsche viewed strict egalitarianism as a moral distortion that expresses the self-interest of mediocre people who feel impotent to strive for greatness. Those who constantly downgrade and criticize as unjust anyone better off than themselves are probably expressing envy:

> You preachers of equality, the tyrannomania of impotence clamors thus out of you for equality: your most secret ambitions to be tyrants thus

shroud themselves in words of virtue. Aggrieved conceit, repressed envy ... erupt from you as a flame and as the frenzy of revenge.[2]

Nietzsche was alarmed by how societies were becoming increasingly uniform and morally bland. Democratic ideals, in his view, were being misused to justify the attitude that everyone is equally virtuous and no one is more noble or heroic than anyone else.

Nietzsche's insights were clarified and developed by the philosopher-sociologist Max Scheler (1874–1928) in a book entitled *Ressentiment*. According to Scheler, *ressentiment* arises not only when we feel inferior, hostile, and impotent to better our situation, but also when we feel unable to confront or express these feelings:

> Revenge, envy, the impulse to detract, spite, *Schadenfreude* [i.e., enjoyment of someone's misfortune], and malice lead to *ressentiment* only if there occurs neither a moral self-conquest ... nor an act or some other adequate expression of emotion (such as verbal abuse or shaking one's fist), and if this restraint is caused by a pronounced awareness of impotence.... *Ressentiment* can only arise if these emotions are particularly powerful and yet must be suppressed because they are coupled with the feeling that one is unable to act them out.[3]

Self-deception results in a loss of conscious supervision over our envy and other forms of hatred, but the hate does not go away. It is merely released through avenues more subtle than Salieri's open campaign of vengeance, for example through snide remarks or by rechanneling hatred toward other objects—we kick the dog or yell at a friend. Its most devastating effect, according to Scheler, is its distortion of our values: Value standards are lowered or corrupted so as to make us look good in our own eyes. One approach is to bring everyone down to the same low level: No one has a better character than anyone else. Another approach is to claim that values are merely subjective, so that one person's values are as good as anyone's. On a more restricted scale, someone might attack the practice of grading on the grounds that it unfairly tries to distinguish and rate work that is essentially all the same, and because professors are all biased anyway.

Hatred

Not all hatred is inherently unjustified in the way that envy and *ressentiment* are. To begin with, there is *simple hatred*: strong aversion toward certain foods, discomforts, types of weather, or disappointing grades. Simple hatreds, like simple loves, are manifestations of strong tastes. In contrast, consider hatred toward persons whom we see as bad: Is such hatred justified when the person really is bad in the way we believe? Some world religions, especially Christianity, have condemned hatred (of persons, rather than of immoral actions) as always unjustified (unlike indignation, which Jesus and the Hebrew prophets sometimes manifested). Should hatred of persons be universally condemned?

Jean Hampton distinguishes three types of hatred (beyond envy and simple hatred), each of which is based on the belief that the hated person is morally bad, perhaps because she or he has personally injured us. *Malice* is the desire to get even with others in such a way that we win over them and are thereby elevated (at least in our eyes). *Spite* is the desire to bring others down to our level. *Moral hatred* is aversion toward persons who identify themselves with immoral causes. All these emotions are unjustified when based on false beliefs about another person, but let us consider cases where the other person really is at fault in the way we believe.

Hampton argues that malice and spite are inherently irrational, although moral hatred is not. Malice and spite embody efforts to assert our self-respect and self-esteem in ways that are self-defeating. Consider a case of malice: Someone has insulted me, and rather than just feeling resentment about the insult, I maliciously hate the person. I set out to vindicate (vindictively!) my damaged or threatened self-esteem by attacking the self-esteem of the other person: "I'll show him!" If, however, I succeed in "putting down" the other person and elevating myself over my enemy, what do I gain? To win in competition with a bad person is to triumph over nothing. This is a theme in Western movies:

> An avenger uses the threat of death to master a hated wrongdoer in order to diminish him. Frequently this involves "making him crawl" before the avenger.... But as he looks upon the wretched and pathetic figure of the wrongdoer, the avenger invariably finds that he is getting no pleasure from his victory. He has shown that the wrongdoer is nothing, so that now he is the lord of nothing.[4]

Spite is even more clearly self-defeating. Spiteful haters seek to pull others down to the same low level with themselves (whereas malicious haters want to achieve superiority over them). Hampton's analysis brings to mind those persons who knowingly infect others with the AIDS virus in order to inflict on them the same fate as themselves. These spiteful haters irrationally believe that their own well-being is somehow improved by imposing undeserved suffering of the same kind they have undergone, and that belief is irrational.

Moral hatred is not so obviously bad, however. Hampton calls it "moral" because it is admirably motivated both by indignation toward persons who have identified themselves with immoral causes or practices, and by a desire to triumph over those persons and their immoral outlooks by acting on behalf of a morally good cause, such as justice. In this way, we might hate

Hitler, Stalin, and terrorists. There need be nothing self-defeating about hatred in such cases. Our hate may motivate us to admirable conduct and lead to deserved self-respect for fighting on behalf of good causes and sometimes enjoying victory over evil. Nevertheless, Hampton asks whether it is better to act on indignation and resentment, rather than hatred, while striving to overcome our hatred through love. Here she is speaking on behalf of the injunction to love and forgive our enemies, even as we justifiably oppose their immorality. Is that injunction a religious principle that transcends our ordinary moral understanding, or is there some basis for it in ordinary morality?

Forgiveness

Forgiveness is the act of relinquishing or avoiding negative attitudes toward someone for a wrong they have committed. Distinct from the outward act of telling others they are forgiven, forgiveness is an inner act or activity; it is a change of heart from ill will (hatred, anger, or contempt) to good will. It need not imply a complete reacceptance of a person, nor a return to the same good relationship we may have had with someone. It does, however, open the door to a renewal or restoration of relationships with acquaintances, friends, or loved ones. That is one reason why it is so important in maintaining personal relationships. We all make mistakes and harm others in ways that threaten relationships. Forgiveness makes it possible for us to restore relationships based on mutual respect or caring. But is forgiveness always required? Is it always desirable? Apparently not.

Victims of rape, wife battering, murder of a family member, major theft, or arson may be fully justified in the bitter resentment (and hate?) they experience. Whether they decide to forgive is their choice, but if they too easily forgive we might wonder whether they lack self-respect and self-esteem. They have been wronged, seriously wronged; to forswear their resentment and hostility without good reasons is not admirable.

What are the reasons that justify forgiveness? Most of the reasons center on the wrongdoer. First, are there mitigating circumstances surrounding the wrongdoing? For example, did the person who interfered with our freedom at least have good intentions? Second, have the wrongdoers felt remorse and made amends, or are they simply enjoying the benefits they received in wronging us? The thief who enjoys stolen goods and even mocks the stupidity of his victims is typically not an appropriate object of forgiveness.

Other reasons for forgiveness concern our special relationship with the wrongdoer. We are more ready to forgive parents, friends, and lovers because of how much they have contributed to our lives in the past and because of the importance of our ongoing relationship with them.

Finally, some reasons for forgiving center on the person who has been wronged. Sometimes the bitterness we experience from a wrong causes us more suffering than the wrong itself. The ordeal of a divorce, for example, can leave lasting wounds of rage and hate. For the sake of our own happiness we may need to forgive, or partly forgive, the former spouse or lover. Again, in this case as in others, we may realize that we are also partly to blame, and hence may be in need of forgiveness ourselves. We may be in no (moral) position to blame, since we have committed similar wrongs (and not repented of them).

We have been discussing the forgiveness of specific wrongs, but there is also the question of general dispositions to forgive. Wholesale, unconditional forgiveness that is oblivious to reasons is objectionable, but the general unwillingness to forgive is equally objectionable. It may reveal a lack of generosity (especially regarding minor offenses), a lack of compassion (toward people who genuinely repent and make amends), or a lack of humility (in failing to recognize our equal faults).

Conflict Resolution and Peacemaking

Mutual respect is especially threatened when anger and hatred enter into conflicts involving clashing interests and values. The peaceful resolution of conflicts is perhaps the greatest moral challenge today, as individuals and groups find it increasingly difficult to maintain ties of community and mutual respect. Violence is a desperate last resort in conflicts, but so is the expulsion of people from the moral community.

Peacemaking, then, becomes an essential activity. Sometimes we think of peace as the absence of all conflict, but perhaps that is an unrealistic or even undesirable goal. Martin Luther King, Jr., was one of the greatest peacemakers of the twentieth century, but he understood the need for conflicts in order to arouse attention to important values. To silence conflicts in order to maintain a racist society yields the kind of peace that is not worth seeking. King used nonviolent civil disobedience as a way to generate creative conflicts that brought concealed injustices to the surface and enabled them to be overcome without violence.

If conflicts are inherent in life, perhaps we should think of peace as a creative way of dealing with conflicts, rather than as a state of nonconflict. We might define peace as the procedural framework in which conflicts are dealt with constructively. Or, following Gray Cox, we might define peace as "a process in which people freely and responsibly cultivate shared commitments to common expressions, projects and practices."[5] Just how this process unfolds depends largely on contexts in which conflicts arise.

Cox offers three examples. First, the context might be collective decision making within groups that have a dominant shared value perspective concerning the good ends in life, as is the case with many religious groups. The Quakers, for example, developed a five-stage procedure for resolving conflicts: (1) pacify impulses by diverting attention from disrupting desires and emotions; (2) address concerns, both by articulating them and through quiet contemplation; (3) gather consensus through dialogue and listen sympathetically to other perspectives; (4) find clarity, in the sense of forming a resolve to improve the problem being addressed; and (5) bear witness to the discovered truth by living rightly.

Second, the context might be the pursuit of justice in situations where one party to a dispute is heavily armed and capable of maintaining unjust policies through the use of force. Gandhi and Martin Luther King, Jr., are examples of how civil disobedience can be used to appeal to the basic decency of the wider community. Protesters engaged in civil disobedience break laws openly and nonviolently and are willing to go to jail to indicate their loyalty to their cause and also to show respect for the law. Their commitment in the face of great opposition draws media attention that sparks sympathetic attention from the community.

Third, most often the opposition is between individuals or groups which have some shared interests (although not as thoroughgoing as in the first context) and some clashing interests (although not on such a scale that civil disobedience is a genuine option). Most conflicts arise in this context. If we assume that the conflicting parties are willing to communicate with each other, *principled negotiation* makes sense.

As explained by Roger Fisher and William Ury, principled negotiation has four components: (1) tackle the problem rather than attacking the person with whom one disagrees; (2) concentrate on interests (of others and of oneself) rather than on stated positions—the game of adopting a negotiating position, then changing positions in response to the opponent, fails to get at the real goods at stake; (3) creatively generate a range of possible solutions, and discuss them, before settling on any one option; and (4) as early as possible, seek to find objective criteria that are acceptable as guidelines for acceptable solutions; especially important are principles of fair procedures in how agreements are pursued.

As an illustration, Fisher and Ury cite the 1978 Camp David Accord between Egypt and Israel. The Accord resolved the long-running hostilities concerning the Egyptian Sinai Peninsula, which Israel had occupied since the 1967 war between the countries. After accepting President Carter's invitation to talk, the leaders of both countries came to Camp David insisting on full sovereignty over the disputed area. During the talks, however, Egypt's President Sadat and Israel's Prime Minister Begin were able to come to understand the deeper interests that lay beneath their official positions. Egypt needed its own territory returned; Israel needed its security protected against Egyptian tanks that could quickly move into Israel. Exploring a range of possible solutions, the leaders were able to reconcile their interests by returning the land to Egypt, with the stipulation that the land would be demilitarized so as to keep Egyptian tanks at a safe distance from the borders of Israel.

Compromise

Conflict resolution often requires compromises, but there are two types of compromises, or even two senses of the word *compromise*. In the negative sense, *immoral compromises* involve a betrayal of one's integrity—"selling out." In the positive sense, *reasonable compromises* are rational accommodations based on making mutual concessions. The willingness to engage in reasonable compromises is a virtue; the tendency to engage in immoral compromises is a vice. What is the difference?

Immoral compromises occur when moral principles and ideals are violated, usually in the pursuit of private gain. Reasonable compromises, by contrast, are those in which we act on moral principles and ideals. The difference becomes somewhat blurred, however, when we consider that reasonable compromises do sometimes require us to limit the overzealous ("uncompromising") pursuit of a valid ideal. The *fanatic* is a person who is unwilling to make adjustments by scaling back or placing limits on the means employed in pursuing an ideal. For example, Palestinian terrorists may be justified in pursuing freedom for their homeland, but not to the point of using terrorism to draw attention to their cause.

To further clarify the difference in the two types of compromise, note that reasonable compromises tend to arise in particular circumstances. According to Martin Benjamin, the circumstances usually involve (1) disagreement about some of the facts relevant to making decisions, (2) moral complexity, involving moral reasons that point in different directions, (3) the need for decisions to be made promptly, rather than postponed indefinitely, and (4) the desirability for the parties involved to maintain an ongoing relationship with each other.[6] The last feature is especially important in understanding what Benjamin calls *integrity-preserving compromises*. Some of the ideals we most value in relationships are mutual respect and mutual caring. In making reasonable compromises we act on these ideals about relationships in placing limits on our pursuit of other important ideals. Reasonable compromises balance, rather than "sell out," our ideals; they also preserve our integrity as persons committed to the ideals.

Reasonable compromisers have good judgment. By contrast, fanatics lack good judgment. They suffer from "tunnel vision," seeing one moral imperative as having unlimited importance while remaining insensitive to the claims of other equally valid moral principles. As a result, their one commitment reveals excess: It is pursued with misguided and intolerant zeal.

SUMMARY

Resentment (in response to an injury) and indignation (in response to a violation of a moral principle) imply a desire to right a wrong. Hatred of persons, by contrast, involves ill will and aversion and implies a desire to hurt. In the form of malicious envy, hatred implies a desire that another's good be destroyed or taken away. *Ressentiment* is self-deceiving envy and hate expressed through unconscious spite or malice. More generally, malicious hatred implies a desire to elevate oneself by bringing down the person one hates, and spiteful hatred implies a desire to bring the other person down to one's low level. By contrast, moral hatred is admirably motivated by the desire to conquer over immoral people and causes.

Envy is overcome or weakened when one of its three aspects is removed or lessened. We can overcome feelings of hate, inferiority, and impotence by strengthening our self-confidence and self-esteem, and also by developing a capacity to appreciate the talents and achievements of other people. Forgiveness is sometimes the best or only way to restore mutual respect after injuries have been suffered, but forgiveness is sometimes inappropriate.

Rational approaches to conflict resolution vary according to contextual features, such as extensively shared values within a group, the potential for violence, and whether opposing parties are willing to build on areas of shared interest despite their conflicting conceptions of the good. Reasonable compromise is an integrity-preserving accommodation in circumstances where cooperation must be preserved amidst factual uncertainty, moral complexity, and urgent decision making. Immoral compromise, by contrast, betrays moral ideals and integrity. To distinguish between reasonable and immoral compromises demands good judgment in balancing moral ideals, including the ideal of maintaining mutual respect.

DISCUSSION TOPICS

1   To covet is to desire another's possessions in some objectionable way. How is covetousness related to envy? How do you interpret the proverb "Envy destroys the good it covets"?

2   This chapter emphasized the bad aspects of envy. Based on your own experience, is this emphasis unjustified? Can you see some possible good effects of envy (such as stimulating us to compete more fiercely)?

3   Read the following passage:

> Consider a relationship stricken by envy. A friend joyfully shares the news of her fine achievement. The less successful friend wishes to, wants to, intends to, and indeed tries to create a sincere congratulation fitting with the excellence of

her accomplishment and the warmth of their friendship. But he botches it. The congratulations come out forced, choked, diminished, and cool.[7]

Describe two possible aftermaths, one in which the envy destroys the friendship and one in which the envy is overcome and the relationship stays intact. What might lead things to develop in the one way rather than the other?

4   Apply the following passage, written by Henry Fairlie, to Salieri:

> The envious man does not love himself, although he begins with self-love. He is not grateful for, or happy in, what he is or what he has. The sin is deadly, less because it destroys him, than because it will not let him live. It will not let him live as himself, grateful for his qualities and talents, such as they are, and making the best and most rewarding use of them. His disparagement of others is a reflection of his disparagement of himself; he regards himself with as much malice as he regards them.[8]

5   Kant wrote that "the three vices which are the essence of vileness and wickedness are ingratitude, envy, and malice. When these reach their full degree they are devilish."[9] What connections do you see among these three vices? Do they perhaps share a common core?

6   Discuss the ideal, usually associated with Christianity, that we should always forgive. Should it perhaps be interpreted to mean that we should be prepared to forgive *if* a person repents or there are other reasons for forgiving? Or is the ideal a religious goal that transcends ordinary morality in requiring people to forgive out of love, for the sake of helping the wrongdoer? Does forgiveness sometimes hurt, rather than help the wrongdoer?

In discussing the last question, consider how, in Eugene O'Neill's play *The Iceman Cometh*, a man finds himself hating his wife for forgiving his drunken binges with prostitutes. Her constant forgiveness made him hate himself all the more. The man remarks, "I even caught myself hating her for making me hate myself so much. There's a limit to the guilt you can feel and the forgiveness and the pity you can take! You have to begin blaming someone else, too."[10]

7   If forgiveness consists of forgoing hostile feelings, mercy consists of forgoing or reducing the punishment that is normally warranted for wrongdoing. With this distinction, can you make sense of the idea of forgiving a drunk driver, but insisting that the driver should receive no mercy in being punished?

8   Apply the Fisher-Ury approach to principled negotiation to each of the following issues that on occasion generate conflict at most campuses. In each case identify at least two opposing positions and how they might be reconciled. (a) What should be the policies—both as written and enforced—on alcohol use in campus dorms? (b) What policies should apply to inviting controversial speakers to campus and paying their fees from student tuition? (c) Should nudity be allowed in college plays?

9   A surrogate mother gives birth to a child conceived through artificial insemination, usually using her ovum but sometimes using another woman's ovum, which is implanted in her uterus after being fertilized. Usually the woman is paid about $10,000 to carry the child to term and then give it up for adoption to the intended parents, who pay the money. Sometimes the surrogate mother bonds

with the child and refuses to give it up for adoption, and occasionally the intended parents refuse to adopt the child once it is born. Describe a particular case involving such conflicts and then explain how you would recommend the conflict be resolved through negotiation. Also, explain why you find the practice of surrogate motherhood morally justifiable or unjustifiable.

10 Sometimes we think of compromise as a sign of weakness of will and cowardice, but that is because we forget the importance of reasonable compromises. John F. Kennedy had in mind reasonable compromises when he wrote, in *Profiles in Courage*, that "compromise need not mean cowardice. Indeed it is frequently the compromisers and conciliators who are faced with the severest tests of political courage as they oppose the extremist views of their constituents."[11] Read a recent newspaper to identify a political issue in which compromise was involved. Do you suspect the compromise was a courageous act, a cowardly "sellout," or perhaps some of both?

SUGGESTED READINGS

Benjamin, Martin. *Splitting the Difference: Compromise and Integrity in Ethics and Politics.* Lawrence, KS: University Press of Kansas, 1990.

Cox, Gray. *The Ways of Peace*. New York: Paulist Press, 1986.

Fairlie, Henry. *The Seven Deadly Sins Today*. Notre Dame, IN: University of Notre Dame Press, 1979.

Farber, Leslie H. *Lying, Despair, Jealousy, Envy, Sex, Suicide, Drugs, and the Good Life*. New York: Basic Books, 1976.

Fisher, Roger, and William Ury. *Getting to Yes: Negotiating Agreement Without Giving In*. New York: Penguin, 1981.

Jacoby, Susan. *Wild Justice: The Evolution of Revenge*. New York: Harper & Row, 1983.

Kant, Immanuel. "Jealousy and Its Offspring—Envy and Grudge." In L. W. Beck (ed. and trans.), *Lectures on Ethics*. New York: Harper & Row, 1963.

McFall, Lynne. "What's Wrong with Bitterness?" In C. Card (ed.), *Feminist Ethics*. Lawrence, KS: University Press of Kansas, 1991.

Murphy, Jeffrie G., and Jean Hampton. *Forgiveness and Mercy*. Cambridge: Cambridge University Press, 1988.

Newman, Jay. *Fanatics and Hypocrites*. New York: Prometheus, 1986.

Nietzsche, Friedrich. "On the Tarantulas." In W. Kaufmann (trans.), *Thus Spoke Zarathustra*, New York: Penguin, 1978. Pp. 99–102.

Nozick, Robert. "Self-Esteem and Envy." In *Anarchy, State, and Utopia*. New York: Basic Books, 1974. Pp. 239–246.

Rawls, John. "The Problem of Envy" and "Envy and Equality." In *A Theory of Justice*. Cambridge, MA: Harvard University Press, 1971. Pp. 530–541.

Richards, Norvin, "Forgiveness." In J. Deigh (ed.), *Ethics and Personality: Essays in Moral Psychology*. Chicago: University of Chicago Press, 1992. Pp. 223–243.

Sabini, John, and Maury Silver. "Envy." In *Moralities of Everyday Life*. Oxford: Oxford University Press, 1982. Pp. 15–33.

Scheler, Max. *Ressentiment*. W. W. Holdheim (trans.). L. A. Coser (ed.). New York: Schocken, 1972.

Schoeck, Helmut. *Envy: A Theory of Social Behavior*. M. Glenny and B. Ross (trans.). London: Secker & Warburg, 1969.

Shaffer, Peter. *Amadeus*. New York: New American Library, 1984.

Shakespeare, William. *Othello*. New York: New American Library, 1963.

Solomon, Robert C. *A Passion for Justice: Emotions and the Origins of the Social Contract*. Reading, MA: Addison-Wesley, 1990.

Taylor, Gabriele. "Envy and Jealousy: Emotions and Vices." *Midwest Studies in Philosophy, Ethical Theory: Character and Virtue*, vol. 13. Notre Dame, IN: University of Notre Dame Press, 1988. Pp. 233–249.

CHAPTER 11

Prejudice

Prejudice, in the sense intended here, is an unfair and unreasonable attitude toward members of a group of people. The attitude is manifested in emotions and conduct of individuals (individual prejudice) or in practices, laws, and institutions (institutional prejudice). The group of people can be identified by racial, ethnic, national, religious, aesthetic (for example, "ugly" people), or ideological criteria. Racism and sexism are the two types of prejudice emphasized here.

The term *racism* was coined during the 1950s to refer to racial prejudice. *Sexism* was adopted during the 1960s to refer to misogyny (hatred of women), patriarchy (socially sanctioned male dominance), and unfair discrimination against women. The term is also now applied to misandry (hatred of men) and unfair discrimination against men. Interestingly, the expression "male chauvinist" was coined during the late 1960s by women working in the civil rights and student movements to apply to male colleagues who relegated women to secondary roles in the fight against racism.

Overt Versus Covert Prejudice

One form of individual prejudice is overt; it is easily discernible and involves consciously held prejudiced attitudes. For example, the racist bigot self-confidently asserts that African-American and Latino people are inferior; the anti-Semite passionately denounces Jews as dangerous; and the male chauvinist insists that women are by nature suited only for homemaking and should be barred from business and politics. Overt prejudice can also take institutional forms. Such prejudice has its origin in widespread negative attitudes toward groups, attitudes that generate or support repressive laws, rules, and practices. Overt prejudice not infrequently involves violence, both in its personal forms (as when a gang of white youths attacks a stranger simply because he is black) and in its institutional forms (as when laws continue to protect wife-battering husbands).

The form of prejudice we will emphasize, however, is more covert or concealed. It is also called "visceral," not just because it is deep-seated and difficult to remove, but because it is somewhat hidden, especially to the prejudiced person. Self-deception often contributes to covert prejudice, but usually such prejudice arises in part from a person's uncritical adoption of prejudiced attitudes or participation in prejudiced social practices.

In this chapter, four manifestations of covert prejudice are discussed: (1) acceptance of stereotypes about people's personalities, character, capacities, or roles, (2) use of prejudicial forms of language, (3) ridicule through bigoted humor, and (4) restriction of social roles available to people. Following a discussion of these forms of prejudice we discuss affirmative action and reverse preferential treatment.

Stereotypes

Ralph Ellison's *Invisible Man* explores how stereotypes prevent white people from understanding black people. The central metaphor of the novel is set forth in the opening passage:

> I am an invisible man. No, I am not a spook like those who haunted Edgar Allan Poe.... I am invisible, understand, simply because people refuse to see me. Like the bodiless heads you see sometimes in circus sideshows, it is as though I have been surrounded by mirrors of hard, distorting glass. When they approach me they see only my surroundings, themselves, or figments of their imagination—indeed, everything and anything except me.... That invisibility to which I refer occurs because of a peculiar disposition of the eyes of those with whom I come in contact. A matter of the construction of their *inner* eyes, those eyes with which they look through their physical eyes upon reality.[1]

These distorting inner mirrors are preconceived beliefs and attitudes about black people. They are the "prejudging" inherent in prejudice. In contemporary psychological terms, they represent biased "cognitive schemas" through which experiences are filtered. In ordinary language, they are negative stereotypes, that is, simplistic views based on false beliefs, incomplete information, or unjustified value judgments.

Later in the novel the Invisible Man relates the incident that forced him to grasp how cognitively distorting mirrors had rendered him invisible. Walking alone at night, he accidentally bumped into a white man who called him "an insulting name." He exploded in rage, attacking the man and demanding an apology. During the ensuing fight the white man continued to shout racist obscenities even after the Invisible Man held a knife to his throat. Suddenly he realized that "the man had not *seen* me, actually; that he, as far as he knew, was in the midst of a walking nightmare" involving an insane assailant who had no reason (that the white man would grasp) for attacking him.[2] He also realized that the man's verbal assault resulted from a stereotypic view that operated outside the man's full awareness.

Was the Invisible Man blameworthy for the violence? In the beginning of the novel he denies responsibility, arguing that "responsibility rests upon recognition."[3] In other words, moral responsibility presupposes a minimal mutual respect among groups of people, and that respect is exactly what the white man refused to give him. By the end of the novel, however, the protagonist modifies this view, accepting partial responsibility for his own invisibility because of his passivity and naïveté.

Is the white man responsible? According to the Invisible Man, that depends on whether he could be expected to recognize the meaning and the danger of his racial slur: "He, let us say, was lost in a dream world. But didn't *he* control that dream world—which, alas, is only too real!—and didn't *he* rule me out of it?"[4] This relates to the question raised in Chapter 6 concerning responsibility for self-deception and preventable ignorance. As was argued there, we are responsible for much of our self-deception and we can be held accountable for unquestioning conformity to social pressures. Rather than repeating that argument, let us turn to the question of how prejudiced stereotypes are supported by self-deception.

Marilyn Frye makes some helpful suggestions about how this occurs. Although she uses the example of sexism, her remarks are easily extended to other forms of prejudice. In her essay "Male Chauvinism—A Conceptual Analysis," Frye first points out sexism and prejudice do not always involve self-deception. Rather, some sexism is unthinkingly absorbed from parents, friends, and society. She offers the example of a man who, in always opening doors for women but not for men, has simply adopted the practice unreflectively. He may not even be a sexist, but merely a participant in a discriminatory practice. People who develop and sustain prejudiced attitudes even when they have every opportunity to abandon them, however, typically engage in some degree of self-deceptive evasion and distortion of facts.

The tactics of self-deceiving prejudice include straightforward deception about the behavior of individuals with whom one comes in contact, either in the form of ignoring or downplaying the abilities they display. One can also disregard the special obstacles others confront. More insidious tactics include the self-deceptive manipulation of the circumstances against a person. Consider, for example, how fathers, in teaching their daughters to throw a baseball, may "go through various superficial maneuvers and declare failure (her failure) without having engaged in anything like the perseverance and ingenuity which would have been engaged in the training of sons."[5] A racist parallel would be an employer who deliberately places a trainee in difficult situations that make poor performance more likely, or who gives less help and attention to a minority trainee than to a white male.

Frye offers a second example of the creation of unfair circumstances. Without acknowledging it to oneself, one refrains from the kinds of personal contact in which one's prejudice might be uncovered or challenged:

> One cannot, for instance, manifest certain kinds of intelligence in inter-
> actions with a person who enters with a prior conviction of one's stu-
> pidity, lack of insight, absence of wit; one cannot manifest sensitivity or
> loyalty in interactions with someone who is distrustful and will not share
> relevant information.... He [the male chauvinist] can in one fell swoop
> avoid seeing the critical central range of a woman's ... abilities simply
> by being uncooperative and uncommunicative, and can do it without
> knowing he has done it by self-deceptively believing he has been coop-
> erative and communicative.[6]

There are parallels here with the ways some people avoid honest personal interactions with those of particular racial groups. If challenged, one might claim to be acting on one's own tastes concerning people. Do we not all have a right to choose our associates? Yet the possession of rights is not the issue; quite simply, it is wrong to exercise our rights in ways that show disrespect for an entire group of people.

Language

A second way in which prejudice is expressed covertly is through language. One form of such prejudice, many people now argue, is the use of certain familiar terms and expressions. Language is used to formulate and express thoughts, but it also shapes thoughts. Words and ways of speaking are to a large extent historical products that embody assumptions, attitudes, and emotional responses. As Ludwig Wittgenstein (1889–1951) argued, linguistic practices are intimately joined to "ways of life" defined by communal practices, beliefs, and attitudes. Wittgenstein's later philosophy emerged after he traced his early errors in doing philosophy to naïveté about how language influences thought. In reflecting on those errors, he remarked, "A *picture* held us captive. And we could not get outside it, for it lay in our language and language seemed to repeat it to us inexorably."[7] Earlier thinkers such as Francis Bacon (1561–1626) were also sensitive to this danger: "People believe that their reason governs words. But words turn and twist the understanding."[8]

One of the most important applications of how language embeds and sanctions misleading "pictures"—that is, perspectives and ways of thinking—has been made by feminists who uncovered sex biases built into language. This linguistic sexism still permeates everyday language use and raises moral questions about whether we should feel comfortable in allowing it to continue. Consider some of the ways in which linguistic practices reflect and reinforce sexist as well as racist biases:

1   Men are referred to as *Mr.* while women are identified by marital status: *Mrs.* or *Miss* (a problem now easily solved by the use of *Ms.*).

2   According to custom and continuing social pressure, after marriage only the woman is encouraged to change her last name, thereby symbolically expressing a new identity oriented toward the man.

3   Everyday locutions place the male first, as in *husband and wife* (not *wife and husband*), *men and women*, and *son and daughter*.

4   Until recently, names for occupations were male-oriented, as in *fireman* (versus *fire fighter*), *mailman* (versus *mail carrier*), *congressman* (versus *member of congress*), and *chairman* (versus *chair* or *chairperson*).

5   Adult women office workers are often referred to as *the girls in the office*, while male workers are called men. (Compare the racist use of *boy* to refer to adult black men.)

6   The same personality traits are labeled positively when found in males and negatively when found in females: Males are assertive but females are bitchy; men are blunt but women can't hold their tongues; men discuss but women gossip.

7   Far more than men, women are referred to with terms that tie them to their anatomy or to animals, often vulgarly so: *broads, chicks, piece*.

8   God is referred to as *He*, even in religions that officially find it blasphemous to ascribe human properties to God.

9   *Man* (versus *humans* or *persons*), its variants (*mankind, men*), and male pronouns (*he, his*) are used in contexts referring to both men and women, while the reverse would not convey the same universal meaning.

Despite the systematic and varied ways in which male biases enter into language, there are some people who see no need to change our ways of speaking. They insist that language should be preserved as it is, and they deny that anyone's thoughts or attitudes are influenced by such trivial linguistic customs. There are two rejoinders to this linguistic conservatism. First, commonsense or naive beliefs about how language affects thought and attitude need to be examined in light of scientific studies. A classic sociological experiment challenges the naive view that using "man" to apply to both men and women has no effect on thought and action:

Some three hundred college students were asked to select from magazines and newspapers a variety of pictures that would appropriately illustrate the different chapters of a sociology textbook being prepared for publication. Half the students were assigned chapter headings like "Social Man," "Industrial Man," and "Political Man." The other half were given different but corresponding headings like "Society," "Industrial Life," and "Political Behavior." Analysis of the pictures selected revealed that in the minds of students of both sexes use of the word man evoked, to a statistically significant degree, images of males only—filtering out recognition of women's participation in these major areas of life—whereas the corresponding headings without "man" evoked images of both males and females. In some instances the differences reached magnitudes of 30 to 40 percent. The authors concluded, "This is rather convincing evidence that when you use the word man generically, people do tend to think male, and tend not to think female."[9]

Second, even those who seek to honor custom must recognize that customs are changing dramatically in this area, and presumably, once established, those emergent customs will warrant the same respect claimed for the older ones. Increasingly, publishers, writers, public speakers, and conversationalists are paying heed to ways to root out sexism in language. In such a climate of change it is, at the least, rude to refuse even to try to adjust one's language, and such a refusal may indicate sexist attitudes.

Ridicule Through Bigoted Humor

A third way covert prejudice is manifested relies on a special use of language: ridicule through bigoted humor. We might think of humor as something arising from our enjoyment of incongruity for its own sake, which is expressed through laughter, pleasant inclinations to laugh, and moments of cheerfulness.[10] To ridicule is to mock or arouse scorn by portraying someone (or something) in a negative way, and often this is done through malicious uses of humor. Ridicule through humor constitutes a seductive and camouflaged way to spitefully mock an individual or a group. It is seductive because it can catch us off guard, evoking spontaneous reactions of amusement. It also camouflages prejudice with apparently innocent pleasures: the physical pleasure of laughter, the social pleasure of sharing laughter with others, and the intellectual pleasure of wittiness. Because it seems good to bring people pleasure, ridicule through humor appears to have at least something good about it; but does it really?

In fact, jokes afford a virtual haven for the expression of covert prejudice. Consider several examples, beginning with the following episode from

American politics. In 1976, Earl Butz resigned as President Ford's secretary of agriculture. The resignation resulted from one joke he told on a flight to Los Angeles following the Kansas City Republican convention: As reported in *Newsweek* magazine,

> Butz found himself sitting with Watergate veteran John Dean (who was covering the convention for *Rolling Stone* magazine) and singer Pat Boone. At one point Boone mused, "It seems to me that the party of Abraham Lincoln could and should attract more black people. Why can't that be done?" The "coloreds," Butz replied jokingly, were only interested in three things, and his punch line hit in a grossly obscene way at their preferences in sex, shoes, and bathroom arrangements.[11]

President Ford reprimanded Butz, and despite Butz's popularity with his constituency in the Farm Belt, he was forced by mounting public pressure to resign.

An example of sexist humor is recorded for all posterity by James Boswell in his *Life of Samuel Johnson*. While walking with Johnson one day, Boswell remarked, "I had been that morning at a meeting of the people called Quakers, where I had heard a woman preach." Johnson replied, "Sir, a woman's preaching is like a dog's walking on his hind legs. It is not done well; but you are surprised to find it done at all."[12]

Light bulb jokes, which became popular in the United States during the late 1960s and 1970s, were used to portray Polish-Americans as stupid: "How many Polacks [to use the offensive slur] does it take to change a light bulb? Three: one to hold the bulb and two to turn the ladder." And anti-Semitic jokes frequently portray Jews as cheap while mocking their physiognomy: "Why do Jews have big noses? Air is free."

Telling these jokes in the presence of members of the groups being ridiculed will generally directly insult those persons and cause both hurt and resentment. If no members of the group are present, however, is any harm done? Whether we tell a bigoted joke or laugh at one, we are usually sharing the prejudiced attitudes expressed in the joke. In finding the joke enjoyable, we embrace, at least for that moment, the derogatory attitudes underlying the negative stereotype of a group of people. Earl Butz insisted that he was not a racist and did not intend to express a racist attitude, he was just having fun. The fun, however, came through "making fun of" all black people by affirming a negative stereotype of black people and inviting his hearers to do likewise. Bigoted humor endorses or condones bigoted attitudes and supports a social climate of disrespect for groups of people. Telling and laughing at bigoted jokes usually joins speaker and hearer in a conspiracy of social oppression.

We should, however, qualify this point with several observations. For one thing, in special circumstances it is possible to tell or enjoy some otherwise bigoted jokes without being prejudiced. Much depends on the context.

For example, there is such a thing as having a *right to laugh* at a particular joke in a particular situation. Members of a minority group often have the right to tell and enjoy a joke about their group that outsiders do not have (unless they have been accepted by the group).

As another example, white people may be justified in laughing at racial jokes told by Richard Pryor, even though laughing at the same jokes told by Earl Butz would be wrong. The two cases are different because the motives and attitudes expressed in telling of the joke are different. Whereas Butz is "putting down" and alienating black people, Pryor is trying to overcome alienation among races through self-understanding about racism, mutual understanding, and sympathetic identification. Butz would have us laugh *at* black people, with contempt and alienation; Pryor would have us laugh *with* him, with good will and shared identification. Even when jokes depend on our perception of someone as inferior or flawed, we can often focus on the incongruity itself as humorous, without expressing degrading attitudes. That makes it possible sometimes to have a right to laugh at otherwise bigoted jokes in special circumstances where it is the incongruity itself, rather than a put-down, we enjoy.

Gender Roles

A fourth way prejudice is manifested is through restrictive social roles. Gender or sex roles represent socially created expectations for males and females, just as racial roles represent socially created expectations for members of particular racial groups. Roles for black and white people were strongly differentiated well into this century. It was only a few decades ago, in 1954, that the Supreme Court ruled in *Brown vs. Board of Education* that "separate but equal" schools were inherently unequal and unfair. In principle, and officially, our society has recognized that it is insulting to keep a minority separated—in schools, restaurants, restrooms, buses, and other public settings—from social interaction with a privileged group.

Although the equal rights of minorities have now been at least officially recognized in our society, the same cannot be said for women. Since the following two dozen words were first formulated in 1923, opponents have continually blocked their addition to the Constitution as the Equal Rights Amendment (ERA): "Equality of rights under the law shall not be denied or abridged by the United States or by any State on account of sex." In 1982 this proposed amendment failed to gain the required ratification of three-fourths of the state legislatures, even though it was passed by the Senate and House of Representatives and had the approval of the majority of Americans.

The defeat of the ERA and the elements of sexism in the grammar of our language have suggested to some thinkers that sexism is more firmly entrenched in our society than racism, although it would be difficult to prove that. It is, however, worth considering some of the differences between racism and sexism, as identified by Richard Wasserstrom in his essay "On Racism and Sexism." Wasserstrom draws attention to the substantial psychological literature documenting how we respond differently to boys and girls from the time they are born. For example, girls are handled more delicately as babies; from infancy on boys are encouraged to be more independent and strong; and girls and women are taught to be dependent and passive and are generally more restricted in the kinds of activities in which they can engage.

Wasserstrom argues that the key difference between racism and sexism lies in the greater complexity of the attitudes and valuations involved in sexism. Racist stereotypes of black people are wholly negative; that is, racists regard black people as having less worth than white people. Sexist attitudes, by contrast, are mixed in a manner that enables sexists to believe they view women as having equal or greater worth than men:

> Women are both put on a pedestal and deemed not fully developed persons. They are idealized; their approval and admiration is sought; and they are at the same time regarded as less competent than men and less able to live fully developed, fully human lives—for that is what men do. At best, they are viewed and treated as having properties and attributes that are valuable and admirable for humans of this type. For example, they may be viewed as especially empathetic, intuitive, loving, and nurturing. At best, these qualities are viewed as good properties for women to have, and, provided they are properly muted, are sometimes valued within the more well-rounded male.[13]

Wasserstrom urges that in order to determine which roles betray sexist and racist attitudes, we must determine which roles would be present in a morally ideal society. As an aid in thinking about this question, he distinguishes three types of gender roles: (1) those concerning political rights, such as the right to vote and hold political office; (2) those pertaining to economic and nonpolitical practices, such as work and marital roles; and (3) those involving personal traits, tastes, interests, and interactions, including the selection of friends and personal entertainment and the encouragement of sex-stereotyped traits of temperament and character.

With respect to all these areas Wasserstrom suggests that a morally ideal society would regard racial and sexual differences as completely irrelevant. Just as eye color is almost entirely ignored in our society (completely so in areas 1 and 2, and mostly so in area 3), so too racial and sex traits would be equally insignificant if our society were morally ideal. Wasserstrom refers to this as the "assimilationist ideal."

For example, concerning the third area of personal characteristics and interactions, Wasserstrom makes the following assertions:

> On the attitudinal and conceptual level, the assimilationist ideal would require the eradication of all sex-role differentiation. It would never teach about the inevitable or essential attributes of masculinity or femininity; it would never encourage or discourage the ideas of sisterhood or brotherhood; and it would be unintelligible to talk about the virtues as well as disabilities of being a woman or a man. Were sex like eye color, these things would make no sense. Just as the normal, typical adult is virtually oblivious to the eye color of other persons for all major interpersonal relationships, so the normal, typical adult in this kind of non-sexist society would be indifferent to the sexual, physiological differences of other persons for all interpersonal relationships.[14]

This is a striking claim. Apparently, in seeking to abolish all differentiation as masculine and feminine, Wasserstrom is recommending a kind of androgynous and bisexual ideal society in which even clothing, hair styles, use of makeup, and sexual preferences would not be developed along sex lines.

Wasserstrom gives two arguments in support of this ideal society. First, he notes that the roles given to women have historically been the lesser, inferior ones in terms of social power. Second, and more important to a consideration of ideal societies, gender roles are inherently harmful: "Sex roles, and all that accompany them, necessarily impose limits—restrictions on what one can do, be or become. As such, they are, I think, at least prima facie wrong."[15]

It will be left for the reader to determine whether Wasserstrom is correct. In doing so, consider a rejoinder to Wasserstrom by Elizabeth Wolgast in *Equality and the Rights of Women*. Wolgast contends that, at the very least, the biological possibility of pregnancy provides one focal difference that should be openly acknowledged in assessing the comparative rights of women and men (for example, rights to guaranteed pregnancy leaves that secure employment at the same job when women return to work, and funded day care for the children of working mothers). Moreover, special economic benefits to widows are justifiable, especially when women have worked at home as homemakers. With respect to Wasserstrom's third category, Wolgast urges that we should not be disturbed by how biological differences encourage some social differentiation in roles:

> *Could* we treat the sexes alike as Wasserstrom proposes? We normally respond differently to members of the opposite sex than to members of our own. Even putting sexual attraction aside, we still have different relations to members of different sexes. With members of our sex, we have and anticipate having, a good deal in common. To a child we say, "When I was a little girl ..." (if we are women) with the implication that we lack the same identification with boys. While with members of the

opposite sex we perceive contrasts and divergent points of view, for some areas of common experience are lacking. Understanding those other perspectives is often a tenuous matter, ignorance and mystery being the conditions it must work against; but it is also one that fascinates, challenges, delights, and amuses us.[16]

Reverse Preferential Treatment

As long as racism and sexism continue, it is essential to promote social practices that counter prejudice. One such practice is affirmative action, which was begun during the 1960s to promote equal opportunity in employment and education. Strictly defined, affirmative action is the pursuit of active measures in advertising, hiring, promotion, training, and education to ensure that prejudice does not deny minorities and women equal opportunities. For example, employers state in their advertisements that they are equal opportunity employers, thereby encouraging all qualified people to apply. Once applications are received, employers make sure that full and fair attention is given to each applicant, making special efforts to counter any possible prejudice that could affect decisions. Distinct from affirmative action, although often confused with it, is *preferential treatment* (or *reverse* preferential treatment): the preference afforded to members of groups that in the past were discriminated against, in particular women and minorities. *Weak* preferential treatment gives an automatic advantage to a woman or minority who is equally qualified as a white male. *Strong* preferential treatment gives an advantage even when the woman or minority is less qualified than a white male, although still competent to succeed (in employment or education). While affirmative action in the strict sense is relatively uncontroversial, both forms of preferential treatment are highly controversial.

Defenders of preferential treatment programs have two main arguments. First, they appeal to *compensatory justice*: the obligation to compensate for past and present injustice in the forms of racism and sexism. As groups, women and minorities have suffered from the subtle forms of bigotry that permeate society. For example, on average they have received fewer educational resources and less encouragement to undertake challenging educational and career options. Preferential treatment balances out this effect. In terms of rights ethics, women and minorities have a right to compensation; in terms of duty ethics, they are owed a duty of compensation; in rule-utilitarian terms, the rule that gives them preference is justified by the overall good it promotes in counting women and minorities equally.

Second, preferential treatment programs have valuable benefits for society as a whole. They bring women and minorities into positions of responsibility and authority, and thereby enrich the mixture of views and talents in the educational system and workforce. New role models are created that encourage additional women and minorities to excel. Society as a whole is encouraged to move toward greater mutual respect and acceptance of cultural diversity. This argument is utilitarian in spirit, although rights ethicists and duty ethicists also emphasize the support for equal respect that derives from a fully integrated society, which preferential treatment promotes.

Opponents of preferential treatment regard it as compounding past injustice with a new form of prejudice—"reverse discrimination"—which is tantamount to an attempt to make two wrongs add up to a right. It is true that equal respect for persons is a demand at the heart of rights ethics, duty ethics, and rule-utilitarianism, and its requirement is straightforward: Give all people the same opportunities to compete according to their qualifications for work and educational opportunities. While it is also true that specific individuals who are denied equal opportunity are owed compensation, opponents of preferential treatment argue that such programs are not focused on specifically wronged individuals. Instead, they target all members of groups, some of whom are already privileged because of their wealthy parents.

In regard to good consequences, opponents contend that preferential treatment is a recipe for lowering excellence at the workplace and in all fields of human endeavor that demand advanced education. In admissions to college, as well as in acceptance for jobs and promotions, they argue that the standard must be excellence, not minimal competence plus extraneous factors such as race and gender. Moreover, they contend, preferential programs foster resentment among white males and their families regarding the denial of equal opportunities. They also create a stigma that women and minorities are incapable of making it on their own, without special breaks. This stigma furthers, rather than counters, prejudice.

Are preferential treatment programs just or unjust? This question is left as a discussion topic.

SUMMARY

Prejudice, in the sense of unfair and unreasonable attitudes toward members of a group, can be overt (consciously held and easily discerned by others) or covert (less conscious and more concealed). Most prejudice has cultural origins, and much covert prejudice is partially caused and supported by self-deceptive beliefs and attitudes. Self-deception supports cultural stereotypes by allowing one to ignore and downplay the abilities of others, disregard the special obstacles they confront, and rig the circumstances so as to deny them fair opportunities to overthrow the stereotypes.

In addition to self-deceptive stereotypes, language is a second potent form of covert prejudice that is institutional in nature. Familiar grammatical practices, such as the use of male pronouns to refer to both women and men, convey language-embedded images of men as superior to women.

Bigoted humor is a third way to manifest and foster prejudice. Humor is based on our enjoyment of incongruity for its own sake, which is expressed through laughter or episodic cheerfulness. It is bad when the enjoyment comes at the expense of others, and malicious when others are intentionally degraded. Bigoted humor expresses prejudice and reinforces negative stereotypes. We have no right to laugh at groups in ways that alienate them, although in special circumstances we can laugh with someone who does have the right to tell an otherwise inappropriate joke. Everything depends on the context and motives.

A fourth form of prejudice, which can be both institutionalized and personal, is covert sexism, by which women and men are encouraged to take differential roles that deny them equal opportunities, just as racism denies to minorities the same opportunities that members of the dominant group in a society enjoy. As the disagreement between Wasserstrom and Wolgast reflects, our society is in the midst of determining whether all differential roles impose unfair and hurtful restrictions.

In the strict sense, affirmative action programs are aimed at ensuring equal opportunity to all individuals. Reverse preferential treatment programs have the further aim of giving preference to women and minorities over equally qualified white males (weak preferential treatment) or more qualified white males (strong preferential treatment). Defenders of the programs emphasize society's responsibility to compensate for the effects of past and present prejudice; they also point to the benefits of a fully integrated society. Critics claim that the programs violate equal opportunity principles and cause additional bad consequences.

DISCUSSION TOPICS

1 Do you agree with Wasserstrom that all gender roles that create different expectations for females and males impose harmful limits on what they can do and become? Or is Wolgast correct in believing that some differential expectations for females and males are both inevitable and desirable? Can women be equal with men but significantly different and complementary? Consider a range of examples of ways we characterize females and males, from dress codes and hair styles to differences in personality traits and character traits (such as those discussed by Carol Gilligan).

2 Is there sexism involved in allowing sports teams to restrict members to one sex? In answering this question, consider each of the following contexts: junior and

little league sports supported by communities; elementary school teams; high school teams; college teams; professional sports. Is your answer the same when you use race as a criterion for team membership?

3   Describe a situation in which the following jokes would be morally objectionable and a situation (if there is one) in which they would not:

What's black and catches flies?
—Willie Mays (former centerfielder of the San Francisco Giants).[17]

Who are the three most dangerous men in the world?
—An Italian with a gun, a Mexican with a driver's license, and a Frenchman with a chipped tooth.[18]

What is the difference between a Jewish Mother and a vulture?
—A vulture waits until you are dead to eat your heart out.[19]

Men have only two faults: Everything they say and everything they do.[20]

4   Rudeness is a major violation of decorum, that is, of the generally accepted standards for proper behavior, dress, and speech in a given culture. It is a matter of both etiquette and morality, at least insofar as rudeness involves disrespect. Is it rude for a man not to open doors for women, or does the practice of opening doors for them (but not for men) express or support the assumption that women are weak and in need of help?

5   Wasserstrom believes that a just society would abandon racial roles as well as gender roles. In fact, he thinks that all racial differences would be irrelevant to how people responded to one another in such a society. Do you agree or disagree? In your answer, consider the objection that, even though racial differences have been used to hurt members of minorities, they need not do so in an ideal society. A perfectly just society might allow a plurality of racial groupings and responses that bring an enriching diversity of subcultures.

6   Elizabeth Wolgast contends that women should have special rights, such as the right to pregnancy leave with a guaranteed job upon return to work. Do you agree? Is her view compatible with the Equal Rights Amendment?

7   Prejudice consists of unfair and unreasonable attitudes toward members of a group. Is the African-American or the Mexican-American who is raised as a second-class citizen in a ghetto or barrio prejudiced if that person is hostile toward white people and chooses to associate with them as little as possible in his or her personal life?

8   In 1988, on the birthday of Martin Luther King, Jr., Jimmy ("the Greek") Snyder commented during an interview that black athletes have special physical prowess because their ancestors were "bred" to have strong thighs during the days of slavery in the United States. In widely quoted remarks, Snyder said that "the slave owner would breed his big black [man] with his big woman so that he would have a big black kid." Snyder, a prominent sports broadcaster, was fired from his job because of these remarks. Some people defended Snyder on the grounds that he had portrayed black athletes as superior, praising them rather than intending to make a racial slur. Is Snyder's remark racist? Is it unfair that he was fired? (In your answer, take account of the fact that there is no evidence supporting his "pop" evolution theory.)

9 In recent years a number of incidents on college campuses created a concern that a "new racism"—that is, renewed racism—confronts black students. For example, a brawl between white and black students occurred at the University of Massachusetts at Amherst following the final game of the 1986 World Series; a fraternity at the New Jersey Institute of Technology held a party advertised with handbills glorifying violence against blacks; a fraternity at the University of Wisconsin at Madison placed a caricature of a black man with a bone through his nose on the fraternity's front lawn; vandals carved "KKK" in a black student's dormitory room at the University of California at Berkeley.[21] Related events occurred elsewhere, such as in the Queens section of New York City, where a black man was killed by a car while fleeing a group of white teenagers who believed they had a right to keep black people away, and in Forsyth County, Georgia, where an all-white community insisted on keeping black people out of the neighborhood. How would you explain this renewal of overt racism in recent years, especially among students at schools that attract well-educated students? What should be done about it?

10 Present and defend your view about whether reverse preferential treatment, in either its weak or strong form, is morally justified.

11 Studies have shown that a large majority of American couples prefer to have boys for their first babies. Is this preference a form of sexism? Is the case different if a couple insists they like boys and girls equally but assert they need a boy in order to carry on the family name?

Suppose that a couple learns the sex of the fetus several months into a pregnancy (as is possible using amniocentesis, the process by which cells from a sample of the fluid surrounding the fetus are analyzed to discover its chromosomes). Upon learning that the fetus is female, they plan to have an abortion because they want a boy and plan to have only one child. Is the abortion an act of sexism?

SUGGESTED READINGS

Baird, Robert M., and Stuart E. Rosenbaum (eds.). *Bigotry, Prejudice, and Hatred: Definitions, Causes & Solutions.* Buffalo, NY: Prometheus, 1992.

Baker, Robert. "'Pricks' and 'Chicks': A Plea for Persons." In R. Baker and F. Elliston (eds.), *Philosophy and Sex.* Rev. ed. Buffalo, NY: Prometheus, 1984.

Boxill, Bernard R. *Blacks and Social Justice.* Rev. ed. Lanham, MD: Rowman & Littlefield, 1992.

Cohen, Marshall T., T. Nagel, and T. Scanlon (eds.). *Equality and Preferential Treatment.* Princeton, NJ: Princeton University Press, 1977.

De Sousa, Ronald. "When Is It Wrong to Laugh?" In *The Rationality of Emotion.* Cambridge, MA: MIT Press, 1987.

Dundes, Alan. *Cracking Jokes: Studies of Sick Humor Cycles and Stereotypes.* Berkeley, CA: Ten Speed Press, 1987.

English, Jane (ed.). *Sex Equality.* Englewood Cliffs, NJ: Prentice-Hall, 1977.

Ezorsky, Gertrude. *Racism and Justice: The Case for Affirmative Action.* Ithaca, NY: Cornell University Press, 1991.

Fausto-Sterling, Anne. *Myths of Gender: Biological Theories About Women and Men.* New York: Basic Books, 1985.

Frye, Marilyn. "Male Chauvinism—A Conceptual Analysis." In M. Vetterling-Braggin (ed.), *Sexist Language: A Modern Philosophical Analysis.* Totowa, NJ: Littlefield, Adams, 1981.

Goldberg, David Theo (ed.). *Anatomy of Racism.* Minneapolis, MN: University of Minnesota Press, 1990.

Lipman-Blumen, Jean. *Gender Roles and Power.* Englewood Cliffs, NJ: Prentice-Hall, 1984.

Jaggar, Alison M., and Paula S. Rothenberg. *Feminist Frameworks: Alternative Theoretical Accounts of the Relations between Women and Men.* 3rd ed. New York: McGraw-Hill, 1993.

Martin, Mike W. "*Invisible Man* and the Indictment of Innocence." *College Language Association Journal,* vol. 25 (1982): 288–302.

Miller, Casey, and Kate Swift. *Words and Women.* Garden City, NY: Anchor, 1976.

Morreall, John (ed.). *The Philosophy of Laughter and Humor.* Albany, NY: State University of New York Press, 1987.

Philips, Michael. "Racist Acts and Racist Humor." *Canadian Journal of Philosophy,* vol. 15 (1984).

Rothenberg, Paula S. (ed.). *Race, Class, & Gender in the United States: An Integrated Study.* 2nd ed. New York: St. Martin's Press, 1992.

Sartre, Jean-Paul. *Anti-Semite and Jew.* New York: Schocken, 1965.

Spender, Dale. *Man Made Language.* Boston, MA: Routledge & Kegan Paul, 1980.

Thalberg, Irving. "Visceral Racism." *Monist,* vol. 56 (1972).

Vetterling-Braggin, Mary (ed.). *"Femininity," "Masculinity," and "Androgyny": A Modern Philosophical Discussion.* Totowa, NJ: Littlefield, Adams, 1982.

Vetterling-Braggin, Mary (ed.). *Sexist Language: A Modern Philosophical Analysis.* Totowa, NJ: Littlefield, Adams, 1981.

Vetterling-Braggin, Mary, Frederick A. Elliston, and Jane English (eds.). *Feminism and Philosophy.* Totowa, NJ: Rowman & Allanheld, 1977.

Warren, Virginia L. "Guidelines for the Nonsexist Use of Language." *Proceedings and Addresses of The American Philosophical Association,* vol. 59 (1986).

Wasserstrom, Richard A. "On Racism and Sexism." In R. A. Wasserstrom (ed.), *Today's Moral Problems.* 3rd ed. New York: Macmillan, 1985.

Wolgast, Elizabeth H. *Equality and the Rights of Women.* Ithaca, NY: Cornell University Press, 1980.

CHAPTER 12

Abortion

Since 1973, when the Supreme Court issued its ruling in *Roe v. Wade*, abortion has become an increasingly divisive issue in the United States.[1] The Supreme Court ruled that women have the right to abortions until the fetus becomes viable, that is, until it can live outside the uterus (the Court also upheld the right to an abortion after viability if the abortion is necessary for the health of the woman).* As a rationale, the Court cited a woman's right to privacy—her right to make decisions without interference by the government.† This ruling made unconstitutional most state laws prohibiting abortion.

In the abortion controversy, much is at stake concerning respect for persons. *Pro-life* ("conservative") groups, who favor prohibition of all or most abortions, claim that abortions kill babies—one and one-half million each year in the United States alone. *Pro-choice* ("liberal") groups, who favor permissive laws on abortion, regard attempts to restrict abortions as assaults on the fundamental freedoms of women. The confrontations between pro-life and pro-choice groups sometimes conceal the "in-between" or moderate

---

*In 1973, the point of viability was about six months, but since then medical technology has made it possible for many fetuses to survive weeks earlier. We will use the word *fetus* to refer to the prenatal (unborn) stage from conception until birth, rather than the narrower medical sense of "fetus," which refers to the unborn from the time when brain waves can be monitored at about eight weeks.

†Refusing to rule on whether the viable fetus is a person with a right to live, the Court instead ruled that states could pass laws forbidding abortions after the stage of viability because of states' "legitimate interest in potential life." Note: "potential life." The Court said it lacked the knowledge to rule on when the fetus becomes an actual person. The Court also ruled that states could pass laws governing where and how a fetus of three months' development can be aborted, because at that time abortions become more hazardous and because states have a legitimate interest in protecting the health of women.

positions. *Moderates* regard some abortions as morally permissible and other abortions as unjustified. Interestingly, more than half of all Americans define themselves (in opinion polls) as moderates, although most also believe that people should be allowed to make their own abortion decisions.[2]

The dichotomy between pro-choice and pro-life groups also conceals the fact that there are *three* important moral issues concerning abortion. First, is the fetus a person, with a right to live? If it is not fully a person, what is its moral status? Second, if we assume that the fetus is a person with a right to life or is otherwise morally valuable, how should that right or value be weighed against other moral reasons, in particular the rights of the woman? Third, what laws and government policies concerning abortion are morally justified?

With regard to each of these issues there are conservative, liberal, and moderate views. Indeed, one might be a conservative or moderate on some of the issues and a liberal on others. This adds to the complexity of the abortion question, and in what follows we can sketch only a few of the many arguments found in the extensive literature on this topic.

Issue 1: Are Fetuses Persons?

The first issues we consider concern whether the fetus is a person (and, if so, when it becomes one) or whether it has some other moral status. For the purposes of this discussion, let us define *persons* as beings who have a moral right to life or who are otherwise defined as full members of the moral community. Where, in the continuous development from conception to birth to infancy, do we "draw a line" and understand the fetus as a person?

Conservatives

Conservatives draw the line at conception, at the moment when a sperm fertilizes an ovum to form a "zygote," a single cell which contains forty-six chromosomes (unless genetic abnormalities occur). Often conservatives have religious beliefs which lead them to view the zygote as a person with a soul, but conservatives also set forth moral arguments for their view. The moral arguments are relevant here, since our concern is with arguments that carry force beyond particular religious faiths.

One argument focuses on the immediate properties of the zygote.[3] The zygote is the product of two humans and it has forty-six chromosomes; therefore it is a human being. Because all humans have a right to life, the fetus is a person with a right to life.

This argument assumes that a zygote is a human being because it is produced by humans and has forty-six chromosomes. Critics disagree and find it odd to think of a single cell as a human being. They point out that every cell in the body has forty-six chromosomes (except for sperm and ova, which have twenty-three chromosomes) and can be viewed as a "living thing" and a product of humans, but of course these cells are not human beings.

Liberals draw a sharp distinction between two senses of "human": (1) a biological or genetic sense, in which a fetus might be counted as a member of the species *homo sapiens* simply because of its chromosomal count inherited from other humans, and (2) a moral sense in which a human is a person with a right to live or otherwise has full membership in the moral community. They charge conservatives with erroneously sliding from the first to the second sense. Liberals claim that the fact that it has forty-six chromosomes may make the fetus human in the biological or genetic sense, but it does not follow that it is therefore human in the moral sense.

A second conservative argument begins not with the zygote, but with the point at which everyone will agree there is a person. Most people (though not all) will agree that a healthy newborn baby is a person. If that fact is challenged, then we can choose a later stage at which everyone will agree the infant is a person, and consider the process which led up to that stage. The process is one of continuous development of a single being, so continuous that, in reverse chronology, it would be arbitrary to draw a line at any point short of the zygote and say there is no longer a person at that point. Therefore, a zygote is a person.

Critics of this argument insist there are nonarbitrary lines that can be drawn at dramatic points along the way. Viability is one such dramatic point, at which the fetus becomes capable of existing outside the uterus. Another dramatic point is marked by the development of brain waves, which suggests the beginnings of or foundation for consciousness. Even if a precise line cannot be drawn, at least a blurry line, sufficient for moral purposes, might be drawn at such points.

A third conservative argument looks to the future of the zygote. In one version this is the potentiality argument: Because the zygote will develop into an infant (that is, a person in its infancy), it is already a person. That is a fallacy: A potential person is not yet a person. More generally, a merely potential anything is not yet that thing. More recent versions of this argument, however, are not so obviously fallacious.

Don Marquis argues that the fetus is morally comparable to you and me in one key respect: It has a future which is valuable. It will have this future, given normal development, whether or not we conclude it is now a person. That is what matters morally, according to Marquis, because that explains why it is wrong to kill you or me: "When I am killed, I am deprived both of what I now value which would have been part of my future personal life, but also what I would come to value....Inflicting this loss on me is ultimately what makes killing me wrong."[4] The same principle which forbids killing creatures that have a valuable future applies to fetuses: "The future of a standard fetus includes a set of experiences, projects, activities, and such which are identical with the futures of adult human beings and are identical with futures of young children. Since the reason that is sufficient to explain why it is wrong to kill human beings after the time of birth is a reason that also applies to fetuses, it follows that abortion is prima facie seriously morally wrong."[5] Is this argument sound? (This question is left as a discussion topic.)

Liberals

Liberals draw the line defining persons at viability, birth, or even much later. Mary Anne Warren, for example, argues that a fetus is not a person because it lacks the five features characteristic of persons:

> (1) consciousness (of objects and events external and/or internal to the being), and in particular the capacity to feel pain; (2) reasoning (the *developed* capacity to solve new and relatively complex problems); (3) self-motivated activity (activity which is relatively independent of either genetic or direct external control); (4) the capacity to communicate, by whatever means, messages of an indefinite variety of types, that is, not just with an indefinite number of possible contents, but on indefinitely many possible topics; (5) the presence of self-concepts, and self-awareness, either individual or racial, or both."[6]

To qualify as a person, according to Warren, at least one of these conditions must be met; but the fetus, even at seven or eight months, does not meet any of these conditions, and therefore is not a person.

Is it true, as Warren contends, that a developed fetus meets none of these conditions? Studies of advanced-stage fetuses suggest they have a capacity for pain and conservatives and moderates suggest that perhaps some of the other criteria are also met. Is it possible to give a more decisive criterion for being a person?

Michael Tooley thinks that self-awareness (Warren's fifth criterion) is both necessary and sufficient for being a person. He argues that "an organism possesses a serious right to life only if it possesses the concept of a self as a continuing subject of experiences and other mental states, and believes that it is itself such a continuing entity."[7] To have a right to something means that if we desire that thing then other people are obligated not to deprive us of it. In particular, to have a right to life means that if we desire to live then others are obligated not to kill us. In turn, to desire life entails that we have a concept of our life, as well as a concept of ourselves as wanting to live (allowing that we have this concept even when asleep, in a coma, or depressed). To have any rights at all, then, one must have self-awareness. Since at no stage is the fetus self-aware, the fetus is not a person.

The obvious objection to Tooley is that newborn babies and even one-year-old infants also fail to meet his criterion, and hence are not persons according to his criterion. Tooley does not see this as an objection, however, for he believes that persons emerge only later in infancy as they develop a self-concept. Does this mean that infanticide—killing of infants—is justified, since the early infant is not a person? Yes, says Tooley, or rather he suggests that in some cases infanticide is justified, namely, those babies with severe birth defects. Healthy and moderately handicapped infants should not be killed, because of utilitarian reasons, such as the interests and concerns of other members of the moral community.

Tooley's view seems astonishing. If anything is clear to most of us, it is that infants are persons—persons in their early infancy. But then, what criterion establishes personhood? Is the criterion viability, the ability to live outside the woman? Or is it arbitrary to draw the line at that point, rather than, say, at a day or two (or week or so) earlier?

Moderates

Moderates adopt one of two approaches. One approach is to "draw a line" between nonpersons and persons at an earlier stage than liberals but at a later stage than conservatives. Some moderates, for example, are struck by the emergence of brain wave activity during the second month of fetal development.[8] They interpret brain wave activity as indicating the beginning of consciousness, or at least the foundation for the conscious life which is characteristic of persons. This view draws some support from the contemporary legal definition of when a person is dead. According to the "brain dead" definition, a person is dead when an electroencephalogram detects no electrical activity in the brain, even though the heart and lungs may continue to function. Since the cessation of brain function signals the death of a person, is it not reasonable to understand the beginning of brain functioning as the beginning of personhood?

A very different approach adopted by moderates is to abandon the effort to draw a line between persons and nonpersons. As Jane English writes, "There is no single core of necessary and sufficient features which we can draw upon with the assurance that they constitute what really makes a person; there are only features that are more or less typical."[9] These typical features include the ones cited by Mary Anne Warren—consciousness, reasoning, self-motivation, communication capacities, and self-awareness. However, they also include physical factors such as genetic makeup and physical appearance, social factors such as the ability to form relationships and interact within communities, and legal factors such as status before the law. There are innumerable distinctive characteristics of persons, but none of them constitutes the defining essence of persons. As a result, there is no reasonable way to draw a line at one point of development and proclaim that there, for the first time, a person exists.

Nevertheless, English suggests that the very early fetus, which is only a cell or clump of cells, is very unlike a person. The fetus gradually becomes more person-like as it develops. Hence the fetus, at least at some of its stages, has an intermediate moral status. It is not yet a person with a full-blown right to live, but neither is it a mere "tumor" that lacks all moral status. Moreover, the moral value of the fetus changes and increases during the course of its development. No precise quantification of that value is possible, but the more-advanced fetus has greater moral significance than the less-advanced fetus.

This second approach by moderates leaves us with ambiguity, uncertainty, and perhaps ambivalence, rather than clear guidelines for understanding the fetus. Does this result amount to being "wishy-washy," or does it capture the vagueness inherent in the concept of persons?

Issue 2: Balancing Moral Reasons

Where does this disagreement over the moral status of the fetus leave us? In disagreement! The above arguments (and others) sometimes do lead individuals to change their attitudes about whether a fetus is a person, but no widespread consensus has emerged on this first issue. Is it possible to make progress by moving to the second issue, which concerns the attempt to balance the moral significance of the fetus against other moral reasons, in particular, against the rights of the woman?

Conflicting Rights: Liberals Versus Conservatives

For a moment, let us stipulate (for the sake of argument) that the fetus is a person with a right to life. With regard to abortion, what follows from this assumption? At first glance it may seem obvious that a person's right to life is momentous enough to outweigh whatever inconvenience a pregnancy might impose on a woman. Pregnancy involves more, however, than a minor inconvenience! This first glance also overlooks the importance of women's rights to autonomy (self-determination) and to decide what happens to their bodies.

Judith Jarvis Thomson argues that a right to life, by itself, does not give anyone a right to use another person's body for nine months. In general, our right to decide what happens to our bodies is not trivial compared with another person's right to life. She asks us to imagine this:

> You wake up in the morning and find yourself back to back in bed with an unconscious violinist. A famous unconscious violinist. He has been

found to have a fatal kidney ailment, and the Society of Music Lovers has canvassed all the available medical records and found that you alone have the right blood type to help. They have therefore kidnapped you, and last night the violinist's circulatory system was plugged into yours, so that your kidneys can be used to extract poisons from his blood as well as your own."[10]

The Society of Music Lovers apologizes to you, but they emphasize the importance of the violinist's right to life, which is in fact of obviously greater importance than any inconvenience to you.

Most of us would be outraged if this happened to us, and we would reject the notion that another person's right to life gives that person a right to use another's body. To allow the violinist to remain hooked up to one's blood supply would be an act of generosity, but the violinist's right to life does not by itself confer an obligation. By analogy, the fetus's right to life does not by itself give it a right to a woman's body. In general, a right to life does not entail an unconditional right to any and all resources that society has available to keep us alive; nor does it give us an absolute right never to be killed (or allowed to die) under any circumstances. It gives only a right not to be killed unjustly, and we need further argument to show whether abortion constitutes an unjust killing of a fetus.

Indeed, conservatives do have a further argument. They argue that, in most instances, a woman tacitly gives the fetus a right to use her body. The violinist case is analogous only to pregnancies caused by rape (as Thomson is also aware). When a woman engages in sexual intercourse she knows of the risk of getting pregnant, or at least she can be expected to know that risk. Hence, she can be held responsible for the pregnancy which results from her conduct, and she implicitly grants the fetus the right to the essential means for its survival until it becomes able to survive outside the uterus. The logical implication is that women unwilling to accept that responsibility—even with accidental pregnancy—should remain sexually abstinent.

Is sexual abstinence an unreasonable demand? Liberals insist it is. By taking every reasonable precaution in using birth control, a woman shows she is not granting a fetus (caused by an accidental pregnancy) the right to use her body. Thus, liberals argue that in these cases, at least, abortion is permissible. Liberals go even further, however. Suppose we could agree that responsible sexual conduct implies the use of birth control (both to prevent unwanted pregnancies and, by means of condoms, to prevent AIDS). We might recognize that a woman who has several abortions—essentially using abortion as a form of birth control—is not acting responsibly. Does it follow that she gives the fetus a right to use her body, and hence that the fetus's right obligates her to give birth to the fetus, as conservatives contend? Liberals argue that the woman's failure to engage in responsible sex does not imply that she has given the fetus the right to her body for nine months. A woman's right to decide what happens in and to her body overrides any right the fetus has.

We have returned to moral gridlock between liberals and conservatives. The assumption that the fetus is a person with a right to life does not bring conservatives and liberals closer together. Conservatives weigh the fetus's right to life more heavily than liberals, and liberals weigh the woman's right to decide what happens to her body more heavily than conservatives. What do moderates have to say at this point?

Moderates

Jane English, who argued that we cannot determine precisely when a fetus becomes a person, asks us to assume for the sake of argument that a fetus is not a person. What follows? It does not follow that we can treat the fetus in any way we like. Animals are not persons, but it is immoral to torture them for fun, and perhaps it is wrong to kill them without a good reason. Just because a living thing is not a person does not mean it has no moral significance at all. Advanced fetuses are at least person-like, and that gives them moral significance. Less-advanced fetuses, at least at intermediary stages of development, may also have some moral significance that demands we have good reasons before aborting them.

Even if we are unhappy with this talk about "some moral significance," we need to attend to certain psychological facts about our response to person-like fetuses. To maintain our moral sensitivity we must preserve a coherence among such moral attitudes as respect, sympathy, and guilt. A casual attitude about abortion can erode that coherence. English writes, "Thus, I think that anti-abortion forces are indeed giving their strongest arguments when they point to the similarities between a fetus and a baby, and when they try to evoke our emotional attachment to and sympathy for the fetus. An early horror story from New York about nurses who were expected to alternate between caring for six-week premature infants and disposing of viable 24-week aborted fetuses is just that—a horror story."[11]

English appeals to the bad consequences that can follow from a failure to recognize some moral significance to fetuses, even if they are not fully persons. In effect, this part of her argument is rule-utilitarian in that it attends to the consequences of adopting certain general attitudes and rules regarding fetuses. Other moderates think in more contextual terms, perhaps act-utilitarian terms. They recommend a case-by-case analysis of each abortion decision, asking: What are the consequences, good and bad, of abortion or childbirth in particular circumstances? This approach bypasses the abstract arguments over rights that characterize the disagreements between conservatives and liberals.

For example, suppose that giving birth would bring into the world an unwanted child whose mother is unable to give loving care to the child. Suppose that having a child would subvert a woman's education and career plans, as well as lead her peers to stigmatize her. Suppose a fetus has been diagnosed with a very serious genetic disease that calls into question whether it will have a meaningful life and adds great hardship to its caregivers. Suppose a woman is willing to give the child up for adoption, but for various reasons the child would be unlikely to be adopted and the government happens to provide inadequate resources to care for orphans. The possible situations are varied, and each example must be examined in its full complexity. As a result, moderates urge that women's rights sometimes, but not always, override the moral status of the fetus.

Issue 3: Laws and Government Policies

Disagreements over the first two issues—the status of the fetus and the balance of moral factors—are reflected in the differences over the third issue: What laws and government policies concerning abortion are morally justified? Liberals support *Roe v. Wade*. They also favor government-funded abortions for women who lack the financial resources for abortion. Conservatives seek to overturn *Roe v. Wade* and to pass laws preventing most abortions. Moderates want abortions to be legal at least up to two or three months, and are open to compromises that would modify *Roe v. Wade*.

The question of legality is a distinctive new issue that invokes new moral reasons. In particular, justified laws must be sensitive to political settings—in particular, to the democratic setting in the United States—and to overall consequences of the laws. Thus, a conservative or moderate on the first two issues might consistently support *Roe v. Wade* on the grounds that in democracies adults should be allowed to make their personal choices, especially in situations where there is no moral consensus about the first two issues. This consistency is especially clear for those conservatives who understand their attitudes on abortion to be grounded in their religious beliefs, which they know cannot be the basis for laws in a democracy which separates church and state.

Again, there are consequences which need to be weighed in assessing which laws are morally justified. In particular, the illegality of abortion would not in itself end abortions, but only reduce them by making them more difficult to obtain, forcing women to travel to places where abortions remain legal. Restrictive laws would also result in death and injuries from illegally performed abortions by unqualified persons. These consequences need to be weighed by all parties in deciding which laws are feasible and desirable, although they do not by themselves settle the issue.

There are also consequences of the legal status of abortion, such as the continuing political turmoil and social disruption since *Roe v. Wade*. Since

1988, for example, the conservative group Operation Rescue has attempted (and often succeeded) in using civil disobedience to block entrance to or to close abortion clinics. Others have engaged in violent acts, including the bombing of abortion clinics. In March 1993, one pro-life activist murdered a Florida gynecologist who performed abortions. Conservatives regard this violence as minor compared with the scale of what they see as the widespread abortion-killings of babies.

Most laws are the products of compromises, and moderates urge that abortion laws clearly exemplify an instance where compromise is desirable. As Martin Benjamin points out, the abortion controversy meets all four conditions for circumstances calling for compromise: (1) The facts are uncertain (about world-views, about the long-term effects of new and traditional ways of life); (2) the moral issues are complex; (3) the disputing parties are in continuing and cooperative relationships as citizens of the same country; and (4) the legal issues must be resolved to maintain community.[12] What compromises concerning abortion laws are reasonable and possible?

Martin Benjamin supports the idea of a compromise that would reject *Roe v. Wade* by restricting abortions after three months or even ten weeks, except for unusual circumstances such as those presented by threats to the woman's health, severe genetic deformities, and cases of rape and incest (where the victim did not make an earlier decision for an abortion). In his view, this change in the law would embody genuine concessions on each side. Yet, the vast majority of abortions take place during the early months of pregnancy, and it seems doubtful that conservatives would endorse a compromise that left the number of abortions essentially unchanged.

Benjamin points out that compromise has proven extraordinarily difficult because abortion is at the center of wider controversies concerning the ethics of sex, love, and gender roles. Indeed, abortion is the lightning rod for disputes between religious conservatives and feminists—two groups which defend clashing ideals surrounding sexual conduct and gender roles.[13] The most vocal part of the pro-life movement sees abortion as violating its religious conviction that the proper role of sex is procreation within marriage. The most vocal part of the pro-choice movement sees the right to abortion as a symbol for diversity of outlook on sex in relation to love, and also as supporting the freedom of women to pursue careers previously closed to them.

One obvious hope for compromise is to find widely acceptable ways to prevent unwanted pregnancies. For example, most people agree that wider education may be helpful (though some conservatives oppose the funding of sex education programs, which in their view encourage sexual promiscuity). Another possible preventive measure would be to make birth control more effective, for instance, by making condoms easily available—a practice that is occurring anyway in order to prevent AIDS. Many conservatives have opposed this practice because it encourages premarital sex, which they find immoral. Another possibility is pregnancy counseling designed to inform women of their options, including adoption. Liberals have been opposed to this because they suspect it leads to coercion, rather than value-neutral counseling. Despite these difficulties confronting compromise, some legislators have managed to develop compromises on education and counseling programs in their states.[14]

Liberals might be open to the possibility of compromises which enable attention and resources to shift away from the preoccupation with abortion and toward other pressing social needs. For example, they might stop pushing for laws which allow public money to be used to fund abortions for women who cannot afford them, knowing that such laws require conservatives to pay taxes to fund acts which conservatives regard as killing.

Finally, there is always the hope for increased tolerance and understanding of opposing world-views that often frame abortion debates. Is that hope realistic, and could it at least lessen the preoccupation with abortion that overshadows other issues which all agree are also important for our society to confront?

SUMMARY

We distinguished three moral issues concerning abortion. First, is the fetus a person with a right to life (or who otherwise possesses full moral status in the community of persons)? Conservatives argue that the fetus is a person because it is genetically human, because the only nonarbitrary place to draw a line identifying personhood is at conception, and because fetuses are just like other humans in their prospects for a valuable future. Liberals argue that fetuses are not persons, because persons have features such as rationality and self-awareness that fetuses do not have. Moderates draw the line between persons and nonpersons at points in between conception and viability; alternatively they argue that no sharp lines can be drawn at all and that the fetus has a partial moral status (some moral worth, but not as much as persons).

The second issue arises when we assume the fetus is a person with a right to life (or otherwise has full moral status in the moral community). How is its right to life to be weighed against the woman's right to autonomy and her right to decide what happens in and to her body? Conservatives see the fetus's right as most important, while liberals regard the woman's right as most important. Moderates insist on examining particular cases and contexts, believing that some, but not all, abortions are morally justified.

The third issue concerns the moral justification of the laws and government policies governing abortion. This issue is closely related to the first two issues, but raises new questions about democratic rights to private decision making and the potentially adverse effects of all laws.

DISCUSSION TOPICS

1   Don Marquis argued that there is a strong moral presumption against abortion because fetuses have valuable futures, just as you and I have, and because it is prima facie immoral to kill creatures with valuable futures. Assess his argument, and in doing so consider the following questions. (a) Marquis does not think his argument applies to sperm and ova, since at the time of conception there are millions of sperm but no entity (sperm or ovum) which we can identify as having a valuable future like our future. Do you agree, or does this pose a problem for his view? (b) Does Marquis's argument assume that the fetus is the same creature as the adult person it may become, rather than just a precursor to that person? If so, does this pose a problem for his view? (c) Is the moral principle he cites justified, or is the justified principle something like: It is prima facie wrong to kill creatures which have a valuable future *and* are already valuable in some way?

2   According to the golden rule, we should do to others what we would have them do to us. Assuming that we value our lives, we are glad that our mothers did not abort us when we were fetuses. To universalize in the spirit of the Golden Rule, does it follow that we should not engage in abortions?[15]

3   Many (though not all) people believe abortion is permissible when a woman is made pregnant by a rapist, thereby recognizing the exceptional burden placed on women (and their husbands) who are victimized twice: once from the rape and again from bringing a rapist's child into the world. Yet, on the assumption that the zygote is a person, the rapist's child is completely innocent—as innocent as any other child. If the conservative allows an exception here, must a consistent perspective allow other exceptions when a woman may suffer great burdens in bringing a child to birth, burdens such as educational and career sacrifices? Or is the case of rape unique and not suitable to generalization?

4   Liberals sometimes point out that nearly everyone agrees that abortion is permissible in order to save the life of a woman, as when a pregnancy threatens a woman's life because of her poor health or because of other medical complications. They then extend the idea of self-defense to include the psychological defense of a woman who would suffer extreme emotional distress or damage to her career (and livelihood) by having an unwanted child. (a) If we assume (for the sake of argument) that a fetus is a person with a right to life, is it obvious that a woman's right to self-defense overrides the fetus's right to life? (b) What would you say about this argument: The woman has had an opportunity to live and hence, in fairness, the fetus should been given a similar opportunity?

5   Do you think a husband or lover who impregnates a woman should have the right to share in the abortion decision? If not, are we consistent when we demand that fathers assume full responsibility for their children? "Why should men share responsibility for child support or childrearing if they cannot share in what is asserted to be the woman's sole decision?"[16]

6   Amniocentesis and other prenatal diagnostic techniques provide detailed information about the genetic nature of developing fetuses at the stage when abortions are legal. This information sometimes influences abortion decisions. Are abortions for any of the following reasons morally acceptable? (a) The fetus has a

severe genetic abnormality, such as spina bifida. (b) The fetus has a significant, but not life-threatening, genetic abnormality, such as Down's syndrome. (c) The fetus is a girl and a couple wants a boy instead (or vice versa).

7   Is abortion so important that it should continue to dominate American politics, especially in light of its present role as a focus for disagreements among religious conservatives and feminists? Or do you agree that, to minimize social turmoil, compromise is needed in the formulation of laws and social policies concerning abortion? If so, can you think of abortion laws that are promising compromises?

8   Anthony Weston views *Roe v. Wade* as already an acceptable compromise which reasonably balances conflicting reasons and views by forbidding some abortions (those after viability) while making others permissible. He also draws attention to what he sees as a "vital asymmetry" between the pro-life and pro-choice positions: "'Pro-choice' is not 'anti-life'; the argument [for it] is only that other values also matter, that the appeal to 'life' does not close the question. 'Pro-life,' however, *is* anti-'choice'; the claim is that the value of one of the lives in question overrides all other values and all other lives, and precludes any other choice."[17] Is Weston correct in seeing a moral asymmetry in the pro-life and pro-choice positions? And does *Roe v. Wade* constitute a reasonable compromise on abortion?

9   One hope is that new medical technologies for birth control will quiet the abortion controversy. In recent years, liberals heralded RU 486, the newly developed French drug, as such a remedy. The drug induces abortions during the early weeks of a pregnancy and has a far lower rate of complication than other abortion techniques. Pressure from conservative groups led President Bush to prevent the Food and Drug Administration from testing the drug; President Clinton reversed that decision. If this or other drugs become available, abortion confrontations may be altered in some ways, if only because fewer abortion clinics—the visible target for anti-abortion groups—would be needed. Would this or other birth control techniques be likely to quell abortion controversies?

SUGGESTED READINGS

Baird, Robert M., and Stuart E. Rosenbaum (eds.). *The Ethics of Abortion*. Buffalo, NY: Prometheus Books, 1989.

Brody, Baruch. *Abortion and the Sanctity of Human Life: A Philosophical View*. Cambridge, MA: MIT Press, 1975.

Callahan, Daniel. *Abortion: Law, Choice and Morality*. London: Collier-Macmillan, 1970.

Callahan, Sidney, and Daniel Callahan (eds.). *Abortion: Understanding Differences*. New York: Plenum, 1984.

Feinberg, Joel, and Barbara Baum Levenbook. "Abortion." In T. Regan (ed.), *Matters of Life and Death*. 3rd ed. New York: Random House, 1993.

Feinberg, Joel (ed.). *The Problem of Abortion*. 2nd ed. Belmont, CA: Wadsworth, 1984.

Garfield, Jay L., and Patricia Hennessey (eds.). *Abortion: Moral and Legal Perspectives.* Amherst, MA: University of Massachusetts Press, 1984.

Kamm, F. M. *Creation and Abortion: A Study in Moral and Legal Philosophy.* New York: Oxford University Press, 1992.

Luker, Kristin. *Abortion and Politics of Motherhood.* Berkeley, CA: University of California Press, 1984.

Noonan, John T., Jr. *A Private Choice: Abortion in America in the Seventies.* New York: The Free Press, 1979.

Petchesky, Rosalind Pollack. *Abortion and Woman's Choice.* Boston, MA: Northeastern University Press, 1985.

Pojman, Louis P., and Francis J. Beckwith (eds.). *The Abortion Controversy: A Reader.* Boston, MA: Jones and Bartlett, 1994.

Schwarz, Stephen D. *The Moral Question of Abortion.* Chicago: Loyola University Press, 1990.

Sumner, Wayne. *Abortion and Moral Theory.* Princeton, NJ: Princeton University Press, 1981.

Tooley, Michael. *Abortion and Infanticide.* Oxford: Oxford University Press, 1983.

Weston, Anthony. *Toward Better Problems: New Perspectives on Abortion, Animal Rights, the Environment, and Justice.* Philadelphia, PA: Temple University Press, 1992.

CHAPTER 13

Rape and Sexual Harassment

Fear of rape is part of the daily life of many women. Tragically, the fear is fully warranted: It is estimated that one in five women alive today will be raped, and the percentage of women raped is even higher in some American cities already. These statistics represent estimates, because only about one in ten rapes is even reported. Recent studies have suggested that sexual harassment is also a problem on a much greater scale than is commonly believed.

Rape is cruel and coercive. Sexual harassment is coercive and frequently cruel. As such, rape and sexual harassment constitute failures to maintain minimal standards of decency; they involve direct assaults on the dignity of people. We will preface our discussion with some general comments on cruelty and coercion.

Coercion and the Right to Personal Autonomy

Coercion entails unjustified interference with the freedom of others. It is an infringement on another's legitimate efforts to determine her or his own destiny, a violation of the right to personal autonomy.

Personal autonomy is a wider notion than moral autonomy, a concept introduced in our discussions of Kohlberg, Gilligan, and Kant. Recall that moral autonomy consists of the ability to make one's own moral judgments based on some degree of moral caring. Moral autonomy focuses on moral reasoning and judgment rather than on action per se, although reasoning, judging, and acting certainly are closely connected. *Personal autonomy*, by contrast, pertains to all reasoning and acting, not just moral reasoning. Its close synonyms are *self-determination* and *self-governance*, and it is a central component of authenticity.

As Lawrence Haworth points out, the term *personal autonomy* (and each of its synonyms) has two senses, one purely descriptive and one normative. The descriptive sense refers to certain facts about people who exercise personal autonomy:

> In some contexts, saying a person is autonomous is a way of attributing to him the personal characteristic of being in charge of his own life. He is not overly dependent on others and not swamped by his own passions; he has the ability to see through to completion those plans and projects he sets for himself. He has, one may say, procedural independence, self-control, and competence. In these contexts, "autonomy" is a descriptive term. It is an empirical [i.e., purely factual] question whether, in what respects, and to what degree a person is autonomous.[1]

According to this definition, personal autonomy has three main aspects. First, it involves "procedural independence." This means that the person's actions are not coerced by force, duress, fraud, deception, or other forms of constraints imposed by individuals or society. The idea is that the procedures used by the autonomous person in making decisions are not undermined by external intervention.

Second, autonomous persons are competent to guide their own lives. They have the ability to choose their actions by making rational decisions and acting on them. Their reasoning is not, for example, distorted by major biases that deflect them from the truth, and they are able to live up to their convictions without frequent weakness of will.

Third, they have "substantive independence" in that they are not excessively dependent on other people. "Excessively dependent" is a vague term, but it refers, for example, to persons who willingly give up any attempt to think for themselves, relying on someone else to think for them. This is vividly illustrated by persons who join cults in order to escape the difficulties they have found in governing their own lives.

The normative sense of personal autonomy refers to the moral right to exercise personal autonomy in the descriptive sense. When we claim that someone has violated our autonomy, we mean they have violated our right to guide our own lives. We can also fail to be autonomous by improperly exercising our right to autonomy: Weakness of will and self-deception undermine personal autonomy just as much as do manipulators and deceivers. In discussing rape and sexual harassment, however, our focus will be on violations of another person's right to personal autonomy.

Why is the right to personal autonomy morally important? In Kant's view, to violate that right is to treat persons as mere means to one's own ends, thereby violating the duty to respect the dignity of others. In Mill's view (expressed in *On Liberty*) personal autonomy is the primary avenue to the pursuit of happiness, and hence to undermine autonomy is to decrease the opportunities for finding happiness. In Locke's view, the right to personal autonomy is essentially the same as the right to liberty—the fundamental human right that needs no further justification. While Locke would view autonomy as a negative right (a right to be free from interference), Melden might say it implies a positive right to have society create an environment where rape and sexual harassment are strongly discouraged.

Haworth believes that personal autonomy is intrinsically good (good in and of itself). The ability and willingness to guide one's own life is desirable for its own sake, apart from any further appeal to duties, happiness, or human rights. We might say it is a virtue: It is a human excellence that should be preserved despite pressures from other people and temptations from within; for it makes possible creativity, individuality, authenticity, and innovative personal relationships.

Cruelty

Our introduction of cruelty will be brief, even though it takes innumerable forms. One form is omitted actions, such as when we speak of the "cruel indifference" of an insensitive bureaucrat or of the callousness of some people concerning world hunger. There are cruel emotions, such as the enjoyment of an innocent victim's suffering (a form of sadism); cruel attitudes, such as those of the racist and sexist; cruel hopes, such as the hope to see an innocent child hurt; and cruel motives and desires, such as the desire to augment one's reputation by unfairly criticizing someone.

The most familiar type of cruelty is deliberate infliction of suffering without justification. When the suffering is one's own, masochism is involved. When the suffering is that of another person, as in rape and some sexual harassment, sadism—that is, the enjoyment of the suffering of another person—may be involved.

Most modern moral perspectives, from the Renaissance on, have regarded cruelty as the worst form of immorality. It is noteworthy, however, that this was not true of the predominant attitudes during the Middle Ages. In particular, medieval Christianity viewed pride, not cruelty, as the worst sin. Cruelty was not even listed as one of the seven deadly sins, even though lesser vices, such as gluttony and lust, were. Much of contemporary moral thought consists of identifying subtle forms of cruelty as well as blatant forms that have been unduly tolerated. Some sexual harassment falls into the first category, while rape falls into the second category.

Motivations to Rape

Most rapes betray a cruelty that has one of the following underlying motivations: (1) maliciousness, that is, cruelty prompted by hatred or the desire to hurt, (2) means-to-end motivation, that is, cruelty intended as the means to some further desired purpose, (3) unintended cruelty that arises incidentally to the pursuit of other purposes, and (4) cruelty based on indifference to the suffering of the victim. (Note: In the following discussion, rapists are referred to in terms of male pronouns because the overwhelming majority of rapes are committed by men against women. Even though homosexual and lesbian rapes do occur, especially in prisons, and rape of men by women is possible, these instances are comparatively rare.)

Malice is the motive when the rapist deliberately seeks to degrade and injure the victim and (sadistically) takes pleasure in dominating her and causing her to suffer. Means-to-end motivation occurs when the rapist seeks some further goal; for example, he may seek peer approval from fellow gang members or fraternity brothers who have dared him to commit the rape. Unintended cruelty results when the rapist thinks he is not using coercion, as when he believes that a woman wants him to engage in forcible intercourse with her despite her protestations. Cruelty based on indifference is illustrated by a sociopathic rapist who is completely indifferent to the feelings of the victim.

According to the traditional male-oriented perspective, the act of rape depended primarily on means-to-end motivation. Rape was regarded as a sex-oriented crime in which the rapist used the victim as the means to attain his own sexual satisfaction. Both feminists and experimental psychologists have refuted this view. The end sought is not sexual satisfaction per se; instead, it is either (1) pleasure in the violence or (2) self-esteem derived from power over the victim (often vicariously experienced as power over all women).

Of course, the rapist often deceives himself about his cruelty and hate. For example, he embraces the myth that women secretly want to be raped and that their protests are not genuine, or he convinces himself that a particular woman invites the rape by her clothing and behavior. As we saw in Chapter 6, self-deception does not mitigate culpability. In fact, in the case of rape it compounds guilt, because the rapist is blameworthy both for cruelty and for easing his conscience at the expense of the victim and the truth.

What Is Wrong with Rape?

Rape is a clear-cut paradigm of immorality, but precisely why is it immoral? Part of the answer concerns motives; in particular, rape is immoral if the rapist's motives are to enjoy illegitimate control over the victim, to degrade an innocent person, or to enjoy the victim's suffering. Most of the answer, however, pertains to the act of rape itself and its effects on the victim.

In an insightful essay, Susan Griffin offered the following explanation of why rape is immoral:

Rape is an act of aggression in which the victim is denied her self-determination. It is an act of violence which, if not actually followed by beatings or murder, nevertheless always carries with it the threat of death. And finally, rape is a form of mass terrorism, for the victims of rape are chosen indiscriminately, but the propagandists for male supremacy broadcast that it is women who cause rape by being unchaste or in the wrong place at the wrong time, by behaving as though they were free.[2]

Griffin suggests that rape is immoral because it causes at least three kinds of harm to women. First, the act is a violation of a woman's right to self-determination or personal autonomy, a view that follows logically from the definition of rape as sexual intercourse against or without a person's consent. Second, rape inflicts suffering of several kinds: terror, fear for one's life, immediate physical pain, and trauma that endures years after the assault. Third, because rape is widespread, it creates warranted fear that restricts the range of women's activities, thereby again violating their right to autonomy.

There is yet another reason why rape is deeply immoral. In our culture sexuality is regarded as central to a person's identity. Sexuality is also an aspect of one's life in which freedom and self-determination are very highly valued. In violating this area of private life, the rapist directly assaults the self-respect of his victim. Usually he is well aware of this fact, and he intends to communicate utter disrespect and contempt for the victim *as* a woman.

Acquaintance Rape Versus Consent

Susan Griffin's essay, which appeared in 1971, focused on rapists who choose their victims indiscriminately. Since then it has been learned that most rapists are acquainted with their victims prior to the rape. This is especially true when the victim is a college student. Such "acquaintance rape" sometimes occurs on dates, as in the following examples of "date rape" taken from studies done by the sociologist William B. Sanders:*

[1] A blind date had been arranged between the victim and suspect. The couple went out to dinner together and then for drinks. At the apartment, the man began making overtures to the victim, and she declined. Then the suspect began slapping the victim and took her into the bedroom where he raped her.

[2] Victim picked up suspect in a bar and drove him in her car to a college parking lot. The suspect propositioned the victim, and the victim

said she was "in the mood for some loving." At the parking lot, the victim changed her mind since the man's demeanor became ugly—he offered her money. The suspect then grabbed the victim and demanded she take her pants off, which she did after repeated demands and in fear for her safety, and he raped her.[3]

In the first case there is clearly no consent at any time. What should be said, however, about the second case, in which there is initial consent that is later withdrawn? Does the victim's initial agreement constitute a tacit consent to the man's subsequent conduct, especially if they had already voluntarily engaged in some sexual activity? Surely not. An agreement to play a game of tennis does not give one's partner consent to force one to finish the game against one's later wishes; the same is even more true of sexual activity. Both a woman and a man have the right to end a sexual encounter at any time, in particular when what is intended as a mutually pleasurable activity ceases to be so.

Gradually, the law has begun to accept what women have been saying for some time: No means no—at any time during a sexual encounter. In 1992, Mike Tyson, heavyweight champion boxer, was found guilty of rape and sentenced to six years in jail. He and the woman had been drinking and then went to his room in the early morning hours. Tyson took for granted that the woman was giving tacit consent, but the courts made it clear that a woman is free to refuse intercourse at any stage of flirting or sexual foreplay.

Is the woman nevertheless partially responsible and blameworthy for "precipitating" a rape when she engages in provocative behavior? Susan Brownmiller offers the following answer in *Against Our Will: Men, Women, and Rape*, a book that has drawn increased attention to rape:

> Some men might consider a housewife who lets a strange man into her house for a glass of water guilty of precipitant behavior, and more men would consider a female hitchhiker who accepts a ride from an unknown male guilty of precipitant behavior. Rape-minded men would consider both actions tantamount to an open invitation. I, on the other hand, consider the housewife and hitchhiker insufficiently wary, but in no way would I consider their actions provocative or even mildly precipitant. Similarly, most men seem to consider a woman who engages in sex play but stops short of intercourse guilty not only of precipitant behavior, but of cruel, provocative behavior with no excuse, yet I and my sister feminists would argue that her actions are perfectly allowable and quite within the bounds of human decency and rational decisions.[4]

Brownmiller here argues that women have the same right to control over their lives and sexual conduct that men take for granted over theirs. The right to self-determination is held equally by women and men, despite the unfair double standard by which our society conventionally affords men greater license in their sexual activities.

This double standard, we might add, has even entered into the traditional legal definition of rape. That definition explicitly excluded forcible and violent intercourse within marriage after a wife has refused her husband's sexual advances. The exclusion was based on the assumption that wives are the sexual property of their husbands, and it also presupposed that a consent to marriage entailed a sweeping consent to sexual intercourse at any time. Laws are changing, but it remains difficult to prove in court that a rape took place when a married or unmarried victim has consented on previous occasions to sexual intercourse with the rapist.

Sexual Harassment

Sexual harassment has received unprecedented national attention since October 1991 when Anita Hill testified at the confirmation hearings for Supreme Court nominee Clarence Thomas. Hill reported that, years earlier, when she worked for Thomas, he had sexually harassed her with lewd remarks and sexual provocations. Hill's credentials were impeccable, and at the time of the hearings she was a respected professor of law. Thomas insisted he was an innocent victim of a "high-tech lynching." The majority of Americans believed him, paving the way for his ratification as the only African-American Supreme Court justice (replacing the retired Thurgood Marshall, who had been the only other African-American Supreme Court justice). About one-third of Americans believed Anita Hill and were convinced that a person who had engaged in sexual harassment had been appointed to the Supreme Court. Debates over this episode continue today, and they have drawn attention to widespread sexual harassment at the workplace and in academia.

Sexual harassment is any sexually oriented act or practice involving intimidation, coercion, or unfair sexual conduct.* In everyday speech the word *harassment* suggests repeated aggravation or persistent annoyance. As part of the expression "sexual harassment," however, it carries the special connotation of misuse of power or authority, where authority consists of institutionally granted forms of power. This can occur in a single episode that is not repeated. The primary habitats of sexual harassment are authority relationships, in particular at work and school. Before focusing on these authority contexts, however, let us mention cases involving unequal power that do not involve authority.

When a man leers, jeers, or whistles at a woman in a public setting, he may be "hassling" her, that is, bothering or irritating her. Hassling becomes

---

*This definition applies to sexual assault, although sexual assault is sometimes treated as an offense distinct from sexual harassment.

sexual harassment when similar acts occur in threatening situations, for instance when the man and woman are strangers alone on an isolated street at night; another such situation occurs when the man is part of a group of men confronting and blocking the woman's path. Whatever the man's actual intentions may be, his conduct is reasonably interpreted in such situations as endangering or disrupting the woman's life.

The Workplace

Sexual harassment by an employer (usually, though not always, male) of an employee (usually female) involves abuse of institutional authority, that is, the abuse of power given to the employer by the institution. Recent legislation and Supreme Court rulings define sexual harassment in the workplace as essentially any sexually oriented practice that threatens jobs or work performance.

Obvious examples include threats to fire or demote an employee unless sexual favors are granted, deliberate touching in unwanted ways, and inappropriate comments on the clothing and physical appearance of an employee. A different kind of sexual harassment occurs when employers reveal details about their personal sex lives to their employees against the employees' wishes. The courts have also ruled that harassment occurs when a male supervisor or colleague posts *Playboy* centerfolds in an office to which women have access. All these forms of behavior are restricted by sex discrimination laws that prohibit differential treatment of women and men in unfair ways.

Academia

Academia, like the workplace, is structured according to authority relationships. This fact is downplayed on campuses where faculty members are encouraged to give personal attention to students, where there is trust between students and professors, and where eccentric behavior is tolerated. Nevertheless, professors do have considerable control over their students through grading practices and their institutional authority to guide the educational process. In addition, professors are granted an exceptionally high degree of personal autonomy in carrying out their functions.

As was noted, sexual harassment need not involve assault on or physical restraint of someone against that person's will. In what way or ways, then, is sexual harassment in academia coercive? Let us consider three types of sexual harassment: (1) threats of penalties, (2) annoyance, and (3) offers of rewards.

Sexual threats are the clearest example of coercion. In extreme cases, professors either hint or directly state that, unless students sleep with them, the students will receive lower grades than their work warrants. This interferes with the agency of the student in that a threat suggests that something unwanted will occur unless one complies. When students do not want to date or have sex with professors, their situation has been worsened by the threat: Either they must accede to a professor's wishes and do something unwanted or they run the risk of receiving an undeserved grade. Even if the student does want to sleep with the professor, the professor is nevertheless trying to manipulate the situation unfairly, using means outside the bounds of understood professional ethics. The threat is coercive, even when the student does not experience it as such.

Sexual annoyance occurs when a professor's sexual overtures cause a student to feel uncomfortable or anxious, or when the overture in any other way creates a climate that distracts from the learning process. Such an overture normally raises (quite reasonable) fears that the professor might retaliate if the student objects to the advance. Sexual annoyance is wrong precisely because it impedes or threatens to impede the learning relationship between student and professor. In this way it also violates the right to self-determination of the student who has chosen to be in that situation to learn. Sexual annoyance is also wrong because of the disrespect demonstrated by focusing attention on one aspect of the student—the sexual one—in a context where that focus is understood to be inappropriate.

Sexual offers represent attempts to influence behavior by promising a benefit. For example, it is unethical for a professor to offer to raise a student's deserved grade from a C to an A on the condition that the student agree to a date. Not only is the professor violating the standards of integrity required in grading, but the professor is treating all students in the class unfairly. Is there, however, coercion involved in such cases? After all, a desired good (the higher grade) is being offered, and the student seemingly is free to accept or reject the offer. Indeed, Michael Bayles argues that such offers are not coercive when the student wants what is offered:

> Assume there is a mediocre woman graduate student who would not receive an assistantship. Suppose the department chairman offers her one if she goes to bed with him, and she does so. In what sense has the graduate student acted against her will? She apparently preferred having an assistantship and sleeping with the chairman to not sleeping with him and not having an assistantship. So it would appear that she did what she wanted in the situation.... The fact that a choice has an undesirable consequence [i.e., having to sleep with the chairman] does not make it against one's will. One may prefer to have clean teeth without having to brush them; nonetheless, one is not acting against one's will when one brushes them.[5]

Bayles concludes that the student's situation is actually improved by the offer because her options are preferable (in her eyes) to what they were before, and in any case Bayles claims that she is free without coercion to choose either way.

This view fails to take account of how these situations generate fear. In particular, there is fear that the professor might penalize the student for refusing the offer, a valid fear considering the professor has already (in making the offer) violated the professional standards of fairness in allocating assistantships. Moreover, such bribes exert an undue influence that distorts the choices the student should have to confront. In addition, as John Hughes and Larry May argue, such offers constitute a form of sex discrimination. As such, they directly hurt the victim, who is usually a woman, and also indirectly hurt all women:

> Sexual harassment is a form of sex discrimination because (1) the policy is based on a ...[sex-specific] criterion of classification, which adversely affects members of only one sex-class, and (2) the policy is based on and perpetuates a sex stereotype [of women as weak and vulnerable] which stigmatizes the class of women and thus, potentially, all of its members.[6]

Here is one final situation: What should be said of the professor who flirts with students and, upon receiving a positive response, asks them to bed? Assume there are no threats, no annoying overtures, and no offers amounting to undue influence. Can we then conclude that this is not sexual harassment, but rather the exercise of free choice in sexual matters? Before we accept that conclusion, let us consider the following argument by Billie Dziech and Linda Weiner:

> Whatever the intent, sexual give-and-take is based on mutual consent of equals. This is obviously not the case in sexual harassment. Normal sexual give-and-take is not possible in student-teacher relationships because the power imbalance and role disparity are too great.[7]

Later, Dziech and Wiener add the following comment:

> Attraction between professor and student may occur, but it is almost impossible for that attraction to be acted on successfully given the average campus environment and the restrictions on student-teacher roles. If legitimate attractions do occur, the couple's regard for the relationship should lead them to restrain themselves until their roles change.[8]

Is this excessive caution? Is it perhaps an infringement of the rights of both students and faculty in matters of sex and love? Or does the risk of coercion in student-faculty relationships warrant the restraint recommended by Dziech and Wiener? We will return to these questions in the "Discussion Topics" section.

SUMMARY

Respect for other people requires us to honor their right to personal autonomy or self-determination. This right creates obligations not to inter-

fere in people's legitimate areas of personal prerogative, as well as obligations to contribute to making society supportive of personal autonomy.
Personal autonomy includes *moral autonomy* (the ability and willingness to
form reasonable moral judgments and to act on them), but it encompasses
much more. It requires procedural independence (the freedom from coercion or deception by others), competence (self-control and the exercise of
rationality), and substantive independence (lack of excessive dependence
on others).

Rape violates personal autonomy by denying sexual choice, an area of
self-determination central to personal identity and self-respect. This is true
of individual acts of rape, which by definition involve the violation of consent. It is equally true, however, of rape as a widespread practice, because
the very real threat of rape forces women to restrict their activities.

Rape is also a form of cruelty in which suffering is deliberately and
without any justification inflicted on a person. The suffering includes immediate physical pain, terror and fear for one's life, and trauma that lasts
for years afterward. The rapist's intentions are violent rather than primarily sexual per se and typically rape is motivated by a derivation of self-esteem
through sexual dominance or an enjoyment of the violent subjugation of
women.

Although sexual harassment often involves cruelty, it is of special interest
because of the ways it violates self-determination. It can be defined as any
sexually oriented act or practice involving intimidation, coercion, or unfair
sexual conduct. Most often it involves abuse of authority relationships at
work and school. Sexual harassment is most commonly exhibited through
sexual threats, sexual annoyance, and sexual offers, each of which creates
conditions that disrupt work and learning.

DISCUSSION TOPICS

1 Date rape sometimes occurs when the rapist is drunk or on drugs, and it also occurs when the victim is intoxicated. Explain what you see as the problems in determining whether there is consent when the victim is partially or completely
   intoxicated. Should it be assumed that when individuals are intoxicated, they
   cannot give voluntary consent to intercourse? Also, is an intoxicated rapist less
   blameworthy than a sober one?

   In answering these questions, identify and discuss the moral issues involved
   in the following rape reported by Robin Warshaw in *I Never Called It Rape*. At
   the time of the rape the woman was in her first year attending a large university
   and living in coed dorms. She met an attractive football player at a dorm party.

   He wasn't drinking, but he was feeding me alcohol. He asked me to come
   back to his room—it was right down the hall from where all of us were
   [partying].... I thought it was just like, "Let's get out of this party." When

we got to his room and I saw there was nobody there, I didn't think I could do anything about it.

We started kissing and then he started taking off my clothes. I kept telling him to stop and I was crying. I was scared of him and thought he was going to hurt me.... He had a hand over my face. I was five foot two and weighed 110 pounds. [He weighed 265 pounds.] I didn't have any choice.[9]

2   According to one study, "the organization and membership of fraternities contribute heavily to coercive and often violent sex."[10] The study cited such factors as fraternity populations of the same sex and same age group; fraternity house locations (private dwellings not under campus supervision); widespread alcohol abuse; competitiveness; secrecy and the unwillingness to inform on each other; recruitment and socialization practices that "emphasize a macho conception of men and masculinity, a narrow, stereotyped conception of women and femininity, and the treatment of women as commodities."[11] Do you know of fraternities of this sort? Do you know of sororities that encourage undesirable stereotypes of women? What can be done to change the climate of such organizations?

3   Widespread rape is a product of cultures like our own in which male violence is tolerated and even encouraged. Studies show that rape is linked to other forms of physical violence on dates—hitting, pushing, squeezing—as well as to verbal abuse. Studies also show that, although women sometimes engage in such violence, they do so much less frequently and with far less intensity. What should society (especially schools and law enforcement) do to create a climate that discourages male violence?

4   What moral differences, if any, are there in the cases of (a) a man who rapes a stranger, (b) acquaintance rape, and (c) a man who forces his wife to have sexual intercourse?

5   Men (and some women) sometimes consider that sexually provocative clothing and conduct justify or excuse sexual harassment and rape. Discuss why they might think this and whether it has any justification. Would the same conclusion apply to men who are sexually provocative?

6   If a woman does not actively resist sexual intercourse, does that entail that she is giving consent? If you think context is important in answering this question, describe several contexts that yield different answers.

7   If a woman does not actively protest another person's unwanted and annoying sexual advances at the workplace or in academic settings, does that mean that she finds the conduct acceptable and that no sexual harassment takes place? What would you say to critics who charge that Anita Hill is blameworthy because she did not explicitly object to Clarence Thomas at the time when she alleges he sexually harassed her?

8   Should there be absolute (that is, exceptionless) prohibitions on sexual relationships between professors and (a) students currently registered for their classes, (b) students attending their school but not registered in their classes, (c) students who are their advisees? Do such prohibitions violate the sexual freedom of consenting adults?

SUGGESTED READINGS

Brownmiller, Susan. *Against Our Will: Men, Women and Rape*. New York: Simon & Schuster, 1975.

Cranor, Carl. "On Respecting Human Beings as Persons." *Journal of Value Inquiry*, vol. 17 (1983).

Downie, R. S., and Elizabeth Telfer. *Respect for Persons*. New York: Schocken, 1970.

Dziech, Billie Wright, and Linda Weiner. *The Lecherous Professor: Sexual Harassment on Campus*. 2nd ed. Chicago: University of Illinois Press, 1990.

Estrich, Susan. *Real Rape*. Cambridge, MA: Harvard University Press, 1987.

Griffin, Susan. *Rape: The Politics of Consciousness*. 3rd ed. New York: Harper & Row, 1986.

Hallie, Philip P. *Cruelty*. Rev. ed. Middletown, CT: Wesleyan University Press, 1982.

Hughes, John C., and Larry May. "Sexual Harassment." *Social Theory and Practice*, vol. 6 (1980).

MacKinnon, Catharine A. *Sexual Harassment of Working Women*. New Haven, CT: Yale University Press, 1979.

Midgley, Mary. *Wickedness: A Philosophical Essay*. Boston, MA: Routledge & Kegan Paul, 1984.

Mill, John Stuart. *On Liberty*. Indianapolis, IN: Hackett Publishing, 1978.

Morrison, Toni (ed.). *Race-ing Justice, En-gendering Power: Essays on Anita Hill, Clarence Thomas, and the Construction of Social Reality*. New York: Pantheon Books, 1992.

Pennock, J. Roland, and John W. Chapman (eds.). *Nomos XIV: Coercion*. New York: Aldine, Atherton, 1972.

Pineau, Lois, "Date Rape: A Feminist Analysis." *Law and Philosophy*, No. 8 (1989): 217–243.

Sanders, William B. *Rape and Woman's Identity*. Beverly Hills, CA: Sage, 1980.

Shafer, Carolyn M., and Marilyn Frye. "Rape and Respect." In M. Vetterling-Braggin, F. A. Elliston, and J. English (eds.), *Feminism and Philosophy*. Totowa, NJ: Rowman & Allanheld, 1977.

Sumrall, Amber Coverdale, and Dena Taylor (eds.). *Sexual Harassment: Women Speak Out*. Freedom, CA: Crossing Press, 1992. A case studies book.

Tomaselli, Sylvana, and Roy Porter (eds.). *Rape*. New York: Basil Blackwell, 1986.

Tong, Rosemarie. *Women, Sex, and the Law*. Totowa, NJ: Rowman & Allanheld, 1984.

Wall, Edmund (ed.). *Sexual Harassment*. Buffalo, NY: Prometheus Books, 1992.

Warshaw, Robin. *I Never Called It Rape: The Ms. Report on Recognizing, Fighting, and Surviving Date and Acquaintance Rape*. New York: Harper and Row, 1988.

Williams, Bernard. "The Idea of Equality." In *Problems of the Self*. Cambridge: Cambridge University Press, 1973.

PART FOUR

Sexual Morality

It is through sex...that each individual has to pass in order to have access to ... [her or his] own identity.... Hence the importance we ascribe to it, the reverential fear with which we surround it, the care we take to know it. Hence the fact that over the centuries it has become more important than our soul, more important almost than our life.[1]

Michel Foucault

Sexual desire, according to traditional attitudes, is a valuable but dangerous force that needs the control of a swarm of prohibitions. Its moral status centers on the biological purpose of producing children and is specified by five mandates: (1) to refrain from sexual activity until marriage, (2) to engage in marital sex without preventing the conception of children, (3) to refrain from sex with anyone but one's spouse, (4) to choose a spouse of the opposite sex, and (5) to love one's sexual partner, that is, one's spouse. A contemporary variation on this traditional view emphasizes that sex is morally significant in expressing and supporting love between married partners, in addition to its role in creating children.

The sexual revolution of the 1960s challenged these mandates by questioning the requirement that sex be joined with love, marriage, and children. New attitudes arose that accepted or advocated sex outside marriage, contraception, sex with more than one person, homosexuality, and sex without love. In the name of freedom (autonomy, self-determination) and respect for the freedom of others, proponents of the sexual revolution accepted virtually all forms of sexual expression by consenting participants.

Philosophical thinking about sex emerged largely in response to the sexual revolution. Before the 1960s, few philosophers regarded sex as a worthy

topic.* Since 1970, however, philosophers have devoted increasing attention to the topics dealt with in the following four chapters: the moral relationships between sex and love, marriage and adultery, homosexuality and
homophobia, and pornography and fantasy, respectively.

Some have argued that the sexual revolution is over and that the horrifying epidemic of AIDS (Acquired Immune Deficiency Syndrome), as well as
the increase in other, albeit less deadly, sexually transmitted diseases, is forcing a renewed interest in more traditional values. Others hope that sexual
attitudes are undergoing a gradual evolution that will bring about a synthesis of the best ideas and attitudes of the sexual revolution and traditional
perspectives. In any case, sexuality is a central topic for everyday ethics,
especially regarding the attempt to understand our personal identities and
the search for meaningful relationships.

---

* A notable exception was Bertrand Russell (1872–1970), whose defense of sex outside
marriage—"free love"—prompted universities to ban him from teaching for over two decades.

CHAPTER 14

Sex and Love

What is the connection between sex, love, and moral values? In particular, is there an obligation to restrict sex to relationships involving love? Or, is the insistence that sex be accompanied by love based on a degrading view of sexuality—that sex is bad and in need of redemption by love? Is romantic (sexual, erotic) love a kind of illusion and trap, or at least so fraught with peril that it is best avoided?

In Marilyn French's novel *The Women's Room*, Val, a thirty-nine-year-old student, contends that sex ought to be separated from love. Val has come to believe that erotic love is a biological illusion and a trap for women:

> Love is insanity.... It is the taking over of a rational and lucid mind by delusion and self-destruction. You lose yourself, you have no power over yourself, you can't even think straight. That's the reason I hate it.[1]

By the time people recover from this insanity—and sooner or later they always do—they are often married and have children. According to Val, this works out well for men who wish to have wives at home with their children, but less well for women, who usually end up getting hurt.

Even though she rejects erotic love, Val is not cynical about sex, once it is freed from love. Indeed,

> for her, sex was almost a philosophy. She saw the whole world in terms of it.... Val slept with people the way other people go out for dinner with a friend. She liked them, she liked sex. She rarely expected anything from it beyond the pleasure of the moment. At the same time, she said it was overrated: it had been so tabooed, she claimed, that we had come to expect paradise from it. It was only fun, great fun, but not paradise.[2]

Definitions of Love

What does Val mean by "love"? In this chapter our interest is in erotic, sexual, romantic love—that is, love involving sexual attraction. Val is talking about erotic love, but she also has in mind a particular conception of erotic love—the Romantic conception. When we speak of Romantic love (with a capital "R"), we will mean the view of romantic love (with a small "r") that was dominant during the nineteenth century, which had as its precursor the courtly love tradition of the Middle Ages (as expressed in the legends of Lancelot and Guinevere, and Tristan and Isolde), and which continues today in certain highly romanticized myths about being destined for one person whom one idealizes and with whom one can live happily ever after. Val seems to have in mind Romantic idealization: the process whereby two lovers each exaggerate the beauty and goodness of the other and become largely oblivious to the other's faults. We sometimes refer to such love as an infatuation that distorts one's normal degree of reasonableness. Is that true love?

Most of us distinguish "true" or "genuine" love—the "real thing"—from a variety of more superficial infatuations. We draw the distinction in different ways, however, reflecting differences in the values we hold. *True love* is a value-loaded expression: It refers to the kinds of responses and relationships (involving sexual attraction) that we consider desirable or ideal. Often we disagree with each other about what it is. Consider, for example, three different ideals of true love (and there are many more).

The Romantic ideal values passion above all else. Passion reflects an intense longing for someone, accompanied by an obsessive preoccupation with that person. In a passionate state one devotes frenzied attention to every aspect of the beloved and finds everything about the beloved glorious. It is the state most often referred to as "falling in love," although we might also call it the "in love" state. This is the conception of love that Val rejects.

A contrasting conception of true love stresses "loving" rather than being "in love." Loving consists of caring and commitment as opposed to passionate attention, although the caring on occasion may be expressed through passion. In *The Art of Loving* the humanistic psychologist Erich Fromm developed a strongly moralized view of love along these lines. Love, he suggests, is the attitude characterized by giving, caring, and acting responsibly and respectfully while also maintaining one's own integrity, self-respect, and individuality. "Falling in love," by contrast, is an immature and selfish preoccupation. In fact, Fromm continues, any form of intense preoccupation with one individual can be a distortion of true love, where true love is a general attitude toward all people:

> Love is not primarily a relationship to a specific person; it is an *attitude*, an *orientation of character* which determines the relatedness of a person to the world as a whole, not toward one "object" of love.... If I truly love one person I love all persons, I love the world, I love life.[3]

It is perhaps difficult, however, to see how Fromm's attempt to view all love as general humanitarian caring (or as he calls it, "brotherly love") can apply to erotic love. Humanitarian caring is inclusive: It is addressed to many people at the same time. Erotic love is exclusive: It focuses great concern and attention on one person (or at most a few persons), excluding most others. Fromm fears that this exclusivity leads to narcissistic distortions and *egoism à deux* (double and shared egotism) in which two people become unhealthily "addicted" to each other. It that an inevitable result?

A third conception of love combines some elements from the Romantic and humanitarian views while discarding other elements. Erotic love involves preoccupation with one individual, but in a caring and committed way, not an unhealthy and selfish way. Thus, according to feminist Shulamith Firestone, in erotic love the personal identities of two equal partners are intermingled and reshaped. Each becomes "psychically wide-open" to the other, in terms of both complete emotional vulnerability and intellectual openness to the experience of the other. Commitment is crucial in order to create the trust and security needed to sustain this vulnerability. Yet the commitment is not entirely selfless; instead, it is based on a mixture of caring and self-interest:

> The self attempts to enrich itself through the absorption of another being.... Love between two equals would be an enrichment, each enlarging himself through the other: instead of being one, locked in a cell of himself with only his own experience and view, he could participate in the existence of another—an extra window on the world.[4]

In addition, Firestone insists that true love involves mutual understanding rather than illusion of the sort typical of romantic infatuation. In fact, love is a form of creative vision in which value is discerned (in the beloved) as well as affirmed and bestowed:

> Because of this fusion of egos, in which each sees and cares about the other as a new self, the beauty/character of the beloved, perhaps hidden to outsiders under layers of defenses, is revealed.... Increased sensitivity to the real, if hidden, values in the other ... is not "blindness" or "idealization" but is, in fact, deeper vision.[5]

Yet Firestone would agree with Val that love is easily distorted in ways hurtful to women. She argues that, until women have economic status and power equal to that of men, true love will remain difficult to achieve. Unequal power tends to make women vulnerable to exploitation by men, who often have difficulty in giving the commitment and the emotional openness required by love.

These three conceptions of love—a Romantic, a humanitarian, and a feminist conception—are intended only as illustrations of how the expression "true love" is used to convey contrasting values. Love is not some simple "feeling," contrary to what contemporary popular music and romance novels often suggest. For the purposes of discussing the relationship between sex and love, however, it will be helpful to develop some minimal (if controversial) definitions.

By *erotic love* we will mean love expressed through sex, which includes sexual arousal, desire, and activity (ranging from a caress to intercourse). The adjective *sexual* thus refers to bodily states involving genital excitement and to thoughts, pleasures, and desires associated with that excitement. By *liking* we mean a positive attitude toward someone based on some attraction—one finds that person "to one's taste." *Affection* is an emotion of concern for another person's well-being, an emotion that may last for a shorter time than does the attitude of liking. *Love* refers to an attitude that involves caring, affection for, and commitment to the good of one's partner in a deeper degree than does liking. As deep caring and commitment are understood to involve further values that guide relationships—perhaps honesty, equality and fairness, responsibilities, and faithfulness—ideals of *true love* acquire further moral content.

With these distinctions in mind, let us consider an argument in favor of valuing sexual expressions without love and then an argument in favor of tightly linking sex and love.

Arguments for Sex Without Love

In his book *Sex Without Love*, Russell Vannoy provides a philosophical defense of Val's attitudes. Vannoy focuses on people whom he calls *authentic* and *humanists*. By *authentic* he refers to people who make decisions based on self-knowledge, under minimal influence from distorting external factors and in full awareness of relevant information. *Humanists* are individuals who value other people for their intrinsic worth and who display sensitivity, simple decency, and some generosity.

Vannoy believes that traditional views of sex are based on a simplistic dualism: Either sex is an expression of love or it is a degrading indulgence for selfish purposes. He argues that there is a large middle ground between these two extremes. For example, sex can express simple affection, liking, friendship, sheer delight in the beauty of another person, and physical recreation based on mutual consent and desire. In these ways, sex need not be degrading or exploitative, but neither must it involve anything as serious as love, which implies deep emotional ties and commitment. Traditionalists, Vannoy argues, have simply failed to acknowledge the full possibilities of nonloving sex:

> It can be an evening of sensuous eroticism that may continue for hours and include all the foreplay, afterplay, kisses and caresses that actual

lovers enjoy, perhaps done simply out of deep mutual admiration for each other's sensuous qualities and out of gratitude for having been chosen by the other for such an evening. Yet the pair may go their separate ways in the morning and never see each other again, perhaps because they prefer their own independence and singlehood to permanent emotional involvement and marriage.[6]

Furthermore, Vannoy defends sex without love outside of romantic relationships. Masturbation and fetishes, for example, provide pleasurable experiences for people who prefer more private modes of sexual expression. In Vannoy's view, to deny that sex has many legitimate forms of expression outside romantic relationships is to embrace a degrading view of sex as something that by itself is bad and that stands in need of redemption through love, marriage, and procreation.

In addition to arguing that sex without love is morally permissible for authentic humanists, Vannoy defends two further theses. On the one hand, he contends that in many cases sex without love is better than sex with love in terms of pleasure and contribution to well-being. The practice of sex without love can yield higher degrees of excitement by allowing greater novelty, variety, and romantic adventure, whereas sex between married partners tends to become boringly routine. Inevitably, the initial romantic intensity fades, leaving at best lukewarm companionship and at worst mutual hostility due to the loss of other romantic options. Also, love burdens sex with demands that partners perform satisfactorily. It threatens the delights of sex by burying them within delicately balanced and emotionally complex love relationships. In this context, affectionate sex without the burdens of commitment is far preferable.

On the other hand, Vannoy attacks erotic love as an incoherent ideal riddled with inconsistent demands and illusions that inevitably cause frustration and unhappiness. For example, love seeks to endure forever ("until death do us part" or "for all eternity") and simultaneously to be ecstatically exciting, but it cannot be both: The initial intensity always fades. Again, lovers want their partners to be overwhelmed with emotions so intense as to blind them to their flaws, and yet simultaneously to choose rationally to love them from an understanding of their true natures. They also want partners who feel deeply dependent on them and who wish to serve their interests out of pure altruism, and yet who are secure and independent individuals with interests of their own that sometimes conflict with the demands of selfless giving.

In short, Vannoy argues for three theses: (1) All sex without love is morally permissible when engaged in by consenting adults who avoid cruelty and exploitation; (2) often sex without love is better than sex with love; and (3) traditional ideals about sexual love are irrational and incoherent. Can defenders of traditional views refute these theses?

Arguments for Sex with Love

Defenses of traditional views of sex often appeal to God's commandments as interpreted by particular religions. It is understandable that religious faith will influence one's views of sexual morality, but is it possible to defend traditional views without appealing to religious doctrines?

Roger Scruton attempts such a defense in his book *Sexual Desire*. His defense is based on the Aristotelian view that virtue and self-fulfillment go together, as well as on the claim that sex has a natural role in contributing to self-fulfillment.

Scruton first reminds us that sexual desire is not merely a desire to engage in intercourse with a *body*. Instead, it is a desire for another *person* who is, like oneself, an embodied consciousness, that is, a consciousness in a body. More specifically, sexual desire entails a longing to unite with a person, whether the longing is focused in a desire for intercourse or whether it is a less focused desire. It also implies a wish to have our partners enjoy being desired by us and to desire us in similar ways.

Sexual desires are satisfied through experiences of shared sexual excitement in which the consciousnesses of both partners are focused on the pleasures of both partners' bodies. Scruton eloquently describes this "mutual embodiment, the other's 'being in' his body and I in mine": "In our excitement we sense each other's animation, and become acquainted with the pulsing of the spirit in the flesh, which fills the body with a pervasive 'I', and transforms it into something strange, precious and possessible."[7]

What moral relevance does this experience have? When joined with love, this experience of embodiment provides a unique way for two people to affirm each other's value. In doing so, it teaches them to appreciate the basis of morality: the value of people as conscious beings with bodies. Without erotic love we would "appreciate less vividly the fundamental premise of morality: that the repository of infinite value which is the other self, exists not in some Platonic supersphere, but here in the flesh."[8] Thus, Scruton asserts, to give and receive this form of appreciation and affirmation is a crucial aspect of self-fulfillment:

> Erotic love involves an element of mutual self-enhancement; it generates a sense of the irreplaceable value, both of the other and of the self, and of the activities which bind them. To receive and to give this love is to achieve something of incomparable value in the process of self-fulfillment. It is to gain the most powerful of all interpersonal *guarantees*; in erotic love the subject becomes conscious of the full reality of his personal existence, not only in his own eyes, but in the eyes of another.[9]

Sex without love cannot yield this mutual affirmation of personal worth, which Scruton thinks is essential for self-fulfillment. Love affirms the interests of the beloved through a long-term commitment to promote them. Within love relationships sex becomes an expression and symbol of this enduring affirmation. In contrast, sex as a one-night stand, as a temporary recreation, or even as an act of affection is incapable of conveying the profound affirmation of the other person. Nor can masturbation or perversions (such as sex with animals and sex with dead people), which do not even involve two mutually excited conscious beings, convey any such affirmation. Moreover, according to Scruton's ideal of "sexual integrity," premarital sex is objectionable. Postponing sexual activity until long-term marital commitments are possible is a way to preserve the connection between sex and love. In short, there is an obligation to join sex and love because that conjunction allows individuals each to affirm the other's moral worth in a singularly important way that contributes to self-fulfillment.

How, then, would Scruton respond to Vannoy's claims that sex without love is more exciting and that erotic love is an incoherent ideal? Recall that Vannoy viewed sex without love as often more exciting because it offers greater variety, novelty, and romance than does sex within long-term loving relationships. A traditionalist might admit there is a loss of newness and romance as partners become well acquainted with each other's bodies, but nevertheless insist that the loss is outweighed by the security and mutual affirmation offered by loving sex. Scruton, however, has a more positive rejoinder. He reminds us that erotic love offers unlimited variety, because sexual desire is focused on a conscious person, and consciousness is not something fixed: "Sexual curiosity...renews itself endlessly; for the object of curiosity is not the bodily region as such, but the region 'as inhabited by a pleased consciousness,' and pleasure is a dynamic thing, which has a constantly shifting significance in the experience of the person who feels it."[10] Sex within long-term relationships is as varied in what it expresses and affirms as are the two consciousnesses it joins together.

Is love an impossible ideal? Scruton might agree that it is when it involves the conflicting desires Vannoy lists: that love both last forever and provide constant ecstasy; that one's partner be overwhelmed by emotion and thereby blinded to one's flaws and yet rationally understand and appreciate one; that one's partner be perfectly altruistic and dependent on one and yet be an interesting and independent individual. Scruton, however, would probably view these desires, in contrast with the rational desires involved in the kinds of self-fulfilling love he describes, as unreasonable and immature.

Scruton might also point out that mature love relationships provide recurring moments of ecstasy interspersed with caring support for one's partner's endeavors, allow for honest recognition of faults, and admit to elements of both strong dependency and independence. Scruton does agree with Vannoy on one point: Love requires a thorough union of interests. Whereas Vannoy finds that union stifling, however, Scruton finds it liberating. This disagreement strikes at the heart of contemporary concerns to reconcile individuality and unity, or distinct and shared identities, in love relationships.

True Love: Obligations or Ideals?

We noted that *true love* is an expression the meaning of which is tied to one's value perspective on human relationships, and we have mentioned several such perspectives. Let us now ask whether the values that enter into conceptions of true love are universal obligations, as Scruton suggests, or moral ideals that individuals are free to embrace but which are not incumbent on everyone.

Scruton's defense of the traditional view of sex rests on the assumption that human sexuality has one "natural" aim in promoting self-fulfillment: to foster erotic love and its unique form of moral affirmation. Drawing on that assumption, he tries to demonstrate a general obligation to link sex and love. Is there, however, any one "natural" role of sex in contributing to human fulfillment? Cannot sex serve many legitimate roles in different lives, or in the same life at different stages?

There are alternative roads to self-fulfillment, and numerous ways to find affirmation of one's moral worth. The suppression or sublimation of sex is perhaps the best avenue for some people, such as priests and nuns, who take vows of chastity as part of a religious commitment. For other people (Vannoy, for example), who value variety and intensity of sexual passion, evasion of long-term commitments may contribute to self-fulfillment. For some, a variety of types of relationships, some long and some short, may be best. For those who value the constancy, support, and depth of long-term relationships, the lifetime commitments advocated by Scruton will be best.

According to this line of thought, there is no universal obligation to link sex and love in any one way. Instead, there are many permissible moral ideals concerning sex that individuals may choose among in seeking self-fulfillment. (The choice, we hope, would be made wisely, on the basis of self-understanding.) These are *moral* ideals in that they express visions of valuable forms of human relationships, ones that may in different ways combine affection, caring, mutual understanding, mutual respect, honesty, and mutual commitments. Moreover, once embraced, some of the ideals generate obligations. In particular, when two people accept Scruton's ideal of long-term commitments and make mutual commitments based on a shared acceptance of the ideal, they incur special obligations to conform to the ideal. There is, however, no single degree of commitment to these ideals that is obligatory for all individuals.

Recognition of a plurality of permissible sexual ideals should not be confused with acceptance of the attitude put forth in the 1960s that anything goes, at least as long as there is mutual consent. The difference arises from the fact that sexual ideals can be evaluated by reference to the self-fulfillment and personal well-being of individuals and couples. There are often very good reasons for certain individuals and couples (given their psychological natures and preferred life-styles) to adopt one ideal rather than another in their pursuit of happiness and meaningful life.

This pluralistic model of sexual morality would certainly complicate sexual relationships, because individuals would bring to relationships different ideals about what is desirable for them; but people do so already to a large extent in our society. In any case, ideals are open to discussion and criticism by couples. They are also open to compromise, in the best sense of the term: reconciliation of differences by mutual concessions. As with all major aspects of loving relationships, the nature of love itself is mutually shaped by couples.

SUMMARY

True love is a term used to express value perspectives concerning what relationships are most desirable. The Romantic perspective focuses on passionate preoccupation with the beloved; Erich Fromm's humanitarian perspective stresses general caring for all people, even when expressed through a relationship with one person; and Shulamith Firestone's feminist perspective emphasizes emotional sharing between equals in a way that reshapes personal identity.

When is sex without love morally permissible? Russell Vannoy argues that it is permissible whenever the participants freely consent. He rejects the simple dichotomy between sex as an expression of love and sex as a selfish indulgence, drawing attention to ways in which sex can express affection, liking, and friendship. Roger Scruton argues that erotic love makes a unique contribution to self-fulfillment through a mutual affirmation of the moral worth of embodied conscious beings. Perhaps, however, sex can contribute in a variety of ways to the fulfillment of individuals and couples, and thus there may be several morally permissible ideals concerning sex.

Is sex without love more exciting, because it allows greater variety and romance with different partners? No doubt it is for some individuals, but as Scruton points out, sexual desire is directed toward persons who have a consciousness as alive as one's own, and this enables long-term relationships to offer unlimited variety in what is enjoyed and expressed through sex.

Is sexual love an incoherent ideal, as Vannoy charges? Must it involve conflicting desires (such as those for constant ecstasy and permanence), overwhelming emotions and calm rationality, dependence and independence for both partners, unity and individuality? Although immature forms of love are characterized by incompatible demands, mature love need not be. As Shulamith Firestone suggests, love involves a profound reshaping of personal identity within a caring relationship with another person.

DISCUSSION TOPICS

1   Is there a universal moral obligation to refrain from sex except when it expresses deep affection and lasting commitment? Or are all forms of sexual expression morally permissible, so long as they are based on consent and respect for one's partner's consent?

2   In what ways is sex with love better (though not necessarily the only acceptable option) than sex without love, and vice versa?

3   Firestone believes that (genuine) erotic love is possible only between individuals who are equal in the kinds of power that mutual economic independence provides. Presumably, two people need not earn the same income, but both must have self-sufficient incomes; otherwise, harmful forms of dependency arise. In contrast, Robert Solomon contends that love requires only equality of consent; that is, both partners agree to the roles they play in the relationship. Do you agree with what he says in the following passage?

> But what does "equality" mean in relations? It does not mean "being the same." It does not exclude all sorts of asymmetrical and uneven roles and relationships, including the absolute domination of one person by the other. It does not require, as such, the equal division of housework or "bread earning" tasks.... Equality in love essentially means a mutually-agreed upon indeterminacy [i.e., lack of fixedness or finality] ... in which one's self-images and personal roles and identity are up for grabs, in negotiation with one other person, in which there are no preordained roles or predestined status relationships.[11]

4   Is it possible to love erotically more than one person at the same time? Before answering this question, first discuss what you understand it to mean. Are we asking whether one person could experience certain emotions at the same time toward more than one person? Are we asking a practical question about whether there is enough time and energy to pursue more than one relationship at a time? Or are we asking a value question concerning which kind of relationships have the highest value?

5   The French Romantic novelist Stendhal (1783–1842) argued that passionate romantic love is the highest form of love and that it always involves an element of illusion: "From the moment he falls in love even the wisest man no longer sees anything *as it really is*. He underrates his own qualities, and overrates the least favour bestowed by his beloved."[12] Love is a combination of illusion and esteem for the beloved and involves a process he called "crystallization." When a tree branch is thrown into the salt mines near Salzburg and remains there for a few months, it is transformed into a shimmeringly beautiful crystalline latticework. Analogously, the lover's imagination ascribes one perfection after another to the

beloved. Does the process of falling in love always or usually involve illusions? Or can the intense preoccupation with the beloved be based primarily on insight into the special value the person has, as both Scruton and Firestone suggest?

If you think that love and illusion are often compatible, are there any limits you would draw concerning extreme illusions? For example, could we experience true love for someone whose gender we are mistaken about? In David Hwang's play *M. Butterfly*, a heterosexual man thinks he is deeply in love with a Chinese opera singer who he learns twenty years later is a man.[13] During the twenty years, the man believed he was deeply in love with the singer, but he later concludes that he loved only a fantasy, not a real person. Do you agree?

6   *True love* is a term used to express a value perspective on the most desirable forms of erotic relationships. Put into words your conception of true (erotic) love. In particular, discuss the moral values, if any, that enter into your conception of love. Include in your discussion a response to the following questions (which combine some of the preceding questions):

   a   Is true love something that has to last a lifetime, or can it exist for a few years (or a few days) and then end?

   b   Can a person love two people at the same time?

   c   To what extent does genuine love require that one share the interests of one's lover?

   d   Is true love purely altruistic, that is, completely selfless? Or does it involve a substantial element of self-concern or self-love mixed with elements of altruism?

   e   In what sense, if any, does true love require equality or fairness in relationships?

   f   Must true love be based on mutual understanding, or does it admit of large degrees of illusion and error about one's partner?

   g   Do we *choose* to love, or does love *happen* to us (as is suggested by such phrases as "falling in love" and "being hit by lightning")?

7   In *The Second Sex* Simone de Beauvoir writes, "The word *love* has by no means the same sense for both sexes, and this is one cause of the serious misunderstandings that divide them. Byron well said: 'Man's love is of man's life a thing apart; 'Tis woman's whole existence.'"[14] Beauvoir then goes on to say that women tend to think of love as unconditional and selfless devotion, whereas men typically do not think of love as requiring this consuming devotion for them, though they seek it from women.

In a variation of this theme, Robert Nozick writes:

> The individual self can be related to the *we* [i.e., a closely bonded couple in an intimate relationship] it identifies with in two different ways. It can see the *we* as a very important *aspect* of itself, or it can see itself as part of the *we*, as contained within it. It may be that men more often take the former view, women the latter. Although both see the *we* as extremely important for the self, most men might draw the circle of themselves containing the circle of the *we* as an aspect *within* it, while most women might draw the circle of themselves within the circle of the *we*.[15]

Do you agree with de Beauvoir and Nozick that, roughly speaking, most women tend to love in different ways than most men do? If so, what do you think might cause this to be? If not, why do you think de Beauvoir and Nozick were led to make their suggestions?

8   Today it is sometimes claimed that AIDS is "changing sexual morality." It is certainly altering many people's behavior patterns, but is this due to prudence about one's self-interest or to fundamental changes in moral beliefs and attitudes concerning sex?

SUGGESTED READINGS

Baker, Robert, and Frederick Elliston (eds.). *Philosophy and Sex*. Rev. ed. Buffalo, NY: Prometheus, 1984.

Bertocci, Peter A. *Sex, Love, and the Person*. New York: Sheed & Ward, 1967.

Brown, Robert. *Analyzing Love*. New York: Cambridge University Press, 1987.

Firestone, Shulamith. *The Dialectic of Sex: The Case for Feminist Revolution*. New York: Morrow, 1970.

Fromm, Erich. *The Art of Loving*. New York: Harper & Row, 1956.

Gilbert, Paul. *Human Relationships: A Philosophical Introduction*. Oxford: Blackwell, 1991.

Hunter, J. F. M. *Thinking about Sex and Love: A Philosophical Inquiry*. New York: St. Martin's Press, 1980.

Martin, Mike W. "Honesty in Love," *Journal of Value Inquiry*, vol. 27. (1993).

Minas, Anne (ed.). *Gender Basics: Feminist Perspectives on Women and Men*. Belmont, CA: Wadsworth, 1993.

Norton, David L., and Mary F. Kille (eds.). *Philosophies of Love*. Totowa, NJ: Rowman & Allanheld, 1983.

Nozick, Robert. "Love's Bond." In *The Examined Life*. New York: Simon and Schuster, 1989). Pp. 68–86.

Nussbaum, Martha C. *Love's Knowledge: Essays on Philosophy and Literature*. New York: Oxford University Press, 1990.

Posner, Richard A. *Sex and Reason*. Cambridge, MA: Harvard University Press, 1992.

Santas, Gerasimos. *Plato and Freud: Two Theories of Love*. New York: Basil Blackwell, 1988.

Scruton, Roger. *Sexual Desire: A Moral Philosophy of the Erotic*. New York: Free Press, 1986.

Singer, Irving. *The Nature of Love*. 3 vols. Chicago: University of Chicago Press, 1984, 1987.

Sircello, Guy. *Love and Beauty*. Princeton, NJ: Princeton University Press, 1989.

Soble, Alan (ed.). *Eros, Agape and Philia: Readings in the Philosophy of Love*. New York: Paragon House, 1989.

Soble, Alan (ed.). *The Philosophy of Sex: Contemporary Readings*. 2nd ed. Savage, MD: Rowman & Littlefield, 1991.

Solomon, Robert C. *About Love: Reinventing Romance for Our Times*. New York: Simon and Schuster, 1988.

Solomon, Robert C., and Kathleen M. Higgins (eds.). *The Philosophy of (Erotic) Love*. Lawrence, KS: University Press of Kansas, 1991.

Sternberg, Robert J., and Michael L. Barnes (eds.). *The Psychology of Love*. New Haven, CT: Yale University Press, 1988.

Vannoy, Russell. *Sex Without Love: A Philosophical Exploration*. Buffalo, NY: Prometheus, 1980.

Verene, D. P. (ed.). *Sexual Love and Western Morality: A Philosophical Anthology*. New York: Harper & Row, 1972.

Weeks, Jeffrey. *Sexuality*. New York: Routledge, 1986.

Wilson, John. *Love, Sex, and Feminism*. New York: Praeger, 1980.

CHAPTER 15

Marriage and Adultery

Despite sharp criticism, marriage continues to be a prevalent form of sexual relationship. Ninety percent of Americans marry. Half of those marriages end in divorce, but 80 percent of divorced people remarry, usually within five years. Perhaps no form of social relationship, however, has greater demands placed on it and, as a result, is burdened with so many difficulties. One difficulty is adultery, which occurs in more than half of all marriages—most husbands and many wives have extramarital affairs at some time during their marriage.

Yet sexual exclusivity in marriage—that is, restriction of sex only to one's spouse—is only one aspect of traditional marriages. Even more central is the lifetime commitment to join one's life intensively and intimately to one other person. As traditionally conceived in Western culture, marriage combines several elements: (1) mutual commitments to life-long companionship and (2) mutual commitments to sexual exclusivity (3) expressed publicly in formal legal or religious ceremonies and (4) made between one male and one female. We will focus on the first three conditions, especially the first two, postponing the question of homosexual marriages to the next chapter. Our primary interest is the moral significance of a formal commitment by two people to life-long companionship and sexual exclusivity.

Is Marriage a Moral Issue?

Some religions regard marriage as a *religious* obligation (assuming the opportunity for it arises). It seems clear, however, that there is no general *moral* obligation to marry. Marriage is an option, not an obligation. Does that mean marriage is primarily a matter of personal preference rather than morality?

In our society, of course, decisions about marriage are based in large part on personal preferences (in contrast to societies favoring arranged marriages). Some people choose to marry because they believe it is the best avenue for finding love, emotional support, sexual satisfaction, an enriched sense of self-worth, and economic security. For example, in *Women and Love*, Shere Hite quotes one woman as reporting, "I didn't like being single. No emotional security, no stability, no financial security, no companionship, no closeness, no love or sharing."[1] For other people, however, marriage is followed by frustration and abuse that bring an end to happiness. Many of the women Hite interviewed reported a preference for being single:

> Life is much better for me as a single woman. I can choose my friends, plan my social life, plan my private life, do and say what I please at home, make my home MINE (reflective of me), and I don't have to answer to anyone or explain my actions to anyone. Isn't it funny how long it takes to find out that freedom feels so good? Why do we rush into marriage like we do?[2]

Marriage decisions, however, are not solely expressions of personal preference and self-interest. They are also moral decisions. Even though there is no obligation to marry, marriage embodies moral ideals and also moral commitments that generate responsibilities. Moreover, there may be an obligation for some people in some circumstances *not* to marry: Unless one is willing in good faith to undertake the commitments involved, one may be guilty of deceit, promise breaking, and betrayal. Perhaps most fundamentally, there is an obligation to make marital decisions wisely, because the good of one's partner, oneself, and often others (especially children) is at stake.

Potential Drawbacks to Marriage

Conventional thought asserts that marriage is worth the sacrifices it requires, because it offers the best hope for most people to find love, emotional richness, satisfying sex, and support and self-esteem. Critics of this view, however, urge that most marriages are bad overall and would not exist if people thought more clearly and honestly. In particular, John McMurtry in "Monogamy: A Critique" argues that marriage is bound to affect adversely most people's chances of finding love and happiness, for three main reasons.

Outside Control

McMurtry's first criticism concerns state and religious control of marriages: "Centralized official control of marriage … necessarily alienates the partners from [taking] full responsibility for and freedom in their relationship."[3] For the Romans, marriage was a matter of personal agreement between the partners, and it automatically dissolved by similar mutual agreement. In contrast, under our tradition, which allows government and churches to control marriage ceremonies and relationships, freedom is restricted and individuals are encouraged to think of their relationship as partly the responsibility of larger social institutions, and are also influenced by peer pressure deriving from those institutions.

Certainly, such external forces do come into play. Social controls over marriages may generate coercive pressures and a sense that marital commitments are not entirely one's own responsibility. Moreover, there continue to be social pressures, especially on women, to marry and to stay married, even in extremely destructive relationships that ought to be dissolved. Yet much has changed since 1972 when McMurtry wrote his essay. There is greater social tolerance for people who live together before marriage (nearly half of recently married couples). Also, changes in divorce laws have made it easier to end a marriage. And when couples do marry, it is usually by choice and with the aim of expressing their commitments through a public ceremony.

Some couples regard public ceremonies and legal ties as superfluous or hurtful in the way McMurtry suggests. They may redefine marriage in purely moral terms as a relationship based on commitments to live together, without the need for legal or religious sanction. For others, however, the symbolism of public ceremonies provides a significant way to solemnize their commitments in the eyes of society and also in their own eyes; it is, or can be, a highly personal mutual expression between partners.

At this point, let us set aside this question about ceremonies in order to focus on a purely moral concept of marriage defined by life-long commitments, whether or not legal and religious rites are involved. McMurtry's other criticisms are directed toward these commitments and their consequences.

Psychological Constriction

In the marriage vows of the sixteenth-century *Book of Common Prayer* of the Church of England, the man is asked: "Wilt thou love her, comfort her, honor and keep her, in sickness and in health; and, forsaking all others, keep thee only unto her, so long as ye both shall live?" In addition to making these same vows, the woman is also asked to obey and serve—an inequality usually avoided in contemporary vows! No doubt some couples speaking these words understand them as a kind of pleasant poetical expression rather than a literal commitment. Most couples, however, fully intend to make the commitment to life-long companionship. Is such a commitment wise? Not according to McMurtry:

> The restriction of marriage union to two partners necessarily prevents the strengths of larger groupings. Such advantages as the following are thereby usually ruled out: (a) the security, range, and power of larger

socioeconomic units; (b) the epistemological [i.e., mental] and emotional substance, variety, and scope of more pluralist interactions.[4]

More recently, feminist critics of marriage emphasize that these losses hurt women more than men. All too often in marriage, even when both partners have jobs, women's identities are based only on their roles as wives (and mothers), whereas men find greater enrichment through their work. For most wives, the result of one-sided dependency is that marriage involves more sacrifice than self-fulfillment. Marriage also provides a veil of privacy that conceals injustices and cruelties, including wife battering, child abuse, and gross imbalances in the benefits and burdens for women.

As Susan Moller Okin writes in a book-long critique of marriage,

> I argue that marriage and family, as currently practiced in our society, are unjust institutions. They constitute the pivot of a societal system of gender that renders women vulnerable to dependency, exploitation, and abuse. When we look seriously at the distribution between husbands and wives of such critical social goods as work (paid and unpaid), power, prestige, self-esteem, opportunities for self-development, and both physical and economic security, we find socially constructed inequalities between them, right down the list."[5]

In particular, Okin documents how husbands receive a far larger share of opportunities for recognition through careers and education. Women are given the bulk of housekeeping chores and child-raising responsibilities, even when they do paid work outside the home. Men exercise more control within relationships because they have greater economic power and because women reasonably fear that divorce would drastically lower their standard of living.

Okin is offering rough generalizations, of course. She is aware that there are exceptions to her claims. Marriage is changing and offers increasing variety and flexibility. If we take such things into consideration, what can we say in defense of (many) marriages, especially concerning the question of freedom? To begin with, while marriage takes away some freedom in the sense that it reduces some options, it need not reduce overall options; instead, it changes options—dramatically. Marriage does close some options. Single (and childless), one can come and go as one chooses without having to notify or negotiate with anyone. That changes with marriage, but marriage creates new options, such as the opportunity for steady companionship and the sharing of daily activities (including sex). Of course, only good marriages offer this; but then, only some forms of being single offer happy options too.

McMurtry and Okin, of course, are concerned more with the quality of options within marriages than with the quantity of options. In their view, marital options are psychologically constrictive: Dependency on just one partner restricts the intellectual and emotional stimulation offered by a wider network of relationships, and also reduces the economic freedom of women in particular. We have all seen marriages in which this constriction occurs; but must it occur, or is marriage a sufficiently flexible practice that couples can avoid this constriction?

Contemporary marriages are extremely diverse and include at least three general types, as distinguished by sociologist Francesca M. Cancian. Cancian suggests that two models have been overemphasized: "(1) the traditional family, based on restricting individual freedom, especially for women, and (2) the contemporary pattern of limited commitments between independent individuals, each focused on his or her own self-development."[6] Yet a third model, which is increasingly popular, views long-term love and self-development as equally important and mutually reinforcing: "(3) Love and self-development both grow from the mutual interdependence of two people, not from extreme independence nor from the one-way dependency of a woman on a man encouraged by traditional marriage."[7] This model of interdependence stresses growth through intimate caring relationships with as much equal sharing as possible. According to Cancian, such relationships tend to break down role differentiation based on gender stereotypes of women as submissive, gentle, sensitive, and supportive, and of men as assertive, dominant, emotionally reserved (except perhaps in showing anger), and economically and intellectually independent. On this model, both marital roles and love itself are *androgynous*.

Interdependent relationships require *mutuality* of effort, sensitivity, and adjustment, as well as a sense of fairness and commitment to mutuality as an on-going process. The philosopher S. I. Benn earlier described this process, which is found among friends as well as spouses:

> It is of the essence of this relation that it is fully participatory. Each respects and values every other as a full partner, and exerts his own effort in the expectation and trust that the other will do likewise.... [The relation is one of] mutuality, the extent to which each is sensitive to the others' response to his own effort, is prepared to monitor his own attitudes to his partners and to the partnership, and to adjust to changes in the interests, tastes, values and personalities of the others.... [The goal of] the enterprise is to keep the partnership moving, to make it a vehicle through which the personalities of the partners can develop autonomously, without destroying it.[8]

This kind of relationship need not foster isolation from other enriching relationships. Rather, it allows marriages to function as emotional anchors that strengthen capacities for friendships and community involvement. A sense of permanence makes partners feel confident that the relationship will not be destroyed by change and disagreements, but rather that they will eventually enter into a sense of shared history together.

Having emphasized that marriage for many people is enriching, not constricting, we can agree that marriage is not good for everyone. Many marriages are harmful, especially to women—much depends on one's partner! Marriages demand an ability and a willingness to join one's activities continuously and intensively with those of another person. Usually, it requires a personal decision to value that relationship over attractive career options and other forms of relationships, and for some individuals that can be constrictive.

Sexual Confinement

Far from supporting erotic love, McMurtry maintains, marriage frustrates it: "Formal exclusion of all others from erotic contact with the marriage partner systematically promotes conjugal insecurity, jealousy, and alienation."[9] It does this by creating "a literally totalitarian expectation of sexual confinement" of one's spouse that is bound to create anxiety about potential violations of the commitment to sexual exclusivity by either spouse. Spouses become fearful of losing their counterparts, jealous about attention paid to others, and emotionally distanced from each other. In any case, the confinement is impractical: Affairs occur, accompanied by deception and antagonism between partners.

Even apart from consequences, McMurtry states, marriage is based on degrading attitudes that spouses "own" the sexual activities of their partners: "The ground of our marriage institution … is this: the maintenance by one man or woman of the effective right to exclude indefinitely all others from erotic access to the conjugal partner."[10] Marriage is a state of "indefinite, and exclusive ownership by two individuals of one another's sexual powers" and as such is "a form of private property" that treats people as if they were things to be possessed.[11]

Once again, McMurtry raises a valid criticism of some marriages. Some husbands do treat their wives as chattel. Yet it is entirely possible for spouses to view themselves as the beneficiaries of mutual gifts of free commitments rather than as possessors of ownership rights. If there is a right, it is the right created by freely given promises and commitments, not by ownership. There is also an awareness and appreciation that each spouse is dependent on the other for on-going renewal of those commitments.

In regard to the charge that marriage promotes insecurity, jealousy, and alienation, no doubt these effects do sometimes occur. Are they, however, the result primarily of the commitment to sexual exclusivity, or are they instead due to the particular characters of the individuals involved? For many couples, commitments provide a stable context that promotes sexual satisfaction by creating both opportunities for regular sex and an atmosphere in which trusting sexual expression can take place. Commitments made in good faith also can dramatically lessen jealousy by allowing partners to feel confident that outside affairs will not occur. The ill effects that McMurtry emphasizes are due primarily to the personalities and characters of individuals rather than to the nature of marital commitments per se.

Perhaps this reply is too hasty, however, since two related topics deserve further discussion: Even if we find value in marriage, we need to consider whether traditional marriages should be rethought so as to (1) permit extramarital love affairs and (2) minimize sexual jealousies that result when partners look beyond their spouses for sex, affection, or other attention.

Extramarital Affairs: Two Cases

Extramarital affairs, or acts of adultery, have always raised moral concern, and they continue to do so in both personal and public life. In 1992, the entire world learned the details about the extramarital affairs involved in the unraveling of the storybook romance of Prince Charles and Lady Diana. Earlier, in 1987, the press exposed the adulteries of Jim Bakker and Gary Hart. The differences between the cases of Bakker and Hart remind us that extramarital affairs take many forms, making it difficult to generalize about their moral status.

Jim Bakker was a successful television evangelist who created and directed the PTL (for "Praise the Lord" and "People That Love") Club. His affair had been a one-night stand six years earlier with Jessica Hahn, a twenty-one-year-old former church secretary. Bakker followers portrayed Hahn as a temptress who seduced Bakker during a troubled time in his marriage to Tammy Faye Bakker. Hahn's version, as recounted in *Newsweek* magazine, differed sharply:

> She was flown to Florida to meet Bakker by another evangelist, John Wesley Fletcher; she had baby-sat with Fletcher's children, and he knew she idolized Bakker. But at a hotel, so the story went, she was given drugged wine. Bakker appeared, dressed only in a white terry-cloth swimsuit, and she was told to give him a back rub. Dazed and sick, she resisted, but was unable to fight off Bakker's advances.[12]

Whichever version is true, the story is sordid—even setting aside the $265,000 in hush money that Bakker paid to Hahn a few years later and the subsequent legal conviction of Bakker for fraud and abuse of ministry funds. The Bakkers' marriage was based on traditional vows of sexual exclusivity, vows that were violated in a sexual episode that involved no love and apparent abuse of religious authority.

In 1987, Gary Hart was the leading Democratic candidate for president. Early in May he challenged reporters to scrutinize his private life by following him around. In mid-May he was seen entering and leaving his townhouse on Capitol Hill with model Donna Rice. The next day it was reported that in March he had gone on an overnight trip to Bimini (aboard a boat named *Monkey Business*) with a male friend and two women, one of whom was Rice. Hart and Rice insisted their relationship was platonic. Yet Hart's friends had worried for years that he was destroying his political career by "womanizing": "'It's no secret among Hart staffers that Hart has had these romances,' said one campaign official. 'But we felt it wasn't anybody's business except his and [his wife] Lee's.'"[13]

Hart's political sense is open to challenge, but is the same true of his sexual ethics? If we assume that Gary and Lee Hart, unlike Jim and Tammy Bakker, did not have a traditional commitment to sexual exclusivity, is there anything immoral about Hart's extramarital sexual romances? In general, are not extramarital affairs immoral when and only when they involve a violation of commitments or promises?

A Defense of Extramarital Affairs

In *Having Love Affairs*, Richard Taylor provides a spirited defense of many extramarital affairs. His basic argument is simple: Love is the highest good, and hence extramarital affairs based on love are intrinsically good, although admittedly their good might occasionally be outweighed by bad effects. Unlike McMurtry, Taylor sees great value in marriages (based on love), but he vigorously defends McMurtry's favorable view of affairs as offering enriching human relationships, even for couples who began their marriages with traditional vows:

> The joys of illicit and passionate love, which include but go far beyond the mere joys of sex, are incomparably good. And it is undeniable that those who never experience love affairs, and who perhaps even boast of their faultless monogamy year in and year out, have really missed something.[14]

Just as marital love offers the special goods deriving from close companionship, extramarital affairs offer a unique combination of excitement, affection, recognition, and strengthened self-esteem. Few things are more flattering and exhilarating than being loved by someone willing to take risks in surmounting conventional pressures against extramarital affairs.

Of course, affairs do sometimes hurt spouses. Jealousy is natural, even though Taylor views it as always bad and destructive. Affairs need not hurt marriages, however: "No good marriage relationship can be threatened by a love affair so long as others keep out of it."[15] Good marriages are based on mutual love, which presumably is strong enough to survive affairs. Taylor admits that love affairs are not for everyone, and certainly not for those who prefer orderliness and security over the excitement and risk offered by affairs. He insists, however, that the risk of harm from affairs can be minimized if spouses and lovers follow some basic rules.

Specifically, spouses who suspect their partners are engaged in affairs should heed the following guidelines: (1) "Do not spy or pry," because to do so both degrades oneself and shows a lack of trust in the spouse's exercise of autonomy. (2) "Do not confront or entrap," because these actions are based on a cruel impulse to humiliate the spouse. (3) "Stay out of it," and cultivate instead an attitude of confidence that the love involved in the marriage will sustain it after the affair has run its course. (4) "Stop being jealous," for jealousy is an inherently ugly and self-torturing emotion.

Spouses engaged in love affairs should in turn heed the following rules, among others: (1) "Stop feeling guilty"; such feelings are irrational products of centuries of prejudice against affairs. (2) "Be aware of the needs of the other" (that is, of one's lover), because that is central to love. (3) "Be honest" (with one's lover), because absolute honesty is required by the special intimacy involved in affairs. (It is especially wrong to lie about one's marital status.) (4) "Do not exhibit and boast," but rather restrain the natural tendency to broadcast the joy the affair has brought.

Taylor's view of extramarital affairs turns traditional morality on its head! What should we say, however, about the deception involved in most affairs? Should we not object to infidelity, betrayal, and violation of marital commitments? Doesn't Taylor's view neglect the virtues of truthfulness and fidelity? Taylor in fact defends concealment of the truth from one's spouse: "Candor is *not* the first obligation of husbands and wives. The first obligation is to love, and a direct consequence of that love is the desire not to injure."[16] When the truth, if revealed, is likely to injure one's spouse and one's marital relationship, love justifies concealment—by means of lies, if necessary. On the issue of fidelity to one's spouse, Taylor is adamant that it has nothing to do with sexual exclusivity: "The real and literal meaning of fidelity is *faithfulness*, and what thinking person could imagine that there is only one way in which someone can fail to keep faith with another? Faithfulness is a state of one's heart and mind," rather than a matter of rules.[17] Infidelity represents a betrayal of love and the commitment to love. It takes many forms, such as when one neglects the sexual needs of one's spouse, is uncaring, or unappreciative of the spouse's talents, or diverts shared money into a secret savings account for one's selfish use. According to Taylor, however, love for one's spouse is not betrayed by extramarital love affairs.

Many extramarital affairs are entered into without serious thought. Taylor is the first major philosopher to view them as so important as to warrant a book-length examination. Whether his defense of affairs is adequate will be left for discussion topics.

Jealousy

Recall (from Chapter 10) that jealousy is different from envy. For one thing, whereas envy centers on hatred, jealousy centers on a sense of injury and loss. We are jealous when we believe we have lost or are threatened with losing the affection, love, or esteem within a relationship we value. Although jealousy may involve hatred, it need not. Frequently, we express a sense of injury or loss through the emotions of anger, sadness, depression, or an aroused desire to assert ourselves in order to regain lost affection.

Furthermore, whereas envy requires only two people, jealousy normally requires three—a triangle. For example, a sister or brother is jealous of a sibling because only one receives what both need: attention and recognition from their parents. A worker is jealous of a co-worker because the latter received an award or bonus from the employer. A lover is jealous because the beloved favors a rival suitor.

Finally, whereas envy is tied to feelings of inferiority, jealousy derives from feelings of insecurity. It entails a fear that one will lose something dear, or it brings a painful collapse after the loss of a hoped-for relationship. The vulnerability caused by love exposes even the most secure person to the insecurities of jealousy. For example, in Shakespeare's tragedy *Othello*, the title character, a socially secure and successful military leader, becomes intensely jealous when he (mistakenly) suspects his wife Desdemona of having an affair with his lieutenant, Cassio. (Note that Iago, who plots to make Othello feel this way, is motivated by envy, not jealousy.) Othello's jealousy and doubts about Desdemona's faithfulness become an obsession. He cannot work, love, or think rationally, and in a final rage he kills Desdemona.

Under this definition, is jealousy, like envy, always bad? It certainly has a bad reputation. Othello reminds us of its potential to foster destructive anger and hate. More recently, the 1960s free-love movement attempted to portray jealousy as based on an ugly attitude of possessiveness. The jealous person was viewed as treating his or her lover as a commodity that can be owned. Love, the free-love movement insisted, must be freely given and received as a gift, never claimed as a property right. Taylor defended this assessment of jealousy:

> Jealousy is the most wrenching and destructive of human passions. Not only is it painful, but the pain is self-inflicted; and unlike most other emotions, no good ever comes from it…. Jealousy always has its source in something almost as ugly as itself; namely, in the attitude of possessiveness towards another person.[18]

Taylor viewed jealousy as destructive of love, or at least of erotic love (which was his main concern):

> Possessive love, as it might be called, is no real expression of love at all, but its perversion. Loving an *object* is not really loving *it* at all; instead, it is an expression of self-love. A person who takes pride in his possessions, who glories in them, quite clearly does not love them for their own sake, but for his. They are just ornaments.[19]

Is this entirely negative evaluation of jealousy warranted? Granted, jealousy can become pathological, involving immoral possessive attitudes toward other people and their affection, but it need not. In fact, jealousy is very often a sign of love! Consider the traditional "love game" designed to test whether someone really cares about us. We contrive a situation in which the person being tested sees us with some attractive rival. Our goal is that the person will show displeasure, thereby confirming our hope that the person desires our affection, and that the person will become more ardent in pursuing us.

Of course, this is a *game*, most often a childish game of the sort encountered in soap operas. It can even cause harm when it backfires, by causing the beloved to feel betrayed or abandoned. Nevertheless, it provides a clue to a deeper truth: Feelings of jealousy show we care about the attention and affection of another, and this is frequently a sign of love. Imagine a married couple who are utterly incapable of feeling jealous of each other. No matter how much time, affection, and sexual attention each partner devotes to others, neither ever feels a twinge of jealousy. Either they are exceptionally confident they will never lose whatever it is they need from each other, or they do not care very deeply about each other.

Jerome Neu puts the point this way: "Behind jealousy lies love.... [For] 'jealousy' includes a positive evaluation of, or attachment to, the person (or thing or property) one is jealous over or about. One can be jealous only of something that it highly valued."[20] As Neu also emphasizes, jealousy may be an inevitable aspect of some personal relationships. Intimate love relationships usually demand large amounts of time and energy, and time and energy are limited quantities. It is understandable that jealousy will play a role when these quantities are too much diverted from the relationship.

Even if we grant that jealousy is frequently a sign of love, and perhaps an inescapable aspect of intimate relationships, does any real good ever come from it? Would anything be lost if all jealousy suddenly disappeared from human experience?

Something might indeed be lost. Two good things can be said about at least some jealousy, if it does not become obsessive and cruel. First, jealousy provides a helpful vehicle for self-discovery: Honest reflection on jealousy can yield insights about whom we love and how deeply we love (as the previous comments imply). Second, jealousy sometimes helps to protect and preserve love and friendship. It functions as an emotional alarm, warning us that caring relationships may be at risk from outsiders. As with the emotion of fear, jealousy can provide a painful but prompt warning before we can even articulate our concern for a relationship. Moreover, jealousy can strengthen, albeit temporarily, the ardor with which love is expressed, because we put more attention into valuable things when we believe they are at risk. In this role it serves on occasion to help sustain intimate and caring relationships.

SUMMARY

The traditional form of marriage in Western culture is based on mutual commitments between a man and a woman to life-long companionship and sexual exclusivity (restriction of sexual relations to one's spouse). While there is no moral obligation to marry, marriage nevertheless raises moral questions. Some questions center on happiness and self-fulfillment and concern decisions whether to marry and whether to stay married. Other questions, especially those concerning extramarital affairs and adultery, center around moral ideals embraced and commitments undertaken by couples who enter into traditional marriages.

Critics argue that traditional marital commitments are inherently harmful in several respects. First, they allow government or churches to exercise regulatory control over marriages, which lessens the spouses' sense of full responsibility for their relationship. Second, the commitments are psychologically constrictive and prevent enriching relationships with people other than one's spouse. Some feminists emphasize especially the economic and psychological damage done to women in particular. Third, the commitment to sexual exclusivity leads to sexual confinement, which causes insecurity and jealousy and betrays a degrading attitude of ownership of the spouse's sexual activities.

Richard Taylor defends extramarital affairs insofar as they are based on passionate love. He argues that such affairs are singularly exciting, supportive of self-esteem, and valuable for the affection and love they provide. They need not involve either infidelity or immoral deception. Infidelity is a betrayal of love, but one can love a partner in an affair while continuing to love one's spouse. Moreover, one's love for a spouse entails a desire not to hurt her or his feelings, and so one may be justified in concealing the affair with secrecy and deception. These provocative claims, however, are open to challenge, as the Discussion Topics below suggest.

Jealousy is the feeling that we have lost or may lose something dear to us, in particular the affection of someone we value. Jealousy is sometimes very bad, as when it becomes obsessive and destroys loving relationships. Sometimes, however, it has good effects: It can aid self-understanding, warn of dangers to relationships, and evoke increased attention to a relationship.

DISCUSSION TOPICS

1   An "open marriage" is one in which spouses mutually agree to permit each other to have extramarital affairs. In some open marriages there is an agreement to tell each other about the affairs; in others, disclosure is left to the discretion of the spouse having the affair; and in still others there is an agreement not to tell each

other about the affairs. Without appealing to religious beliefs (about divine commandments), can you find anything immoral about any of these forms of open marriage?

2   One objection to traditional marriages is that they are based on unrealistic commitments. No matter how intense one's feelings may be at the time of the marriage, no one can know for sure whether one will still love one's spouse twenty or fifty years, or even one year, later, because feelings are not entirely under one's control. Therefore, such commitments are either foolish or dishonest (based on pretense). Do you agree? In presenting your answer, clarify what you mean by "love." Also, compare and contrast marriage vows to other lifetime promises, such as a promise made to a parent that one will become (and stay) a doctor, or a promise made to God to undertake a lifetime of humanitarian service.

3   Comment on sayings like "True love will last," "Love is all we need" (to make our relationship work), and "Love will keep us together." Distinguish different things that might be meant by "love" (some of which perhaps make the cliché false, and some true). In particular, does your conception of love incorporate the effort to cultivate such virtues as patience, persistence, flexibility, willingness to compromise, sensitivity, honesty, courtesy, and even a sense of humor? Does it include the willingness to "fight fair" during disagreements by not attacking one's partner in emotionally vulnerable areas, as well as the skill not to allow daily problems to escalate out of all proportion? How is the virtue of wisdom—which enables us to know when a marriage has become hopeless and is best dissolved—related to love?

4   Taylor argues compellingly that marital infidelity can take forms having nothing to do with sexual exclusivity. That does not prove, however, that violation of marriage vows of sexual exclusivity is not also infidelity. Isn't it a form of infidelity to have a sexual affair after one has promised (to one's spouse) not to have such affairs? If it is, can the obligation of fidelity sometimes be overridden by other considerations that justify sexual affairs?

5   Taylor contends that affairs do not threaten good marriages based on love. If by "love" he includes the willingness to indulge a spouse's affairs, the claim is true by definition; but Taylor seems to be making an empirical claim (one based on experience) about the effects of affairs on marriages characterized by a deep sense of caring. He bases the claim on his own experience, together with over sixty questionnaires filled out by people who answered an ad he placed in three newspapers. (The ad stated that a professor of philosophy was researching extramarital love affairs and called for people willing to answer a questionnaire.) Do you agree with Taylor's claim that extramarital affairs do not threaten good marriages? What kind of scientific studies of marriages are needed to determine whether Taylor is correct?

6   Many people are currently experimenting with various forms of "marriage contracts." For example, before marrying, a couple might sign a legal document specifying the distribution of money and property in the event of divorce. (See Lenore Weitzman's book *The Marriage Contract*... for details.) Critics of these contracts contend that they convey doubts about whether the relationship will survive, and thereby weaken the hope for a permanent relationship based on

trust. (Such contracts might even constitute a kind of self-fulfilling prophecy.) Defenders believe that the contracts are based on an attitude of realism (in facing the fact that one in two marriages ends in divorce) and that such an attitude may actually benefit the relationship. What is your view and why?

7 Does the fact that traditional marriages involve commitments to life-long companionship imply that divorce automatically represents a kind of moral failure? Isn't it possible to be morally justified in withdrawing a lifetime commitment in light of major changes in one's life and the relationship with one's spouse? Is divorce sometimes a very good thing, even when children are involved?

8 Present and defend your view about whether sexual jealousy is good or bad. Bring to mind several examples from your experience and experiences of your friends. If jealousy is natural, how is it best dealt with?

SUGGESTED READINGS

Bayles, Michael D. "Marriage, Love, and Procreation." In R. Baker and F. Elliston (eds.), *Philosophy and Sex*. Rev. ed. Buffalo, NY: Prometheus, 1984.

Bernard, Jessie. *The Future of Marriage*. New York: Bantam, 1973.

Cancian, Francesca M. *Love in America: Gender and Self-Development*. New York: Cambridge University Press, 1987.

Clanton, Gordon, and Lynn G. Smith (eds.). *Jealousy*. Lanham, PA: University Press of America, 1986.

Friday, Nancy. *Jealousy*. New York: Morrow, 1985.

Friedman, Marilyn. "The Social Self and the Partiality Debates." In C. Card (ed.), *Feminist Ethics*. Lawrence, KS: University Press of Kansas, 1991.

Graham, Gordon. "Commitment and the Value of Marriage." In G. Graham and H. LaFollette (eds.), *Person to Person*. Philadelphia, PA: Temple University Press, 1989. Pp. 199–212.

Gregory, Paul. "Against Couples." *Journal of Applied Philosophy*, vol. 1 (1984).

Hite, Shere. *Women and Love: A Cultural Revolution in Progress*. New York: Knopf, 1987.

Hunter, J. F. M. *Thinking about Sex and Love*. Toronto, Ontario: Macmillan of Canada, 1980.

Martin, Mike W. "Adultery and Fidelity." *Journal of Social Philosophy*, vol. forthcoming (1994).

Martin, Mike W. "Love's Constancy." *Philosophy*, vol. 68 (1993): 63–77.

McMurtry, John. "Monogamy: A Critique." *The Monist*, vol. 56 (1972). Reprinted in R. Baker and F. Elliston (eds.), *Philosophy and Sex*. Rev. ed. Buffalo, NY: Prometheus, 1984.

Neu, Jerome. "Jealous Thoughts." In A. O. Rorty (ed.), *Explaining Emotions*. Berkeley, CA: University of California Press, 1980.

O'Driscoll, Lyla H. "On the Nature and Value of Marriage." In M. Vetterling-Braggin, F. A. Elliston, and J. English (eds.), *Feminism and Philosophy*. Totowa, NJ: Rowman & Allanheld, 1977.

Okin, Susan Moller. *Justice, Gender, and the Family.* New York: Basic Books, 1989.

Palmer, David. "The Consolation of the Wedded." In R. Baker and F. Elliston (eds.), *Philosophy and Sex.* Rev. ed. Buffalo, NY: Prometheus, 1984.

Russell, Bertrand. *Marriage and Morals.* New York: Liveright, 1929.

Sommers, Christina Hoff. "Philosophers Against the Family." In G. Graham and H. LaFollette (eds.), *Person to Person.* Philadelphia, PA: Temple University Press, 1989. Pp. 82–105.

Steinbock, Bonnie. "Adultery." In A. Soble (ed.), *The Philosophy of Sex.* Rev. ed. Savage, MD: Rowman & Littlefield, 1991. Pp. 187–192.

Taylor, Richard. *Having Love Affairs.* Buffalo, NY: Prometheus, 1982.

Tov-Ruach, Leila. "Jealousy, Attention, and Loss." In A. O. Rorty (ed.), *Explaining Emotions.* Berkeley, CA: University of California Press, 1980.

Wasserstrom, Richard A. "Is Adultery Immoral?" In R. A. Wasserstrom (ed.), *Today's Moral Problems.* 3rd ed. New York: Macmillan, 1985.

Weitzman, Lenore J. *The Divorce Revolution: The Unexpected Social and Economic Consequences for Women and Children in America.* New York: Free Press, 1985.

Weitzman, Lenore J. *The Marriage Contract: A Guide to Living with Lovers and Spouses.* New York: Free Press, 1981.

CHAPTER 16

Homosexuality and Homophobia

Homosexuality is the sexual orientation in which one's primary attraction is to members of one's own sex. Gays are men primarily attracted to men, and lesbians are women primarily attracted to women. In heterosexuality the primary sexual attraction is to members of the opposite sex, and in bisexuality the attraction is to both men and women. Sexual orientation is defined by predominant patterns of sexual desires, emotions, fantasies, behavior, and the cues or stimuli that lead to sexual arousal. Sexual orientation differs from biological sex type (male versus female) and gender identity (one's conviction of being male or female and masculine or feminine).[1] It also differs from sex roles, that is, the social roles conventionally expected for men and women (as defined by physique, voice, clothing, personality, occupation, parenting styles, and so on).

Classical Greek culture accepted male homosexuality, but most Western societies have treated homosexuals with contempt and oppression. For a long while, homosexuality was viewed as a sickness, and today many people continue to condemn homosexual acts as deeply immoral. In this chapter we discuss whether those negative attitudes are justified or whether they are based on ignorance, prejudice, and fear, that is, homophobia. Homophobia is the excessive and unjustified fear and hatred of homosexuality, homosexual acts, and homosexuals. Often, homophobia leads to acts of prejudice and persecution: ridicule, discrimination, support of social policies that oppress homosexuals, and violence against gays and lesbians. Is homosexuality immoral, or is hatred of homosexuality an irrational prejudice (homophobic)? Is the moral problem homosexuality or homophobia? In this chapter we consider the arguments on each side of this issue.

Closets and Coming Out

Let us begin with two case studies illustrating the difficulties confronting gay and lesbian people. Negative social attitudes lead many homosexuals to live "closeted" lives of sexual isolation, loneliness, fear, and frustration. Not only does this compound the normal difficulties associated with finding sexual partners, it also encourages short-lived affairs rather than long-term relationships, which are publicly visible and hence dangerous in a climate of social oppression of homosexuality. Public affirmation of a homosexual identity—"coming out"—usually incurs the risk of reprisals: rejection, derisive laughter, physical assault, and violation of rights in gaining and retaining employment, in buying or renting homes, and in purchasing life insurance.

Social pressure also can make it difficult to "come out to oneself," that is, to acknowledge and affirm to oneself one's sexual orientation. Whatever one's sexual identity, adolescence is a turbulent time in terms of awakening to, accepting, and expressing one's sexuality. For gays and lesbians, however, the obstacles are multiplied. The difficulties continue well into adulthood, as is illustrated in the autobiography of Malcolm Boyd, *Take Off the Masks.*

During the 1960s and 1970s, Boyd was well known as a nonviolent civil rights activist, Vietnam War protester, and religious thinker. As a prominent Episcopalian priest he crusaded for the rights of women to enter the priesthood, and he also sought to strengthen ties between Christians and Jews. Yet his acceptance of his own sexuality required a painful and gradual process.

At age ten he knew he was attracted to boys and men, but he suppressed the thoughts and impulses accompanying that attraction. During high school, he took a rare (and spontaneous) gamble in hinting to his closest friend that he was attracted to him. The friend never spoke to him again. In college and early adulthood he grew contemptuous of homosexuals and was willing to laugh derisively at them. Yet later he occasionally experimented with gay relationships, which led only to feelings of intense guilt and self-contempt.

Boyd was thirty-three when he began to accept his sexual orientation. He was able to do so through a love relationship with a man who reciprocated his feelings. The affair lasted eight months, until circumstances forced the two men apart. About the experience Boyd wrote:

> Could I not stand, alone before my God, and say, "This is who I am. I can be no other." Wasn't this the essence of Christianity—a direct and personal relationship between a human being and God? "Listen, for whatever reason you made me, I am part of your creation. I have found a capacity to love. I do not believe that that is sin."[2]

During the next decade Boyd fell in love twice more, but again it was impossible to pursue the affairs publicly in a way that would enable them to last. Gradually, he was able fully to accept his homosexuality and the form of love it made possible:

I cannot recall a sexual relationship that was ever simply casual for me. Always I felt an intensity, a yearning to belong and love, and an awesome sense of universal meaning in *this* act. Surely this has brought me sadness as well as joy.[3]

For lesbians, acceptance of homosexuality can be a process even more difficult, because of additional general social pressures against assertiveness in women in overcoming their expected social roles. Those individuals who achieve self-acceptance without major trauma tend to be unusually strong. One such woman is Martina Navratilova, the champion tennis player. Navratilova says she is bisexual (although she hates that "creepy sounding" label), but her primary adult sexual attachments have been with women.

During her early teenage years, Navratilova had crushes on both female and male teachers. Later, she felt strong attachments to a few women tennis players. Only when she turned eighteen, however, did she recognize and accept that these crushes involved a sexual interest. At that time she also had her first love relationship, one initiated by an older and more assertive woman:

> When it finally happened, I said, this is easy and right. And the next morning—*voilà*—I had an outright, head-over-heels case of infatuation with her. When will I see you again? What will we do with our time together? I was in love, just like in the story books, and everything felt great.[4]

Things were not so great when her parents learned about the affair. Her father immediately referred her to a book about "her sickness." There were vehement arguments. During one argument her father said he would rather see her become a prostitute than a lesbian (and he meant it). Navratilova also worried that her sexual orientation would disrupt her attempts to become an American citizen after defecting from her native country, Czechoslovakia (where, incidentally, gays were sent to insane asylums and lesbians never came out of the closet).

The Reproductive Purpose of Sex

Is there anything immoral about homosexual acts? One view, held by the Catholic church and some other major religions, is that homosexuality is *unnatural* in that it departs from (or "perverts") the proper role of sex in human life. Sex is properly viewed as the means of procreation—of having children. Because homosexual acts do not have the potential to generate children, they constitute a misuse of sex and are therefore immoral. According to Leviticus in the Old Testament, homosexual acts are an abomination warranting death by stoning.[5] And according to Romans in the New Testament, homosexuals are guilty of a "vile affection" that alters "the natural use [of sex] into that which is against nature"[6] (although it is noteworthy that Jesus never himself condemns or even mentions homosexuality).

If homosexual acts are immoral simply because they cannot lead to children, then it follows that all other kinds of sexual acts that cannot lead to children are also immoral. Masturbation and heterosexual intercourse using contraceptives, for example, would also have to be condemned. If we leave aside certain religious views, it is hard to see how such acts could be immoral; and if we accept that masturbation and sexual intercourse using effective contraception are not inherently immoral, the statement that all nonreproductive sex is immoral becomes false. Therefore, the mere fact that homosexual acts cannot generate children does not make them immoral.

This type of argument is known as *reductio ad absurdum* (reduction to absurdity), which is an attempt to refute a view by showing that it entails a falsehood, drawing on the logical point that true views do not entail falsehoods. The argument should be convincing for anyone who believes that masturbation and the use of birth control devices are not immoral per se. What could be said, however, to persuade someone who does not hold these beliefs?

For example, Saint Thomas Aquinas would not be convinced by the *reductio ad absurdum* argument. According to him, all use of sex except for procreation is immoral:

> The emission of semen ought to be so ordered that it will result in both the production of the proper offspring and in the upbringing of this offspring.

> It is evident from this that every emission of semen, in such a way that generation cannot follow, is contrary to the good for man. And if this be done deliberately, it must be a sin.... For which reason, sins of this type are called contrary to nature.[7]

In fact, Aquinas believed that masturbation and homosexuality constituted sins even worse than heterosexual rape, because rape could at least generate children. Today, the Catholic church does not share that view, nor does it agree with Aquinas that the *sole* legitimate use of sex is procreation: Sex also should express love. Nevertheless, the official Catholic view concurs with Aquinas that masturbation, use of contraceptives in heterosexual sex, and homosexual acts are all immoral for the same reason: They are not the type of acts that can lead to reproduction.

One way to proceed at this point is to argue that masturbation is surely morally permissible when it leads to pleasure and has no bad side effects; and that intercourse with contraceptives is morally permissible and often desirable when it supports loving relationships and yields no harmful side effects (as are other nonreproductive sex acts based on mutual consent, such as oral sex). Support for this view seems to be offered, at least on the surface, by utilitarianism (in emphasizing mutual pleasure and happiness), duty ethics (in emphasizing mutual respect and autonomous consent of adults), and rights ethics (in emphasizing freedom that does not harm others).

Let us shift the burden of proof, however, by asking whether there are any good reasons for believing that nonreproductive sex is bad. What could be morally objectionable about using sex solely to express affection and love, at least within long-term relationships of the sort that Boyd and Navratilova sought to establish in their lives? Doesn't sex have several natural and legitimate uses in addition to procreation, enabling us, for instance, to obtain pleasure, relieve stress, strengthen self-esteem, show affection, and express love?

Notice that the question about moral reasons does not disappear if we appeal to God or stipulate that "natural" means "what God commands" and "unnatural" means what God forbids. Even if we set aside religious disagreements about what God commands and whether God exists, recall the point raised in Chapter 1: It makes sense to ask *why* God commands certain things rather than others. Presumably, a morally perfect being would make commandments on the basis of good moral reasons rather than on whim or from prejudice. Are there any good reasons to believe that a morally perfect being would forbid all nonreproductive types of sex acts? This is essentially the same question as above: Are there any good reasons for believing that all nonreproductive sex acts are bad? This question will be left as a discussion topic.

Other Senses of "Unnatural"

If we set aside the senses of "unnatural sex" that mean "nonprocreative" and "contrary to God's commands," are there any other senses in which homosexuality is unnatural—senses that have some moral relevance? The words *natural* and *unnatural* do have other meanings, but it is doubtful that they have any moral significance or relevance for thinking about homosexuality.

First, one could define *natural* in terms of "the *primary* biological function." Thus, the natural function of the digestive system and of eating is to provide nutrition for the body; similarly, the natural function of genitals and sexual intercourse is procreation. If we adopt this definition, nonreproductive sex is unnatural (assuming the most important evolutionary role of sex is reproduction); but even though this may be true, critics argue that it is morally irrelevant to the topic of homosexuality. Just because the primary function of the digestive system and of eating is nutrition, it does not follow that it is immoral sometimes to eat just for pleasure or during an enjoyable luncheon with a friend or spouse, even though one is not hungry or in need of food. Similarly, even if the primary biological purpose of sex is procreation, it does not follow that it is bad to use sex solely for pleasure or for expressing love.

Second, *natural* might mean "healthy," both mentally and physically. Is homosexuality a mental illness? Here the expert testimony of health professionals is relevant (if not decisive). Before 1974, the American Psychiatric Association (APA) viewed homosexuality as a mental disorder and listed it as such in its *Diagnostic and Statistical Manual of Mental Disorders*. In 1974, however, the APA acknowledged that it had made a mistake and emended the *Manual*. Did the mistake arise because psychiatrists misinterpreted the anxieties they sometimes observed in homosexuals as symptoms of an illness rather than as largely the product of special societal pressures on homosexuals? Did the mistake perhaps express homophobia among health professionals of the time? Today, most health professionals—the vast majority—do not view homosexuality as unhealthy. Insofar as homosexuals suffer from any greater anxiety or depression, the cause is now understood to be society's rejection of homosexuality.

The physical health of many gays, of course, has been devastated by AIDS. Homosexuality is not, however, the cause of AIDS, and homosexual acts by themselves do not cause AIDS. AIDS is spread by the failure to use precautions (especially condoms) during homosexual *or* heterosexual intercourse (as well as by the shared use of needles by drug addicts and transfusions of contaminated blood).

Third, some people see a kind of naturalness in how genitals "fit together" during heterosexual intercourse. Here *natural* seems to mean "geometrically complementary." Is the notion of genital geometry, however, relevant to the debate over homosexuality as unnatural? Or does it express a heterosexual bias against homosexual experiences, especially in view of the fact that the alleged geometrical problem is never voiced by homosexuals?

Fourth, *natural* might mean "common" or "usual." Again, critics argue that this sense is also irrelevant morally. The fact that most people are heterosexual does not make it immoral to be in a sexual minority. If it did, then by analogy all left-handed people would be immoral too, because they represent a minority orientation to space and activities; likewise, windsurfing would constitute an immoral use of the sea.

Fifth, *natural* might be used to characterize something that "feels natural," in the sense that it is based on an inclination that one feels and with which one identifies. True, many heterosexuals do lack or are uncomfortable about homosexual impulses, which seem alien and repulsive, but isn't this only a statement about heterosexual tastes and orientation, a statement that lacks moral force? To illustrate, many people are repelled at the thought of eating snails, but it does not follow that a passion for escargot is immoral. Tastes in food, wine, books, and friends—and sex—involve deep feelings that can be as strong as moral emotions. For this reason, it is sometimes easy to confuse issues of taste and morality, but they are distinct.

Sixth, *natural* might be defined as that which conforms to the appropriate roles for men and women. Homosexuality, it is claimed, is morally objectionable because gays tend to be effeminate in gesture and voice, violating masculine role models; conversely, lesbians tend to be unfeminine. Critics point out that this argument falsely stereotypes the mannerisms of gays and lesbians, most of whom do not fit this profile. (For example, Rock Hudson was gay but not effeminate.) The argument also assumes that all males and all females have a moral obligation to fit a particular gender role, and it apparently misappropriates the word *natural* by applying it to what are primarily socially created (not naturally created) sex roles.

Promiscuity

Another stereotypic view of gays—that all gays are promiscuous due to something inherent in male homosexuality—merits a separate discussion. Whereas lesbians tend not to be promiscuous, there are in fact gay men who have many hundreds of sexual partners during a lifetime. Yet most gays have fewer partners than this stereotype suggests, and of course many heterosexual males are also promiscuous, and have sex as often as they can find a willing partner.

Nevertheless, Roger Scruton argues that male homosexuality *tends* to encourage promiscuity and thereby discourages long-term love relationships of the kind he values (see Chapter 14). According to Scruton, all males have a strong natural tendency to sexual predation, which means they will desire many sexual partners during a lifetime. This instinct is tamed through attraction to the "mystery" of the opposite sex. Because members of the opposite sex are radically unlike oneself (physically, mentally), in pursuing sexual relationships with them one knowingly undertakes great risks—the risks of the unknown. These risks encourage commitment and fidelity that form the basis for long-term relationships grounded in erotic love.

> The opening of the self to the mystery of another gender, thereby taking responsibility for an experience which one does not wholly understand, is a feature of sexual maturity, and one of the fundamental motives tending towards commitment. This exposure to something unknown can resolve itself, finally, only in a mutual vow. Only in a vow is the trust created which protects the participants from the threat of betrayal. Without the fundamental experience of the otherness of the sexual partner, an important component in erotic love is therefore put in jeopardy. For the homosexual, who knows intimately in himself the generality that he finds in the other, there may be a diminished sense of risk. The move out of the self may be less adventurous, the help of the other [within a long-term relationship] less required.[8]

In short, Scruton thinks that mystery heightens risk, and risk encourages the partners to make a mutual commitment that sustains them in taking the risk. Homosexual relationships offer less mystery because the participants are already familiar with the gender of their partners; therefore, the need for commitment is decreased, and promiscuity is encouraged.

Is this a sound argument? Scruton is sensitive to one difficulty: If the argument works for gays, why should it not also work for lesbians? Lesbian promiscuity is rare, and Scruton implies that the real problem lies in the sexual predatoriness of all males. But his "mystery of the opposite sex" argument seems to imply that lesbians would be less inclined to form commitments than other women, and no evidence supports that conclusion. A second difficulty is that the promiscuity of some gays can be explained in another way, which Scruton does not consider. As previously mentioned, the harsh social condemnations of homosexuality have made it very risky (often dangerous) for gays to be identified publicly, which discourages open, long-term relationships and encourages brief and secretive sexual encounters.

In assessing the "mystery and risk" argument, two further points need to be considered. There may be deep mysteries (and unknowns worth exploring) between any two lovers, whatever their sexual orientation. Were society to remove its taboo on homosexuality, couldn't the emotional and intellectual differences between two individuals suffice to encourage trust and commitment? Furthermore, shouldn't heterosexuals allow the possibility that homosexuality may contain its own domains of new and "mysterious" experience for those who choose to explore it? In this connection, consider the words of the poet and feminist Adrienne Rich concerning lesbian experience:

> Lesbian existence comprises both the breaking of a taboo and the rejection of a compulsory way of life. It is also a direct or indirect attack on male right of access to women. But it is more than these.... I perceive the lesbian experience as being, like motherhood, a profoundly *female* experience, with particular oppressions, meanings, and potentialities.[9]

Homophobia and Sexual Tastes

At this point we leave for discussion whether there are any convincing moral reasons against homosexuality. Let us conclude with some comments about homophobia. Whatever one's considered views about homosexuality, it is one thing to believe that homosexual acts are bad; it is quite another to hate, detest, degrade, and condone repression of homosexual persons.

Not everyone who objects to homosexuality (perhaps because of religious beliefs) is homophobic. They might object to hatred of homosexuals as much as they object to homosexuality itself. Many people, however, feel justified in "putting down" gays and lesbians in a variety of ways, ranging from tasteless jokes and derisive laughter to indifference to their legal rights. Is this not a form of prejudice as bad as prejudice based on race, religion, or physique?

Imagine someone arguing that the hatred involved in homophobia is no more immoral than hatred involved in other phobias. According to this argument, it is not immoral to have and to act upon phobias about spiders or snakes, about open spaces or closed spaces, or about heights and airplane rides. Similarly, nothing is immoral about hating gays and lesbians (whatever the moral status of homosexual acts). In fact, this argument is based on a weak analogy. Homophobia is directed toward people, not animals, spaces, special locations, or modes of transportation. The argument is akin to the assertion that one is not a racist, rather one simply has a phobia about black or Jewish people.

Consider another argument that appeals to the right to pursue one's own tastes. Just as we have tastes in food, sex, and clothing, we all have tastes in the kinds of people with whom we interact. Some people, so the argument goes, are uncomfortable with gay people and have a right to dislike them, avoid them, and joke about them. We do, of course, have a right to pursue our tastes, including those concerning people; but there are limits to those rights, and they do not justify violating the rights of others.

An equally important point is this: The existence of a right to pursue a taste does not imply that the taste is "all right" (i.e., morally permissible). The right to pursue our tastes implies that others should not attempt to coerce us to act otherwise; our tastes and actions may nevertheless be objectionable because they are prejudiced. Hatred of all homosexuals is a form of dismissing and shutting out people on the basis of one of their attributes, their sexual orientation. In that respect, at least, it is similar to racism and sexism.

SUMMARY

Homosexuality is the sexual orientation in which one is primarily attracted to members of one's own biological sex. Homophobia is the irrational fear and hatred of homosexuality, homosexual acts, and homosexuals.

The primary traditional ethical argument against homosexual acts is that they are unnatural or perverted in that they cannot result in reproduction. Sexual intercourse and orgasm, it is contended, are morally permissible only when they involve the kinds of acts that could lead to children. If this view were true, masturbation and sexual intercourse with contraceptives must likewise be condemned as unnatural or perverted.

Various other arguments supporting the idea that homosexual acts are unnatural include the following: (1) The primary biological function of sex is reproduction; (2) homosexual acts are unhealthy; (3) only in heterosexual acts is there genital geometry; (4) heterosexual acts are usual or most common; (5) only heterosexual acts are based on an inclination with which most people identify; and (6) only heterosexual acts conform to gender roles. In each case we raised questions suggesting that these senses of *unnatural* lack moral relevance.

Roger Scruton argues that male homosexuality encourages promiscuity, which makes it objectionable in light of the traditional view that sex should be joined to long-term erotic love relationships. His argument is that homosexuals miss out on the mysteries involved in a relationship with a member of the opposite sex (with whom one is less familiar than with one's own sex type). Yet, the main mysteries of sex derive from an exploration into the unknown of another person, whatever that person's sexual orientation, and the stronger tendency to promiscuity in some gays may be due to social pressures against publicly visible, long-term gay relationships.

Homophobia is unlike most phobias in that it is directed toward people. There are limits to how far one can go in acting on one's tastes. Even when one has a right not to be interfered with by others in pursuing one's tastes, those tastes may involve prejudice based on religion, race, or sexual orientation.

DISCUSSION TOPICS

1   Are there good reasons for believing that the only morally permissible sex acts are procreative kinds, that is, acts of the general kind that could lead to children?

2   Sexual orientation is something that, unlike sexual activities, is usually not chosen. (If you are heterosexual, did you ever choose to be so?) The causes of heterosexuality and homosexuality are still uncertain, although scientists are exploring genetic and environmental causes and, more recently, hormone balances during early stages of (fetal and neonatal) development. Moreover, sexual orientation is usually impossible to change completely, because it involves fundamental patterns of desires, fantasies, and interests that are not easily altered. Do these facts have any moral relevance to the question of whether homosexual and heterosexual acts are morally permissible?

3   One objection raised against homosexuality is that, if everyone (or most people) became homosexual, there would not be enough children to sustain society. Is this a good argument?

4   Heterosexuals take for granted the legal right to marry in any state in the United States, but homosexuals are denied this right (except in a few cities). Is this unjust discrimination? In your answer, take note of the fact that even if homosexuality is believed to be immoral, that does not settle the question about the right of homosexuals to marry. (Consider as well the following analogous situation: Many people believe that the use of contraceptives is immoral but do not believe that laws should prohibit their use or prohibit people who use them from marrying.)

5   One of the earliest controversies in President Clinton's administration concerned whether acknowledged homosexuals should be allowed to serve in the armed

forces. Are there any good reasons for prohibiting gay and lesbian soldiers from serving in the military, or has their past exclusion resulted from homophobia?

6 Some people say that, although they have nothing against homosexuals, they morally object to homosexuals "flaunting" their sexuality, for example, by holding hands or kissing in public. Often the same people do not object to heterosexuals engaging in similar conduct in public. What would you say to these people?

7 Homosexuals are often prevented from serving as scout leaders and camp counselors. Is this practice permissible, or is it a form of unjustified discrimination? In your answer, consider this: The practice is often defended by citing fears that homosexuals will molest young people, but it is now known that child abuse occurs at roughly the same rate among heterosexuals and homosexuals.

8 Assess the following claim: "Homosexuality is immoral because homosexuals caused the AIDS epidemic in the United States." In your assessment, take account of the fact that the existence of the AIDS virus was not even suspected (by homosexuals or by anyone) during the early years in which the epidemic spread. Also take account of the fact that, long after the gay community has taken decisive steps to control this epidemic, the drug culture and heterosexuals still are not taking adequate precautions.

SUGGESTED READINGS

Aquinas, St. Thomas. *On the Truth of the Catholic Faith.* Book 3: *Providence*, Part I, trans. V. J. Bourke. New York: Doubleday, 1956.

Batchelor, Edward (ed.). *Homosexuality and Ethics.* New York: Pilgrim Press, 1980.

Bentham, Jeremy. "An Essay on 'Paederasty.'" In R. Baker and F. Elliston (eds.), *Philosophy and Sex.* Rev. ed. Buffalo, NY: Prometheus, 1984.

Boyd, Malcolm. *Take Off the Masks.* Philadelphia, PA: New Society, 1984.

Card, Claudia. "Why Homophobia?" *Hypatia*, vol. 5 (Fall, 1990): 110–117.

Elliston, Frederick. "Gay Marriage." In R. Baker and F. Elliston (eds.), *Philosophy and Sex.* Rev. ed. Buffalo, NY: Prometheus, 1984.

Engelhardt, H. Tristram. "The Disease of Masturbation: Values and the Concept of Disease." In T. L. Beauchamp and L. Walters (eds.), *Contemporary Issues in Bioethics.* 2nd ed. Belmont, CA: Wadsworth, 1982.

Hoagland, Sarah. *Lesbian Ethics: Toward New Value.* Palo Alto, CA: Institute of Lesbian Studies, 1988.

Koertge, Noretta (ed.). *Philosophy and Homosexuality.* New York: Harrington Park Press, 1985.

Kosnik, Anthony, et al. *Human Sexuality: New Directions in American Catholic Thought.* New York: Paulist Press, 1977.

Levin, Michael. "Why Homosexuality is Abnormal." *The Monist*, vol. 67 (1984).

Levy, Donald. "Perversion and the Unnatural as Moral Categories." In A. Soble (ed.), *The Philosophy of Sex.* Totowa, NJ: Littlefield, Adams, 1980.

Mohr, Richard D. *Gays/Justice: A Study of Ethics, Society, and Law.* New York: Columbia University Press, 1988.

Rich, Adrienne. "Compulsory Heterosexuality and Lesbian Existence." *SIGNS: Journal of Women in Culture and Society*, vol. 5 (1980). Reprinted in C. R. Stimpson and E. Spector (eds.), *Women: Sex and Sexuality*. Chicago: University of Chicago Press, 1980.

Ruse, Michael. *Homosexuality*. Oxford: Basil Blackwell, 1988.

Scruton, Roger. *Sexual Desire: A Moral Philosophy of the Erotic*. New York: Free Press, 1986.

Weinberg, George. *Society and the Healthy Homosexual*. Garden City, NY: Anchor, 1973.

CHAPTER 17

Pornography and Fantasy

Sexually explicit magazines, books, and movies pervade our society. During the sexual revolution of the 1960s, supporters argued that such materials liberated sexual repressions and affirmed sex as good. In 1970, the President's Commission on Obscenity and Pornography concluded that pornography is not harmful but instead is a positive influence in releasing inhibitions, helping married couples with sexual difficulties, and encouraging frank discussions between parents and children about sex. Critics of this attitude were regarded as puritanical reactionaries who would have us retreat into the sexual hypocrisy and repression of the 1950s.

A decade later, however, these comfortable generalizations were subject to serious challenge (for different reasons) by two groups that had little else in common. Conservatives and some liberal feminists were both alarmed by the sheer magnitude of the multibillion-dollar pornography industry that was churning out obscenity on an alarming scale. Of greatest concern were two dramatic trends: the combination of sexual and violent images and the use of children in pornography. Liberation, it seemed to many, had turned into degradation of women and exploitation of children.

During the past decade, attempts have been made to control pornography through legislation against its makers, civil suits against its distributors, and by support for economic boycotts and demonstrations against its merchandisers. Debates over such attempts address important and complex issues; yet they should not deflect attention from everyday questions we all face concerning the use of pornography. Whether or not censorship of pornography violates rights to expression and privacy, we still need to examine the moral effects of pornography on our lives. Even if legal and moral rights forbid others from interfering with the use of pornography, we still need to ask whether that use is sometimes morally harmful. A right to use something does not automatically imply it is all right to use it.

We begin with a question of definition: Just what is pornography? We then ask several specific questions concerning use of pornography. Because many anxieties about pornography pertain to wider issues about fantasy pleasures, we next raise those concerns. The chapter concludes with a categorization of pornography to enable readers to pinpoint which kinds they find morally objectionable.

A Definition of Pornography

Disputes over pornography, whether between friends or among legislators, are often hamstrung by lack of clarity about the meaning of the term. It would be unreasonable to expect a definition to resolve uncertainties about what material is pornographic: There will always be difficult cases, whatever definition we adopt. Yet, in order to avoid verbal disputes—disputes based on misunderstandings about the meaning of a term—it is crucial to begin with some shared definition. At the same time, we should bear in mind that in public debates substantive issues are often blurred by the use of different definitions by different parties to the debate. When participating in those debates, we should be prepared to deal with contrasting definitions.

Conservative thinkers and many lawyers and judges use *pornography* as a close synonym for *obscenity* in the sense of something disgustingly offensive to decency. In this usage, to label something as pornography is to condemn it or to express a negative attitude toward it as "lacking a redeeming social value." For example, in 1986, Attorney General Meese's Commission on Pornography wrote a letter to the owners of 7-Eleven stores suggesting that, by selling *Playboy* and *Penthouse* magazines, they were distributing pornography. It was understood that this was intended as a criticism of the magazines as obscene, and for a while it caused the stores to stop selling them.

Some feminists (not all) have also built negative attitudes into their definitions of pornography, usually defining it as any sexual material that degrades women and exploits children. They invoke the term *erotica* to refer to morally acceptable sexually arousing material—including some material that the conservative Meese Commission might label obscene. One definition of pornography along these lines is given by Helen Longino:

> I define pornography as verbal or pictorial explicit representations of sexual behavior that ... have as a distinguishing characteristic the degrading and demeaning portrayal of the role and status of the human female ... as a mere sexual object to be exploited and manipulated sexually. In pornographic books, magazines, and films, women are

represented as passive and as slavishly dependent upon men. The role of female characters is limited to the provision of sexual services to men.[1]

Other feminist definitions are even narrower and specifically single out images of sexual violence against women. Robin Morgan implied such a definition in an essay with a title that quickly became a feminist slogan: "Theory and Practice: Pornography and Rape."[2]

These conservative and feminist definitions are "persuasive definitions" in that they define *pornography* in a way intended to persuade us to view pornography with a negative attitude. In the discussion that follows, however, we do not presuppose negative attitudes toward pornography. In fact, a more neutral definition is employed by most philosophers, literary critics, social scientists, and other feminists (who disagree with attempts to censor pornography). According to this neutral sense, *pornography* refers to sexually explicit material that is intended primarily to be sexually arousing, rather than, say, to serve some literary or educational purpose. Nudity shown in medical textbooks would not count as pornography, because its intended use is educational. Similarly, explicit depictions of highly erotic scenes in serious works of fiction, such as James Joyce's *Ulysses* or Philip Roth's *Portnoy's Complaint*, would not be considered pornographic, because the intended role of these depictions has a serious aesthetic purpose (beyond sexual arousal). As used here, *pornography* refers to any writing or image (in pictures, film, sculpture, music, and so on) that is sexually explicit and created with the primary intention of sexually arousing the reader, viewer, or audience. We will also speak of a *pornographic use* of nonpornography to refer to the use of any sexually explicit nonpornography (such as a photograph in a medical textbook, a scene in a serious novel, or an ad for lingerie) for purposes of sexual arousal.

These definitions are somewhat vague. They do not, for example, spell out what *sexually explicit* means. In any case, however, there will always be some uncertain or borderline instances of pornography, and this definition will at least enable us to proceed with some shared understanding.

Examples of Pornography

When is the use of pornography, or the pornographic use of sexual material, morally permissible, and when is it morally objectionable? Let us replace this general question with a few more specific questions, using several examples.

First, consider a married couple watching an X-rated video about another couple, who in real life happen to be married. The movie follows them from their first meeting through their honeymoon. The last half of the movie is devoted to graphic depictions of honeymoon lovemaking scenes. The love-making is lively, involves a remarkable variety of physical positions and loca-tions, is visually explicit and somewhat exaggerated in terms of the moaning and exclamations of pleasure, and depicts mutual assertiveness and equal ec-stasy for the two participants. The viewers struggle to contain themselves until the movie is over, at which time they jump into bed to engage in a considerably shorter version of what they have just seen.

This example is atypical. Very few X-rated movies depict men and women as sexual equals, or focus on sex between married people, or use actors who are married in real life. The example, however, provides a useful starting point for reflection. Is it at all morally objectionable for the couple to view the movie, or for the actors to perform in the movie? Assuming that both partners wanted to watch the film and did so in order to enhance their rela-tionship, is there anything problematic about watching another couple make love on film? Would your answer change if the actors in the example were not a married couple?

Here is another situation. A high school student buys photographic art magazines containing nude pictures that art critics would consider to be in good taste. The student appreciates the beauty of the models and has a strong interest in imagining what the women are like in real life. In his own mind, at least, the pictures depict people with whom he feels some sense of personal connection. He is especially attracted to those models who convey in their fa-cial expressions and bodily postures a sense of warmth, love, and ease with their bodies. Nevertheless, his use of the magazines is pornographic in that he buys them primarily because they are sexually exciting and he uses the pic-tures as the basis for his fantasies about making love and for masturbation.

Examples of this sort are part of the personal histories of most people. If the student is criticized for treating the models as "mere sex objects," then some account must be given of the role of the personal dimension of the fantasies. No doubt some individuals come to rely on fantasies to such an extent that they lose touch with reality, or else they allow the fantasies to foster distorted expectations of or attitudes toward women or men. When that does not occur, however, is there anything morally objectionable about this pornographic use of material, or is it instead a healthy form of sexual ex-pression and a normal aspect of developing a gender identity? Would your answer change if, instead of art magazines, the young man were viewing the pictures in *Playboy*?

Suppose about once a week a young woman reads a romance novel which contains some sexually explicit scenes. She takes some interest in the plot and character development, but she regards such elements primarily as a prelude to the more sexually arousing scenes involving explicit sexual depic-tions. Her main use of the novels is pornographic. Occasionally, the scenes form the basis for sexual fantasies, but for the most part they heighten her sexual life with her husband. Is there anything morally problematic about the fact that married partners may enjoy fantasies about having love affairs with people other than their spouses? If so, are the objections mitigated when the overall effects on the relationship are beneficial?

Next consider a single, middle-aged man who subscribes regularly to several hard-core pornography magazines because they feature close-ups of female genitals. His sex life consists of occasional affairs and regular masturbation sparked by fantasy images of the sort depicted in the magazines. He may or may not wish he had a richer sex life, but he has found a satisfactory compromise for the time being. Is it immoral to have a fantasy about one part of the body? Is it immoral to become preoccupied with such fantasies to the point where they become the center of one's sexual life?

Finally, let us consider a man who takes intense pleasure in watching snuff films, that is, films in which actresses play characters who are murdered ("snuffed out"). His all-time favorite is the 1976 film *Snuff*, which was advertised as showing the actual murder of a woman, although its distributors denied a real murder was filmed (and let us assume they were right). The film is about a man named Satan who leads a South American cult of young women who are allowed to enter the group only after an initiation involving torture. The cult plans a slaughter of a mother and her near-birth fetus. Following the graphic and violent scene in which the mother and baby are stabbed, the camera pulls back to show the production crew. A young production assistant tells the film director that she was greatly aroused by the scene, and the director responds by asking her to bed to play out her fantasies about the stabbing scene. Here is what follows, in the words of Beverly LaBelle, who saw the film:

> They start fumbling around in bed until she realizes that the crew is still filming. She protests and tries to get up. The director picks up a dagger that is lying on the bed and says, "Bitch, now you're going to get what you want." What happens next goes beyond the realm of language. He butchers her slowly, deeply, and thoroughly. The observer's gut revulsion is overwhelming at the amount of blood, chopped-up fingers, flying arms, sawed-off legs, and yet more blood oozing like a river out of her mouth before she dies. But the climax is still at hand. In a moment of undiluted evil, he cuts open her abdomen and brandishes her very insides high above his head in a scream of orgasmic conquest.[3]

Beverly LaBelle felt revulsion, but the male viewer in our example felt intense sexual arousal. Is our horror of this man due to a belief that he is likely to harm women? Or is there not something inherently immoral about someone's delight in such movies and fantasies, and about the attitudes toward women that underlie such fantasy pleasures?

Fantasy

Is pornography immoral insofar as it stimulates pleasurable fantasies about immorality, especially of the sort found in the last example? To answer this question we must first ask a more basic question: Is a fantasy immoral when (and because) it consists of pleasurable thoughts about immorality (whether or not pornography is involved)? Does the immorality of what is fantasized transfer in some way to the fantasy itself?

Fantasy as Morally Neutral

We do sometimes *feel* guilty or ashamed for enjoying thoughts about doing something we believe is wrong; but it does not follow that we actually are guilty of wrongdoing. Feelings, after all, can be inappropriate, excessive, and irrational (as we saw in Chapter 5). According to one view, familiar in popular psychology books, fantasies are harmless passing thoughts about which people should not feel guilt and for which they should not be criticized. Insofar as fantasies produce pleasure, they are good, and by themselves they cannot cause harm.

Furthermore, according to this view, fantasies are involuntary—they happen to us—and in this respect they are unlike voluntary actions with which morality is concerned. To be anxious about fantasies reflects a superstitious attitude. It is akin to the unreasonable anxieties of children who believe their nightmares or daydreams can magically cause events without further actions of their own. Indeed, criticism of fantasies on moral grounds is actually harmful, for it encourages repression of thoughts that should be freely brought to consciousness as aids to self-awareness.

This view is expressed by Nancy Friday in *My Secret Garden: Women's Sexual Fantasies*. According to Friday, fear of one's enjoyment of sexual fantasies is a sign of inhibitions that have been forced on women. Some sexual fantasies provide a healthy outlet (*catharsis*) for unrealized sexual desires, for desires for greater variety of partners and experiences or greater intensity of pleasure, for desires to control sexual encounters, and for the need for sexual approval and esteem.

Other sexual fantasies, according to Friday, do not express serious desires to do what is imagined:

> Fantasy need have nothing to do with reality, in terms of suppressed wish-fulfillment. Women ... whose fantasy life is focused on the rape theme, invariably insist that they have no real desire to be raped, and would, in fact, run a mile from anyone who raised a finger against them, and I believe them.[4]

Women who have such fantasies are expressing only a desire for a ravishing sexual experience, while maintaining in their imaginations full control over what happens (unlike what happens in rape).

Fantasy as Sometimes Immoral

A sharply opposed religious view, however, does not accept all sexual fantasies as morally neutral. In a familiar passage in the New Testament we read:

> Ye have heard that it was said by them of old time, Thou shalt not commit adultery:

> But I say unto you, that whosoever looketh on a woman to lust after her hath committed adultery with her already in his heart.[5]

Whatever the intent of the author of these lines, many Christians have held that they condemn as immoral pleasurable fantasies about certain sexual activities.

Is this religious view excessively moralistic? In his essay "Real Guilt and Neurotic Guilt," Herbert Fingarette finds some basis for it. Fingarette points out that, according to both Freudian psychoanalysis and common sense, fantasies express and are caused by wishes and desires. These wishes and desires, rather than fantasies per se, are subject to moral appraisal:

> Moral guilt accrues by virtue of our wishes, not merely our acts.... The question of moral guilt does not wait for acts; it is in profound degree a question of what one harbors in one's heart.... One only need wish evil in order to be genuinely guilty.[6]

Fingarette adds some important qualifications, however, that bring him somewhat closer to Friday's view. First, he is sensitive to the complexities involved in interpreting fantasies in order to uncover the wish or desire they express. As Freud emphasized, wishes are often distorted and disguised before they reach consciousness as fantasies and daydreams. Hence, the wish expressed in the fantasy may not be a wish actually to do what is fantasized; this notion is compatible with Friday's view that women's rape fantasies do not express a desire to be raped.

Second, Fingarette develops his thesis primarily with respect to neurotics who deceive themselves about their wishes. He emphasizes that, in order to confront these wishes, individuals must be willing to bring them to consciousness and reflect on them honestly. Here again he would agree with Friday about the importance of exploring rather than repressing dreams, daydreams, and fantasies of all sorts. He would also agree that an excessively harsh judgmental attitude toward fantasies can prevent honest self-exploration.

Third, the degree of guilt entailed in the act of wishing is obviously far less than that entailed in the actual commission of an immoral act. Common sense alone tells us that to murder someone is infinitely worse than to wish to murder them: The murder harms another person, whereas the wish need not affect others at all. Moreover, the murderer, by acting, has accepted and endorsed the wish to kill, which makes him or her far worse in character than the fantasizer.

This last comment suggests that guilt should be measured in part by the extent to which a person endorses and identifies with wishes to do immoral things. Although Fingarette might agree with this point concerning healthy people, he draws attention to a complication: Neurotics refuse to acknowledge and identify with troublesome wishes and instead deceive themselves about them. In this connection Fingarette notes that the disavowed wishes can wreak havoc in the neurotic's life, as well as harm others through actions that express those wishes. Hence, Fingarette suggests that the degree of guilt for wishes depends not just on how far one identifies with one's wishes, but also on the degree to which the wishes have harmful effects. We should take into account the actual effect the wish has on individuals and their relationships.

A Synthesis of Opposing Views

Which is correct, Friday's complete demoralization of fantasies or Fingarette's guarded moralization of them? However we answer this question, three points seem clear.

First, the crux of the matter, as both Friday and Fingarette agree, lies in the extent to which fantasies influence lives; in particular, how they influence actions, attitudes, emotions, and relationships. Fantasies vary considerably in how they function within individuals' personalities, characters, and relationships. Perhaps Friday is too optimistic in her effort to make us more accepting of sexual fantasies, and Fingarette unduly somber, perhaps as a result of focusing on neurotics.

Second, Friday and Fingarette also agree that we must take care in interpreting exactly what wish is being expressed in fantasies. Consider, for example, adultery fantasies. Some of them involve desires to hurt one's spouse, and therefore raise moral concerns. Others, perhaps most, involve no desire to hurt. They merely express a wish for an exciting experience, and they need have no adverse effects on relationships. Many adultery fantasies do not express a serious desire for an affair, but merely represent a wish to enjoy a pleasurable thought. These fantasies generate moral concern only when they become obsessive and strengthen strong desires that add to temptations to have affairs in which a spouse is betrayed.

Third, we have varying degrees of control over our fantasies. Some fantasies arise involuntarily and then drift out of consciousness, never to reappear. A censorious attitude toward them is surely inappropriate, not only because they come uninvited and have no further implications in our lives, but also because preoccupation with judging them deflects attention from matters of greater importance.

Other fantasies are intentionally brought to mind or reveled in once they enter consciousness. Occasionally, this provides an effective release for an impulse that would otherwise boil within and eventually cause outward harm. To deliberately feed the imagination with images of violence, however, is more likely to have the opposite effect of strengthening impulses. It is not prudishness, but common sense, to believe that at least some men who eagerly and repeatedly seek out violent sexual pornography are fostering desires and attitudes that they should instead work to overcome.

In sum, the moral status of sexual fantasies about immoral acts is complex. These fantasies are not automatically immoral; neither are they always immune from moral criticism. Similarly, the moral status of the use of pornography to stimulate fantasy is equally complex. We must all assess our fantasies and the fantasies of others in light of overall patterns of behavior and attitude, avoiding the extremes of viewing fantasies either as always harmless or always subject to moral criticism. In making these assessments, we need to bear in mind that the pleasure we derive from fantasies can serve as a motive for self-deception about the subtle ways in which indulgence in certain fantasies can shape our attitudes, which in turn are expressed in conduct.

Obscenity

Private fantasies represent only one dimension of pornography use. There is another: the public reality of massive amounts of pornographic material. Pornography entails explicit *depiction* of sex through words or images intended to arouse sexually. Depiction requires the use of a medium or representational form—books, magazines, pictures, movies, taped telephone recordings, computer programs, and so forth. The extensive purchase, rental, and use of pornography contributes to this social practice. It would seem that repeated use of violent and degrading forms of pornography for pleasure constitutes a tacit endorsement of the objectionable attitudes underlying immoral forms of pornography.

Most of us do not object to all pornography, but we do regard some pornography as obscene. Obscenity is not defined solely in terms of the emotions it provokes, such as disgust, nausea, and abhorrence; after all, we can recognize obscenity even after becoming desensitized and jaded toward it. Obscenity refers to that which goes beyond decency, and hence refers to standards of decency and beliefs about those standards.

Obscenity is a wider concept than pornography. An action or a remark as well as a depiction may be regarded as obscene. Also, obscenity may take nonsexual forms. There are obscene ways of eating (gluttonously), and obscene depictions of excretion and defecation. Although *obscene* can be used as an aesthetic term alluding to nonmoral standards of beauty and taste, in discussions of pornography it has moral connotations. Obscene kinds of pornography violate standards of *moral* decency.

When is pornography obscene, that is, morally objectionable? And when does use of pornography constitute participation in a morally objectionable practice?

These questions will be left as discussion topics, but before we conclude this chapter, a few additional comments should be made. First, it is important to distinguish between the depiction of something indecent and the depiction of something in an indecent way. Obscene things can be depicted in nonobscene ways. For example, depictions of rape and other forms of extreme sexual violence can be decent if they reveal the horror of the act, and good literature and art does just that. Conversely, nonobscene things can be depicted in obscene ways. Human nudity is not obscene, but in much pornography it is depicted obscenely.

Furthermore, our discussion suggests that pornography comes in many forms. Four general categories—loveless sex, child pornography, nonviolent sexist pornography, and violent sexual imagery—deserve separate consideration.

First, much pornography is intended to convey the message that sex without love, affection, or commitment is permissible and desirable. It sympathetically portrays and tacitly endorses sex solely for pleasure, sex outside marriage, casual and anonymous sex, group sex, or public sex. Conservatives' objections to pornography have tended to center on this category, alleging that all such pornography is obscene. Is it?

Second, pornography that uses children as sex objects and that involves child nudity is immoral. It exploits the children used as models, and it condones and encourages child abuse. This is the one area in which conservatives and liberals can agree on the need for strict censorship laws. Yet many forms of advertising and modeling use sexually provocative pictures of children. Is the use of twelve- and thirteen-year-old models in sexually suggestive poses morally objectionable? Is it so for fifteen- or sixteen-year-olds? Is it objectionable to use adult models who look as if they were children?

Third, much pornography falls into the category of nonviolent but potentially sexist. The difficult question here is, What is sexist? Is it always sexist to portray a nude woman with a snake wrapped sensuously around her or with bunny ears (or with other animal suggestions)? Is every picture that emphasizes or exclusively shows women's sex organs sexist and degrading? Should we regard as sexist the nude photos in *Playboy* that show a complete figure in poses suggesting that women are primarily sexual playmates for men?

Finally, much pornography features the use of violent sexual images. In recent years this form of pornography has proliferated, and mostly involves obscene and violent images of women. With good reason, feminists have directed most criticism against it and have struggled to define it with sufficient precision to pass laws against it. One influential definition of obscene pornography (or what the authors call simply *pornography*) was developed by Andrea Dworkin and Catharine MacKinnon. It was presented as part of a model civil rights statute authorizing civil suits against makers and distributors of obscenity. A version of the model statute was adopted in Indianapolis, but in 1984 the Supreme Court declared it an unconstitutional restriction of free speech. Nevertheless, the definition remains morally valuable and reminds us of the kinds of violent pornography that are mass produced today:

1. *Pornography* is the graphic sexually explicit subordination of women through pictures and/or words that also includes one or more of the following: (i) women are presented dehumanized as sexual objects, things, or commodities; or (ii) women are presented as sexual objects who enjoy pain or humiliation; or (iii) women are presented as sexual objects who experience sexual pleasure in being raped; or (iv) women are presented as sexual objects tied up or cut up or mutilated or bruised or physically hurt; or (v) women are presented in postures or positions of sexual submission, servility, or display; or (vi) women's body parts—including but not limited to vaginas, breasts, or buttocks—are exhibited such that women are reduced to those parts; or (vii) women are presented as whores by nature; or (viii) women are presented being penetrated by objects or animals; or (ix) women are presented in scenarios of degradation, injury, torture, shown as filthy or inferior, bleeding, bruised, or hurt in a context that makes these conditions sexual.

2. The use of men, children, or transsexuals in the place of women in (1) above is pornography for purposes of this law.[7]

Defenders of the violent forms of pornography contend that it provides a healthy release or catharsis, rather than encouraging violence. Although the full scientific evidence necessary to address such viewpoints has not yet been gathered, this generalization has been seriously challenged by recent experiments. For example, there is now solid evidence that long-term exposure to images of gross violence does strengthen negative attitudes toward women. Men are affected by repeated exposure to the myth that women want to be raped, a familiar theme in violent pornography. Anyone who reviews studies such as those in *Pornography and Sexual Aggression*, edited by Neil Malamuth and Edward Donnerstein, cannot be altogether complacent about the influence of violent pornography. At the same time, other studies reveal that most males are not aroused by violent pornography and instead find it revolting.

Finally, whatever the general experiments show about overall tendencies, it remains true that the use of pornography is a personal matter in the following sense: Its effect on individuals varies. Each of us must achieve a self-understanding of its sometimes beneficial and sometimes harmful effects on our lives.

SUMMARY

The word *pornography* has several different meanings. In a pejorative sense, pornography is obscene (immoral) smut. In a neutral sense, pornography is sexually explicit material intended primarily to be sexually arousing. We have used the second sense. Nonpornographic materials (such as nude pictures in medical books) also can be used pornographically in the sense of being used primarily for sexual arousal.

Is the use of pornography morally objectionable? No simple answer is possible, because the uses of pornography are too varied. This general question is best replaced by a series of more focused questions about specific uses of pornography. Such types of uses include: (1) married couples' use of pornography for enrichment of their sexual relationship; (2) use of nude photos for sexual arousal by someone who regards them (through imagination) as representing people for whom he feels affection; (3) a spouse's use of romance novels to stimulate adultery fantasies; (4) preoccupation with "hard-core" pornography centered on genital pictures of members of the opposite sex; and (5) repeated use of violent pornography that portrays women as objects to be abused.

One way to evaluate these and other uses of pornography is to explore the role of the fantasies they produce in individuals. Nancy Friday argues that sexual fantasies are in general a healthy sexual expression, while Herbert Fingarette defends the New Testament view that fantasies about immoral acts frequently express immoral wishes. Both agree, however, on several points: Sexual fantasies should be evaluated in light of how they affect an individual's life and relationships; care must be taken in interpreting the wish expressed in a fantasy (because unconscious wishes are often disguised before they are manifested in a conscious fantasy); and the degree to which fantasies are voluntary may vary (ranging from a spontaneous nonvoluntary fantasy to deliberate, repeated recourse to a fantasy).

The second way to evaluate pornography is as mass-produced and mass-consumed public objects that, by permeating our society, influence attitudes, especially about women. Obscene pornography is sexually explicit material that violates standards of moral decency. Four categories of pornography are often regarded as obscene: (1) material that conveys a message that sex without love is desirable, (2) material that portrays children as sex objects, (3) nonviolent sexist pornography, and (4) violent sexual imagery.

DISCUSSION TOPICS

1   We assumed that it is "prudish" (that is, excessively proper or modest about sexuality) to object to all uses of sexually explicit material for sexual arousal. Is this

assumption perhaps unjustified? In defending your view, explain how this question (about moral justification) might be approached within each of the main types of ethical theory: utilitarianism, duty ethics, rights ethics, and virtue ethics.

2   A frequent criticism of pornography is that it treats women (and sometimes men) as "mere sex objects." What do you think is meant by this expression, and is it a valid complaint? Relate your answer to Kant's proscription against treating other people merely as a means to our own ends.

3   Are some fantasies, sexual or otherwise, inherently immoral, even though they do not lead to immoral actions? In giving your answer, comment on the views set forth in the New Testament and the views of Nancy Friday and Herbert Fingarette.

4   Discuss whether there is anything immoral about each of the following:
    a   A rape fantasy spontaneously enters a man's mind and is quickly dismissed from attention.
    b   A man deliberately and frequently brings to mind rape fantasies, even though he never has any strong urge to rape (and never does so).
    c   Occasionally (about once every few months), a woman has the fantasy of being raped.
    d   A woman has and enjoys recurring fantasies of being raped, even though she sincerely denies any desire to be raped.

5   Five different examples of pornography (or pornographic uses of nonpornography) were presented early in this chapter. Present and defend your answer to the questions raised at the end of each example.

6   Four general categories of pornography are most often criticized as obscene and immoral: (1) that which recommends sex without love or affection, (2) that which portrays children as sex objects, (3) nonviolent sexist pornography, and (4) violent sexual images, usually of women. Present and defend your view concerning whether each of these types of pornography is obscene.

7   While feminists are united in condemning any pornography that contributes to violence against women, they are sharply divided over the issue of whether pornography should be censored. One major concern of feminists opposed to censorship is that if governments (which are often patriarchal) are allowed to regulate pornography, they could use that power to repress nontraditional forms of sexual expression that the majority of citizens may object to, such as homosexual pornography and pornography in which women are portrayed as assertive, eager, and equal sexual partners. Present your view on whether any pornography involving adults should be banned by law, and defend it by appeal to an ethical theory. If you think some pornography should be banned, can you formulate a law which would not be so inclusive as to ban morally permissible types of pornography?

SUGGESTED READINGS

Attorney General's Commission on Pornography: Final Report. 2 Vols. Washington, DC: U.S. Department of Justice, 1986.

Baird, Robert M., and Stuart E. Rosenbaum (eds.). *Pornography: Private Right or Public Menace?* Buffalo, NY: Prometheus, 1991.

Burstyn, Varda (ed.). *Women Against Censorship*. Vancouver, British Columbia: Douglas & McIntyre, 1985.

Copp, David, and Susan Wendell (eds.). *Pornography and Censorship*. Buffalo, NY: Prometheus, 1983.

Davis, Murray S. *Smut: Erotic Reality/Obscene Ideology*. Chicago: University of Chicago Press, 1983.

Fingarette, Herbert. "Real Guilt and Neurotic Guilt." In *On Responsibility*. New York: Basic Books, 1967.

Friday, Nancy. *Men in Love: Men's Sexual Fantasies, The Triumph of Love over Rage*. New York: Dell, 1980.

Friday, Nancy. *My Secret Garden: Women's Sexual Fantasies*. New York: Pocket Books, 1973.

Garry, Ann. "Pornography and Respect for Women." *Social Theory and Practice*, vol. 4 (1978).

Hill, Judith M. "Pornography and Degradation." *Hypatia*, vol. 2 (1987): 39–54.

Kimmel, Michael S. (ed.). *Men Confront Pornography*. New York: Meridian, 1991.

Lederer, Laura (ed.). *Take Back the Night: Women on Pornography*. New York: Morrow, 1980.

MacKinnon, Catharine A. *Feminism Unmodified*. Cambridge, MA: Harvard University Press, 1987.

Morgan, Robin. "Theory and Practice: Pornography and Rape." In L. Lederer (ed.), *Take Back the Night: Women on Pornography*. New York: Morrow, 1980.

Report of the President's Commission on Obscenity and Pornography. Washington, DC: U.S. Government Printing Office, 1970.

Segal, Lynne, and Marry McIntosh (eds.). *Sex Exposed: Sexuality and the Pornography Debate*. New Brunswick, NJ: Rutgers University Press, 1993.

Singer, Jerome L., and Ellen Switzer. *Mind-Play: The Creative Uses of Fantasy*. Englewood Cliffs, NJ: Prentice-Hall, 1980.

Soble, Alan. *Pornography: Marxism, Feminism, and the Future of Sexuality*. New Haven, CT: Yale University Press, 1986.

Talese, Gay. *Thy Neighbor's Wife*. New York: Dell, 1980.

Tong, Rosemarie. *Women, Sex, and the Law*. Totowa, NJ: Rowman & Allanheld, 1984.

Zillman, D., and J. Bryant (eds.). *Pornography Research: Advances and Policy Implications*. Hillsdale, NJ: Lawrence Erlbaum Associates, 1989.

PART FIVE

Caring Relationships and Community

*The epithets **sociable, good-natured, humane, merciful, grateful, friendly, generous, beneficent**, or their equivalents, are known in all languages, and universally express the highest merit, which **human nature** is capable of attaining.[1]*

David Hume

Caring for others entails that we desire their well-being and, when appropriate, seek disinterestedly to promote their good. Caring consists of more than respect for them and their rights; we want those we care for to prosper, and we enjoy helping them prosper.

To care for someone need not be "purely" or "solely" altruistic in the sense that we are concerned only with another's good, and not ours. Nor must it be entirely "selfless" in the sense of involving self-sacrifice. On the contrary, people who are most caring tend to see their own good as intimately tied to the good of those for whom they care. In caring for others, they see their own good promoted as well.

In this way, caring and self-interest can be compatible and reinforce each other. When we sustain relationships based on care, we promote both the good of others and of ourselves. That does not, of course, make caring "selfish." Selfishness is excessive concern for oneself at the expense of others. Caring is the opposite of selfishness, but it can also differ from self-sacrificial forms of "selflessness."

Caring relationships involve two or more conscious beings, at least one of whom cares about the other. They take many forms beyond the relationships of sexual love discussed in Part Four. In Part Five, we discuss caring relationships between parents and children, friends, colleagues at work, and community members.

CHAPTER 18

Parents and Children

Relationships between parents and children are as morally perilous as they are momentous. They are the source of much suffering and even cruelty, yet they can also be full of caring and love. At least, we think they *ought* to be paradigms of relationships based on care and love. This "ought" raises interesting questions. Does it mean there is a "duty to love" one's children and, reciprocally, a duty for children to love their parents? Can there in fact be a duty to love? Isn't love something that must emerge spontaneously or not at all, rather than something that can be cultivated as a matter of duty? Does the "ought" perhaps express a moral ideal that is better understood in terms other than duties?

Surely parents have some duties to children, but what is the basis of those duties, and which duties are most important? Do all grown children have obligations to their parents? In thinking about children, should we emphasize their rights rather than their duties, as the recent children's rights movement insists?

Although it is impossible to generalize about family structures, especially with respect to contemporary society, it will help focus our discussion of these issues if we begin with two examples.

Two Examples

When he was thirty-six, the writer Franz Kafka (1883–1924) composed a forty-five-page letter to his father in which he sought to understand and to heal the emotional chasm between them. The letter is a vivid reminder of how relationships with parents have an influence well into adulthood. It begins: "You asked me recently why I maintain that I am afraid of you. As usual, I was unable to think of any answer to your question, partly for the very reason I am afraid of you."[1]

The fear arose from the father's thorough domination in raising his son: "From your armchair you ruled the world. Your opinion was correct, every other was mad."[2] The father defined the rules of the household, the children's behavior away from home, the family business, and the acceptable attitudes toward the world outside the family. His views were the final authority in determining everything important. They were also frequently self-contradictory or even preposterous, and this generated in Kafka the painful awareness of irrational authority that permeates his writings, for example in "The Metamorphosis" and *The Trial.*

His father's edicts were backed by threats, shouts, rage, and spiteful laughter at any sign of disobedience. Young Franz viewed such behavior as more than sheer bluster, as indeed a recurring condemnation of himself. When the rage was not followed by the threatened punishment, his feelings of guilt and failure were only compounded.

Even worse was his father's difficulty in showing simple affection and providing emotional support. On his return from school, Franz's excitement over his ideas or achievements would be disparaged by the father as childish and petty. He received encouragement only when he conformed to his father's image of manliness—a business-oriented, soldiery, beer-drinking tough guy. Franz's gradual development as a sensitive artist and writer was met with contempt or disregard.

Not surprisingly, Kafka developed a personality grounded in self-doubt and a sense of worthlessness: "Ever since I could think I have had such profound anxieties about asserting my spiritual existence that I was indifferent to everything else."[3] Even as an adult he continued to judge himself in the harsh terms set by his father. Marriage, for example, which he accepted as the sign of full maturity in his society, became impossible for him. Shortly before writing the letter, he could still be deflated by his father's critical view of his fiancée as a mediocre girl who seduced his son by wearing a fancy blouse.

After writing the letter to his father, Franz asked his mother to deliver it. This messenger role was in keeping with her subservient status within the family as go-between for the father and the children. She was a paragon of kindness, but always within the limits of her husband's dominance. This kindness served the cruel function, Kafka realized in retrospect, of the beater during a hunt. By constantly seeking to reconcile Franz with his father, his mother drove him back under the father's domination.

The Kafkas were typical of the nineteenth-century family, in which the father's authority was both unlimited and unquestioned by wives and children, a situation much rarer today. The authority of contemporary parents is now limited by the powerful influences of peers, teachers, and mass media, and is also undermined by greatly increased freedom for children. In fact, according to the Carnegie Council on Children, modern parents are like corporate executives responsible for loosely coordinating the activities of others who shape their children's lives. Confronted with an array of professionals who claim to understand their children better than they do, parents are also each like "a maestro trying to conduct an orchestra of players who have never met and who play from a multitude of different scores, each in a notation the conductor cannot read."[4]

Nevertheless, the fundamental parental role in providing early guidance and emotional support for children remains the same as in previous centuries. In fact, as the Carnegie Council also noted, this role has become even more important. In a world where work is increasingly impersonal, where ties with neighbors are weak, and where religions have lost their grip, the family can be a haven for emotional and moral nurturing of all family members.

Tragically, too often that does not occur. Political conservatives discern a breakdown of traditional parental responsibility, and political liberals point to a barrage of increasing pressures on parents. Both trends are illustrated in the parents of Maya Angelou, the distinguished African-American writer. Angelou's parents separated when she was three and sent her and her brother to be raised by their grandmother in Stamps, Arkansas.

The grandmother was exceptionally effective as a parent. With limited resources and within a society that was both racist and parochial, she gave Angelou a loving upbringing: "Her world was bordered on all sides with work, duty, religion and 'her place.' I don't think she ever knew that a deep-brooding love hung over everything she touched."[5] The grandmother reminds us that a family is defined as a circle of deep caring rather than any particular configuration of relatives.

When Angelou was eight she was sent to visit her mother in St. Louis. Because she suffered from nightmares, she was allowed to sleep in the bed with her mother—and her mother's boyfriend. One morning, after her mother left early for an errand, she was awakened by the boyfriend, who sexually abused her by touching her between the legs. At the time, Angelou did not understand this episode (and a later one) as sexual abuse because the boyfriend was gentle and seemingly affectionate. That changed when the boyfriend raped her. He warned her that if she told anyone he would kill her brother (whom she adored).

Angelou's mother sensed something was wrong and, while confronting the boyfriend, learned what had occurred. She kicked the boyfriend out and had him prosecuted for rape. Before the man could serve a one-year jail term, members of the local community killed him. Angelou, who was then eight years old, felt responsible for the man's death and punished herself by refusing to speak for years. Various relatives construed her silence as impudent sullenness and thrashed her. She was sent back to live with her grandmother until she turned thirteen, at which time she was sent again to stay with her mother.

With these examples in mind, we can turn to the question, What are the primary responsibilities of parents toward their children?

Parental Responsibility: Respect Versus Abuse

By *parents* we mean individuals who have primary responsibility and authority in raising a child. They may be biological parents, foster parents, or "significant others" who replace legal guardians as primary providers and protectors. Parents are those people who, by assuming responsibility for a child's development, serve as primary caretakers.

Parents' fundamental duty to their children is to respect them as persons—persons undergoing various stages of development. This may sound odd at first, because we expect so much more from parents than the respect that all people owe to children. Yet, just as parents are in a unique position to nurture and support their children, so too are they uniquely well placed to harm them by failing to show them even minimal respect, as we saw in the cases of Kafka and Angelou. Furthermore, precisely because parents do contribute so much to their children's development, it is easy for them to rationalize away the harm they do under the guise of exercising parental responsibility. Such rationalization frequently characterizes parents' actions in the areas of discipline, affection, and encouragement.

First, child abuse is sometimes rationalized as discipline or excused as an attempt to teach a lesson. Thus, a spanking turns into a beating without the parent's awareness of the transition. Kafka reported a related example in recalling his only direct memory from infancy. He had been whimpering for water, and ignoring several warnings to be quiet, when suddenly his father carried him outside and locked him out for a while on a cool evening when he was wearing only a nightshirt. This was devastating to Kafka, who remembered the episode as ultimate proof that he was worthless in his father's eyes.

Second, even gross abuse can occur in the guise of affection. Father-daughter incest and other forms of sexual abuse, which are estimated to occur to one of every six girls, rarely result from the use of overt force. Typically, at first there is enticement: kind words ("Daddy loves you") and gentle touching as in the case of Angelou. Threats aimed at keeping the child quiet usually come after the sexual abuse. Sexual abuse, which so clearly exploits the vulnerability and trust of children, is sometimes rationalized by alleged paternal rights to the sexual satisfaction that the wife "fails" to give, combined with the self-serving belief that no real harm is done. Such beliefs have even been publicly defended: There is a lobby of incest advocates, the René Guyon Society, which publicly espouses parent-child sex in the name of the sexual liberation of children.

Third, a great deal of psychological manipulation takes place under the guise of guidance and encouragement. Parents do have the right and responsibility to convey their own sense of moral decency to their children—within limits. That sense of decency may be prejudiced and narrow, and in some respects it almost always is. Nevertheless, it provides the essential foundation of values that children can subsequently modify. What is objectionable—obviously so in the case of Kafka's father—is the use of tactics that crush a child's attempts to assess those values and to modify them as the child develops capacities for autonomous reasoning. Furthermore, overzealous parental concern can mask an attempt to live vicariously through children, to derive esteem and vent frustrations by pressuring children in harmful ways.

Definitions of Child Abuse

Child abuse takes many subtle forms, which prompts us to define it carefully in regard to parental duties to children. Traditional definitions of child abuse were developed in the legal context, because courts needed a criterion for justifiable forced removal of children from homes. Studies showed that forced removal of children does more harm than good, except when abuse is very severe. This fact, coupled with a concern for preserving family unity, led courts to define child abuse very narrowly as a pattern of either severe battery or deprivation of necessities such as food, shelter, clothing, affection, and education. Hence, the legal definition does not apply to an array of moral harms that are less severe or unsolvable through legal remedies.

At the opposite extreme is a definition of child abuse as any failure to promote the child's best interests. This definition, however, is much too wide. For one thing, there is always some alternative home where the interests of a given child might be better promoted. This would make most parents abusers because they lack ideal resources for maximizing their child's interests! Another objection is that, according to this definition, parents would be abusers each time they failed to place a given child's interests above all others; yet those interests must always be balanced against the needs and interests of other family members, including parents.

If the definition of child abuse as extreme deprivation is too narrow, and the definition of child abuse as a failure to maximize the child's interests is too wide, then perhaps child abuse should be defined as a failure to meet the child's basic needs which handicaps the child's basic development. This definition would have to be linked to a theory about needs, development, and growth toward maturity. Because these are all value concepts, such a theory would draw on both psychological and value assumptions about mature and responsible conduct, which is the goal of healthy psychological development.

Although this definition is an improvement over the others, Natalie Abrams suggests it is still too limited. Abrams points out that abuse of people in general consists of more than simply harm to their development. In a legal context, for example, the term *battery* refers to an infringement on the liberty of another against that person's will or choice. This is wrong, because battery also constitutes an assault on the person's dignity, even if it does not actually handicap development. Similarly, Abrams suggests, abuse of children is best conceived as an assault on their dignity as persons:

> It is this concept of an affront to dignity that is totally omitted in the definitions of child abuse or neglect, which focus solely on actual or risked harmful consequences. It is not enough simply to say that the harmful consequences constitute assaults on one's dignity and, therefore, that the child's dignity is indirectly being protected. Although harmful consequences must be prohibited in order to ensure the possibility of the child's development, the prevention of these harms does not amount to respect for the child's dignity, any more than it would amount to respect for adult dignity.[6]

This definition, which is plainly inspired by Kantian rather than utilitarian thought, coheres with our earlier emphasis on respect for children as persons. Yet there is a problem with the definition, Abrams acknowledges. The dignity of adults is defined by reference to their consent. Violation of their rights without their consent, that is, without their voluntary and informed agreement, constitutes an assault on their dignity. How can this standard be applied to young children, who lack the capacity to give consent?

Abrams offers the following suggestions. The concept of consent is indeed inapplicable to very young children, and a minimum standard for the decent treatment of children should be established. Even young children can express their wishes, verbally or nonverbally. These wishes should be respected as far as possible, except when to do so would be detrimental to the child's development or prohibited by the needs of other family members. Thus, this standard does not require that maximum amounts of money be spent on the child, as the best-interests standard might imply. It requires only that a fair share of family resources be spent in the direction indicated by the child's wishes, except when that would harm the child's development.

It follows from this standard that there are limits on how far parents can justifiably manipulate their children to adopt particular interests, values, careers, religious beliefs, and tastes. The appeal to their best interests, for example, does not automatically justify coercion of older children to adopt particular religious practices. Nor are parents warranted in coercing children to pursue careers that, in the parents' judgment, are in the children's best interests. Instead, parents should help provide the conditions that will enable children to make their own career choices.

Beyond their basic physical needs, the essential ingredients for children's well-being are the skills and enthusiasm for independent thought and action. Note that this is also at the heart of personal and moral autonomy: the active capacity to create and pursue a rational and moral plan of life. Hence, one of the primary duties of parents is to provide conditions that foster the growth of autonomy.

Before turning to the reciprocal duties that children owe to parents, let us briefly consider two further objections to Abrams's emphasis on consent as a moral limit on how children can be treated. The first objection is that the emphasis is hollow because it allows exceptions whenever harm to the child is involved and parents will inevitably apply their own views of what this harm is. Thus, for example, parents will continue to force their religious beliefs on their children in the name of the children's interests, even when the children clearly refuse consent.

This objection highlights a practical difficulty in applying Abrams's standard, although the objection should be qualified. The standard Abrams has in mind is not parents' views of the proper development of the child, but instead the actual healthy development of the child. Parents are required to become informed and intelligent about what that development is! Moreover, the consent requirement clearly does imply increased respect for the child's own views about proper development as the child matures. Eventually, at the morally vague stage of "maturity," the parent should recognize the consent of the son or daughter as final. Between early infancy and maturity, however, children have a gradually developing capacity for consent that should be respected in such matters as religion.

The second objection to an emphasis on consent concerns incest. Suppose there are rare instances when incest does not harm a child's development and when an older child of fifteen years or more gives consent. Does it follow that the incest is permissible and is not an assault on the child's dignity? If so, this might imply that we should no longer regard incest as taboo, that is, as absolutely prohibited.

In response to this objection we should emphasize that the chances of psychological and developmental harm from incest are so high, and the degree of possible harm so enormous, that it makes sense to retain an absolute ban on it. (This is a rule-utilitarian argument that recognizes the need for all to adhere to a general rule because of the important good consequences that follow from doing so.) Furthermore, there is the question of whether even a fifteen-year-old child (or young adult) is capable of giving consent freely in a situation that combines sexual inexperience on the child's part and psychological authority on the part of a parent or older relative. Finally, there remains the ideal that parents ought to love their children as parents, not as sexual partners. Incest threatens the kind of love that for children is both inherently valuable and the basis of self-respect in adult life.

Filial Duties and Gratitude

Let us now shift the moral focus from parental responsibilities to children's duties. What is the appropriate moral attitude of children, especially grown sons and daughters, toward their parents? Recent social thought has stressed that the relationship is largely one of rights. Reacting to the horrors of child abuse and neglect, members of the children's rights movement, such as Abrams, have emphasized children's rights to be given what is necessary for proper development ("positive rights") and their rights to have as much freedom as possible without interference from others ("negative rights"). These human rights are viewed as one justification for claiming that parents have duties toward children, that is, duties to respect their children's rights.

Duties

Young children, of course, also have duties to obey and cooperate with parents once they grow beyond infancy. The duties are limited, because there is no duty to do everything—however immoral or inappropriate—a parent commands. Nevertheless, children's duties are important because other members of the family have needs that must be recognized and balanced. Young children are not able to balance these other needs and hence should generally defer to their parents' judgment. As they grow older, however, they should be allowed an increasing voice in family decisions in order to aid development of their autonomy. Furthermore, children's own sense of autonomy can arise only on a foundation of early development guided by their parents.

The traditional Judeo-Christian view of what is owed to parents goes far beyond this, however. Children and adults alike are enjoined, according to one of the Ten Commandments, to "Honor thy father and thy mother." This is usually interpreted as a requirement to respect them and be grateful to them, and is a prescription for a lifetime, not just during childhood. Failure to be grateful reflects the vice of extreme ingratitude. Thus, Franz Kafka was accused by his father of ingratitude for becoming estranged from him.

This traditional view has been challenged on several counts. First, gratitude is an emotion, and emotions are not under our direct control. Therefore, we cannot have a duty to feel gratitude, because we do not have duties to do things beyond our control. One possible reply to this challenge is that the duty of gratitude refers more to *showing* gratitude than to *feeling* grateful. To show gratitude is to perform acts that manifest or express gratitude, and these are under our control.

Perhaps, however, this preliminary reply is superficial. The duty of gratitude is a duty to show genuine or sincere gratitude, which entails that one actually feel grateful rather than merely pretend to be. Can there, then, be a duty to be grateful if such a duty entails a duty to have certain emotions?

Gratitude

In order to answer this question, we need to know what the emotion of gratitude is. If it is an inner sensation or feeling (for instance, a warm glow inside) over which we have no control, then it would seem absurd to speak of a duty of gratitude. Fortunately, it is not! Like other important and complex emotions, gratitude is not a set of inner twitches and tingles, but instead a structure involving beliefs, attitudes, and desires.

Gratitude has the following ingredients: (1) a belief that one or more people voluntarily did something good for us, or at least intended it to be good for us, (2) a positive attitude of goodwill toward those benefactors (such as a hope for their well-being), and (3) a desire to show them appreciation (in an appropriate way, whether with a reciprocal gift, a simple thank you, or any number of other signs of appreciation). In addition, when we have received a gift that is actually good for us, gratitude also requires us (4) to appreciate and properly use the gift. With "white elephant" gifts, however, which we cannot be expected to appreciate, this last condition does not apply. We are free to dispose of the gift with discretion, that is, without hurting the feelings of the giver.

Understood in this way, gratitude is somewhat under our control; to some extent we can influence our beliefs, attitudes, and desires. We can often allow (or refuse to allow) gratitude to develop within us by attending to the benevolent motives of the giver, dwelling on the value or intended value of the gift, and reminding ourselves of the importance of sustaining our relationship with the person by acknowledging his or her kindness.

Admittedly, there are some occasions when one either cannot or should not foster gratitude in this way. Perhaps, for example, to do so would add to an already harmful sense of dependence on a parent whose motives in giving were as much an attempt to manipulate as to help. The following statement illustrates this point: "If you do not complete medical school and stay active in our church, then you are an ingrate for all we have given you!" Gratitude, even for benefits received, is sometimes inappropriate and misplaced.[7]

A second challenge to the traditional view that children owe gratitude to their parents is the assertion that parents, in giving their children the necessities for development, are merely doing their duty. Gratitude, it is implied, is owed only when people do something good that is not required by duty. This argument is unsound. Sometimes, we owe gratitude for acts on our behalf that were required by duty. It would, for example, be callous for someone who was saved by a lifeguard or police officer to dismiss that act as undeserving of gratitude on the ground that the rescuer had a duty as a professional. When we benefit from a great good, we should be grateful. For most of us, the greatest goods we receive include those from our parents. Moreover, parents are usually motivated far more by love than by a sense of duty. Raising children requires sacrifices, and parents usually make those sacrifices voluntarily and lovingly. To fail to respond with gratitude as the beneficiary of this love and these sacrifices is a moral failure as well as a betrayal.

A third and more forceful challenge to the view that parents are owed honor and gratitude was given by Jane English, who found it objectionable to talk about *owing* parents for their sacrifices. The notion of owing is appropriate in regard to repaying debts, meeting contracts, and returning favors; adult children, however, ought not to think of their relationship with their parents in such ways:

> Parents' voluntary sacrifices, rather than creating "debts" to be "repaid," tend to create love or "friendship." The duties of grown children are those of friends and result from love between them and their parents, rather than being things owed in repayment for the parents' earlier sacrifices.[8]

English makes an important point: The adult son or daughter does not owe parents in the same way he or she might owe an unpaid debt or owe a favor in return for having received one. This legalistic way of thinking actually threatens the kind of mutual caring about one another's needs that underlies loving relationships.

Moreover, when parents sever an ongoing loving friendship with their children, they should not expect gratitude for the earlier sacrifices they made. As English notes, if biological parents who are fully able to raise their child decide instead to give it up for adoption, they should not expect gratitude for any sacrifices they made in having the child. Again, if parents disavow their children because they refuse to marry within a preferred religion or to pursue careers favored by their parents, and the parents thereafter have nothing to do with them, the children have no obligation years later to pay their medical bills in old age. For similar reasons, Franz Kafka's father had no right to expect gratitude from him.

Perhaps, however, we may hesitate to embrace English's emphasis on friendship in the relationship between parents and grown children. Notice that a consequence of her view is that, once friendship ceases on the part of either party, duties of friendship also cease. Is there not, however, a stronger obligation to try to sustain a loving relationship with one's parents than there is to sustain friendships? More basically, isn't it inappropriate to construe the relationship with parents either as primarily friendship *or* as primarily a matter of rights and duties? What about love?

Love

As we saw in Chapter 14, love is as complex conceptually and morally as it is complicated in real life. Here we will mention an aspect of love that warrants further discussion. The issue is whether most of what has been said thus far in this chapter is inappropriate because the relationship between parents and children ought to be one of love, rather than duties and rights. Parents, ideally, have children out of love and out of a desire to create an intimate loving relationship. Moreover, to be a successful parent one must raise children with love, and in such a way that children know they are deeply loved and singularly important to the parents.

The failure of Kafka's father was a failure to love, as well as a failure of duty (and perhaps the same is somewhat true of Franz Kafka with respect to his father). On the same principle, the idea of a child's duty of gratitude is insulting to many parents precisely because they seek love, not dutiful respect and gratitude, from their children. For a similar reason, mere friendship is not sufficient to capture the hoped-for relationship between parents and children.

Perhaps to a large extent this emphasis on love need not undermine the relevance of the preceding discussion of duties, rights, and responsibilities. The *kind* of parent-child love that is most important and worth promoting encompasses and transcends, without replacing, the duties of mutual respect and caring. Love is the aim and ideal of parent-child relationships. It is itself an ideal, not a duty.

The important question at this point is, What kind of love represents the ideal? Is mutual caring for one another's interests sufficient? Is self-sacrifice implicit in the ideal? Is the desire for love a desire for an unconditional love that does not depend on any particular achievements or traits of character in the family members? These questions will be left as discussion topics.

Surrogate Motherhood

Medical technology has added a new dimension to traditional concerns about parenting: surrogate motherhood. In one case, a woman is artificially inseminated with sperm of a man who contracts with the woman—the surrogate mother—to bring the child to term and give it up to the man (and usually his wife) for adoption. In another case, a man's sperm inseminates his wife's ovum and the fertilized ovum is then implanted in the uterus of a second woman, who carries the child to term and transfers its custody to the couple whose genetic material was used to create it. In both cases, a contract is signed by all parties whereby the adoptive parents pay the surrogate mother about $10,000 (in addition to paying medical costs and costs of agencies which arrange the contract, often another $30,000).

Surrogate motherhood generates disturbing moral questions, several of which we will raise and leave for discussion. First, does surrogate motherhood constitute a form of baby selling (and buying)? Baby selling is illegal, and for good reason: It degrades a human child by treating the child as an object to be transferred on the market like other objects. In surrogate motherhood, at least one genetic parent receives the child, and to that extent it is unlike traditional baby selling. Nevertheless, it also involves payment of money to receive from another woman a baby that is not generated in traditional ways. Supporters of surrogate motherhood view the $10,000 as a compensation for inconvenience, of the sort that a Peace Corps volunteer receives for voluntary service. Opponents, however, see the exchange of money for babies as simply a variation of baby selling, and they point out that the money is a strong incentive for many women to make money through surrogacy (just as traditional forms of baby selling posed incentives for lower-class women to make money by giving up their babies for adoption).

Second, supporters of surrogate motherhood view it as a straightforward extension of normal parental practices that takes advantage of new medical technology. Opponents object that the surrogate mother is essentially deciding to have children without assuming responsibility for the child (and instead is carrying the child simply for the purposes of transferring it to others). They point to the importance of sustaining the traditional tie between having a child and assuming personal responsibility for its care.

Third, supporters of surrogate motherhood (including some feminists) emphasize the autonomy of women to make their own decisions about engaging in this practice, whatever their motives, without government interference. To prohibit the practice would constitute objectionable paternalism, that is, an interference with the autonomy of adults in order to promote their good (as the government sees that good). Opponents (including other feminists) view the practice as a new form of exploitation of women. The practice is essentially a form of "renting a uterus" (usually that of a lower-class woman who needs the money), and thus treats women as objects to be used.

Fourth, what are the effects of surrogate motherhood on children? Supporters argue that there is not yet good scientific data about any harmful side-effects to children. They predict that there will no doubt be some psychological problems, but no more than in other cases of adopted children. Opponents argue that the risk is too great and point to cases that have already gone seriously wrong. For example, in the famous "Baby M" case, Mary Beth Whitehead, the surrogate mother, changed her mind and decided she wanted to keep the child, thereby provoking a lengthy court battle for custody of the child. (The New Jersey Supreme Court eventually awarded custody to the genetic father, while entitling Mary Beth Whitehead to visitation rights; the court's reasoning centered on which party would best be able to give parental care to the child. The decision also voided legal contracts which did not leave the surrogate mother ample time to change her mind about whether to keep the child.) In other cases, the child may have genetic deformities or for other reasons may be rejected both by the individuals contracting for the child and by the surrogate mother, thereby making the child a ward of the taxpayers. Additionally, when a surrogate mother has other children of her own, those children may feel great anxiety that they too are vulnerable to being given away.

SUMMARY

Parents are any persons who assume responsibility for the primary caretaking of a child. Their most fundamental duty to the child is respect, which includes a duty to provide the basic necessities of life during the time when the child is completely dependent on the parents. In regard to discipline, affection, and encouragement, this duty requires parents to avoid abuse and forms of manipulation that restrict the child's potential for subsequent autonomous growth.

Child abuse is an assault on the dignity of children, in the form of actions that either disregard their needs, undermine their autonomy as they move toward adulthood, or in other ways unjustifiably harm them. Respect for children requires parents to refrain from imposing their own convictions on them, but rather to provide conditions that enable children to develop a capacity for creating and pursuing their own rational plans of life.

Children have obligations of gratitude for the benefits and the benevolence received from parents. Gratitude has the following ingredients: belief that someone voluntarily did something intended to be good for us, usually motivated by a concern for our good; a consequent feeling of goodwill toward the benefactor; a desire to show appreciation; and appreciation and proper use of the gift. Gratitude is under our control and is appropriate even though parents have an obligation to promote their children's good.

Although there are mutual obligations involved in parent-child relationships, the ideal form of the relationship is centered on mutual love and mutual caring about one another's good.

A surrogate mother is a woman who carries a fetus to birth and then transfers it to other individuals who have made a contract with her to adopt the child and who pay her about $10,000, plus medical expenses. Does the practice of surrogate motherhood treat babies as objects and thereby amount to a high-tech form of baby selling? Does surrogate motherhood erode the connection between having children and responsibly caring for them? Does it exploit women? Are its effects on children morally objectionable?

DISCUSSION TOPICS

1 What kind of love between parents and adult children do you see as most desirable? Is it a form of friendship (as Jane English suggests) or is it more like identity-shaping romantic love?

2 Do adult children have an obligation to feel and show gratitude to parents who have greatly contributed to their good? Or is sincere gratitude to one's parents a moral virtue that is highly desirable but not obligatory?

3 Is there an obligation to give financial support to one's parents in their old age, should they need it? Does the obligation depend on whether one's parents were caring and loving? Is there an obligation of parents not to become a financial burden on their children?

4 Evaluate the following argument: Parents should not raise their children in any particular religion, because that brainwashes them in a matter of great importance. Instead, parents should take them to several churches in order to lay a foundation for children to make up their own minds about religion later. Is your view on this issue the same with respect to early moral training?

5 Given the enormous potential for parents to cause harm, should the government require that parents take courses on parenthood before they are permitted to have children? Should the state be allowed to decide who can be a parent (as is presently the case with respect to adoption of children)?

6 Two parents who believe that homosexuality is immoral learn that their son or daughter is homosexual. In a rage they sever all ties with their child—those of emotion, finance, communication, and so on. The last time they talk with their child, they disavow their identity as parents, exclaiming, "You are no longer our child." Have the parents done anything immoral? If so, which ethical theory best captures what is wrong: utilitarianism, duty ethics, rights ethics, or virtue ethics?

7 During 1986 and 1987, there were several widely publicized cases of children (teenage and preteenage) who reported their parents to the police for using illegal drugs. Some of the children were given recognition awards by police departments. Identify and discuss the moral issues you see raised by these cases. Are the issues the same or different with respect to parents who turn in their adult children for drug use?

8 Decisions about whether to have children include decisions to beget, to bear, to keep, and to adopt a child. We speak of such decisions as "deciding to have a baby," which reflects our preoccupation with cuddly, dependent infants (rather than merely reflecting the biological fact that babies are children in the early stages of development). Yet the decision to have a child is or should be a decision to enter into a long-term, complex, changing, and largely unpredictable intimate relationship with another person. Discuss the main moral considerations that should be weighed by prospective parents in deciding whether to have a child. At the time when the decision is made to beget a child, are there obligations to the future child (who does not yet exist)?

9 Ideally, parent-child relationships are based on mutual trust. Does that make it worse to lie to one's parents than to lie to a stranger? Consider several examples, and also review the discussion of lying in Chapter 4.

10 Present and defend your view concerning surrogate motherhood. (a) Is the practice morally acceptable, or should it be discouraged or even prohibited by law? (b) Should the government regulate the practice in any way, or should it permit all contracts among adults, thereby permitting the cost of surrogate motherhood to be set by whatever the market will pay (so as to entitle women to earn whatever they can through surrogate motherhood)?

SUGGESTED READINGS

Abrams, Natalie. "Problems in Defining Child Abuse and Neglect." In O. O'Neill and W. Ruddick (eds.), *Having Children: Philosophical and Legal Reflections on Parenthood*. New York: Oxford University Press, 1979.

Aiken, William, and Hugh LaFollette (eds.). *Whose Child? Children's Rights, Parental Authority, and State Power*. Totowa, NJ: Littlefield, Adams, 1980.

Berger, Fred R. "Gratitude." *Ethics*, vol. 85 (1975): 298–309.

Blustein, Jeffrey. *Parents and Children: The Ethics of the Family*. New York: Oxford University Press, 1982.

Card, Claudia. "Gratitude and Obligation." *American Philosophical Quarterly*, vol. 25 (1988): 115–127.

Daniels, Norman. *Am I My Parents' Keeper?: An Essay on Justice Between the Young and the Old*. New York: Oxford University Press, 1988.

English, Jane. "What Do Grown Children Owe Their Parents?" In O. O'Neill and W. Ruddick (eds.), *Having Children: Philosophical and Legal Reflections on Parenthood*. New York: Oxford University Press, 1979.

Feinberg, Joel. "The Child's Right to an Open Future." In W. Aiken and H. LaFollette (eds.), *Whose Child?: Children's Rights, Parental Authority, and State Power*. Totowa, NJ: Littlefield, Adams, 1980. Pp. 124–153.

Gostin, Larry (ed.). *Surrogate Motherhood: Politics and Privacy*. Bloomington, IN: Indiana University Press, 1990.

Janeway, Elizabeth. "Incest: A Rational Look at the Oldest Taboo." In *Cross Sections from a Decade of Change*. New York: Harcourt Brace Jovanovich, 1977.

Jecker, Nancy. "Are Filial Duties Unfounded?" *American Philosophical Quarterly*, vol. 26 (1989): 73–80.

Keniston, Kenneth, and The Carnegie Council on Children. *All Our Children: The American Family Under Pressure*. New York: Harcourt Brace Jovanovich, 1977.

McConnell, Terrance. *Gratitude*. Philadelphia, PA: Temple University Press, 1993.

Neu, Jerome. "What Is Wrong With Incest?" *Inquiry*, vol. 19 (1976).

O'Barr, Jean F., Deborah Pope, and Mary Wyer (eds.). *Ties That Bind: Essays on Mothering and Patriarchy*. Chicago: University of Chicago Press, 1990.

O'Neill, Onora, and William Ruddick (eds.). *Having Children: Philosophical and Legal Reflections on Parenthood*. New York: Oxford University Press, 1979.

Pagelow, Mildred Daley. *Family Violence.* New York: Praeger, 1984.

Poster, Mark. *Critical Theory of the Family.* New York: Seabury Press, 1978.

Purdy, Laura. "Surrogate Mothering: Exploitation or Empowerment?" *Bioethics,* vol. 3 (1989): 18–34.

Ruddick, Sara. *Maternal Thinking: Toward a Politics of Peace.* Boston, MA: Beacon Press, 1989.

Schoeman, Ferdinand. "Rights of Children, Rights of Parents, and the Moral Basis of the Family." *Ethics,* vol. 91 (1980).

Trebilcot, Joyce (ed.). *Mothering: Essays in Feminist Theory.* Totowa, NJ: Rowman & Allanheld, 1983.

Wringe, C. A. *Children's Rights: A Philosophical Study.* Boston, MA: Routledge & Kegan Paul, 1982.

CHAPTER 19

Friendship

Ethics books emphasizing theories about right conduct rarely give friendship more than passing mention. At best, they treat it as one of many sources of obligation or as a context in which moral dilemmas might arise. At worst, they dismiss it as a source of private pleasure that poses a threat to justice in that it involves a kind of favoritism seemingly incompatible with the demands of impartiality and fairness.

A shift in emphasis to character and personal relationships, however, invites a different perspective that is closer to common sense. We do, after all, ordinarily think of the caring involved in friendship as having special significance morally; moreover, we are uneasy about people who strike us as incapable of friendship. These considerations led Aristotle to devote two of the ten books of his *Nicomachean Ethics* to friendship. In this chapter we examine the moral value of friendship, the responsibilities accompanying friendships, and the moral limits on friendship.

An Example of Friendship

Each of us will have in mind personal examples of friendship, but it may be helpful to cite one example here. In her memoirs, titled *Pentimento*, the American playwright Lillian Hellman describes her friendship with a person she calls Julia. Hellman and Julia were close friends from the time they were twelve until Julia's death almost twenty years later. Their friendship began with mutual interests and enjoyment of each other's company and deepened through shared activities and experiences. Hellman recalls, for example, the first time she was allowed to sleep overnight at her friend's house on a New Year's Eve in New York when they were both twelve:

Each New Year's Eve of my life has brought back the memory of that night. Julia and I lay in twin beds and she recited odds and ends of poetry...Dante in Italian, Heine in German, and even though I could not understand either language, the sounds were so lovely that I felt a sweet sadness as if much was ahead in the world, much that was going to be fine and fulfilling if I could ever find my way.[1]

Hellman and Julia spent many hours together, often seeing each other daily. Although their conversations were permeated by their shared love of literature, they "also talked like all young people, of possible beaux and husbands and babies, and heredity versus environment, and can romantic love last, mixing stuff like that in speeches made only for the pleasure of girls on the edge of growing up."[2] They went on several camping trips near Lake Champlain, including a particularly memorable one when they were sixteen. On that trip Julia captured a rabbit that the two young women skinned, cooked, and ate for dinner. The experience left a permanent mark on Hellman: "Even now, seeing any island, I am busy with that rabbit and fantasies of how I would make do alone, without shelter or tools."[3]

As with most friendships, there were disagreements and frictions that periodically strained their closeness, but these were relatively mild. By the time they turned eighteen, however, circumstances separated them: Julia moved to Oxford for undergraduate studies and later to Vienna for medical school, while Hellman attended college in New York, where she began writing plays. Yet their feelings for one another never diminished, and they continued to write and occasionally to see each other. During the 1930s, Julia had become a socialist and had moved to Berlin to join the anti-Hitler underground and fight fascism. Her socialist principles led her to distribute her considerable wealth to the poor she met in Berlin. Contrary to those principles, she sent frequent and extravagant gifts to Hellman whenever she saw anything she might like.

In 1937, while visiting Paris, Hellman accepted an invitation to attend a theatre festival in Moscow and called Julia to arrange a brief meeting on the way. To her surprise, Julia asked her to stay in Paris a few days longer until she could send a messenger with a special request. Despite the mystery, Hellman immediately agreed to wait: "It would not have occurred to me to ignore what Julia told me to do because that's the way it had always been between us."[4] When the messenger arrived, he requested that Hellman carry to Berlin $50,000 of Julia's money from her Paris bank, to be used to buy the freedom of Jews and other victims of Nazi persecution. The messenger also said that, even though every precaution was to be taken, there would be some danger, and Julia would completely understand if Hellman was unable to grant her request.

Hellman agreed to the request and, not without intrigue, smuggled the money into Berlin. For safety's sake, she was allowed to meet with Julia only briefly in a restaurant. There she burst into tears when she saw that one of

Julia's legs had been amputated following an injury sustained in a Nazi attack. Less than a year later she was informed by telegram that the Nazis had murdered Julia. It was twenty-five years before Hellman was able to write about the incident, and then, out of respect, she withheld Julia's true name in order to protect her family and friends who were still alive.

Definition of Friendship

The example of Hellman and Julia illustrates many features typical of friendship. Yet friendship comes in many forms, and it would be futile to try to define it with a simple set of conditions that sharply distinguish it from other relationships based on caring. The best we can do here is to indicate several criteria that characterize central (or "paradigm") examples of friendship.

First, friendship entails mutual liking, where liking is understood as a special affection for and delight in a person. Friends each enjoy the other's company, enjoy hearing news about the other, accept the other's imperfections, and delight in the other's particular characteristics. In some of the deepest friendships the affection is an instance of love (usually, though not always, nonerotic love). As with other forms of love, even the deepest friendships permit times of emotional distance, irritation, or anger. Hence, the relevant sense of *liking* implies a general attitude and a disposition to affection, rather than a continuous feeling.

Second, friendship involves sharing: mutual activities, shared experiences, reciprocal interests in each other, and intimate communication. This was notable in the early years of the Hellman-Julia friendship, and it continued during the years when an exchange of letters was the main shared activity.

Third, friendship involves reciprocal giving. Hellman and Julia gave freely of their time, attention, and energy, in addition to their exchanges of material gifts. The reciprocal nature of the giving was not diminished by Julia's ability to give far more materially because of her inherited wealth.

Fourth, the motive for sharing and giving is mutual caring, which consists of both friends' desire for the well-being of the other, as well as an especially deep affirmation of the other person's importance. It is true that Julia made a request that placed Hellman at risk, but the request derived from a matter of extraordinary moral importance, and Julia took every possible precaution to protect her.

Fifth, friendship is built on a sense of mutual understanding, understanding based on direct acquaintance with each other and shared personal knowledge. In part this understanding arises from the time spent together, and in part from personal conversation and correspondence. The relationship is "intimate" not only in the sense that it involves close emotional ties, but also in the willingness of friends to disclose more about themselves than they would to most other people.

Sixth, there is trust on the part of both friends. The trust is based on mutual commitments to care about the other's well-being, together with mutual understanding that friends can count on each other in difficult circumstances.

Seventh, friends share mutual respect, especially respect for the other's needs for freedom and self-respect. The friendship is entered into and sustained voluntarily. It is not based primarily on a desire to dominate and manipulate, nor on a desire to be submissive.

Eighth, friendships are (in part) chosen. To be sure, they begin and are sustained on a foundation of feelings of affection that are not wholly under our immediate control: As with erotic love, we cannot simply choose by fiat to be friends with just anyone. Nevertheless, for a friendship to be developed and sustained, friends must make a series of voluntary decisions. Because of this element of volition, friendships reflect important aspects of our personalities that may not be developed through family relationships (which often result from choices made by others rather than by ourselves, such as the decision to have or adopt children).

Ninth, in friendship there is mutual acknowledgment and affirmation of the relationship (as characterized by the preceding features). Each friend is aware of the ties joining them, hopes that the ties will be maintained, and is committed to making an effort to preserve the friendship. In fact, to some extent the high degree of caring involved depends on an anticipation that the friendship will continue.

The Value of Friendship

Why, and when, is friendship valuable, in particular morally valuable? Aristotle stated that friendship is most valuable when based on the friend's admiration for the good traits of character in each other, rather than on mutual usefulness or mutual pleasure, because friendship reinforces and develops good character through mutual inspiration and edification. The same value might accrue when the shared activities joining the friends are altruistic causes, such as helping the poor, promoting world peace, or working to preserve human rights. However, let us set aside these special cases for a moment and require only that the shared activities be morally permissible (not necessarily admirable) and that the mutual liking not be centered on immoral traits.

In moral terms, the most significant aspect of friendship is the mutual caring based on mutual respect and understanding. Each friend is especially concerned about the other's well-being, and each willingly expresses that concern without losing either self-respect or respect for the freedom of the other person. This is morally desirable and admirable in and of itself—as virtue ethicists would emphasize, as well as those utilitarians who count friendship as an especially important intrinsic good. Moreover, the degree of moral goodness involved in friendship depends on the degree of caring.

This view contrasts with Kant's narrow claim that the only thing morally good in and of itself is the desire to act for the sake of duty. It also differs sharply from all theories based on Kant's definition of the "moral point of view" as impartial regard for all people equally. The caring involved in friendship is morally valuable precisely because it is grounded in especially deep concern based on an appreciation of what is unique in the friend. It constitutes a singularly important recognition of the worth of individuals, and fulfills the human need to feel liked on the basis of another's intimate knowledge about oneself.

Friendship is also morally valuable because of its consequences, as utilitarians emphasize. Friendship offers primary support for self-respect and self-esteem: Our sense of self-worth is more vulnerable than we like to think, and nothing can help it more than supportive friendships (with the possible exception of erotic love). In times of difficulty, friends provide emotional support, sometimes more effectively than immediate family.

Friendship contributes in further ways to happiness and personal well-being. It affords friends delight in each other's company, in working and playing together on the basis of mutual concern. To be sure, friendship (like other forms of love) puts us at risk to suffer. The agonies of friendship include grief at the harm that befalls a friend, sadness at the inability to help when circumstances prevent us, and anguish at our failure to help because we are apathetic or selfishly preoccupied. Even when friendship is painful, however, it usually adds to the sense of worth of our lives. It also evokes our interests and enlivens our activities to know that they matter to our friends.

Moreover, friendship often increases our capacities for understanding and appreciating people who are not our friends, but who are either friends of our friends or people they otherwise care about. It can provide a quickened sense of why people have moral worth and thereby augment our sensitivity to the needs of strangers.

Marilyn Friedman has drawn attention to an especially important contribution of friendship to moral growth. Moral development is a lifelong process in which we come to see the world in new ways. Friendship, because it involves trust and intimacy, facilitates this awakening to new perspectives. This happens in both directions: We learn directly from our friends about their responses and attitudes, and we learn about ourselves as we are able to explore our own responses and values through conversations and shared activities.

Friendship makes possible special ways of learning, often unlike learning in more formal contexts such as the classroom or reading. In part this is due to *what* friends reveal, due especially to the detailed richness with which friends express their experiences and attitudes to each other. In part it is due to *how* they reveal it: "In friendship, there is a substantial measure of trust in the ability of our friends to bear what I call reliable 'moral witness' to their own experiences."[5] That is, because of the framework of mutual trust, we are able to appreciate our friends' values internally, from within their frame of reference: "[F]riendship, that is, a relationship of some degree of mutual intimacy, benevolence, interest, and concern, constitutes a context of trust and shared perspectives which fosters *vicarious participation in the very experience of moral alternatives.*[6] Not only do we gain detailed knowledge about our friends' perspectives, thereby widening the range of our own experience, we also enter sympathetically into alternative conceptual and value perspectives which widen our appreciation of human reality. We take seriously our friends' outlooks because we deeply value them as individuals.

Of course, if we were to choose only friends who shared our values in detail, friendship could not open our eyes to new perspectives. In fact, however, friends rarely (if ever) share precisely the same tastes, attitudes, and principles. Even if friendships are formed during periods when individuals have much in common, friendships which endure through time must inevitably accommodate changes in friends. Indeed, often the friendship helps the friends to adjust and change in the course of changes in education, jobs, and marriages. A close friend helps us understand parts of our life which may be very different from the friend's.

Our acknowledgment of these good consequences of friendship does not imply that we should be preoccupied with them. Although they may serve as reminders of the value of friendship, they cannot provide the primary reasons for having friends. To repeat, friendship is based on care and concern, and its origins lie in spontaneous liking. Motivation that derives primarily from an attitude of self-interest only inhibits or erodes friendship.

Responsibilities

A similar remark applies to the idea of duties, obligations, and responsibilities to friends: A primary motivation of duty is for the most part consistent with friendship. A sense of duty motivates us to pay our taxes and not to cheat; by contrast, affection motivates us to give presents to our friends. Nevertheless, there are responsibilities that accompany friendship.

Consider this illustration from David B. Annis:

> For example, if you have an important job interview, but when you start to leave for it, your car won't start, you might legitimately expect your friend, who can easily drive you, to help. If your friend refuses,

you would justifiably feel hurt and betrayed, and not understand how your friend could treat you this way.... Not helping seems inconsistent with the friendship, and if it happens often, the friendship has been abandoned. Notice that we wouldn't in general expect a stranger to drive us."[7]

One response to this example is that, at most, there is what Kant called a *hypothetical* duty: "If you want to maintain the friendship, then you ought to help the friend." This is not a moral (*categorical*) duty, however, but is instead only a counsel of prudence concerning how to satisfy a desire to keep a friend. This response will not do, however: Unless one has a good excuse, failure to help the friend violates the understanding and trust involved in the friendship (we are assuming there is a genuine friendship at the time). In some situations, where much is at stake, we speak of *betraying* the friend— not just of letting the friend down—and also of violating one's own integrity.

How can friendships generate special responsibilities, obligations owed to the friend in particular, but not to just any stranger? Utilitarians will attempt to trace these obligations to the good consequences accruing from friendships. Act-utilitarians encounter difficulty here, since it is not clear that one's aid to a friend will generate the best overall consequences in every situation. Act-utilitarians can still argue, however, that in general it is morally obligatory to help a friend, and in other cases one would have an excuse for not helping. Rule-utilitarians have a more promising approach in emphasizing the general benefits of maintaining the trust so essential to valuable friendships.

Annis, however, suggests that a still more promising approach to understanding the basis of duties of friendship is to emphasize the elements of voluntary choice and commitment typical in friendships: "Friendship involves various voluntary and consented to interactions and shared activities. As the friendship develops, an intricate web of reciprocal and mutual dispositions, beliefs, understandings, feelings, etc., develops."[8] This web of understandings generates trust, including trust that the friend cares and can be relied on to help in some situations. Usually there is no explicit promise to give help (or to maintain a friendship); but there are tacit commitments that arise as a friendship develops, and those tacit commitments generate obligations.

Moral Limits on Friendship

Praise for friendship has sometimes been excessive. Writing in the sixteenth century, for example, Montaigne asserted that "a single dominant friendship dissolves all other obligations" and that in an ideal friendship "each one gives himself so wholly to his friend that he has nothing left to distribute elsewhere."[9] This suggests that deep friendships generate paramount or absolute obligations which can never be overridden by other moral responsibilities. Responsibilities to a friend, however, like virtually all responsibilities, are prima facie; they sometimes have justified exceptions when other pressing obligations conflict with them, including obligations to other friends.

Montaigne's assertion represents harmful hyperbole in view of the numerous moral obligations limiting the claims of friendship. Earlier we assumed that the shared activities in friendships were of a morally permissible nature; now consider situations in which they are immoral. For example, there is friendship among criminals and in the "brotherhood" of organized crime. Insofar as these relationships involve genuine mutual caring, they have moral worth. That worth may be overshadowed, however, by the harm to which the friendship contributes.

It would be moral idolatry to elevate friendship to moral supremacy. No simple general ranking system dictates when the loyalties of a friendship should outweigh or temper loyalties to other friends, to family, or to one's community. Julia provides an interesting illustration of this. In her gifts for Hellman, she allowed personal affection to override her socialist principles of egalitarianism, which prohibit exorbitant gifts to financially secure friends. In response to the possibility of saving innocent human lives, however, she was willing, on the basis of higher principle, to request that Hellman make the personal sacrifice of putting herself at risk.

Strict egalitarians sometimes object that friendship preferentially bestows what they believe is owed equally to all other human beings, or at least to those having the greatest need. For them, the designation of a few individuals for special attention conflicts with the ideal of universal love for all. As our earlier discussion of the value of friendship might imply, we strongly disagree with that position. Nevertheless, there are special contexts in which the claims of justice for all people—the imperatives of impartiality and fairness—ought to restrict the exercise of generosity to friends. When a public official is responsible for appointing the best person for a job that requires the utmost competence (for example, police chief or chief surgeon), a selection influenced by friendship represents a violation of public trust.

At the same time, even in public life—in politics, business, and the professions—we place a high value on friendship and its special loyalties. It is often desirable to work with colleagues who are also friends, and we may give some preference to friends when we are not strictly prohibited by professional responsibilities. Even the competitive world of profit-making business recognizes the importance of "mentor relationships" involving friendship, whereby an established member of a company helps a younger one to advance in the company. Is this aid unjustified? Not insofar as friendships serve to humanize work situations that would otherwise be impersonal and even degrading.

In a famous passage, the novelist E. M. Forster expressed a sentiment related to Montaigne's view of friendship:

> I hate the idea of causes, and if I had to choose between betraying my country and betraying my friend, I hope I should have the guts to betray my country. Such a choice may scandalize the modern reader, and he may stretch out his patriotic hand to the telephone at once and ring up the police. It would not have shocked Dante, though. Dante places Brutus and Cassius in the lowest circle of Hell because they had chosen to betray their friend Julius Caesar rather than their country Rome.[10]

It is impossible to assess Forster's remark without first knowing about the particular context: the kind of country, the kind of friendship, the kinds of betrayal at issue and their probable consequences. If the country, for example, were a totalitarian state of the sort George Orwell described in *1984* (in which the government suppressed personal relationships as a threat to its absolute power), then Forster's remark is an admirable call for heroism. If, however, one's friend belonged to a terrorist group bent on destroying a democratic society, then Forster's remark is morally grotesque.

In *A Passage to India*, Forster portrays an example that supports his emphasis on the responsibilities of friendship. The example concerns a situation in which one's country is at fault, but one is placed under extreme pressure to support the country rather than a friend. Mr. Fielding, principal of an English college in India, had become a friend of Dr. Aziz, an Indian. As colonialists trying to maintain their dominance over India, the English were discouraged from forming such friendships, and the friendship emerged through natural affection despite differences, such as Aziz's Muslim faith and Fielding's atheism. When Aziz is falsely accused of assaulting an English woman while taking her on a tour of the Marabar Cave, the entire English community unifies to prosecute him, based on flimsiest evidence (and confusion) of the English woman. Fielding, however, maintains a firm faith in his friend's innocence and takes his side in the social upheaval that ensues. When Fielding is asked, "You actually are on our side against your own people?" he answers "Yes. Definitely."[11] Despite pressures from many directions, including threats to his career, Fielding vigorously helps Aziz prove his innocence. We admire him for that, and we might doubt his integrity had he acted otherwise. Subsequently, the friendship is suspended when Aziz comes to believe that Fielding has stopped caring about the injustice done to him, but, after nearly two years, shared understanding is restored.

In addition to illustrating the strength of the responsibilities involved in friendship, the example reinforces Friedman's earlier point about how friendships widen our understanding and appreciation of the world. Fielding comes to understand India and Indians far more than most of the other English characters in the novel because of his capacity for friendship. There is an important lesson here for those who live in a world where multicultural understanding becomes increasingly important.

SUMMARY

Friendship has several characteristic features: mutual liking (i.e., the fact that each has affection for and finds enjoyment in the other); sharing and reciprocal giving motivated by caring (i.e., the desire of each to promote the well-being of the other); mutual understanding, trust, and respect; and mutual choice, recognition, and affirmation of the friendship.

Because it involves mutual caring, friendship has moral worth. Not only does it represent an important way to appreciate and affirm the worth of other individuals, it also frequently results in good consequences: It contributes to happiness, increases our capacity to understand people in general, and affords us new insights based on a friend's enriching perspective. Friendship entails special responsibilities, although it can be harmful when it leads to the violation of other important obligations.

DISCUSSION TOPICS

1   Philosophers influenced by Kant argue that morality, by definition, requires impartiality in our treatment of other people. Consider, for example, the following comment:

> Morality is, at the very least, the effort to guide one's conduct by reason—that is, to do what there are the best reasons for doing—while giving equal weight to the interests of each individual who will be affected by one's conduct.[12]

Present and defend your view of whether friendship has a moral importance that justifies (indeed, requires) a lack of complete impartiality in some contexts. Also, identify several contexts in which morality does require strict impartiality and forbids us to allow friendships to bias decisions.

2   Just as we speak of *true love*, we sometimes speak of *true friendship*. Presumably, true or genuine friendships meet some criteria that distinguish them from less valuable relationships. In your view, what are these criteria? That is, what features of some friendships make them especially valuable?

3   Lillian Hellman was willing, out of friendship, to undertake a course of action that involved some danger. What does this willingness indicate about the nature of the friendship she had with Julia? Also, in requesting that Hellman undertake the action, did Julia act disloyally toward Hellman or violate their friendship in any way?

4   Friendship requires mutual caring. Does that mean it requires "pure altruism" in the sense of a desire for the friend's well-being for its own sake, without any ulte-

rior motives of self-interest? Or is friendship ultimately a matter of promoting someone's good in order to get something good for oneself in return? In your answer, take account of Lawrence Blum's view in the following passage, and give examples of what you think he means:

> Caring and the acts of beneficence in friendship are not separate from my own interests, from what is personally a good to me; it is not, in that sense, "disinterested." In fact, friendship is a context in which the division between self-interest and other-interest is often not applicable. The friendship itself defines what is of importance to me, and in that sense what is in my interest. In that sense I do not generally sacrifice my own interest in acting for the good of my friend. I act with a sense of the friendship's importance to me, even though it is the friend whose benefit I directly aim at (i.e., which is my motive for acting), and not my own.[13]

5   We can be friendly toward a great many people, but we can be close friends with far fewer people at any given time. Explain why this is, and in doing so, clarify the distinction between friendliness and friendship. At the same time, discuss whether the idea of having many friends simultaneously is less problematic than having many simultaneous erotic love relationships.

6   Express in your own words Aristotle's argument in the following passage:

> Whatever existence means for each class of men, whatever it is for whose sake they value life, in *that* they wish to occupy themselves with their friends; and so some drink together, others dice together, others join in athletic exercises and hunting, or in the study of philosophy, each class spending their days together in whatever they love most in life; for since they wish to live with their friends, they do and share in those things which give them the sense of living together. Thus the friendship of bad men turns out an evil thing (for because of their instability they unite in bad pursuits, and besides they become evil by becoming like each other), while the friendship of good men is good, being augmented by their companionship.[14]

Is Aristotle's argument a good one?

7   When is it permissible or even obligatory to express to a friend your view about the friend's faults, especially those which threaten the friend's well-being (for example, the friend's drug problem, overeating, surliness to others, dishonesty at school or work, etc.)? And when, if ever—and in particular if you believe that the friend will benefit in the long run—is it permissible to report a friend's wrongdoing to the relevant authorities? If you find these questions difficult to answer (in the abstract), discuss whether you think the answer turns (in part) on differences among friendships, including differences in what friends want or require from each other.

8   Is friendship gender-linked? Do men and women tend to display different patterns of friendships? Does your experience support or oppose the following observation by Lillian B. Rubin? "At every life stage between twenty-five and fifty-five, women have more friendships, as distinct from collegial relationships or work-mates, than men.... Generally, women's friendships with each other rest on shared intimacies, self-revelation, nurturance and emotional support.... In contrast, men's relationships are marked by shared activities."[15]

SUGGESTED READINGS

Annis, David B. "The Meaning, Value, and Duties of Friendship." *American Philosophical Quarterly*, vol. 24 (1987): 349–356.

Aristotle. *Nicomachean Ethics*. Trans. W. D. Ross. In R. McKeon (ed.), *The Basic Works of Aristotle*, Books 8 and 9. New York: Random House, 1941.

Badhwar, Neera Kapur (ed.). *Friendship: A Philosophical Reader*. Ithaca, NY: Cornell University Press, 1993.

Bernikow, Louise. "Friends." In *Among Women*. New York: Harper & Row, 1981.

Blum, Lawrence A. *Friendship, Altruism and Morality*. Boston, MA: Routledge & Kegan Paul, 1980.

Cooper, John M. "Aristotle on Friendship." In A. O. Rorty (ed.), *Essays on Aristotle's Ethics*. Berkeley, CA: University of California Press, 1980.

Forster, E. M. "What I Believe." In *Two Cheers for Democracy*. New York: Harcourt, Brace & World, 1951.

Friedman, Marilyn. *What Are Friends For: Feminist Perspectives on Personal Relationships and Moral Theory*. Ithaca: Cornell University Press, 1993.

Friedman, Marilyn. "Friendship and Moral Growth." *Journal of Value Inquiry*, vol. 23 (1989): 3–13.

Hellman, Lillian. *Pentimento*. New York: New American Library, 1974.

Kant, Immanuel. "Friendship." In *Lectures on Ethics*. Trans. L. Infield. New York: Harper & Row, 1963.

Meilander, Gilbert C. *Friendship: A Study in Theological Ethics*. Notre Dame, IN: University of Notre Dame Press, 1981.

Montaigne. "Of Friendship." In *The Complete Essays of Montaigne*. Trans. D. M. Frame. Stanford, CA: Stanford University Press, 1971.

Pakaluk, Michael (ed.). *Other Selves: Philosophers on Friendship*. Indianapolis, IN: Hackett, 1991.

Pogrebin, Letty Cottin. *Among Friends*. New York: McGraw-Hill, 1987.

Porter, Roy, and Sylvana Tomaselli (eds.). *The Dialectics of Friendship*. New York: Routledge, 1989.

Raymond, Janice G. *A Passion for Friends: Toward a Philosophy of Female Affection*. Boston, MA: Beacon Press, 1986.

Solomon, Robert C., and Kristine R. Hanson. "The Personal Side of Business." In *Above the Bottom Line: An Introduction to Business Ethics*. New York: Harcourt Brace Jovanovich, 1983.

Sharp, Ronald A. *Friendship and Literature*. Durham, NC: Duke University Press, 1986.

Sherman, Nancy. *The Fabric of Character: Aristotle's Theory of Virtue*. Oxford: Clarendon Press, 1989. Pp. 118–156.

Telfer, Elizabeth. "Friendship." *Proceedings of the Aristotelian Society*, vol. 71 (1970–1971).

Thomas, Laurence. *Living Morally: A Psychology of Moral Character*. Philadelphia, PA: Temple University Press, 1989. Pp. 97–158.

Welty, Eudora, and Ronald A. Sharp (eds.). *The Norton Book of Friendship*. New York: W. W. Norton, 1991.

CHAPTER 20

Meaningful Work

In a wide sense, work is any activity that yields products or services that have value, whether or not one is paid for it. In this sense, the unpaid homemaker who spends over eighty hours a week tending children, cleaning, cooking, ironing, and running errands certainly works. In the narrower sense used here, however, work is an activity for which one receives financial compensation.

Because most people work out of the necessity to earn a living, we tend to think of the morality of work as simply the responsible performance of a job in return for money. Yet work is equally important as a context for caring relationships with colleagues, clients, and members of the public. Although a few types of work are conducted largely in isolation, most work requires shared activities, cooperation, and mutual respect. Collegiality is a virtue essential for both successful and enjoyable work. Moreover, most work situations involve caring relationships with people for whom one performs a service (clients and the public), and these require a range of virtues, from conscientiousness (in performing one's job) to loyalty. Caring relationships provide much of the meaning of work, as the following examples illustrate.

Examples of Two Workers

In his book *Working*, Studs Terkel records more than a hundred interviews with workers from many occupations. The first interview is with a thirty-seven-year-old steelworker named Mike Lefevre, who describes his job as "strictly muscle work ... pick it up, put it down, pick it up, put it down."[1] His steel mill handles from forty to fifty thousand pounds of steel each day, steel that has a final destination unknown to him. Lefevre takes no pride in

303

his work, he explains, because "it's hard to take pride in a bridge you're never gonna cross, in a door you're never gonna open. You're mass-producing things and you never see the end result of it."[2] He is also nagged by a fear that he is replaceable at any time by a machine that can do his work more efficiently.

From his supervisor he receives neither respect nor recognition for his endeavors. Instead, the boss "spies" on him, thereby compounding the monotony of the work with anxiety. Nor is there recognition from co-workers or the public: "It's the non-recognition by other people. To say a woman is *just* a housewife is degrading, right? Okay. *Just* a housewife. It's also degrading to say *just* a laborer."[3]

For Lefevre, work lacks intrinsic value: there is nothing in it worth doing for its own sake, nor are there any personal relationships to give it some meaning. Indeed, from his point of view, the work is inherently bad. He sees nothing in it that evokes his talents and interests: "My attitude is that I don't get excited about my job. I do my work but I don't say whoopee-doo. The day I get excited about my job is the day I go to a head shrinker. How are you gonna get excited about pullin' steel?"[4] Work for him represents a long series of daily humiliations, frustrations, and resentments that periodically erupt into after-work barroom brawls. He works solely for a livelihood and for the sake of his family, especially in order to send his children to college.

Matters are very different, however, with other workers Terkel interviewed. They do not find their jobs demoralizing, even though their work is seemingly as repetitive and difficult as that of the steelworker. Consider Dolores Dante, a waitress in the same restaurant for twenty-three years, working from 5 P.M. to 2 A.M., six days a week. She suffers from arthritis and on many days goes home physically and emotionally exhausted. Nevertheless, she enjoys her work and takes great pride in serving people.

To outside observers, many aspects of her work seem boringly routine, in particular waiting on an endless stream of customers. But Dante takes great interest in her work: "I have to be a waitress. How else can I learn about people? How else does the world come to me?"[5] She creates variety in her work through conversations with customers, and she takes pride in the considerable talents she has developed as a conversationalist.

She also introduces pleasing variations on routine work, for example, by developing a repertoire of ways to ask for a customer's order. She also values her skills in dealing diplomatically with temperamental cooks. At times she even creates an imaginative personal drama in her work: "To be a waitress, it's an art. I feel like a ballerina, too. I have to go between those tables, between those chairs.... I do it with an air."[6]

Like Lefevre, Dante is annoyed by people who reduce her to her work-role by treating her with the attitude that she is *just* a waitress. She takes the view, however, that those individuals fail to see the genuine value in the service she has to offer. She too has to contend with "spying" supervisors and the fear that she is replaceable by others who want her job. Yet she deals with these problems as she does with other difficult aspects of the work, without submitting to a sense of being superfluous or unimportant.

Unlike Lefevre, Dante finds her work inherently valuable, in addition to being instrumentally valuable (that is, valuable as a means to other good things, such as an income for herself and her children). A large part of the inherent value derives from the personal relationships she has with co-workers and members of the public she serves. These relationships bring recognition and a sense of cooperative endeavor and are for the most part based on mutual respect. She works with a clear sense of the connection between her work and the good of the people she serves and works with.

Alienation and Work Ethics

We can state that Lefevre *feels* and *is* alienated from his work, the things he produces, and the people with whom he works. He does not *identify with* his work, nor can he affirm its worth. This subverts the possibility for caring relationships in the workplace; conversely, the absence of those relationships also contributes to worker alienation, as do some attitudes toward one's work.

Karl Marx (1818–1883), who introduced the concept of worker alienation, describes alienation from work activities in terms that fit Lefevre perfectly:

> What constitutes the alienation of labor? First, that the work is *external* to the worker, that it is not part of his nature; and that, consequently, he does not fulfill himself in his work but denies himself, has a feeling of misery rather than well being, does not develop freely his mental and physical energies but is physically exhausted and mentally debased. The worker therefore feels himself at home only during his leisure time, whereas at work he feels homeless.... [Work] is not the satisfaction of a need, but only a *means* for satisfying other needs.[7]

In addition to this characterization of alienation from the activity of working, Marx also analyzes alienation from the product of one's labor (as exemplified by Lefevre's inability to experience the steel products as a personal self-expression), alienation from co-workers (the feeling that one is disconnected from colleagues), and alienation from other human beings in general. All these forms of alienation involve a lack of connection with and personal affirmation of the thing from which one is alienated. In Marx's view, work should be central to our self-esteem, self-respect, and sense of identity—that is, our sense of who we are. Hence, alienation from work is ultimately alienation from ourselves.

Marx argued that worker alienation was an inevitable product of capitalism, whereby workers sell their labor to someone else for money, which is then used to purchase things that satisfy the workers' desires. As the case of Dolores Dante suggests, however, the causes of worker alienation are probably more complicated. In subsequent sections we will focus on one such cause: the nature of the personal relationships at work.

Before continuing, however, we should note a few other attitudes toward work—other *work ethics*—than those of Lefevre (work as a necessary evil), Dante (work as a source of enjoyment through personal relationships), and Marx (work as the primary avenue to self-fulfillment). One is the *Protestant work ethic*, which the sociologist Max Weber saw as underlying the historical development of capitalism. According to this ethic, people are obligated to refrain from pleasures by engaging in work, however onerous and distasteful it may be. This enables us to serve the community, to avoid becoming a social burden, and to accumulate wealth in the service of God. Weber quotes an influential Protestant minister:

> If God shows you a way in which you may lawfully get more than in another way (without wrong to your soul or to any other), if you refuse this, and choose the less gainful way, you cross one of the ends of your calling, and you refuse to be God's steward, and to accept His gifts and use them for Him when He requireth it: you may labour to be rich for God, though not for the flesh and sin.[8]

As this ethic later became secularized, it tended to encourage the pursuit of wealth for its own sake. Perhaps it also formed a rationale for "workaholics" who devote themselves to work beyond reasonable bounds. Both the Protestant work ethic and compulsive attitudes elevate work over personal relationships (whether at work or in personal life).

An opposing work ethic is suggested by Gilbert Meilaender, who rejects the idea that we should "live in order to work" and favors instead "working in order to live." Whether work is inherently pleasant or unpleasant, its primary role in human life is to be an instrumental good. Work provides the leisure time necessary to sustain personal relationships with family and friends:

> When work as we know it emerges as the dominant idea in our lives—when we identify ourselves to others in terms of what we do for a living, work for which we are paid—and when we glorify such work in terms of self-fulfillment, it is time for Christian ethics to speak a good word for working simply in order to live. Perhaps we need to suggest today that it is quite permissible, even appropriate, simply to work in order to live and to seek one's fulfillment elsewhere—in personal bonds like friendship.[9]

Probably there is no single work ethic that is obligatory for all people; rather, various attitudes toward work seem morally permissible and warranted (depending on the worker's situation). Nevertheless, three features of work improve its moral worth whenever they are present: collegiality, loyalty, and caring for members of the public who benefit from one's work.

Collegiality

Collegiality requires that one do more than refrain from unjustly defaming, insulting, harassing, or degrading colleagues. It is a more positive ideal and virtue. Craig Ihara defines it this way:

> The conclusion I have reached is that collegiality is a kind of connectedness grounded in respect for professional expertise and in a commitment to the goals and values of the profession, and that, as such, collegiality includes a disposition to support and cooperate with one's colleagues.[10]

According to this definition, the key ingredients of collegiality are mutual respect, connectedness, and cooperation. These ingredients, and hence collegiality, can be present in all forms of work, not just professions such as law, medicine, and teaching, which require advanced education.

Respect for one's colleagues is an attitude, not simply a pattern of conduct. One who respects one's co-workers values them for their expertise and their devotion to serving some public good. As with friendship, Ihara claims that respect must be reciprocal; however, it seems possible for one person to display collegiality toward a colleague who does not reciprocate with the same attitude.

Connectedness consists of an awareness of being part of a social structure and a community of people who together pursue some shared good. It is a sense that the involvement of others makes one's endeavors possible. There must be at least a minimal sense of shared values concerning the goal that is collectively pursued.

Cooperation is the willingness to work together and to support one another in pursuit of the common goal. Although cooperation is compatible with moderate degrees of competitiveness in which co-workers help stimulate each other in their endeavors, it is undermined when competition with co-workers becomes cutthroat.

Collegiality, which thus encompasses the three elements of mutual respect, connectedness, and cooperation, is a moral virtue for two reasons, according to Ihara. One concerns the benefits to the public and the other concerns a benefit to workers. First, collegiality enables professionals (and, we would add, workers in general) to serve the public good because it strengthens their motivation at work. It does this by creating an environment that supports mutual endeavors, enlivens shared commitments, and encourages responsible work. Second, collegiality contributes to making work inherently worthwhile for those who engage in it. Dolores Dante found significance in her work in part because of the attitudes of goodwill and shared endeavor of co-workers. Mike Lefevre found work hateful in part because he lacked a sense of collegiality with co-workers.

Loyalty

Collegiality is one expression of the wider virtue of loyalty. Loyalty in the workplace has several dimensions: loyalty to colleagues, to one's employer, to one's corporation, and to the clients and public one serves. Many of the difficulties of professional life arise because of conflicts among two or more of these loyalties and the obligations they engender.

Loyalties involve obligations or role-defined duties, but they have other elements as well. To be loyal is to wish to meet one's obligations because of a concern for a person or group. One is motivated by something more personal than Kant's "acting for the sake of duty." There must be caring and concern for the person, group, or cause to which one is loyal.

Josiah Royce (1855–1916) proposed the following definition of loyalty: "Loyalty is the willing and practical and thoroughgoing devotion of a person to a cause."[11] As such, according to Royce, loyalty is inherently good. He recognizes that loyalty as practiced by fanatical devotees to evil causes can have very bad consequences, which make it "instrumentally bad" (i.e., bad as a means to bad effects). Nevertheless, it is always inherently good in relation to a person's character:

> Whoever is loyal whatever be his cause, is devoted, is active, surrenders his private self-will, controls himself, is in love with his cause, and believes in it. The loyal man is thus in a certain state of mind which has its own value for himself. To live a loyal life, whatever be one's cause, is to live in a way which is certainly free from many well-known sources of inner dissatisfaction. Thus hesitancy is often correct by loyalty; for the cause plainly tells the loyal man what to do. Loyalty, again, tends to unify life, to give it centre, fixity, stability.[12]

It is true, of course, that devotion to either moral or immoral causes can have some good effects on the personalities of particular individuals. That does not, however, make it inherently (always) good, as Royce goes on to suggest. In fact, insofar as the unity and stability that loyalty brings to a personality strengthen an individual's commitment to immoral causes, they are not desirable.

After raising similar criticisms against Royce, John Ladd suggests that we redefine loyalty. His definition makes loyalty a virtue, and hence inherently good, without implying there is anything good about immoral fanatics. His definition builds moral duties into the concept of loyalty:

Loyalty, strictly speaking, demands what is morally due the object of loyalty.... Loyalty includes fidelity in carrying out one's duties to the person or group of persons who are the object of loyalty; but it embraces more than that, for it implies an attitude, perhaps an affection or sentiment, toward such persons. Furthermore, at the very least, loyalty requires the complete subordination of one's own private interest in favor of giving what is due.[13]

Because there are no moral duties to pursue immoral ends, the immoral fanatic cannot be called loyal. For example, there cannot be "loyal Ku Klux Klan members." The KKK cause is immoral, and there are no (moral) duties to serve it; hence, the crucial idea of fidelity to one's duties is missing. Loyalty presupposes that the group, individual, or cause to which one is loyal is morally good or permissible.

With the awareness that different writers develop different persuasive (value-loaded) definitions of the word *loyalty,* let us distinguish two general senses of the word. As an attitude and disposition, loyalty is the strong identification with and dedicated caring for a cause, institution, or person. As a virtue, loyalty is a desirable trait of character—desirable in some important respect, though not necessarily in all respects. In relation to work, the primary good of the virtue of loyalty is in shaping character—inducing us to be conscientious, responsible, and caring with regard to both the work itself and relationships at work. At this point, however, we must consider an objection: Is loyalty obsolete and even harmful in today's work environment?

Modern corporations, at least American profit-making ones, are abstract and impersonal entities. Employers have little or no loyalty toward employees: They fire them whenever they deem it necessary for the corporation. This makes it seem unfair to expect loyalty from employees. All that should be required is that employees do a responsible job in return for fair wages. (Such corporations contrast sharply with others—for example, many nonprofit American corporations, and also Japanese corporations, foster close employer-employee relationships.)

Furthermore, loyalty can have bad consequences. When combined with employees' self-interest in keeping their jobs, it can lead workers to do whatever the boss orders, often at the expense of the public good. For example, many employees engage in or know about unethical practices at work about which they remain silent, motivated by a combination of self-interest and loyalty to the corporation. Only rarely do individuals, at great personal risk, "blow the whistle" by informing someone outside the corporation of dangers to the public.[14]

To develop this criticism, there are innumerable instances when whistle-blowing would serve the public good. One example concerns the first crash of a fully loaded jumbo jet, which occurred in 1974 when a cargo door blew open in midair. The open cargo door depressurized the cargo area, collapsing the floor of the passenger area, along which ran the pilot's steering mechanism. All 346 people on board were killed. Two years before the crash it was known that the door was unsafely designed. The senior engineer in charge of the design wrote a memo to his boss stating, "It seems to me inevitable that, in the twenty years ahead of us, DC-10 cargo doors will come open and I would expect this to usually result in the loss of the airplane."[15] Without disagreeing with the engineer's judgment, top management decided on financial grounds that nothing would be done. The engineer did not whistle-blow to the government or to a journalist, and neither did any other engineers or managers who knew about the safety defect.

Do such tragedies suggest that loyalty to companies, colleagues, and employers is harmful? Perhaps not. Recall that Ladd's definition of loyalty places moral limits on what is required by loyalty. In his view, loyalty consists of the faithful and caring fulfillment of one's (prima facie) duties to one's corporation and to the people with whom one works. However, there are also (prima facie) duties not to harm innocent members of the public. In the airplane case, the duties to the public seem to override those to the employer.

There is, however, some truth in the objection that it is unfair to expect loyalty from employees when employers show little or no loyalty. Insofar as corporations encourage an entirely impersonal contract relationship with employees, the conditions for reciprocal loyalty and care are subverted, resulting in the depersonalized and alienated work relationships illustrated in the case of Mike Lefevre. Corporations do in fact vary greatly in the extent to which this occurs.

Altruism and Career Choice

Most careers, and all professions, have some effect on the public good. To become a professional is to acquire duties to the public. These duties place limits on duties to the corporation for which one works, as we saw in the case of the airplane disaster. Is there, however, a duty to embark on any particular kind of career? More generally, should any moral considerations enter into decisions about careers?

Two points are obvious. First, there is an obligation not to pick careers that are likely to cause more harm than good. This rules out "careers" in crime, and it also rules out careers that violate one's conscience. If one believes that the tobacco industry or the nuclear armaments industry is harmful, then one should not work in those industries. The argument that "if I don't take this job, someone else will" is not an excuse for doing something one views as harmful.

Second, individuals have a moral right to select their own careers, at least within a democratic society that values individual liberty. We have a human right to pursue our career interests given the available options, and we are also most qualified to judge what those interests are.

Nevertheless, the right to select a (morally permissible) career does not entail that one will select the morally best career available. Should we think in terms of the moral good we can achieve through a career, or is career choice entirely a matter of self-interest (as is commonly thought)?

Norman Care contends that the good of the community should enter into career decisions; that is, careers should be selected in light of our membership in a community. Each of us, he urges, is responsible for other people who share this world with us. Obviously, we live in a world where millions of people are destitute, where gross inequities exist, and where not nearly enough is done to help people in need. Caring for the public good should enter heavily into career decisions.

In developing this view, Care contrasts three approaches to career choice. A purely *self-realization ethics* would regard personal fulfillment as the sole principle guiding career choice. A purely *service ethics*, by contrast, suggests that careers should be selected on the basis of the maximum good we can do for people. Service to others should have a higher priority than self-realization. A *mixed ethics* states that self-realization has priority in career selection but that, once careers are chosen, they should be pursued in ways that serve the public good as much as possible.

Care argues that service ethics is the correct view. A purely self-realization ethics reflects and encourages callousness. It is based on the false assumption that we are in the world for ourselves rather than as participants in a community of people of equal worth and importance. The mixed-ethics view errs in making caring relationships with other people secondary to self-interest, when in fact they ought to have priority, at least as long as we live in a world where "relatively few are able to realize themselves, relatively many suffer destitution in some or many of its desperate forms, and no effective general ameliorating scheme is in place at all."[16]

A problem with this view, however, was voiced much earlier by Hastings Rashdall (1858–1924). Rashdall was a utilitarian who thought we are obligated to select careers that promote the most good for the most people. This would seem to commit him to a service ethics, but in fact Rashdall defended what Care calls a mixed ethics. He reminded us that careers extend over many years and make great demands. These demands can generate frustration and harm unless they fit our talents and interests. Thus, people who wish to succeed in a service career must have a "calling" for it, because to select a service career out of a sense of duty is probably harmful:

> Certain social functions require for their adequate fulfillment that they should be done in a certain spirit. Such functions demand the possession of certain qualities of mind or heart or character which cannot be summoned up at the command of the will, and cannot be satisfactorily performed merely as a matter of duty.... It is for the general good that every

man should do the work for which he is most fitted; and as a general rule, a natural liking for the work or kind of life adopted is one of the most important qualifications for it.[17]

Using this line of reasoning, Rashdall concluded that it is morally permissible, in selecting careers, to place greater emphasis on self-realization than on service. Nevertheless, once a career is selected, caring relationships should be sought and sustained as much as possible in order to promote as much good as possible. Whether Care or Rashdall is correct will be left as a discussion question.

SUMMARY

There are various work ethics, that is, attitudes concerning the meaning of work. They include the attitudes that work is a necessary evil (Lefevre); work is (in part) inherently enjoyable (Dante); work is a primary avenue to self-fulfillment (Marx); maximization of personal wealth through disciplined work is socially desirable (the Protestant work ethic); and the main purpose of work is to support an independent life in which meaning comes primarily from relationships outside work (Meilaender).

Most work involves caring relationships, at least potentially, and these relationships add to the meaning derived from work. The meaning of work is subverted when workers become alienated from their work activities, the products of their work, or the people with whom they work. Alienation, as Karl Marx analyzed it, involves the inability to identify with something, that is, to see it as a personal involvement or self-expression, and to value it. The absence of caring relationships in the workplace is a major cause of alienation.

Collegiality as a virtue has three aspects: respect for one's co-workers and reciprocation of that respect, an attitude or sense of being connected with colleagues in a shared enterprise serving some public good, and cooperativeness in the sense of willingness to work together with colleagues. Collegiality is inherently good as one form of a caring relationship, and also as a means to whatever public good is served by work.

Loyalty can refer either to strong and caring identifications with persons, causes, or institutions, or to the virtue involved when these identifications are morally valuable in some way—especially when the identifications engender faithful devotion to the fulfillment of one's moral duties. Loyalty to colleagues, employers, and companies is appropriate if there is reciprocal loyalty and if genuine duties and goods are served by that loyalty. Loyalties frequently come into conflict in the workplace, however, and balanced reflection is needed to identify the primary duty in a given situation.

How far should moral reasons enter into the selection of a career? Self-realization ethics states that, unless the work is inherently immoral, one's self-interest is the only consideration. Service ethics states that careers should be selected on the basis of the maximum good we can do for people. Mixed ethics states that self-realization is most important but that, once a career is chosen, it should be pursued so as to maximize the public good.

DISCUSSION TOPICS

1   What moral considerations should be taken into account in choosing a career? On this issue, do you agree with Norman Care, with Hastings Rashdall, or with neither of them?

2   You are working with a colleague who confesses to you that he has been charging personal long-distance phone calls to the company for several years, against company regulations, but that he recently stopped doing so. Does collegiality obligate you to say nothing about the infraction to your employer? Does loyalty to the company obligate you to report the infraction? What should you do?

3   With respect to the case of the airplane crash in 1974, we stated that the obligation to warn the public of dangers should override the duty to the company to obey one's employer. However, it is likely that if the engineer had gone outside the company to inform the public of the dangerous cargo door ("blown the whistle"), he would have been fired. Most whistle-blowers are fired or demoted, and frequently they are "blacklisted"; that is, they are prevented from obtaining a comparable job because they are given negative evaluations when prospective employers call to check on the fired individual's references. Do these facts excuse the engineer from warning the public in view of the extreme self-sacrifice that would be required?

4   In a similar connection, consider the tragic explosion of the space shuttle *Challenger* on January 29, 1986. The disaster was due largely to unsafe seals joining segments of a booster rocket. A number of engineers for Morton Thiokol, the designer and builder of the rocket, argued against making the launch. One engineer, Allan McDonald, had been a critic of the seals long before the disaster. He urged both Thiokol and NASA officials to postpone the launch because the seals had not been tested under temperatures comparable to those at the launch site. Unfortunately, his protests were rejected by the Thiokol management, which had authority for making the final launch recommendation to NASA. Identify the obligations and loyalties relevant to McDonald's situation. Which should have priority? In vigorously protesting the launch, did McDonald do everything morally required?

5   Professions are occupations requiring advanced education, sophisticated skills, and service to some important public good. Usually, they involve special caring relationships with clients. Moral dilemmas arise for professionals when two or more professional duties or loyalties come into conflict, or when a professional obligation conflicts with personal conscience. Defend your view about what ought to be done in each of the following cases, basing your answers on an ethical theory about right action. Also, what virtues are at stake in each case?

a   Judges are responsible for upholding the laws. Suppose, however, that a
    judge views a particular law as grossly immoral, such as a law requiring exces-
    sive punishment for people convicted of using marijuana. Is the judge oblig-
    ated to enforce laws that violate his or her personal conscience? Can a judge's
    concern for a particular individual justify a departure from the law?

b   Physicians have obligations to alleviate suffering and promote life. American
    physicians also work within a legal tradition that forbids euthanasia (that is, the
    intentional infliction, motivated by benevolence, of death on a hopelessly ill or
    injured patient). Consider a physician who disagrees with this tradition and
    who has a patient suffering from terminal cancer. Safe dosages of morphine are
    no longer sufficient to stop the pain, and the patient begs for increased dosages,
    knowing they will hasten death. If the physician's motivation is concern for the
    patient's good, is the physician justified in granting the patient's request?

c   Politicians sometimes are asked to lie in order to protect national security.
    One example occurred in 1980 during the U.S. attempt to save fifty-three
    Americans held hostage in Iran.[18] President Carter believed that if the rescue
    attempt was to have a chance of success, the Iranians had to believe that no
    military action was being planned. As a decoy, he sent Secretary of State
    Cyrus Vance to assure U.S. allies publicly that the United States would not
    engage in military action if the allies would participate in enforcing economic
    sanctions against Iran. Vance made these deceitful assurances to people with
    whom he had previous relationships of trust. Before doing so, he submitted a
    confidential letter of resignation to President Carter, effective after the rescue
    attempt. Was his resignation inappropriate? Do you think he should have re-
    fused President Carter's order?

6   We suggested that the attitude "If I don't do it (this work) then someone else
    will" does not excuse participation in morally objectionable work. Is this sugges-
    tion perhaps mistaken? Consider this example from Bernard Williams:

> George, who has just taken his Ph.D. in chemistry, finds it extremely difficult
> to get a job.... His wife has to go out to work to keep them, which itself causes
> a great deal of strain, since they have small children and there are severe prob-
> lems about looking after them. The results of all this, especially on the chil-
> dren, are damaging. An older chemist, who knows about this situation, says
> that he can get George a decently paid job in a certain laboratory, which pur-
> sues research into chemical and biological warfare. George says that he cannot
> accept this, since he is opposed to chemical and biological warfare.[19]

Suppose an act-utilitarian tells George that it is all right to accept the job because
someone else will take the job if he does not. Is that an adequate excuse (or even
justification) for taking the job? Are there other adequate justifications for taking
the job in George's situation?

SUGGESTED READINGS

Anthony, P. D. *The Ideology of Work.* New York: Methuen, 1978.
Baron, Marica. *The Moral Status of Loyalty.* Dubuque, IA: Kendall-Hunt, 1984.

Beauchamp, Tom L., and Norman E. Bowie (eds.). *Ethical Theory and Business.* 4th ed. Englewood Cliffs, NJ: Prentice-Hall, 1993.

Best, Fred (ed.). *The Future of Work.* Englewood Cliffs, NJ: Prentice-Hall, 1973.

Bolles, Richard Nelson. *What Color Is Your Parachute? A Practical Manual for Job Hunters and Career Changers.* Berkeley, CA: Ten Speed Press. New edition each year.

Callahan, Joan C. (ed.). *Ethical Issues in Professional Life.* New York: Oxford University Press, 1988.

Care, Norman S. "Career Choice." In *On Sharing Fate.* Philadelphia, PA: Temple University Press, 1987.

Ezorsky, Gertrude (ed.). *Moral Rights In the Workplace.* Albany, NY: State University Press of New York, 1987.

Flores, Albert (ed.). *Professional Ideals.* Belmont, CA: Wadsworth, 1988.

Fletcher, George P. *Loyalty: An Essay on the Morality of Relationships.* New York: Oxford University Press, 1993.

Frankena, William K. "The Philosophy of Vocation." *Thought*, vol. 51 (1976): 393–408.

Glover, Jonathan. "Work." In *What Sort of People Should There Be?* New York: Penguin, 1984.

Goldman, Alan H. *The Moral Foundations of Professional Ethics.* Totowa, NJ: Rowman & Littlefield, 1980.

Ihara, Craig K. "Collegiality as a Professional Virtue." In A. Flores (ed.), *Professional Ideals.* Belmont, CA: Wadsworth, 1988.

Martin, Mike W., and Roland Schinzinger. *Ethics in Engineering.* 2nd ed. New York: McGraw–Hill, 1988.

Marx, Karl. *Economic and Philosophical Manuscripts.* In E. Fromm, *Marx's Concept of Man.* Trans. T. B. Bottomore. New York: Ungar, 1966.

O'Toole, James, Jane L. Scheiber, and Linda C. Wood (eds.). *Working: Changes and Choices.* New York: Human Sciences Press, 1981.

Rashdall, Hastings. "Vocation." In *The Theory of Good and Evil.* Vol. 2. Oxford: Clarendon Press, 1907.

Sessions, Robert, and Jack Wortman (eds.). *Working in America: A Humanities Reader.* Notre Dame, IN: University of Notre Dame Press, 1992.

Solomon, Robert C. *Ethics and Excellence: Cooperation and Integrity in Business.* New York: Oxford University Press, 1992.

Terkel, Studs. *Working.* New York: Avon Books, 1975.

Weber, Max. *The Protestant Ethic and the Spirit of Capitalism.* Trans. T. Parsons. New York: Scribner, 1958.

Windt, Peter Y., et al. (eds.). *Ethical Issues in the Professions.* Englewood Cliffs, NJ: Prentice-Hall, 1989.

Work. Special issues of *The Philosophical Forum.* Vol. X, Nos. 2–4.

CHAPTER 21

Community Service

Community service can refer to paid or unpaid service, as well as to the national service program in which community work provides a way to repay student loans. Here we will focus on unpaid service and giving, often referred to as philanthropy or voluntary service.

The word *philanthropy* often brings to mind large gifts made by very rich donors, but in fact the word now applies to all giving for community or public purposes. The expression *voluntary service* has a similar wide meaning, although it often connotes contributions of time rather than money. At least among professional fundraisers, both terms have largely replaced the word *charity*, which has several more limited meanings: (1) the legal sense of tax-deductible gifts, (2) the biblical sense of love, and (3) the pejorative sense of condescending gifts that suggest pity (rather than compassion), whereby the donor feels superior rather than equal to the beneficiary.

Here we will use the terms *philanthropy* and *voluntary service* interchangeably to refer to voluntary giving for community purposes, whether the gifts are large or small, or consist of money, time, talent, used clothing, blood, or take some other form. By *community purposes* we will include virtually all giving beyond one's circle of family and friends—for example, gifts to the arts, humanities, sciences, world hunger organizations, environmental and animal causes, political causes, churches and synagogues, hospitals, museums, libraries, and colleges. We will not assume that either the motives or the purpose of the gift is admirable; those are topics left open for inquiry in specific cases. We will also include giving to communities that are local, regional, national, and international in scope.

Voluntary service to communities occurs on a massive scale in the United States. It is not, however, the exclusive domain of a few rich people and wealthy foundations—they account for only 10 percent of private donations. The remaining 90 percent comes from individuals, half of them in families whose income is under $39,000. Moreover, about half of Americans over age thirteen volunteer an average of 3.5 hours of their time each week.[1]

This aspect of everyday morality—voluntary contribution to communities—deserves more attention in ethics. When philosophers discuss moral community, they often have in mind an abstraction. The most famous such abstraction is Kant's "kingdom of ends": an imaginary situation in which all rational beings respect the autonomy and dignity of others. Here, by contrast, moral community refers to the moral ties that should be sustained by groups of people identified by their place of residence, shared traditions and culture, or common way of life within a neighborhood, state, country, religion, profession, or institution.

Consider, for example, a college. As a moral community, it is defined by the moral relationships that do or should exist among students, professors, staff, trustees, local citizens, and alumni (living and dead). These relationships involve *special* ties of loyalty, shared value, and meaning—*special* in that they center on the aims of the college rather than on the general connections among all rational beings to which Kant referred. These ties, in turn, provide a context for moral activity and virtue for members of that community. In fact, with respect to morally concerned individuals—those having a reasonable degree of moral caring—it is plausible to argue that self-fulfillment requires some voluntary service and giving to the community. A dramatic illustration is the life of Jane Addams.

An Example of Community Service

Jane Addams was a pioneer in modern social work, a profession that did not exist in 1889 when she founded Hull-House. Hull-House was a "settlement house," that is, a community center created to serve the immigrant population in Chicago. In 1889, Addams and her friends renovated an old tenement building in an impoverished part of Chicago, moved in, and began to offer a variety of services in response to the needs of the local community. Initial services included first aid, a public kitchen for people lacking income, and a day-care service for children of working parents (most of whom worked twelve to fourteen hours a day). Later, many new buildings were built, including an art museum, a theatre, and a gymnasium. They recruited hundreds of college students and professors (including John Dewey, the leading American philosopher at the time) to help serve and teach over two thousand people each day.

It became clear to Addams that the immigrants had greater needs than even this monumental enterprise could fulfill. She initiated and supported a variety of legal reforms to reduce working hours, prohibit child labor, fund school playgrounds, improve sanitation, support women's voting rights, and create the first juvenile court in the country. Later, as World War I approached, she devoted her energies to peace activism, the role for which she was the first woman to receive the Nobel Peace Prize.

What motivated Addams and her colleagues at Hull-House? According to her own account, three motives were primary. First, they shared a conviction that democracy is more than a matter of political rights; it is the ideal of universal participation in the community. This ideal is based on the awareness that in a democracy the good of individuals is interwoven with the good of the masses: "The good we secure for ourselves is precarious and uncertain, is floating in the mid-air, until it is secured for all of us and incorporated into our common life."[2]

Second, Addams (like David Hume) believed that an innate sense of humanity generates altruistic desires. She thus found it entirely natural to help others.

Third, Addams asserted, community service connects us with people in ways that evoke our talents and lead to self-fulfillment:

> Nothing so deadens the sympathies and shrivels the power of enjoyment as the persistent keeping away from the great opportunities for helpfulness and a continual ignoring of the starvation struggle which makes up the life of at least half the race. To shut one's self away from that half of the [human] race['s] life is to shut one's self away from the most vital part of it; it is to live out but half the humanity to which we have been born heir and to use but half our faculties. We have all had longings for a fuller life which should include the use of these faculties.[3]

Individualism and Community

For Addams, community service was selfless, in the sense of unselfish; but it was not a matter of pure "selflessness" in the sense of a sacrifice of one's own interests and needs. Community involvement helped unfold her interests and capacities so as to create a richer self through relationships within a community. In this sense there are, and should be, mixed motives for volunteerism, and also for giving. Self-interest (concern for one's own good) and altruism (concern for the good of others) combine in ways that are mutually strengthening. The combination in no way lessens the virtue involved in the acts of altruism. Mixed motives are objectionable only when self-interest so dominates service that one's ability to help others is threatened.

Pursuit of individual self-interest and commitment to the good of the community have more often been seen as opposed rather than complementary in American traditions, according to the sociologist Robert Bellah and his co-authors in *Habits of the Heart*.... The lone individualist, whether a cowboy or a corporate entrepreneur, is glorified. Social involvement is mistakenly equated with conformity, the passive acceptance of given social practices. The social rebel excites our imagination, while the community participant strikes us as a drudge. Jane Addams reminds us, however, that stunning individual expression is fully compatible with community service; indeed, community service can be an ideal forum for individual expression. Addams was an extraordinary individualist in precisely the sense honored in American traditions: self-reliant, independent in thought, innovative, and tenacious in pursuit of her ideals.

In their studies of a wide cross-section of Americans, Bellah and his colleagues found many individuals who were engaged in community service of the sort Addams pursued. To mention just one, they discovered Cecilia Dougherty, an activist in the Campaign for Economic Democracy, which educates, advises, and organizes interracial tenement dwellers in Southern California. Her involvement in the group resulted from her sustained concern for the plight of the underprivileged, a concern that stemmed from her family's tradition of participating in worker reforms.

In reflecting on Dougherty and others like her, Bellah points out that individualism and commitment are creatively intertwined in their lives:

> It is characteristic of Cecilia Dougherty and the others ... that they define themselves through their commitments to a variety of communities rather than through the pursuit of radical autonomy [i.e., separateness from community]. Yet Cecilia, like the others, exhibits a high degree of self-determination and efficacy. She exemplifies a form of individualism that is fulfilled *in* community rather than against it. Conformism, the nemesis of American individualism, does not seem to be a problem for Cecilia and the others. Their involvement in practices of commitment makes them able to resist pressures to conform.[4]

By *community* Bellah means a group of interdependent (mutually dependent) people with a shared history, who jointly participate in social practices, have a common forum for discussion and mutual decision making, and look to the future with a sense of shared hope. Understood in this way, a community is changing and responsive to individual initiative. In turn, it enables individuals to acquire extended and enriched identities through relationships with other people.

How Much Should We Give?

It might be objected, however, that individuality can be enriched and extended in many ways other than through community involvement. Rather than give our time and resources to the community, why should we not focus them entirely on our careers, our families, and our hobbies? After all, is it not the role of government to sustain community, and do we not satisfy our community duties by voting and paying taxes so that government can fulfill that role?

Moreover, the idea of a duty to give to the community (beyond the minimal requirements of citizenship) seems perplexing in that there seems to be no way such a duty can be structured and focused. To whom or to what are we obligated to give? Should our money go to the poor or to the fine arts? How much of our resources should we give? Does the amount (if anything) depend on our personal preferences, and, if so, how can something so personal or subjective have anything to do with morality?

One way to approach these questions is to apply Kant's distinction between *perfect* and *imperfect* duties. Perfect duties are those that hold for all situations: One ought to keep one's promises, be truthful, pay one's debts, not kill innocent people, and so on. Kant thought there were no exceptions to such duties; a more plausible view, however, as we saw in Chapter 4, is that these are prima facie duties that sometimes have legitimate exceptions when more pressing duties override them. Imperfect duties, by contrast, allow us discretion about when to act on them. In particular, the duty of beneficence or benevolence, which implies a specific duty of mutual aid— the duty to help other people who are in distress—allows us considerable discretion in deciding when and how much of our time and money we donate to philanthropic causes.

A difficulty with this view is that it provides no guidance for how our "moral discretion" should be exercised in helping other people. Apparently, we can give much or give little, depending on personal choice. In addition, because those who give much and those who give little both fulfill their "imperfect duty," they can be placed on an equal moral level.

If Kant seems to require too little from us in the way of community involvement, act-utilitarians seem to require an enormous amount. They state that we ought to give as much as we can in order to promote the most good for the most people, regarding each person as equal with ourselves. Complete impartiality should be our guide in dealing with others in need, and we should not give preference to ourselves or our families.

Peter Singer defends an extreme version of this doctrine. He argues that we should sacrifice luxuries in our lives in order to help save the thousands of people—at least thirty thousand people, most of them children— who die from starvation each day and the many others who live impoverished lives in countries such as Bangladesh, Ethiopia, and Somalia. All humans are part of a worldwide community, or "global village," and they make a legitimate claim on our wealth. We should respond to that claim by acting on the following utilitarian-inspired principle: "If it is in our power to prevent something bad from happening, without thereby sacrificing anything of comparable moral importance, we ought, morally, to do it."[5] The amount of giving required by this principle, as Singer insists, is considerable:

> I and everyone else in similar circumstances [of having great wealth compared to starving people] ought to give as much as possible, that is, at least up to the point at which by giving more one would begin to cause serious suffering for oneself and one's dependents—perhaps even beyond this point to the point of marginal utility, at which by giving more one would cause oneself and one's dependents as much suffering as one would prevent in Bengal [and other impoverished regions].[6]

Some utilitarians, especially rule-utilitarians, object that Singer's conclusion is too extreme. They allow that we can give some emphasis to our own needs and those of our families, and that to do so is compatible with the doctrine of impartiality. They believe that such conduct will actually lead to more overall good, because each of us is in the best position to promote her or his own good. Also, contributions in the extraordinary quantities recommended by Singer will erode one's long-term ability to help others. In adopting this position, however, utilitarians fail to resolve the same question that Kant faced: Just how much ought we to give to others?

Rights ethics offers two answers, depending on the kinds of rights recognized. If only negative rights are recognized—rights to be free from interference—then very little giving seems to be required of us. According to this libertarian theory of rights, we have a right to keep what we earn, and, apart from our families, no one has a right to share our resources unless we decide to share them.

A very different conclusion is reached if we recognize positive rights—rights to have the goods needed for a minimally decent standard of living. If each human has these rights, then impoverished people in this country and throughout the world have basic rights to shelter, clothing, and food. Those rights place on people who are advantaged obligations to provide assistance. This positive-rights view leaves open the question of whether giving should be accomplished through governments or by individuals, but it seems to require in any case that we give more than most of us do now, although precisely how much is again unclear.

Virtue ethics is often criticized as the theory least helpful in providing guidance for action in that it does not offer precise rules about how we ought to act or how much we ought to give. This criticism mistakenly assumes, however, that guidance must come in the form of rules. In fact, it can come in the form of ideals that inspire and focus our efforts. In particular, we can be guided by the virtue and the ideal of generosity in giving to the community more than is required by the minimal duties of morality, as we will see in the next section.

Generosity and Supererogation

Kant placed all actions into three categories: those required by duty (right), those forbidden by duty (wrong), and those morally neutral (permissible or "all right"; for example, the act of brushing one's teeth):

> A *duty* is an action to which we are obligated.... An action that is neither commanded nor forbidden is merely permissible, since there is ... no duty with regard to the action. An action of this kind is called morally indifferent.[7]

This threefold classification, however, overlooks actions that are morally admirable—and hence not "morally indifferent"—but which are not required by duty. These acts are supererogatory, that is, morally good in ways that go beyond the requirements of duty.

David Heyd points out that *supererogation* refers to acts that exceed what is required by duties *to others* rather than to oneself. It is defined in terms of an altruistic aim or intention. To be sure, there may be mixed motives involved, such as a desire for fame coupled with a desire to help. If a person is to be generous, however, there must be an intention (aim, purpose) to promote the good of others. Accordingly, Heyd defines a supererogatory act as one that meets the following conditions:

1 It is neither obligatory nor forbidden.
2 Its omission is not wrong, and does not deserve sanction or criticism—either formal or informal.
3 It is morally good, both by virtue of its (intended) consequences and by virtue of its intrinsic value (being beyond duty).
4 It is done voluntarily for the sake of someone else's good and is thus meritorious.[8]

Generous actions meet these conditions, and generous persons have a disposition to perform generous acts. Generous actions go beyond what is morally required or obligatory, and they are done voluntarily with the intention to promote someone else's good. Admittedly, they may not be good in all respects: Generous acts sometimes fail to help others despite the best intentions; but they are intended to help and as such are admirable.

Generous giving of oneself—of one's time, talents, and money—to the community is one ideal worth pursuing. It represents an important virtue worthy of admiration precisely because, in sharing one's resources in benevolent and caring ways, one goes beyond the minimal moral requirements. This ideal also provides an answer to the question of how much to give: We should give generously—if we want to be generous persons! Although this answer shares the vagueness of the answers offered by duty ethics, utilitarianism, and rights ethics, the vagueness is in a way morally fruitful. As a positive ideal, generosity recognizes and praises higher degrees of benevolent giving, and, by allowing flexibility, it takes account of the personal aspect in giving.

"Degrees" of benevolent giving are frequently understood in terms of greater and lesser quantities: The more generous person seems to be the one who gives greater quantities. This view is reflected in James Wallace's definition of acts of what he calls *economic generosity* (which contrasts with generosity in judging other people):

1 The agent, because of his direct concern for the good of the recipient, gives something with the intention of benefiting the recipient.

2 The agent gives up something of his that has a market value and that he has some reason to value and, therefore, to keep.

3 The agent gives more than one is generally expected, because of moral requirements or custom, to give in such circumstances.[9]

The third condition places an emphasis on giving in quantities beyond what is obligatory or usual. This emphasis on quantities, however, overlooks an insight expressed in a well-known passage in the New Testament:

And Jesus sat over against the treasury, and beheld how the people cast money into the treasury: and many that were rich cast in much. And there came a certain poor widow, and she threw in two mites, which make a farthing. And he called unto him his disciples, and saith unto them, Verily I say unto you, That this poor widow hath cast more in, than all they which have cast into the treasure: For all they did cast in of their abundance; but she of her want did cast in all that she had, even all her living.[10]

In other words, the widow is more generous than are the rich donors, even though she gives a vastly smaller quantity. This suggests that degrees of generosity must be measured in relation to the resources of the giver rather than primarily in terms of custom or moral rules about what is required. It also suggests that Wallace's third condition needs to be modified:

3' The agent gives more than is expected of someone having her or his resources and financial situation.

To Whom Should We Give?

Mere endorsement of generosity as an admirable ideal does not indicate to whom and to what we should give. Community has many dimensions. Should we give our resources to humanitarian efforts to feed and clothe the poor and to provide shelter for the homeless? Or should we give to the arts, to education, and to environmental causes? Should we give lots of small gifts or combine our resources into a few large gifts? (The same question could be asked about how we allocate the time we give in volunteering.)

Here we need to remind ourselves that generosity is fully voluntary and beyond the requirements of duty. Thus, it is up to each of us to whom and to what extent we give. We also need to remind ourselves that, wherever we draw the line between generous and required giving, there remains a large area of discretion in how we meet our imperfect duties to help others. Neither generous nor required giving is a matter of whim. On the one hand, we can give generously only when we are moved by benevolent concern for the good of others; that is, we should give thoughtfully in situations in which caring is evoked genuinely and in very personal ways. On the other hand, to meet our general duties to help others, we must exercise good judgment about how best to help—in which situations, in which ways, to which ends—so as contribute to the world in meaningful ways.

To a significant degree, the occasions and objects of giving reflect, and should express, our *personal* interests. Some people are most deeply committed to humanitarian goals, some to educational goals, some to the arts, some to scouting and Little League baseball. Pursuit of these personal loyalties expresses the donor's concern about community better than impartial giving could. In fact, each of us participates in many communities of different sizes, ranging from a school, company, or church to a city, nation, or the world community. Most of us are able to give generously only to some of these overlapping communities. There seems to be no abstract duty to focus our energies on any one such community (say, the largest one), and hence, here again, much is left up to individual judgment and interests.

There is, in short, a large element of highly *personal* morality in decisions about where and how we display virtues like loyalty and generosity, and how best to meet our duties of mutual aid. However, *personal* does not mean *arbitrary*. Our judgment and interests are evoked and exercised thoughtfully, not whimsically, as we engage in intelligent and benevolent giving to help others.

SUMMARY

Philanthropy or voluntary service is voluntary giving for community or public purposes, whether gifts are large or small, in the form of money or time, or for purposes that are humanitarian, political, religious, environmental, educational, or cultural (among other possibilities). A community is a group of people related by shared history and hopes, location and interactions, interests and values. Loyalty to community is shown by actions that exceed such minimal participation as meeting one's responsibilities as a citizen. It is shown in voluntary contributions of one's time, talents, and resources to help others.

America's tradition of individualism is misconstrued when community involvement is equated with mere social conformism. As the life of Jane Addams exemplifies, service to community can express creative individual initiative and development of personality. Moreover, benevolent giving need not be "selfless" in the sense of actions done solely for the good of others. Mixed motives of self-interest and altruism do not negate or diminish the moral worth of giving to help others. The volunteer who, in helping others, also develops personal skills and expresses personal interests is often more vigorously motivated because of the mixed motives.

How much should we give, and to whom? Duty ethics, rights ethics, and utilitarianism do not provide clear-cut answers; neither does virtue ethics, but it does at least set forth generosity as an ideal that guides and focuses giving. Generosity is supererogatory in the sense that it exceeds what is required by moral duty and respect for others' rights. Generosity entails giving with the intention to benefit others, out of concern to promote their welfare. Degrees of generosity are measured by reference to one's resources and ability to help, as well as in terms of the quantities one gives beyond the customary or required amount. Basic duties to help others also take into account one's resources and ability to help.

DISCUSSION TOPICS

1 Present and defend your view (by appealing to an ethical theory) regarding how much one is obligated to give to help save starving people around the world. Should the homeless and starving people in one's local community or within one's country be given priority, or should they be considered equally with other disadvantaged people around the world? Is it obvious that the cause of world hunger should have priority over other worthy causes, such as education or the arts?

2 Consider the following observation by Brian O'Connell:

> There are some disturbing signs that giving and volunteering may not be held in high esteem by young adults. A recent study ... has found that people between the ages of 18 and 34 do not place community service high on their lists of values. The Gallup survey confirms that. It found that volunteering declined 11 percent from 1980 to 1985 among people 18 to 24 years of age and 19 percent among single people.[11]

Is this observation supported by your own view of people in this age range, and do you agree with O'Connell that there is something disturbing about it? Does it suggest, for example, that people in this age group are more selfish than previous generations have been?

3 What, if anything, is wrong about a failure ever to make any philanthropic contribution or engage in any voluntary service to help others?

4 Ralph Waldo Emerson was a classic advocate for American individualism. Do you agree or disagree with what he says about philanthropy in the following passage?

> Do not tell me, as a good man did to-day, of my obligation to put all poor men in good situations. Are they *my* poor? I tell thee, thou foolish philanthropist, that I grudge the dollar, the dime, the cent I give to such men as do not belong to me and to whom I do not belong. There is a class of persons to whom by all spiritual affinity I am bought and sold; for them I will go to prison if need be; but your miscellaneous popular charities; the education at college of fools; the building of meeting-houses to the vain end to which many now stand; alms to sots, and the thousand-fold Relief Societies;—though I confess with shame I sometimes succumb and give the dollar, it is a wicked dollar, which by and by I shall have the manhood to withhold.[12]

5 Is it better to give many small philanthropic gifts or one or two that are large? In answering this question, respond to the following claims:

> There are so many good causes that if we try to respond to them all, we dilute our ability to make a difference to any. But more important is the fact that we dilute ourselves. We run the risk of losing touch with what is really important to us.[13]

6 Assess the following argument: All the concern about motives and intentions in giving is entirely irrelevant. All that matters is the good done by acts of giving. Donations to relieve world hunger, for example, keep people alive no matter what motives or intentions lead people to make the donations.

7 One person regularly donates blood to the Red Cross without receiving any payment, while a second person gives blood only to commercial blood banks that pay for the blood. What moral good is exemplified by the first person that is absent in the second? In general, what distinctive moral goods are made possible by voluntary service and giving?

8 Women have traditionally been encouraged (far more than men) to engage in voluntarism and philanthropy. Do you see any objections to this? In particular, does it or could it lead to exploitation of women who could be doing paid work that has greater economic benefits for them?

9 Sometimes philanthropy is immoral, other times it is foolish, and sometimes it combines good and bad. Evaluate the following examples: (a) donations of cash to a homeless person who uses the money to buy alcohol or drugs (as opposed to donations to a local organization that feeds the homeless); (b) donations to a world-hunger organization that has no plans for long-term solutions versus donations to an organization that does have such plans; (c) donation of a large gift to a private college in order to gain influence in how it is governed; (d) donations of money or time in support of the Ku Klux Klan. Comment especially on the role of respect for persons—in particular respect for persons' autonomy—in promoting effective philanthropy.

SUGGESTED READINGS

Aiken, William, and Hugh La Follette (eds.). *World Hunger and Moral Obligation*. Englewood Cliffs, NJ: Prentice-Hall, 1977.

Bellah, Robert N., et al. *Habits of the Heart: Individualism and Commitment in American Life*. Berkeley, CA: University of California Press, 1985.

Bellah, Robert N., et al. (eds.). *Individualism and Commitment in American Life*. New York: Harper & Row, 1987.

Boyte, Harry C. *Community Is Possible*. New York: Harper & Row, 1984.

Bremner, Robert C. *American Philanthropy*. 2nd ed. Chicago: University of Chicago Press, 1988.

Douglas, James. *Why Charity?: The Case for the Third Sector*. Beverly Hills, CA: Sage Publications, 1983.

Ellis, Susan J., and Katherine H. Noyes. *By the People: A History of Americans as Volunteers*. San Francisco, CA: Jossey-Bass, 1990.

Evers, Williamson M. (ed.). *National Service: Pro & Con*. Stanford, CA: Hoover Institution Press, 1990.

Heyd, David. *Supererogation*. Cambridge: Cambridge University Press, 1982.

Kohn, Alfie. *The Brighter Side of Human Nature: Altruism and Empathy in Everyday Life*. New York: Basic Books, 1990.

Ladd, John. "Loyalty." In P. Edwards (ed.), *The Encyclopedia of Philosophy*. New York: Macmillan, 1967.

Martin, Mike W. *Virtuous Giving: Philanthropy, Voluntary Service, and Caring*. Bloomington, IN: Indiana University Press, 1994.

Mellema, Gregory. *Beyond the Call of Duty: Supererogation, Obligation, and Offence*. Albany, NY: State University of New York Press, 1991.

O'Connell, Brian (ed.). *America's Voluntary Spirit*. New York: Foundation Center, 1983.

Oldenquist, Andrew. *The Non-Suicidal Society*. Bloomington, IN: Indiana University Press, 1986.

Nisbet, Robert. *The Quest for Community*. New York: Oxford University Press, 1970.

Paul, Ellen Frankel, Fred D. Miller, Jr., Jeffrey Paul, and John Ahrens (eds.). *Beneficence, Philanthropy and the Public Good*. New York: Basil Blackwell, 1987. Also published as a special issue of *Social Philosophy and Policy*, vol. 4, Issue 2 (Spring 1987).

Royce, Josiah. "The Nature of Community." In *The Problems of Christianity*. New York: Macmillan, 1913.

Wallace, James D. "Benevolence." In *Virtues and Vices*. Ithaca, NY: Cornell University Press, 1978.

Wolff, Robert Paul. "Loyalty" and "Community." In *The Poverty of Liberalism*. Boston, MA: Beacon Press, 1968.

Wuthnow, Robert. *Acts of Compassion*. Princeton, NJ: Princeton University Press, 1991.

PART SIX

Animals and the Environment

In the relations of humans with the animals, with the flowers,
with the objects of creation, there is a whole great ethic scarcely
seen as yet, but which will eventually break through into the light
and be the corollary and the complement to human ethics.[1]
                                                    Victor Hugo

What responsibilities do we have toward (nonhuman) animals and the environment? Are these responsibilities owed directly to creatures and ecosystems because they have inherent value? Or do we have responsibilities only to human beings (and to any other beings with similar or higher degrees of rationality)?

Traditional ethics has been human-centered and grounded in the conviction that humans have inherent moral worth. At most, traditional ethics has recognized indirect duties to avoid inflicting needless suffering on conscious animals and causing needless destruction of the environment that makes human life possible. The extent to which suffering and destruction are "needed" has been understood essentially in terms of human interests.

In our time, this traditional orientation is being challenged by views that expand the moral community and see inherent moral worth in conscious animals, in all living things, or in natural ecological systems. Even within traditional frameworks which restrict moral value to human beings, responsibilities concerning the environment have been taken much more seriously. Chapter 22 explores moral responsibilities concerning conscious nonhuman animals. Chapter 23 discusses whether the scope of ethics needs to be widened further, or whether traditional ethics can accommodate the increased need for protecting the environment.

CHAPTER 22

Animals

About half of all Americans and Europeans have pets whom they regard as companions. Generally, they devote large amounts of attention and significant financial resources to them, often more than they give to their neighbors. They are sensitive to their pets' needs and emotions and interact with them in caring ways that have moral significance, or so it will be argued here.

Our attitudes toward pets contrast sharply with our typical attitudes toward animals in general. Most people eat animals daily without a qualm and see no objections to the use of animals in experiments that help humans; yet the thought of eating their pets or allowing them to be used for experimentation may be as horrifying as the thought of eating or experimenting on a human stranger. Clearly, we attribute to our pets an importance that sets them apart from other animals. Do we perhaps exaggerate the importance of pets, or conversely, underestimate the value of animals we eat or conduct medical experiments on?

Animals as Companions

When John Steinbeck approached sixty, the age at which he would receive the Nobel Prize for literature, he felt the need to travel extensively in order to regain contact with the people he wrote about. He planned a trip around and through America in a camper truck, leaving his family during the months he traveled alone. His excitement about the planned trip, however, was dampened by "a very lonely, helpless feeling at first—a kind of desolate feeling."[1] The cure was to take along as a traveling companion his large French poodle, named Charles le Chien, or Charley for short. *Travels with Charley*, the literary offspring of the trip, is in part a record of Steinbeck's interactions with Charley.

Steinbeck already knew Charley well, but on the trip he came to know him better. He was previously aware, for example, that Charley was diplomatic rather than confrontational in dealing with other animals. In Yellowstone Park, however, Charley betrayed his usual good sense by trying to charge a bear: "Bears simply brought out the Hyde in my Jekyll-headed dog."[2]

The trip also led Steinbeck to a greater appreciation of Charley's superior intelligence in some matters. Charley lived in an entire world of smells to which Steinbeck and other humans were oblivious. More interestingly, Charley had an exceptional intuitive understanding of people. He would show contempt for incompetent veterinarians who mishandled him and spontaneous trust in skillful ones. He also avoided people who addressed him using baby talk, revealing, according to Steinbeck, a certain pride in not being a human infant. Yet he displayed a humanlike pride in being well groomed, a vanity Steinbeck shared concerning his own beard.

Charley had an equally subtle knowledge of Steinbeck. His understanding extended well beyond responses to verbal commands, for he could easily anticipate with excitement when he would be included in Steinbeck's plans or discern with chagrin that he would be left alone to guard the camper. His talents included several techniques for awakening Steinbeck in the morning: "He can shake himself and his collar loud enough to wake the dead. If that doesn't work he gets a sneezing fit. But perhaps his most irritating method is to sit quietly beside the bed and stare into my face with a sweet and forgiving look on his face."[3]

Like most people with pets, Steinbeck talked to Charley frequently and on a variety of occasions. He routinely spoke to Charley—greeting him, saying goodbye, comforting him when he was nervous, and relaxing both of them by chatting about a problem. Charley was also the object of conversations with strangers and served as an ambassador for Steinbeck in meeting people: "A dog, particularly an exotic like Charley, is a bond between strangers. Many conversations en route began with 'What degree [that is, pedigree] of a dog is that?'"[4]

Steinbeck and Charley were emotionally attuned to each other. On one occasion, for example, Steinbeck became depressed following a conversation with someone who had a special knack for sarcastically demolishing the simple pleasures of a sunny afternoon. Charley cheered him up by initiating puppylike games. On another occasion Charley was sick, and Steinbeck postponed the trip for an entire week while he recuperated. During this time Steinbeck reports feeling compassion for the suffering of his traveling companion as well as helplessness at being unable to alleviate the suffering.

The relationship with Charley that Steinbeck reports involves several elements that common sense recognizes as possible for human-animal interactions. Common sense suggests that animals are capable of beliefs and emotions, and also that animals of a given type are not alike—they have distinctive personalities. All these features enter into human-animal interactions in selective and personal ways akin to friendships among humans. It is true that in a few places Steinbeck lapses into anthropomorphization of animals— that is, he ascribes human traits where they are inappropriate—as when he speaks of Charley's pride in not being a human. Nevertheless, Steinbeck's descriptions of his interactions with Charley, rather than striking us as poetic fancies, for the most part ring true. Human relationships with animal companions are far more akin to caring relationships among persons than they are to children's relationships with dolls. Four points deserve emphasis in this connection.

First, companionship between humans and animals has moral importance. It affords humans comfort, security, and daily cheerfulness, and it obviously benefits specific animals. However, it also creates a bond or relationship based on caring. The importance of this relationship is especially rich within families in which there is an interaction between several humans and pets that exerts a unifying force. The pet becomes a focus of shared concern, including shared activities (petting, feeding, exercising, conversing, playing, and so on). Psychologists also emphasize that pets provide a sense of peace and security. (This is true for cats as well as for guard dogs!) Pets serve as surrogate children for adults, fantasized babies for children, and real friends for all. Pets also generate problems, of course, but even in that regard they are like people, reminding us that all valuable caring relationships require effort.

Second, relationships with animals enliven a sense of kinship with other animals and nature. Living with animals adds to our delight in the simple aspects of biological existence, including pleasure in a good meal or playing a game. The relatively short life spans of pets remind us of the contingency and fragility of our own lives.

Third, caring for animals can add to a capacity to care for people. This is not always true, to be sure; occasionally, pets are used as a means to escape from caring about people. We recognize such cases, however, as unhealthy distortions rather than as typical products of relationships with animals. As Mary Midgley emphasizes, it is a misconception to think that caring for animals somehow detracts from the care available for other people. Such an argument would imply that we should not aid a suffering dog hit by a car, because our energies could in principle be used to help a human at that moment. As Midgley writes, "The reason why this would be odd is that compassion does not need to be treated hydraulically in this way, as a rare and irreplaceable fluid, usable only for exceptionally impressive cases. It is a habit or power of the mind, which grows and develops with use."[5]

Fourth, reflection on our relationships with pets prompts us to reconsider the capacities which bestow moral significance on creatures. The capacities for feelings and social interactions take on greater importance than the traditionally emphasized capacities for rational thought and conduct.

At this point, however, we need to reflect more generally on the moral status of all sentient (conscious) animals, not just those we choose to make our pets. Do such animals have any inherent moral worth, beyond what they contribute to us?

No Moral Worth

The attitude of most classical philosophers was that animals, including nonhuman higher mammals, have no intrinsic moral worth of any kind. They acquire value and moral relevance only insofar as humans choose to value them for human purposes. It follows that nothing is inherently wrong in hurting animals. For example, hunting becomes wrong only when the hunted animals are the property of other humans whose property rights would be infringed by hurting the animal; and the use of animals for food or in medical experiments that have human benefits raises no moral questions.

According to this attitude, attachment to animals may alleviate loneliness, induce calm, and provide delight—but so does television. Deep emotional attachment to or caring for animals is sentimental; that is, it reflects excessive and inappropriate emotional involvement. Pets are like pens or cars to which one might also become sentimentally attached, but they have value only insofar as humans give them value. They are household curios, not caring companions.

The philosophical basis for this attitude was uncompromisingly set forth by both René Descartes (1596–1650) and Benedict de Spinoza (1632–1677). Descartes viewed animals as "thoughtless brutes," sophisticated machines lacking consciousness.[6] Spinoza, by contrast, recognized that they could feel pain and pleasure, but he joined Descartes in banishing them from the realm of moral concern:

> The rational quest of what is useful to us further teaches us the necessity of associating ourselves with our fellow-man, but not with beasts, or things, whose nature is different from our own.... Still, I do not deny that beasts feel; what I deny is, that we may not consult our own advantage and use them as we please, treating them in the way which best suits us; for their nature is not like ours, and their emotions are naturally different from human emotions.[7]

Surely the attitude of Descartes and Spinoza is wrong, tragically wrong. Many animals do feel emotions and have desires and beliefs very similar to our own. Certainly, this is true of the higher mammals on which we will focus. Of course, we admitted the conceptual danger in anthropomorphizing animals by ascribing unwarrantedly complex mental states to them; but the forms of behavior that warrant ascribing at least simple psychological states to people are also manifested by mammals. Moreover, numerous studies in comparative anatomy and neurophysiology also indicate similarities in the mental activities and functions of humans and higher mammals. Indeed, much of the ordinary rationale for using animals in scientific experiments is that their neurological structure, which makes possible conscious activities, resembles that of humans.

At the very least, it is wrong to torture animals for fun. Some philosophers have recognized that many animals feel pain and yet have refused to grant them any inherent moral worth. In particular, Immanuel Kant agreed that torture of animals was clearly immoral, but he also shared the view of Descartes and Spinoza that animals have no moral worth. According to Kant, only rational beings (humans, and possibly other beings such as angels and God) have inherent value. Rational beings are ends in themselves in the sense that they are autonomous beings who place moral limits on the actions of other rational beings. Everything else in the universe merely serves to gratify the reasoned purposes of rational beings. Animals in particular lack the capacity to reason about general principles of conduct that ought to guide rational living. Hence, we owe them no moral respect and have no moral duties to them.

Nevertheless, Kant believed there are duties *to humanity* and to ourselves that generate indirect duties to treat animals humanely. That is, we have duties concerning animals, but not to animals:

> So far as animals are concerned, we have no direct duties. Animals are not self-conscious and are there merely as a means to an end. That end is man.... Our duties towards animals are merely indirect duties towards humanity.... Thus, if a dog has served his master long and faithfully, his service, on the analogy of human service, deserves reward, and when the dog has grown too old to serve, his master ought to keep him until he dies. Such action helps to support us in our duties towards human beings.... Tender feelings towards dumb animals develop humane feelings towards mankind.[8]

Kant's idea is that tenderness with animals helps foster kindness toward humans, whereas cruelty to animals encourages cruelty to humans. Humane responses are a kind of practice exercise for kindness to people.

This is an interesting suggestion, but is it always true? Perhaps some individuals are actually kinder to people because they vent their hostilities on animals, which, in Kant's view, would justify their cruelty to animals. In any case, Kant mislocates the basis for condemning cruelty to animals. It is wrong to torture a dog or cat not because such acts may indirectly influence one's subsequent behavior toward people, but because it harms the dog or cat! Furthermore, the act itself reveals cruelty in one's character, even if that cruelty is not also expressed toward people.

Full Moral Status

Without engaging in subtle debates about the precise degree to which various mammals are self-conscious or capable of rational endeavors and communication, we can recognize their capacity for social life and also their capacity for feeling. What follows from this acknowledgment? Some philosophers believe that these capacities give animals full moral status as valuable members of the moral community.

Jeremy Bentham (1748–1832) drew attention to the importance of the capacity to feel when he charged that the refusal of Descartes and Spinoza to grant any moral status to animals was akin to the sweeping blindness of racists. He drafted the following passage shortly after France prohibited slavery in French colonies:

> The French have already discovered that blackness of the skin is no reason why a human being should be abandoned without redress to the caprice of a tormentor. It may one day come to be recognized that the number of the legs, the villosity of the skin, or the termination of the *os sacrum* [i.e., the tail bone] are reasons equally insufficient for abandoning a sensitive being to the same fate. What else is it that should trace the insuperable line [between humans and animals]? Is it the faculty of reason, or perhaps the faculty of discourse? But a full-grown horse or dog is beyond comparison a more rational, as well as a more conversable animal, than an infant of a day or a week, or even a month, old. But suppose they were otherwise, what would it avail? The question is not, Can they *reason*? nor Can they *talk*? but Can they *suffer*?[9]

Mammals do indeed suffer, feel pleasure and delight, and have interests based on their desires and needs. They care for their young, interact with sensitivity to one another and sometimes to humans. Does it follow that this gives them full moral worth, in the sense of counting equally with humans in the moral community?

Let us turn to two contemporary philosophers who have drawn attention to the plight of animals in a human-centered world. Both are prominent members of the "animal rights movement" that has gained momentum in recent decades, and both sharply disagree with Kant's refusal to grant animals any direct moral status. Yet they offer very different defenses of the humane treatment of animals.

Peter Singer has been called the father of the modern animal rights movement, principally because of his influential book *Animal Liberation*. There is irony in this, however, because Singer denies that animals have rights! Even though in a few passages in *Animal Liberation* he speaks loosely about animal rights, he has since made it clear that, for him, talk of moral rights should be translated into talk about utility, whether one ascribes rights to animals or persons. Like Bentham, Singer is a utilitarian who believes that acts are right or wrong only insofar as they maximize or fail to maximize good consequences, evaluated with respect to all conscious beings affected by the acts. Rights are essentially those areas of freedom and benefit which should be protected in order to maximize utility. Mammals are conscious beings and as such should be taken into account in maximizing utility. Usually, it is wrong to cause suffering to animals because such suffering is rarely justified by some greater good produced for humans.

Animals who are conscious, and hence who are capable of feeling pain or pleasure, have preferences and interests just as humans do. In this respect, according to Singer, their interests should be considered equally with those of humans. To think otherwise is to be guilty of *speciesism*, which he defines as "a prejudice or attitude of bias toward the interests of members of one's own species and against those of members of other species."[10] Speciesism has caused harm as terrible as that of sexism and racism: "This tyranny has caused and today is still causing an amount of pain and suffering that can only be compared with that which resulted from the centuries of tyranny by white humans over black humans."[11] In Singer's view, animals are entitled to equal consideration, although not necessarily equal treatment. Our treatment of (behavior toward) particular animals should depend on their specific needs and capacities—as does our behavior toward humans. Nevertheless, sentient animals deserve to be considered equally in making utilitarian calculations.

Two major conclusions follow if Singer is right. First, just as we do not eat humans (except in extraordinary and tragic circumstances that might justify cannibalism), we should not eat sentient animals when there is any alternative. Since vegetarianism is a healthy alternative, it is immoral to eat animals. It is especially immoral to eat the majority of animals who are raised with mass meat-production techniques. Singer carefully shows how those techniques cause enormous suffering to animals who are raised in unnatural conditions that frustrate normal needs and desires.

Second, most contemporary medical experiments on sentient animals are immoral. In some instances we could use alternative modes of testing, such as computer simulation, that avoid the terrible suffering inflicted on animals. In other instances, the experiments cannot be justified in terms of educational purposes or the pursuit of new knowledge. Admittedly, some experiments are justified from a utilitarian point of view, but they are rare if we recognize animals' interests as worthy of equal consideration with human interests: "So whenever experimenters claim that their experiments are important enough to justify the use of animals, we should ask them whether they would be prepared to use a brain-damaged human being at a similar mental level to the animals they are planning to use."[12] Few (if any) experiments would pass this test.

Ethicists who regard moral rights, rather than utilitarian considerations, as the foundation of morality have developed a different argument for

Singer's conclusions. Perhaps the most careful argument that animals have moral rights is presented by Tom Regan in *The Case for Animal Rights*. Regan begins with the premise that mammals (at least those of age one or older) have inherent value. They have this value not just because they are capable of feeling pain and pleasure, but also because they have beliefs, desires, memories, a sense of the future, preferences, the ability to act purposefully in pursuing their preferences, and a welfare (or set of interests) that goes beyond their potential uses for humans.

Regan contends that inherent value is not a matter of degree; one either has it or one does not. Hence, the value of mammals is equal to the value of humans. Moreover, this inherent value ought to be respected because it creates a valid claim on us. Because these valid claims are what is meant by moral rights, it follows that mammals have moral rights. Their inability to speak for their rights does not alter this fact; it merely makes animals dependent on surrogate agents for the defense of their rights. Their moral situation is in this respect exactly analogous to human babies, infants, and severely mentally handicapped people, who are also dependent on guardians to defend their rights.

For Regan, our goals should be to abolish completely experiments on animals that cause suffering or lead to their deaths, to bring an end to commercial animal agriculture, and also to end sport hunting and trapping (topics we shall consider in the next chapter). Above all, we must end the callous and cruel attitude that animals are mere things to be manipulated for human purposes.

Partial Moral Status

The philosophers we have considered up to this point share a common assumption: Either animals share full moral status with humans or, like rocks and other material objects, they lack any moral status. Kant, Descartes, and Spinoza reasoned that, because animals lack the rational capacities of humans, they are mere things undeserving of any respect. According to Singer, either animals' interests do not matter at all or else they matter equally with those of humans. Similarly, Regan asserts that either animals have no rights or else their rights are as important as those of humans.

Yet there is a middle ground to be considered. It affirms that, insofar as animals are conscious beings, they have some inherent worth, but human beings nevertheless have greater inherent worth. This position recognizes in human consciousness greater degrees of value and potential value, in the same way that John Stuart Mill distinguished degrees of quality among pleasures. This view might also grant that animals have important rights but deny that they have all the rights of human beings. Thus, although they have the right to be treated humanely and not to be tortured, they lack rights to social support through our welfare system. Moreover, even with respect to the same rights—say, a right to life—human rights are to be counted more heavily when they come into conflict with animal rights.

This view also distinguishes degrees of inherent worth among animals, depending on the extent of their capacities to feel pain and pleasure, to act purposefully, and to interact socially with one another and with humans. This would support the special status we have granted to higher mammals, who possess these capacities in greater degrees than do many other animals. It provides a rationale for developing laws to protect dolphins, whales, chimpanzees, and gorillas. Such laws are designed to protect individual animals, unlike other laws aimed at preserving an entire species (of fish, crab, and so on).

What does this "moderate" view imply concerning vegetarianism? The answer depends on the degree of moral importance conferred by "partial moral status." For some, the emphasis shifts to eating less meat, rather than no meat, on the theory that even partial measures (on a wide scale) can substantially reduce the amount of suffering caused to animals. For others the emphasis shifts to eating only meat that is not mass-produced, since the conditions of animals raised on traditional farms does not involve anything comparable to the degree of suffering in the mainstream meat industry.

What does the moderate view imply concerning medical experimentation on animals? It makes the standards for acceptable experiments much more rigorous. For example, it prohibits experiments designed to confirm what is largely already known. It also requires that the promise of new knowledge be established by a greater burden of proof before experiments are permitted by Institutional Review Boards (IRBs: screening committees which are now required at all universities and which must follow federal and state guidelines for humane uses of animals).

Singer and Regan would reject this last approach as "speciesist" in that it explicitly shows unjustified favoritism for humans. Undoubtedly it constitutes favoritism, but is the favoritism unjustified or immoral? Mary Midgley, who explored this middle ground in *Animals and Why They Matter*, cautions us about the term *speciesism*. As typically used, the word is ambiguous, referring to either of two views: (1) Animals have no inherent moral significance, or (2) animals have inherent worth, although not as much as humans. Midgley rejects the former view while affirming the latter. It is not, she urges, a sheer prejudice akin to racism and sexism to give some preference to the interests of members of one's own species in situations where interests conflict. There are genuine moral differences between humans and nonhuman animals—not absolute differences of the sort Kant believed in, but differences in degree which justify us in regarding animals as partial (not fully equal) members of the moral community. Precisely when and in what degree preference is justified should be explored without the presumption either that animals lack all moral significance or that they have moral worth equal to that of humans.

Midgley also recognizes some special significance in the capacity of animals to interact with humans. Underlying this attitude is a clear acknowledgment of the special worth of humans, but also a sensitivity to genuine differences among animals that give them capacities we equally value among humans. Such a position helps make sense of our attitudes toward pets, as does the fact that a history of personal interactions with specific animals adds to the value of relationships with them.

SUMMARY

Most traditional ethical theories have been exclusively human-centered, regarding animals as mechanical playthings that were incapable of feelings (Descartes). Alternatively, they regarded animals' feelings as radically dissimilar to human emotions and insufficient to give them moral worth, which only "rational" beings have (Spinoza, Kant). Responses to animals, according to these theories, have moral relevance only as they affect responses to other humans. Thus, torture of animals is bad only because it encourages cruelty to humans, and gentleness to animals is good only insofar as it reinforces gentleness to humans.

Jeremy Bentham, however, stressed that the ability to reason and to experience complex emotions links humans and animals. In his view, it is morally significant that animals can suffer as well as feel pleasure. To torture an animal for fun is to do moral harm to it and to manifest a character that is cruel, no matter what further implications there are for one's treatment of humans. Contemporary philosophical advocates of humane treatment of animals differ over whether animals have rights, but they share Bentham's view that torture of an animal is a direct moral wrong—to the animal.

Bentham's view also lays a philosophical basis for the recognition of caring relationships between humans and animal companions. Insofar as animals have emotions and needs, it makes sense to care for them and to promote their interests, in the way people do with their pets or "animal companions." Moreover, caring relationships with animal companions take on increased worth insofar as animals are capable of reciprocal responses and interactions with humans.

Does a recognition of the value of animals require us to recognize their worth as equal with that of humans? According to some philosophers it does, and to treat them as moral inferiors is a form of prejudice that they call *speciesism* (Singer, Regan). Recognition that animals have inherent worth, however, is compatible with a position that allows that humans' moral worth is greater and that human interests may legitimately be given greater weight when they conflict with those of animals (Midgley).

DISCUSSION TOPICS

1 Respond to the following argument: People treat their pets *as if* they were people. Much the same is true, however, of fictional characters in plays and movies: It is appropriate to respond with fear, affection, anger, and other emotions to characters whom we pretend are real people. In both cases, however, a game of pretense is involved. Neither pets nor fictional characters are real people, and we know this even at times when we pretend they are. Neither has any kind of inherent moral worth that makes them *deserve* to be treated as people.

2 Many pet owners spend more on their pets than they do on world hunger, even though their money for pet food and supplies could help save human lives. Discuss your view of whether this is morally permissible. If you think it is permissible to spend substantial amounts of money on pets, are there any limits to how much should be spent?

3 It is not uncommon for farmers to become emotionally attached to one animal of a species whose other members they are willing to eat. An example of this millennia-old practice is found in the Old Testament:

> The poor man had nothing, save one little ewe lamb, which he had bought and nourished up: and it grew up together with him, and with his children; it did eat of his own meat, and drank of his own cup, and lay in his bosom, and was unto him as a daughter.[13]

Is there anything morally inconsistent about having a caring relationship with this one sheep while being willing to eat other sheep?

4 Is it morally permissible to eat sentient animals? Jeremy Bentham thought it was, even though (as we saw) he affirmed the moral worth of animals that can feel pain and pleasure:

> There is very good reason why we should be suffered to eat such of them [i.e., animals] as we like to eat; we are the better for it, and they are never the worse. They have none of those long-protracted anticipations of future misery which we have. The death they suffer in our hands commonly is, and always may be, a speedier, and by that means a less painful one, than that which would await them in the inevitable course of nature.[14]

Contemporary mass production of meat, however, does involve considerable suffering for animals. One example that Peter Singer describes in *Animal Liberation* concerns the raising of calves for veal.[15] The calves are taken from their mothers at a very young age and placed in wooden stalls one foot and two inches wide. This prevents them from turning around during the thirteen to fifteen weeks before slaughter. During that time their diet is entirely liquid, which denies them their need for roughage. The lack of exercise and grass keeps their flesh tender. In addition, they are kept anemic to produce the pale pink flesh preferred by gourmets (even though the color does not affect taste). To reduce restlessness, some producers keep them in the dark at all times except for about two hours during feeding. Thus, the calves live in an environment without visual stimulation, physical activity, interaction with their mothers, or social interaction of any other kind. Is their suffering outweighed by the human pleasures in eating them? Would you agree with Bentham about other cases in which suffering to animals is far less extreme?

5   The Food and Drug Administration requires that many kinds of new substances be tested on animals before they are marketed for human use. For example, new cosmetics must be tested for possible eye or skin damage on humans. One test involves using unanesthetized rabbits whose heads are held firmly in place by a neck brace and whose eyes are kept open with metal clips. Concentrated solutions of the substance are dripped into the rabbits' eyes, often repeatedly for several days, and eye damage is measured. Peter Singer writes of such experiments that

> while it may be thought justifiable to require animal tests of potentially life-saving drugs, the same tests are done for products like cosmetics, food colorings, and floor polishes. Should hundreds of animals suffer so that a new kind of lipstick or mouthwash can be put on the market? Don't we already have enough of these products? Who benefits from their introduction, except the companies that hope to make a profit from their new gimmick?[16]

Do you agree or disagree with Singer? What general criteria would you endorse to morally justify experiments on animals?

6   Is bullfighting, which is still practiced in some parts of the world, morally permissible? In your answer, research the values by which other cultures justify the practice.

SUGGESTED READINGS

Bentham, Jeremy. *Introduction to the Principles of Morals and Legislation.* Chapter 17. New York: Hafner, 1948. First published 1789.

Clark, Stephen R. L. *The Nature of the Beast: Are Animals Moral?* New York: Oxford University Press, 1984.

Fox, Michael Allen. *The Case for Animal Experimentation.* Berkeley, CA: University of California Press, 1986.

Frey, R. G. *Rights, Killing and Suffering: Moral Vegetarianism and Applied Ethics.* New York: Basil Blackwell, 1983.

Hearne, Vicki. *Adam's Task: Calling Animals by Name.* New York: Vintage, 1987.

Kant, Immanuel. "Duties Towards Animals and Spirits." In *Lectures on Ethics.* Trans. L. Infield. New York: Harper & Row, 1963.

Levinson, Boris M. *Pets and Human Development.* Springfield, IL: Thomas, 1972.

Midgley, Mary. *Animals and Why They Matter.* Athens, GA: University of Georgia Press, 1984.

Regan, Tom. *The Case for Animal Rights*. Berkeley, CA: University of California Press, 1983.

Regan, Tom (ed.). *Earthbound: New Introductory Essays in Environmental Ethics*. New York: Random House, 1984.

Regan, Tom, and Peter Singer (eds.). *Animal Rights and Human Obligations*. 2nd ed. Englewood Cliffs, NJ: Prentice-Hall, 1989.

Rollin, Bernard E. *Animal Rights and Human Morality*. Buffalo, NY: Prometheus, 1981.

Singer, Peter. *Animal Liberation*. Rev. ed. New York: Avon Books, 1990.

Singer, Peter (ed.). *In Defense of Animals*. New York: Basil Blackwell, 1986.

Spinoza, Benedict de. *The Ethics*. Trans. R. H. M. Elwes. New York: Dover, 1955.

CHAPTER 23

The Environment

Environmental alarms have been sounded on many fronts: polluted lakes and oceans, depleted natural resources, acid rain, endangered species, destruction of rain forests, pesticide poisoning, chemical dump sites, nuclear waste, global warming, and depletion of the ozone layer surrounding the earth. These alarms challenge us to expand our circle of moral concern to include the natural environment. Human survival, not just beautiful scenery, is at stake in the pursuit of a sustainable environment.

Each of us in our daily lives has the capacity to benefit or harm the environment through everyday choices made as consumers (for example, by buying energy-efficient appliances and cars); through habits such as recycling, ride sharing, and conserving electricity and water; through voting patterns; and through philanthropic giving to and voluntary service on behalf of effective environmental organizations. It is possible for us, as the environmental maxim enjoins, to "think globally, act locally." Is it also, however, a moral responsibility? If so, how strong is the responsibility and what is its foundation?

During the 1970s, environmental ethics emerged as a new branch of applied ethics, signaled especially with the creation in 1979 of the journal *Environmental Ethics*. In this chapter we sketch several answers to an issue central to that field of thought: Should ethics be rethought in a fundamental way so as to abandon its traditional human-centered (*anthropocentric*) focus? In addition to this theoretical question, there are numerous practical issues that must be addressed in balancing competing interests, human and nonhuman alike.

Human-Centered Ethics

Western civilizations have largely regarded the environment as a resource to satisfy human desires. In this view, the environment has no intrinsic or inherent moral worth. Rather, its worth is purely instrumental—the means for serving the interests of intrinsically valuable human beings. Some of those interests are *economic*: the management and conservation of resources essential for a productive economy. Other interests are *aesthetic*: the enjoyment of natural beauty and sublime vistas, waterfalls, and mountain ranges. Still others are *recreational*: for example, the enjoyments of backpacking or mountain climbing in wilderness areas. In addition, there are *scientific* interests: the ongoing study of the "natural laboratories" of wilderness areas. Increasingly important is the interest of sheer *survival*. Population has dramatically increased and resources have become scarcer, including resources essential to human life. Each of these interests provides a human-centered moral justification for restrictions on what individuals and corporations do to the environment.

From the perspective of rights ethics, humans have a right to life, liberty, and the pursuit of their happiness. That implies that other persons must not destroy the prerequisites for satisfaction of those rights, in particular, that they must not destroy the common resources of drinkable water, breathable air, and edible food. As William T. Blackstone argued, the basic rights to live and to pursue a fulfilling life imply a *right to a livable environment*:

> The answer then to the question, Is the right to a livable environment a human right? is yes. Each person has this right *qua* being human and because a livable environment is essential for one to fulfill his human capacities. And given the danger to our environment today and hence the danger to the very possibility of human existence, access to a livable environment must be conceived as a right which imposes upon everyone a correlative moral obligation to respect.[1]

A (prima facie) obligation not to damage the environment in ways that harm people can also be derived from duty ethics and utilitarianism. Duty ethics implies a duty not to erode the environment in ways that threaten the ability of people to lead autonomous and meaningful lives. Utilitarianism, with its goal of maximizing the well-being of all people, implies an obligation to avoid harming people and to promote the environmental conditions essential for human life.

Each of these theories of conduct takes into account not only people living today, but future generations as well. The same value that resides in our lives now will someday reside in the lives of others not yet born, and their welfare makes a claim on us now not to undermine their prospects for meaningful life.[2] To deny this by using up the world's resources for the benefit of our own generation would constitute a form of bigotry, a presumption that our lives have greater value than the lives of later generations. Such an attitude would also betray the special obligations of loyalty to the children and grandchildren of members of our present community.

What does virtue ethics, with its focus on the kinds of people we should become, have to say about responsibilities concerning the natural environment? Thomas E. Hill, Jr., begins his answer to this question with a story: "A wealthy eccentric bought a house in a neighborhood I know. The house was surrounded by a beautiful display of grass, plants, and flowers, and it was shaded by a huge old avocado tree. But the grass required cutting, the flowers needed tending, and the man wanted more sun. So he cut the whole lot down and covered the yard with asphalt."[3] Hill compared this action to strip mining and the destruction of redwood forests. He asks, "What sort of person ... would cover his garden with asphalt, strip mine a wooded mountain, or level an irreplaceable redwood grove?"[4]

First, such a person lacks the virtue of moral humility. Humble individuals appreciate their place in nature, understood as a complex interconnected network of plants and animals. They live with an attitude that they are part of a wider organic unity, and they value nature apart from considerations of how it affects themselves.

Second, such a person lacks a sense of aesthetic sensitivity to the beauty of natural objects. This aesthetic sensibility is not a moral virtue per se, but the capacities it reflects—sensitivity, wide emotional interest, and empathy—are also important elements of the moral virtue of sensitivity to persons. It is likely that the failure to respond to natural beauty is a sign of failures to appreciate human beings.

Third, such a person shows a failure of gratitude toward the natural world that makes life possible. This sense of gratitude may be understood in religious terms, as gratitude toward the creator of the natural world, or as a moral virtue, that is, an appreciation for the beauty and the life-support provided by the natural world. In addition, ingratitude regarding the natural world is likely to be reflected in ingratitude toward other persons.

Hill's focus is primarily human-centered in that it explores environmental responsibilities in terms of human ideals concerning human character. Nevertheless, Hill believes that those ideals imply an attitude of valuing nature for itself. We cannot manifest the virtues of humility, sensitivity, and gratitude unless we cherish nature, that is, care for natural things in themselves. This brings us to the question, central to the development of environmental ethics, of whether we should shift the locus of moral value to something wider than human beings.

Nature-Centered Ethics

Aristotle, Locke, Kant, Mill, and most other traditional ethicists took for granted that human beings were the exclusive focus of moral concern because they have an inherent worth missing from other natural creatures. Is that true? After all, humans are natural creatures. We are animals, and like all animals our survival and prospects for healthy lives depend entirely on numerous interdependencies with nonhuman animals, plants, and even the nonliving world.

Thinking along these lines, some environmentalists have reformulated moral philosophy by beginning with one of three proposals: (1) All conscious life has inherent moral value (consciousness-centered or *sentientist ethics*); (2) All life has inherent moral value (life-centered or *biocentric ethics*); (3) Ecosystems have inherent moral value (ecology-centered or *ecocentric ethics*).

Sentientist Ethics

The consciousness-centered perspective, which can be viewed as an extension of traditional moral theories, was broached in the last chapter. There we asked, Why is the torture of animals immoral? Is it (prima facie) wrong solely because it harms other people, either directly (e.g., by harming someone's pet) or indirectly (e.g., by harming our characters and thus influencing us toward cruelty to other people)? Or is it wrong because of the direct harm to the animal? If we believe torture is wrong because the animal is harmed, we are implying that conscious animals have inherent worth.

Conscious beings suffer, feel pleasure, and experience a range of other emotions. That gives them moral significance, whether we understand that significance within the framework of utilitarianism, rights ethics, or duty ethics. As a result, it is immoral to shoot animals solely for sport or to trap them to make fashionable fur coats (especially when the traps cause slow and painful deaths). Moreover, the well-being of sentient animals should be a serious consideration of commercial development that threatens the natural habitats of animals. Every effort should be made to minimize harm and to allow "green areas" where animals can flourish. According to sentientist ethics (as sketched in the discussion of Peter Singer and Tom Regan in the previous chapter), conscious animals should be killed only rarely, when there are no alternatives and only when basic human needs are at stake.

Biocentric Ethics

A life-centered perspective goes much further by affirming the intrinsic worth of all living things, including nonsentient animals and plants. This perspective is not an extension of traditional theories, but is instead a radical reconsideration of ethics.

Albert Schweitzer (1875–1965) encapsulated this view with his phrase "reverence for life." He contended that the most immediate intuition that each of us has is that "I am life which wills to live, in the midst of life which wills to live."[5] If I find goodness in acting on my will to live, consistency requires that I make a similar affirmation for all living things. The ethical person "does not ask how far this or that life deserves one's sympathy as being valuable, nor, beyond that, whether and to what degree it is capable of feeling. Life as such is sacred to him. He tears no leaf from a tree, plucks no flower and takes care to crush no insect. If in summer he is working by lamplight, he prefers to keep the window shut and breathe a stuffy atmosphere rather than see one insect after another fall with singed wings upon his table."6 Killing any living thing is permissible only when "unavoidable" or "necessary." (Schweitzer leaves these criteria somewhat vague, and, contrary to his intentions, they seem to suggest that human interests have priority over those of lower forms of life.)

Some biocentric philosophers reject Schweitzer's refusal to rank the value of various living things. For example, Kenneth Goodpaster allows that different life forms have different degrees of value, and in particular that human interests often outweigh the interests of plants. Nevertheless he shares Schweitzer's sense that all living things have intrinsic value and should be the object of moral concern. They all have "interests" in being alive and pursuing the kinds of life available to them: "the core of moral concern lies in respect for self-sustaining organization and integration in the face of pressures toward high entropy" (disintegration and loss of available energy).7 A tree is an organism with biological needs, and to that extent it is akin to sentient beings. From an evolutionary perspective, consciousness is merely one of many biological functions (however important) which enable organisms to pursue their interests effectively.

Ecocentric Ethics

The ecocentric outlook sees intrinsic value even in nonliving aspects of nature, which, after all, are the evolutionary source of all life. This perspective sees inherent worth in ecosystems: systems of organisms as they interact with their environments.

Aldo Leopold, in his influential version of this view, calls ecosystems "biotic pyramids": systems composed of layers, in which soil is the bottom layer and other layers are composed of the food chains of energy-absorbing plants, plant-eating insects, insect-eating birds, and (eventually) carnivorous mammals. To have an "ecological conscience" implies a respect for the health of biotic pyramids, and therefore a respect for their capacities for self-renewal. Leopold affirmed a "land ethic" which "enlarges the community [of moral concern] to include soils, waters, plants, and animals, or collectively: the land."8 As an alternative to our domination of nature, Leopold urges that we learn to see ourselves as members of the "land-community" or "biotic community" by heeding the following standard of conduct: "A thing is right when it tends to preserve the integrity, stability, and beauty of the biotic community. It is wrong when it tends otherwise."9

Ecocentric ethics has a more holistic emphasis than sentientist and biocentric ethics, accenting entire systems and environments rather than individual creatures. For example, one of the primary concerns of ecocentric ethics is to preserve species (as a whole), especially more developed species, rather than to preserve each plant or animal. This holistic emphasis leads critics to charge ecocentrists with insensitivity to individual organisms because they are more preoccupied with the "whole" rather than its "parts." Critics fear that this bias results in insensitivity to individual persons and that efforts to protect the land may result in the sacrifice of basic needs of persons.

In reply, ecocentrists such as Holmes Rolston III and J. Baird Callicott have emphasized that priorities need not be abandoned in expanding the circle of moral concern—including priorities which sentientists sometimes overlook. Their writings affirm the paramount worth of human beings and recognize that responsibilities to humans are more stringent, while still extending to natural ecosystems a recognition of their inherent worth. Thus, Callicott writes:

> Nor does an ecocentric environmental ethic replace or cancel previous socially generated human-oriented duties—to family and family members, to neighbors and neighborhood, to all human beings and humanity.... The moral sphere, growing in circumference with each stage of social development ... does not expand like a balloon—leaving no trace of its previous boundaries.... The discovery of the biotic community simply adds a new outer orbit of membership and attendant obligation. Our more intimate social bonds and their attendant obligations remain intact.[10]

Native American tribes provide a model for the sort of widened respect for nature that retains respect for persons. Native Americans learned to live in harmony with nature, using what was essential for their lives while maintaining attitudes of respect and even reverence for the environment. Members of traditional tribes lived with a sense that they were members rather than exploiters of a natural community, and they did so without losing a primary respect for one another.

Rules of Conduct

Even if we find meaning in the idea of intrinsic value in nonhuman animals, all life, or ecosystems, does a nature-centered ethics provide clear guidance in dealing with nature? Much turns on the specific version of nature-centered ethics, since different versions have different practical implications. For example, sentient-centered ethics advocates concern for each individual conscious animal, whereas biocentrism proscribes the wanton killing of any living thing, and ecocentrism focuses more on protection of species (as a whole) within their environments.

Suppose that a herd of wild sheep is overgrazing an island so as to threaten several plant species and the ecosystem as a whole. Under the assumption that the sheep cannot be moved elsewhere, ecocentrism would imply selective killing of the sheep, sentientism would imply not killing them (since each animal has value, but the plants do not), and biocentrism seems on the surface to imply that nothing should be done (nature should take its course).

Even more pressing than conflicts within nonhuman nature are conflicts between humans and the natural environment, and here again the theories give different emphases. For example, ecocentrism would have us restrict construction and consumer products which threaten ecosystems, but sentientism would not place a priority on the ecosystems (except when the species therein affect the lives of conscious animals), and biocentrism would be concerned only with preservation of life rather than ecosystems per se. Clearly what is needed is a detailed elaboration of particular versions of nature-centered ethics.

As one example of the complexity to be found in new theories in environmental ethics, consider Paul W. Taylor's biocentric perspective set forth in his book *Respect for Nature*. Taylor locates inherent worth in each living organism, rather than in ecosystems, because each organism is "a teleological center of life, striving to preserve itself and realize its good in its own unique way."[11] The key idea is that each organism—plants, animals, and even one-celled creatures—has a good of its own, something that enables it to survive and flourish as the type of creature it is. Nonconscious (and even many conscious) creatures cannot envision that good, but we can. Our consciousness enables us imaginatively to see the world in terms of what helps the organism flourish, and to take into account what is good for it and weigh it against the good of humans. Our consciousness (and reason) does not, however, give our lives greater moral worth than other creatures. We are exactly like other living organisms in being members of a complex interdependent community of organisms, each of which has a good of its own to be pursued in its unique way.

The attitude of respect for nature consists of valuing all life and refusing to place ourselves above it. It implies four duties toward other life. (1) Nonmaleficence is the duty not to kill other living things. Nonmaleficence is the most important duty to organisms and it forbids wanton killing of animals and plants, such as the killing of elephants to obtain decorative ivory, or fishing for sheer recreation (rather than for food). (2) Noninterference is the duty not to interfere with the freedom of organisms. This rules out, for example, the capture of tropical birds for sale as pets. (3) Fidelity is the duty not to violate the trust of wild animals (as occurs in deception used in hunting, trapping, and fishing). (4) Restitutive justice is the duty to make amends for violations of the other duties, if only by helping to promote the life of other organisms than those we have harmed.

All these duties are prima facie: They have some justified exceptions. In particular, they have some exceptions when they conflict with responsibilities to ourselves and to other human beings. How are these priorities to be set within Taylor's perspective, which refuses to place the inherent worth of humans above that of other animals and plants? Taylor formulates five additional principles of priority.

First, the principle of self-defense permits us to kill when we must in order to protect ourselves against dangerous organisms that threaten our lives. Second, the principle of proportionality asserts that priority is to be given to organisms the basic interests of which are most affected. Basic interests are survival needs, as well as the needs for living a life distinctive to a particular kind of organism. Third, the principle of minimum wrong asserts that we should minimize harm done to all organisms affected. Fourth, the principle of distributive justice asserts that the basic interests of all organisms should be treated as equally important. And fifth, the principle of restitutive justice asserts that, when any of the previous four principles have been violated, some compensation must be made to similar organisms.

What do these priority principles imply? Their implications must be unfolded contextually, but that is equally true of all moral principles applying to humans. They clearly imply, however, that the good of animals and plants must be weighed in decisions about whether to engage in new construction that would destroy indigenous plants and animals. These principles also demonstrate that a nature-centered ethics can provide some guidance in dealing with practical decisions.

Practical Conflicts and Consensus

The contrast between human-centered and nature-centered ethics is theoretically important and also has practical implications. Some environmental activists have used it as support for their sharp confrontations in the courts designed to block or slow commercial development, logging of redwood trees, strip mining, fishing (especially in forms that kill dolphins and whales), and destruction of natural habitats for recreational purposes. They have used it to justify civil disobedience, and even occasional violence, on behalf of their causes. In response, representatives of industry regard nature-centered ethics as the source of environmentalism gone mad, especially in the overwhelming number of new laws and regulations which threaten to strangle business. Not just profits, but thousands of jobs are at stake.

There are no easy solutions to these political and practical confrontations (although the discussion of conflict resolution in Chapter 10 is pertinent). Much is at stake, and moral convictions are deep on both sides. Nevertheless, as these conflicts are pursued we need to appreciate that all informed and caring individuals should have concern for both the environment and for human communities. Balance and good judgment are required, with the object of finding the most reasonable accommodations possible among people of good will. It is important to get beneath slogans, stereotypes, and superficial characterizations of environmental disagreements. Often the fundamental differences cut across these disputes and concerns. In particular, clashes between environmentalists and business often reflect underlying differences between short- and long-term views of human good, differences which nature-centered ethicists can use in appealing to majorities who remain human-centered in their ethical perspectives. In this connection we make a few concluding comments.

The economist Adam Smith argued that self-seeking within a free enterprise system created a self-correcting mechanism that benefited the entire community. He called this the "invisible hand" of free enterprise, but in outline there is nothing mysterious about it. In the pursuit of profits, entrepreneurs create businesses which attract employees, who are motivated by the wages offered. Consumers benefit because competition leads to lower-priced and higher-quality products and services. In response to Smith's argument, the biologist Garrett Hardin argues that in the long run individual self-seeking harms the entire community.

Hardin describes the "tragedy of the commons."[12] The commons was literally a pasture at the center of town which farmers would use as a common grazing area. Ranchers were motivated to add additional cattle or sheep in order to maximize proceeds from their herds. Eventually, however, the commons was overgrazed and all ranchers were hurt as herds died off. Extending this image to current environmental concerns, the commons becomes usable air, water, forests, and other shared resources. If each person thinks only in terms of narrowly conceived self-interests, these commons will eventually be destroyed. Hence, there is a rationale in terms of long-term self-interest for each of us to agree to a reasonable degree of regulation, what Hardin calls mutually agreed-upon public coercion.

Consider the intense controversy between the logging industry in the Pacific Northwest and environmentalists who defended the endangered spotted owl. During this controversy, environmentalists were criticized for caring more for animals than for people. Yet their concern was not just to protect the appealing owl, but to protect the entire ecosystem in which the owl lived. The owl was scientifically determined to be an *indicator species*, that is, a species whose well-being accurately reflects the well-being of an entire ecosystem. Destruction of the owl's ecosystem can have numerous long-term effects on human well-being, if only the loss of a renewable source of timber—a loss that would in the long run harm the logging industry and the people who conduct and benefit from that industry.

Concern for the owl, then, can be viewed as part of the concern for persons. The disagreement turned on long-term versus short-term harm to people, and hence was a conflict within a framework of human-centered ethics as well as nature-centered ethics. In fact, eventually it became clear that the salmon industry was threatened by the muddied waters caused by logging, thereby pitting industries against industries (a conflict within human-centered ethics).

Finally, just as we noted that nature-centered ethics takes many forms, we should note that human-centered ethics does too. Even in rough terms we can contrast a strong and weak version of anthropocentrism (paralleling the distinction between two types of speciesism discussed in Chapter 22). The strong version asserts that only human satisfactions are relevant to decisions concerning the environment and that nonhuman creatures have no intrinsic value at all. The weak version allows that human beings have much greater value than nonhuman creatures, but it recognizes some inherent worth in nonhuman creatures, especially in higher mammals. This weaker version opens the door to a reconciliation with nature-centered perspectives, especially those which themselves give priority to basic human interests when they conflict with the interests of nonhumans.

SUMMARY

Human-centered ethics, which locates inherent moral worth only in rational creatures such as humans, tends to endow other living creatures with only instrumental value for humans. For example, rights ethics values the environment because humans have a right to a livable environment, and because nature has economic, aesthetic, recreational, and scientific uses. Virtue-centered ethics, however, while still human-centered, stresses the virtues of humility, gratitude, and sensitivity to the aspects of nature that have intrinsic value of their own; this view approaches the beginnings of a nature-centered ethics.

Nature-centered ethics, which locates inherent value beyond rational human beings, can take three forms: consciousness-centered ethics (sentientism, as defended by Peter Singer and Tom Regan), life-centered ethics (biocentrism, as defended by Albert Schweitzer, Kenneth Goodpaster, and Paul Taylor), and ecology-centered ethics (ecocentrism, as defended by Aldo Leopold, J. Baird Callicott, and Holmes Rolston III). Taylor's biocentrism, which illustrates how detailed such outlooks have become, formulates principles of duty to living organisms such as nonmaleficence, noninterference, fidelity, and restitution, as well as priority principles for balancing duties to humans and to nature, such as self-defense, proportionality, minimum wrong, distributive justice, and restitution.

Finally, the differences apparent in the practical implications of human- and nature-centered ethics reflect differences—possibly even more important—between long-term and short-term thinking about human good.

DISCUSSION TOPICS

1 Do you agree with Hill's assessment of his neighbor? Exactly what was objectionable in the neighbor's conduct? Was it the destruction of the avocado tree and the other extant plants, or their replacement with concrete? Would the neighbor be open to criticism if, after removing the greenery, he had replaced it with new plants, perhaps ones that required less maintenance? Similarly, are strip mining and the harvesting of redwood trees objectionable only when the land is not later restored?

2 Is there anything morally objectionable about hunting for sport (rather than for food)? In your answer, discuss the attitudes of the hunter who (in 1850) wrote the following description of shooting an elephant:

> The elephant stood broadside to me, at upwards of one hundred yards, and his attention at the moment was occupied with the dogs.... I fired at his shoulder, and secured him with a single shot. The ball caught him high on the shoulder-blade, rendering him instantly lame; and before the echo of the bullet could reach my ear, I plainly saw the elephant was mine.... I resolved to devote a short time to the contemplation of this noble elephant before laying him low; ... I quickly kindled a fire and put on the kettle, and in a few minutes my coffee was prepared. There I sat in my forest home, coolly sipping my coffee, with one of the finest elephants in Africa awaiting my pleasure beside a neighbouring tree....
>
> Having admired the elephant for a considerable time, I resolved to make experiments for vulnerable points.... [He bungles this again and again; eventually, after even he has become a little worried, he succeeds in wounding the elephant fatally.] Large tears now trickled from his eyes, which he slowly shut and opened, his colossal frame quivered convulsively, and falling on his side, he expired.[13]

3 Do you find anything morally objectionable in the following practice? If so, give your reasons and state whether they are human-centered, consciousness-centered, life-centered, or ecology-centered. "Certain rare species of butterflies occur in hummocks (slightly elevated forested ground) on the African grasslands. It was formerly the practice of ... collectors to go in, collect a few hundred specimens and then burn out the hummock with the intention of destroying the species, thereby driving up the price of their collections."[14] Is the destruction of any species of organism objectionable (given that thousands of species disappear each year through natural causes), or only the destruction of certain types of species?

4 Human-centered environmental ethics relies heavily on the idea that we have an obligation to pass on a livable environment to future generations of human beings. Yet those human beings (by definition) do not yet exist. How could nonexistent persons make moral claims on us now? Do nonexistent persons have rights to the preservation (by us) of the environment? (In your answer, consider the analogy with parents' decisions to have children: The future children do not yet exist, and yet the parents have an obligation to prepare to give them meaningful lives before bringing them into existence. That responsibility includes the obligation not to use drugs or engage in other practices that might cause genetic deformities.)

5   What do you think Schweitzer means when he says that all living things have a "will to live"? Do the following organisms have a will to live in exactly the same sense: human beings, squirrels, mosquitoes, protozoans, grass, trees?

6   The tragedy of the commons results not just from the extraction of resources from a shared environment, but also (in reverse) from pollution of the environment. Identify an example from your local community of how the seemingly innocent (nonmalevolent) pursuit of self-interest by many individuals results in pollution that harms the community as a whole.

7   "Eco-feminists" have argued that there are important connections, both in theory and in historical practices, between the attitudes of male dominance involved in exploitation of women and exploitation of nature. Do you agree? In particular, respond to the following passage from Rosemary Ruether:

> Women must see that there can be no liberation for them and no solution to the ecological crisis within a society whose fundamental model of relationship continues to be one of domination. They must unite the demands of the women's movement with those of the ecological movement to envision a radical reshaping of the basic socioeconomic relations and the underlying values of this society.[15]

8   Some of the worst environmental problems have been caused in developed Western countries, but developing countries have begun to cause equally severe problems; examples include the destruction of Brazilian rain forests in order to clear land for farms and cattle, the widespread use of heavily polluting coal in China, the encroachment on wilderness areas in India, and expansion of populations in Third World countries. Given the increasingly global effects of environmental changes, Western countries have put increasing demands on Third World countries to conform to Western standards. Does fairness require that these demands be backed by economic support, which is likely to require higher taxes and self-sacrifice by Western populations? Should Americans be willing to offer what Vice-President Al Gore calls (in his book *Earth in the Balance*) a Global Marshall Plan on behalf of the environment?

9   What would you say to someone who refused to conserve electricity, gasoline, or water on the grounds that such acts are so insignificant in scale that it makes no difference to the overall environmental problems? As part of your answer, consider (a) the virtues of authenticity and integrity, (b) utilitarianism, and (c) rights ethics.

SUGGESTED READINGS

Armstrong, Susan J., and Richard G. Botzler (eds.). *Environmental Ethics: Divergence and Convergence.* New York: McGraw-Hill, 1993.

Buchholz, Rogene A., Alfred A. Marcus, and James E. Post. *Managing Environmental Issues: A Casebook.* Englewood Cliffs, NJ: Prentice-Hall, 1992.

Callicott, J. Baird. *In Defense of the Land Ethic: Essays in Environmental Philosophy.* Albany, NY: State University of New York Press, 1988.

Cooper, David E., and Joy A. Palmer (eds.). *The Environment in Question: Ethics and Global Issues.* New York: Routledge, 1992.

DesJardins, Joseph R. *Environmental Ethics: An Introduction to Environmental Philosophy.* Belmont, CA: Wadsworth, 1993.

Hargrove, Eugene C. *Foundations of Environmental Ethics.* Englewood Cliffs, NJ: Prentice-Hall, 1989.

Hill, Thomas E., Jr. "Ideals of Human Excellence and Preserving Natural Environments." In *Autonomy and Self-Respect.* Cambridge: Cambridge University Press, 1991. Pp. 104–117.

Hypatia: A Journal of Feminist Philosophy, vol. 6 (1991). Special issue on Ecological Feminism, ed. K. J. Warren.

Newton, Lisa H., and Catherine K. Dillingham. *Watersheds: Classic Cases in Environmental Ethics.* Belmont, CA: Wadsworth, 1994.

Passmore, John. *Man's Responsibility for Nature: Ecological Problems and Western Traditions.* New York: Scribner, 1974.

Partridge, Ernest (ed.). *Responsibilities to Future Generations.* Buffalo, NY: Prometheus, 1980.

Rolston, Holmes, III. *Environmental Ethics: Duties to and Values in the Natural World.* Philadelphia, PA: Temple University Press, 1988.

Scherer, Donald. *Upstream/Downstream: Issues in Environmental Ethics.* Philadelphia, PA: Temple University Press, 1990.

Taylor, Paul W. *Respect for Nature: A Theory of Environmental Ethics.* Princeton, NJ: Princeton University Press, 1986.

VanDeVeer, Donald, and Christine Pierce (eds.) *People, Penguins, and Plastic Trees: Basic Issues in Environmental Ethics.* Belmont, CA: Wadsworth, 1986.

VanDeVeer, Donald, and Christine Pierce (eds.). *The Environmental Ethics and Public Policy Book: Philosophy, Ecology, Economics.* Belmont, CA: Wadsworth, 1994.

Notes

PART ONE   *Character, Conduct, and Ethical Theories*

1 Iris Murdoch, *The Sovereignty of Good* (Boston, MA: Ark Paperbacks, 1985), p. 52.

2 Ibid., p. 46.

CHAPTER 1   *Moral Reasons*

1 Martin Gansberg, "38 Who Saw Murder Didn't Call Police," in C. Sommers and F. Sommers (eds.), *Vice and Virtue in Everyday Life* (San Diego, CA: Harcourt Brace Jovanovich, 1989), pp. 51–54.

2 David Hume, *A Treatise of Human Nature* (Oxford: Clarendon Press, 1888), pp. 468–469.

3 This discussion is based on James Rachels, *The Elements of Moral Philosophy*, 2nd ed. (New York: McGraw-Hill, 1993), ch. 5; and Gregory S. Kavka, *Hobbesian Moral Philosophy* (Princeton, NJ: Princeton University Press, 1986), ch. 2.

4 Ruth Benedict, "Anthropology and the Abnormal," *The Journal of General Psychology*, vol. 10 (1934): 59–82. Also see *Patterns of Culture* (Boston, MA: Houghton Mifflin Co., 1934).

5 Richard Borshay Lee, *The !Kung San: Men, Women, and Work in a Foraging Society* (Cambridge: Cambridge University Press, 1979). The "!" in "!Kung" stands for a clicking sound. The !Kung were formerly called Bushmen or Hottentots by anthropologists.

6 Jeffrey Stout, *Ethics After Babel* (Boston, MA: Beacon Press, 1988), p. 98.

7 Plato, *Euthyphro*, trans. L. Cooper, in E. Hamilton and H. Cairns (eds.), *The Collected Dialogues of Plato* (Princeton, NJ: Princeton University Press, 1961), p. 178.

8 Gen. 22:1–2, 9–10, King James version.

9 Jean-Paul Sartre, "Existentialism Is a Humanism," trans. P. Mairet, in W. Kaufmann (ed.), *Existentialism from Dostoevsky to Sartre,* rev. ed. (New York: New American Library, 1975), p. 351.

10 Soren Kierkegaard, *Fear and Trembling,* trans. A. Hannay (New York: Penguin, 1985).

11 Gen. 1:31, King James version.

CHAPTER 2   *Authenticity*

1 See Charles Taylor, *The Ethics of Authenticity* (Cambridge, MA: Harvard University Press, 1991).

2 Jeffrey Stout, *Ethics After Babel* (Boston, MA: Beacon Press, 1988), p. 212.

3 John Stuart Mill, *On Liberty* (Indianapolis, IN: Hackett, 1978), p. 54. First published in 1859.

4 Isaiah Berlin, "The Pursuit of the Ideal," in *The Crooked Timber of Humanity* (New York: Vintage, 1992), p. 11.

5 See John Kekes, *The Examined Life* (Lewisburg, PA: Bucknell University Press, 1988); and Elizabeth Telfer, *Happiness* (New York: St. Martin's Press, 1980).

6 John Stuart Mill, *The Autobiography of John Stuart Mill* (Garden City, NY: Doubleday), p. 110.

7 Jean-Paul Sartre, *Being and Nothingness,* trans. H. E. Barnes (New York: Washington Square Press, 1966), p. 76.

8 Jean-Paul Sartre, "Existentialism Is a Humanism," trans. P. Mairet, in W. Kaufmann (ed.), *Existentialism from Dostoevsky to Sartre,* rev. ed. (New York: New American Library, 1975). The example of the student is also presented in this essay. For a discussion of Friedrich Nietzsche's earlier use of the art analogy in understanding authenticity, see Alexander Nehamas, *Nietzsche: Life as Literature* (Cambridge, MA: Harvard University Press, 1985).

9 Plato, *Apology,* trans. G. M. A. Grube, in *The Trial and Death of Socrates* (Indianapolis, IN: Hackett, 1975), p.26.

10 Ibid., p. 39.

11 Ibid., pp. 32–33.

12 Matt. 5:44, King James version.

13 A phrase used by Martin Luther King, Jr. (among other places) in his dedication to *Why We Can't Wait* (New York: New American Library, 1964), p. vi.

14 Elizabeth Cady Stanton et al., "Declaration of Sentiments," in A. S. Rossi (ed.), *The Feminist Papers* (New York: Bantam, 1973), p. 416.

15 Elizabeth Cady Stanton and The Revising Committee, *The Woman's Bible* (Seattle, WA: Coalition Task Force on Women and Religion, 1974), p. 131. First published in two parts in 1895 and 1898.

16 Carol Gilligan, "Moral Orientation and Moral Development," in E. F. Kittay and D. T. Meyers (eds.), *Women and Moral Theory* (Totowa, NJ: Rowman & Littlefield, 1987), p. 25.

17 Lawrence Kohlberg, "Indoctrination Versus Relativity in Value Education," in G. Sher (ed.), *Moral Philosophy: Selected Readings* (New York: Harcourt Brace Jovanovich, 1987), p. 88.

18 Plato, *Euthyphro,* trans. G. M. A. Grube, in *The Trial and Death of Socrates* (Indianapolis, IN: Hackett, 1975), p. 6.

19 Mary Midgley, "Creation and Originality," in *Heart and Mind: The Varieties of Moral Experience* (New York: St. Martin's Press, 1981), p. 57.

CHAPTER 3   *Theories of Virtue*

1 Cf. Richard Norman, *The Moral Philosophers* (New York: Clarendon Press, 1983), pp. 22–28; and Anthony Kenny, "Mental Health in Plato's Republic," in *The Anatomy of the Soul* (Oxford: Oxford University Press, 1973).

2 Aristotle, *Ethics,* trans. J. A. K. Thomson and H. Tredennick (New York: Penguin, 1976), p. 108.

3 Ibid., p. 104.

4 For further discussions, see John M. Cooper, *Reason and Human Good in Aristotle* (Indianapolis, IN: Hackett, 1986); and Nancy Sherman, *The Fabric of Character: Aristotle's Theory of Virtue* (Oxford: Clarendon Press, 1989).

5 Aristotle, *Ethics,* pp. 108–109.

6 Ibid., pp. 101–102.

7 Cf. Annette C. Baier, "Hume, the Women's Moral Theorist?" in E. F. Kittay and D. T. Meyers (eds.), *Women and Moral Theory* (Totowa, NJ: Rowman & Littlefield, 1987).

8 David Hume, *Hume's Ethical Writings,* Alasdair MacIntyre (ed.) (New York: Macmillan, 1965), p. 29.

9 Alasdair MacIntyre, *After Virtue* (Notre Dame, IN: University of Notre Dame Press, 1981), p. 204.

10 Ibid.

11 Ibid., p. 178.

12 Ibid., p. 204.

13 Ibid.

14 Edmund L. Pincoffs, *Quandaries and Virtues* (Lawrence, KS: University Press of Kansas, 1986), p. 78.

15 Ibid., p. 85.

16 Ibid., p. 89.

17 Plato, *The Republic,* trans. F. M. Cornford (New York: Oxford University Press, 1945), pp. 141–142.

CHAPTER 4   *Theories of Right Action*

1 Immanuel Kant, *Foundations of the Metaphysics of Morals,* trans. L. W. Beck (New York: Liberal Arts Press, 1959). Printed in A. I. Melden, *Ethical Theories: A Book of Readings,* 2nd ed. (Englewood Cliffs, NJ: Prentice-Hall, 1967), p. 345.

2 Ibid., p. 339.

3 Ibid., p. 348.

4 David Ross, *The Right and the Good* (Oxford: Clarendon Press, 1930), p. 19.

5 Ibid., pp. 21–22.

6 John Stuart Mill, *Utilitarianism* (Indianapolis, IN: Hackett, 1979), pp. 22–23, 25.

7 Ibid., pp. 8–9.

8 Ibid., p. 10.

9 Immanuel Kant, "On a Supposed Right to Lie from Altruistic Motives," in L. W. Beck (trans. and ed.), *Critique of Practical Reason and Other Writings in Moral Philosophy* (Chicago: University of Chicago Press, 1949), pp. 346–350.

10 Fyodor Dostoevsky, *Crime and Punishment,* trans. C. Garnett (New York: Bantam, 1981), pp. 58–59.

PART TWO   *Self-Respect and Integrity*

1 Immanuel Kant, *Lectures on Ethics,* trans. L. Infield (New York: Harper & Rowe, 1963), p. 126.

CHAPTER 5   *Valuing Oneself*

1 Immanuel Kant, *Foundations of the Metaphysics of Morals,* trans. L. W. Beck (Indianapolis, IN: Bobbs-Merrill, 1959), p. 47.

2 Immanuel Kant, *Lectures on Ethics,* trans. L. Infield (New York: Harper & Row, 1963), pp. 117–118.

3 John Rawls, *A Theory of Justice* (Cambridge, MA: Harvard University Press, 1971), p. 440.

4 Ibid.

5 Stephen L. Darwall, "Two Kinds of Respect," *Ethics,* vol. 88 (1977): 36–49.

6 Robin S. Dillon, "Toward a Feminist Conception of Self-Respect," *Hypatia,* vol. 7 (1992): 52–69.

7 Erich Fromm, *The Art of Loving* (New York: Harper & Row, 1956), pp. 48–53; and Joel Feinberg, "Absurd Self-Fulfillment," in P. van Inwagen (ed.), *Time and Cause* (Dordrecht, Holland: D. Reidel, 1980).

8 Fyodor Dostoevsky, *The Brothers Karamazov*, trans. A. H. MacAndrew (New York: Bantam, 1970), p. 697. The example of Lise is used by Irwin Goldstein in "Pain and Masochism," *Journal of Value Inquiry*, vol. 17 (1983): 219–223.

9 Fyodor Dostoevsky, *The Brothers Karamazov*, p.703.

10 Theodore Isaac Rubin, *Through My Own Eyes* (New York: Macmillan, 1982), p. 171.

11 Virginia Woolf, "The New Dress," in *A Haunted House and Other Stories* (New York: Harcourt Brace Jovanovich, 1972), p. 47.

12 Nathaniel Hawthorne, *The Scarlet Letter* (New York: Norton, 1978), p. 107.

13 William M. Thackeray, *The Book of Snobs*, in W. P. Trent and J. B. Henneman (eds.), *The Complete Works of William M. Thackeray*, Vol. XIV (New York: Crowell, undated), p. 63.

14 Spiro T. Agnew, speech given on October 19, 1969, in New Orleans, Louisiana, printed in John R. Coyne, Jr., *The Impudent Snobs: Agnew vs. the Intellectual Establishment* (New Rochelle, NY: Arlington House, 1972), p. 248.

15 Quoted by John R. Coyne, Jr., ibid., p. 38.

16 Judith N. Shklar, "What Is Wrong with Snobbery?" in *Ordinary Vices* (Cambridge, MA: Harvard University Press, 1984), pp. 135–136.

17 Thomas E. Hill, *Autonomy and Self-Respect* (New York: Cambridge University Press, 1991), p. 171.

18 Robert C. Solomon, *The Passions* (Notre Dame, IN: University of Notre Dame Press, 1983), p. 295.

CHAPTER 6 *Self-Knowledge and Self-Deception*

1 Sigmund Freud, *The Complete Introductory Lectures on Psychoanalysis*, trans. J. Strachey (New York: W. W. Norton & Co., 1966). Also see Charles Brenner, *An Elementary Textbook of Psychoanalysis*, rev. ed. (Garden City, NY: Anchor, 1974). Roy Schafer translates Freud's language of defense into the more familiar talk about self-deception in *A New Language for Psychoanalysis* (New Haven, CT: Yale University Press, 1976).

2 Herbert Fingarette, *Self-Deception* (Atlantic Highlands, NJ: Humanities Press, 1969), p. 141.

3 Bishop Joseph Butler, "Upon Self-Deceit," in W. E. Gladstone (ed.), *The Works of Joseph Butler* (Oxford: Clarendon Press, 1896), pp. 177–178.

4 Samuel Johnson, *The Rambler*, in A. Murphy (ed.), *The Works of Samuel Johnson*, Vol. 2 (London: S. and R. Bentley, 1823), pp. 181–187.

5 Ibid.

6 Fyodor Dostoevsky, *The Brothers Karamazov*, trans. C. Garnett (New York: New American Library, 1957), p. 49.

7 Sonia Johnson, *From Housewife to Heretic* (Garden City, NY: Anchor, 1983), p. 94.

8 Ibid., pp. 160–161.

9 Immanuel Kant, *The Doctrine of Virtue*, trans. M. J. Gregor (Philadelphia, PA: University of Pennsylvania Press, 1964), pp. 92, 95.

10 Jack W. Meiland, "What Ought We to Believe? or the Ethics of Belief Revisited," *American Philosophical Quarterly* (1980): 15–16.

11 Reinhold Niebuhr, *The Nature and Destiny of Man*, Vol. 1 (New York: Scribner, 1964), p. 203.

CHAPTER 7   *Self-Control and Courage*

1 See Thomas E. Hill, Jr., "Weakness of Will and Character," in *Autonomy and Self-Respect* (Cambridge: Cambridge University Press, 1991), pp. 120–122; and Gwynneth Matthews, "Moral Weakness," in G. W. Mortimore (ed.), *Weakness of Will* (London: Macmillan, 1971).

2 Plato, *Apology*, trans. G. M. A. Grube, in *The Trial and Death of Socrates* (Indianapolis, IN: Hackett, 1975).

3 Plato, *Protagoras*, trans. W. K. C. Guthrie, in E. Hamilton and H. Cairns (eds.), *The Collected Dialogues of Plato* (Princeton, NJ: Princeton University Press, 1963), p. 344.

4 Aristotle, *Nicomachean Ethics*, trans. W. D. Ross, in R. McKeon (ed.), *The Basic Works of Aristotle* (New York: Random House, 1941), p. 1041.

5 Alfred R. Mele, *Irrationality: An Essay on Akrasia, Self-Deception, and Self-Control* (New York: Oxford University Press, 1987), pp. 51–52.

6 Friedrich Nietzsche, *The Gay Science*, trans. W. Kaufmann (New York: Vintage, 1974), pp. 232–233.

7 Our discussion will rely on the important psychological study by C. R. Snyder, Raymond L. Higgins, and Rita J. Stucky, *Excuses* (New York: Wiley, 1983).

8 Elizabeth Glaser and Laura Palmer, *In the Absence of Angels* (New York: Berkley Books, 1991), p. 141.

9 Ibid., p. 157.

10 As reported in the local television news in Orange County, California.

11 Aristotle, *Ethics*, trans. J. A. K. Thomson and H. Tredennick (New York: Penguin, 1976), p. 103.

12 James D. Wallace, "Courage, Cowardice, and Self-Indulgence," in *Virtues and Vices* (Ithaca, NY: Cornell University Press, 1978), pp. 78–81.

13 Douglas N. Walton, *Courage: A Philosophical Investigation* (Berkeley, CA: University of California Press, 1986), p. 191.

14 W. D. Falk, "Morality, Self, and Others," in H. Castaneda and G. Nakhnikian (eds.), *Morality and the Language of Conduct* (Detroit, MI: Wayne State University Press, 1965), p. 103.

15 Mark Twain, *The Adventures of Huckleberry Finn* (New York: Dell, 1960), p. 122.

16 The term *dependent virtues* is used by Michael Slote in *Goods and Virtues* (Oxford: Clarendon Press, 1983), pp. 61–75.

CHAPTER 8   *Suicide and Euthanasia*

1 Albert Camus, *The Myth of Sisyphus* (New York: Vintage, 1955), p. 3.

2 Howard I. Kushner, *American Suicide: A Psychocultural Exploration* (New Brunswick, NJ: Rutgers University Press, 1991).

3 R. G. Frey, "Did Socrates Commit Suicide?" *Philosophy*, vol. 53 (1978): 106–108.

4 Howard I. Kushner, *American Suicide*, pp. 119–120.

5 St. Thomas Aquinas, *Summa Theologica*, Vol. 2 (New York: Benziger Brothers, 1925), Part 2, Question 64, A5.

6 Thomas E. Hill, Jr., *Autonomy and Self-Respect* (Cambridge: Cambridge University Press, 1991), p. 95. Italics removed.

7 John Stuart Mill, *On Liberty* (Indianapolis, IN: Hackett, 1978), p. 9.

8 Glanville Williams, *The Sanctity of Life and the Criminal Law* (New York: Knopf, 1957), p. 27.

9 Quoted by Ronald Munson, *Intervention and Reflection: Basic Issues in Medical Ethics*, 4th ed. (Belmont, CA: Wadsworth, 1992), p. 148.

10 *Cruzan v. Director, Missouri Department of Health*, United States Supreme Court 110 S. Ct. 2841 (1990).

11 Marcia Angell, "Euthanasia," *The New England Journal of Medicine*, vol. 319 (November 17, 1988): 1348–1350.

12 James Rachels, "Active and Passive Euthanasia," in Ronald Munson, *Intervention and Reflection: Basic Issues in Medical Ethics*, p. 165.

13 See Bonnie Steinbock, "The Intentional Termination of Life," in B. Steinbock (ed.), *Killing and Letting Die* (Englewood Cliffs, NJ: Prentice-Hall, 1980), pp. 69–77.

14 Margaret Pabst Battin, "Euthanasia," in D. Van DeVeer and T. Regan (eds.), *Health Care Ethics* (Philadelphia, PA: Temple University Press, 1987), pp. 62–63.

15 Ibid., p. 73.

16 These examples are from William E. Tolhurst, "Suicide, Self-Sacrifice, and Coercion," *The Southern Journal of Philosophy*, vol. 21 (1983): 109–121.

17 Stephen G. Potts, "Looking for the Exit Door: Killing and Caring in Modern Medicine," *Houston Law Review*, vol. 25 (1988): 504–511.

PART THREE   *Respect for Others*

1 John Rawls, *A Theory of Justice* (Cambridge, MA: Harvard University Press, 1971), pp. 178, 337.

CHAPTER 9   *Drug Abuse*

1 The statistics cited in this chapter are drawn primarily from: Ken Liska, *Drugs and the Human Body, With Implications for Society*, 3rd ed. (New York: Macmillan, 1990); Erich Goode, *Drugs in American Society*, 3rd ed. (New York: McGraw-Hill, 1989); and Robert E. Goodin, *No Smoking: The Ethical Issues* (Chicago: University of Chicago Press, 1989).

2 James B. Bakalar and Lester Grinspoon, *Drug Control in a Free Society* (Cambridge: Cambridge University Press, 1984), pp. 46–47.

3 Eugene O'Neill, *Long Day's Journey Into Night* (New Haven, CT: Yale University Press, 1956), p. 93.

4 James B. Bakalar and Lester Grinspoon, *Drug Control in a Free Society*, p. 33.

5 Herbert Fingarette, *Heavy Drinking: The Myth of Alcoholism as a Disease* (Berkeley, CA: University of California Press, 1988), p. 104.

6 Ibid., p. 92.

7 Robert E. Goodin, *No Smoking: The Ethical Issues*, p. 95.

8 See David Boaz (ed.), *The Crisis in Drug Prohibition* (Washington D. C.: Cato Institute, 1990).

9 Erich Goode, *Drugs in American Society*, p. 236.

10 Ibid., p. 275.

11 Mathea Falco, *The Making of a Drug-Free America: Programs that Work* (New York: Times Books, 1992).

12 Immanuel Kant, *Lectures on Ethics*, trans. L. Infield (New York: Harper Torchbooks, 1963), p. 118.

13 Joseph R. DesJardins and Ronald Duska, "Drug Testing in Employment," in J. R. DesJardins and J. J. McCall (eds.), *Contemporary Issues in Business Ethics* (Belmont, CA: Wadsworth, 1990), pp. 202–207.

14 David A. J. Richards, "Drug Use and the Rights of the Person," in S. Luper-Foy and C. Brown (eds.), *The Moral Life* (Fort Worth, TX: Harcourt Brace Jovanovich, 1992), p. 406.

CHAPTER 10   *Interpersonal Conflicts*

1 John Rawls, *A Theory of Justice* (Cambridge, MA: Harvard University Press, 1971), p. 531.

2 Friedrich Nietzsche, *Thus Spoke Zarathustra*, trans. W. Kaufmann (New York: Penguin, 1978), p. 100.

3 Max Scheler, *Ressentiment*, trans. W. W. Holdheim (New York: Schocken, 1972), p. 48.

4 Jean Hampton, "Forgiveness, Resentment and Hatred," in J. G. Murphy and J. Hampton, *Forgiveness and Mercy* (New York: Cambridge University Press, 1988), pp. 73–74.

5 Gray Cox, *The Ways of Peace* (New York: Paulist Press, 1986), p. 129.

6 Martin Benjamin, *Splitting the Difference: Compromise and Integrity in Ethics and Politics* (Lawrence, KS: University Press of Kansas, 1986), pp. 24–32.

7 John Sabini and Maury Silver, *Moralities of Everyday Life* (Oxford: Oxford University Press, 1982), p. 29.

8 Henry Fairlie, *The Seven Deadly Sins Today* (Notre Dame, IN: University of Notre Dame Press, 1979), pp. 67–68.

9 Immanuel Kant, *Lectures on Ethics*, trans. L. Infield (New York: Harper & Row, 1963), p. 218.

10 Eugene O'Neill, *The Iceman Cometh* (New York: Vintage, 1957), p. 239.

11 John F. Kennedy, *Profiles in Courage* (New York: Harper & Row, 1956), p. 17.

CHAPTER 11   *Prejudice*

1 Ralph Ellison, *Invisible Man* (New York: Vintage, 1972), p. 3.

2 Ibid., p. 4.

3 Ibid., p. 14.

4 Ibid.

5 Marilyn Frye, "Male Chauvinism—A Conceptual Analysis," in M. Vetterling-Braggin (ed.), *Sexist Language: A Modern Philosophical Analysis* (Totowa, NJ: Littlefield, Adams, 1981), p. 17.

6 Ibid., p. 18.

7 Ludwig Wittgenstein, *Philosophical Investigations*, 3rd ed., trans. G. E. M. Anscombe (New York: Macmillan, 1953), p. 115.

8 Francis Bacon, *Novum Organum*, T. Fowler (ed.) (Oxford: Oxford University Press, 1889).

9 Quoted from a study done by Sally Hacker and Joseph Schneider in 1972, in C. Miller and K. Swift, *Words and Women* (Garden City, NY: Anchor, 1976), p. 21.

10 Arthur Schopenhauer, *The World as Will and Representation*, trans. E. F. J. Payne (New York: Dover, 1969), Vol. I, pp. 58–61, Vol. II, pp. 91–101. Compare Mike W. Martin, "Humor and Aesthetic Enjoyment of Incongruities," in J. Morreall, *The Philosophy of Laughter and Humor*, pp. 172–186.

11 *Newsweek*, October 11, 1976.

12 James Boswell, *The Life of Samuel Johnson* (New York: Dell, 1960), p. 121. First published in 1791.

13 Richard A. Wasserstrom, "On Racism and Sexism," in R. A. Wasserstrom (ed.), Today's Moral Problems, 3rd ed. (New York: Macmillan, 1985), p. 7.

14 Ibid., p. 21.

15 Ibid., p. 28.

16 Elizabeth H. Wolgast, *Equality and the Rights of Women* (Ithaca, NY: Cornell University Press, 1980), pp. 33–34.

17 Alan Dundes, *Cracking Jokes: Studies of Sick Humor Cycles and Stereotypes* (Berkeley, CA: Ten Speed Press, 1987), p. 53.

18 Ibid., p. 105.

19 Ibid., p. 74.

20 Elizabeth Mehren, "'New Sexism': Men Cry Foul at Male Jokes," *Los Angeles Times* (December 14, 1987), part V, p. 1.

21 Charles S. Farrell, "Black Students Seen Facing 'New Racism' on Many Campuses," *The Chronicle of Higher Education*, vol. 34, no. 20 (January 27, 1988): 1.

CHAPTER 12   *Abortion*

1 *Roe v. Wade, United States Reports*, vol. 410 (1973), pp. 113–178.

2 Nancy (Ann) Davis, "Abortion," in L. C. Becker (ed.), *Encyclopedia of Ethics* (New York: Garland, 1992), pp. 2–6.

3 See Paul Ramsey, "The Morality of Abortion," in D. H. Labby (ed.), *Life or Death: Ethics and Options* (Seattle, WA: University of Washington Press, 1968); and John Noonan, "Abortion and the Catholic Church: A Summary History," *Natural Law Forum*, vol. 12 (1967): 125–131.

4 Don Marquis, "Why Abortion is Immoral," in S. J. Gold (ed.), *Moral Controversies: Race, Class, and Gender in Applied Ethics* (Belmont, CA: Wadsworth, 1993), p. 25. First published in *The Journal of Philosophy*, vol. 86 (1989): 183–202.

5 Ibid., p. 26.

6 Mary Anne Warren, "On the Moral and Legal Status of Abortion," in J. Feinberg (ed.), *The Problem of Abortion*, 2nd ed. (Belmont, CA: Wadsworth, 1984), pp. 111–112.

7 Michael Tooley, "In Defense of Abortion and Infanticide," in R. M. Baird and S. E. Rosenbaum (eds.), *The Ethics of Abortion* (Buffalo, NY: Prometheus, 1989), p. 49. First published in *Philosophy & Public Affairs*, vol. 2 (1972): 37–65.

8 See Baruch Brody, *Abortion and the Sanctity of Human Life: A Philosophical View* (Cambridge, MA: MIT Press, 1975).

9 Jane English, "Abortion and the Concept of a Person," in J. Feinberg (ed.), *The Problem of Abortion*, 2nd ed. (Belmont, CA: Wadsworth, 1984), p. 153. First published in the *Canadian Journal of Philosophy*, vol. 5 (1975): 233–243.

10 Judith Jarvis Thomson, "A Defense of Abortion," in J. Feinberg (ed.), *The Problem of Abortion*, p. 174. First published in *Philosophy & Public Affairs*, vol. 1 (1971): 47–66.

11 Jane English, "Abortion and the Concept of a Person," in J. Feinberg (ed.), *The Problem of Abortion*, pp. 158–9.

12 Martin Benjamin, *Splitting the Difference: Compromise and Integrity in Ethics and Politics* (Lawrence, KS: University Press of Kansas, 1990), pp. 151–171.

13 See Kristin Luker, *Abortion and the Politics of Motherhood* (Berkeley, CA: University of California Press, 1984).

14 For an example, see Beth Maschinot, "Compromising Positions," *In These Times*, vol. 10 (November 20–26, 1985): 4.

15 See R. M. Hare, "Abortion and the Golden Rule," *Philosophy and Public Affairs*, vol. 4 (1975): 201–222; and Harry J. Gensler, "A Kantian Argument Against Abortion," *Philosophical Studies*, vol. 49 (1986): 83–98.

16 Sidney Callahan, "Abortion and the Sexual Agenda," in R. M. Baird and S. E. Rosenbaum (eds.), *The Ethics of Abortion* (Buffalo, NY: Prometheus, 1989), p. 137. First published in *Commonweal* (25 April 1986): 232–238.

17 Anthony Weston, *Toward Better Problems: New Perspectives on Abortion, Animal Rights, the Environment and Justice* (Philadelphia, PA: Temple University Press, 1992), p. 55.

CHAPTER 13   *Rape and Sexual Harassment*

1 Lawrence Haworth, *Autonomy: An Essay in Philosophical Psychology and Ethics* (New Haven, CT: Yale University Press, 1986), p. 1.

2 Susan Griffin, *Rape: The Politics of Consciousness*, 3rd ed. (New York: Harper & Row, 1986), pp. 23–24.

3 William B. Sanders, *Rape and Woman's Identity* (Beverly Hills, CA: Sage, 1980), pp. 50–51.

4 Susan Brownmiller, *Against Our Will: Men, Women, and Rape* (New York: Simon & Schuster, 1975), p. 354.

5 Michael D. Bayles, "Coercive Offers and Public Benefits," *Personalist*, vol. 55 (1974): 142–143.

6 John C. Hughes and Larry May, "Sexual Harassment," *Social Theory and Practice*, vol. 6 (1980): 273–274.

7 Billie Wright Dziech and Linda Weiner, *The Lecherous Professor: Sexual Harassment on Campus* (Boston, MA: Beacon Press, 1984), p. 25.

8 Ibid., p. 77.

9 Robin Warshaw, *I Never Called It Rape: The Ms. Report on Recognizing, Fighting and Surviving Date and Acquaintance Rape* (New York: Harper & Row, 1988), pp. 29–30.

10 Patricia Yancey Martin and Robert A. Hummer, "Fraternities and Rape on Campus," in S. J. Gold (ed.), *Moral Controversies: Race, Class, and Gender in Applied Ethics* (Belmont, CA: Wadsworth, 1993), p. 324. First published in *Gender & Society*, 3 (1989): 457–473.

11 Ibid., pp. 331–332.

PART FOUR *Sexual Morality*

1 Michel Foucault, *The History of Sexuality*, Vol. I, trans. R. Hurley (New York: Vintage, 1980), pp. 155–156.

CHAPTER 14 *Sex and Love*

1 Marilyn French, *The Women's Room* (New York: Summit Books, 1977), pp. 361–362.

2 Ibid., p. 407.

3 Erich Fromm, *The Art of Loving* (New York: Harper & Row, 1956), pp. 38–39.

4 Shulamith Firestone, *The Dialectic of Sex: The Case for Feminist Revolution* (New York: Morrow, 1970), p. 145.

5 Ibid., p. 149.

6 Russell Vannoy, *Sex Without Love: A Philosophical Exploration* (Buffalo, NY: Prometheus, 1980), p. 26.

7 Roger Scruton, *Sexual Desire: A Moral Philosophy of the Erotic* (New York: Free Press, 1986), p. 30.

8 Ibid., p. 251.

9 Ibid., p. 337.

10 Ibid., p. 87.

11 Robert C. Solomon, "Love and Feminism," in R. Baker and F. Elliston (eds.), *Philosophy and Sex*, rev. ed. (Buffalo, NY: Prometheus, 1984), p. 66.

12 Stendhal (Marie Henri Beyle), *Love*, trans. G. Sale and S. Sale (New York: Penguin, 1975), p. 60.

13 David Henry Hwang, *M. Butterfly* (New York: Penguin, 1989).

14 Simone de Beauvoir, *The Second Sex* (New York: Vintage, 1952), p. 712.

15 Robert Nozick, *The Examined Life* (New York: Simon and Schuster, 1989), pp. 73–74.

CHAPTER 15   *Marriage and Adultery*

1 Shere Hite, *Women and Love: A Cultural Revolution in Progress* (New York: Knopf, 1987), p. 325.

2 Ibid.

3 John McMurtry, "Monogamy: A Critique," in R. Baker and F. Elliston (eds.), *Philosophy and Sex*, rev. ed. (Buffalo, NY: Prometheus, 1984), p. 111.

4 Ibid., p. 112.

5 Susan Moller Okin, *Justice, Gender, and the Family* (New York: Basic Books, 1989), pp. 135–136.

6 Francesca M. Cancian, *Love in America: Gender and Self-Development* (New York: Cambridge University Press, 1987), p. 3.

7 Ibid.

8 S. I. Benn, "Individuality, Autonomy and Community," in E. Kamenka (ed.), *Community as a Social Ideal* (London: Edward Arnold, 1982), p. 58.

9 John McMurtry, "Monogamy: A Critique," p. 111.

10 Ibid., p. 112. Italics deleted from original.

11 Ibid., p. 113.

12 Larry Martz, Vern E. Smith, Daniel Pedersen, Daniel Shapiro, Mark Miller, and Ginny Carroll, "God and Money," *Newsweek*, April 6, 1987, pp. 18–19.

13 Tom Morganthau, Margaret Garrard Warner, Howard Fineman, and Erik Calonius, "The Sudden Fall of Gary Hart," *Newsweek*, May 18, 1987, p. 23.

14 Richard Taylor, *Having Love Affairs* (Buffalo, NY: Prometheus, 1982), p. 12.

15 Ibid., p. 138.

16 Ibid., p. 158.

17 Ibid., p. 59.

18 Ibid., pp. 142–143.

19 Ibid., p. 146.

20 Jerome Neu, "Jealous Thoughts," in A. O. Rorty (ed.), *Explaining Emotions* (Berkeley, CA: University of California Press, 1980), pp. 454–455.

CHAPTER 16   *Homosexuality and Homophobia*

1 Frederick Suppe, "Curing Homosexuality," in R. Baker and F. Elliston (eds.), *Philosophy and Sex*, rev. ed. (Buffalo, NY: Prometheus, 1984), pp. 394–395.

2 Malcolm Boyd, *Take Off the Masks* (Philadelphia, PA: New Society, 1984), p. 78.

3 Ibid., p. 5.

4 Martina Navratilova and George Vecsey, *Martina* (New York: Ballantine, 1985), p. 154.

5 Lev. 18:22, King James version.

6 Rom. 1:26–27, King James version.

7 Saint Thomas Aquinas, *On the Truth of the Catholic Faith*, Book 3: *Providence*, Part 1, trans. V. J. Bourke (New York: Doubleday, 1956). Quoted in R. Baker and F. Elliston (eds.), *Philosophy and Sex*, rev. ed. (Buffalo, NY: Prometheus, 1984), p. 15.

8 Roger Scruton, *Sexual Desire: A Moral Philosophy of the Erotic* (New York: Free Press, 1986), pp. 307–308.

9 Adrienne Rich, "Compulsory Heterosexuality and Lesbian Existence," *SIGNS: Journal of Women in Culture and Society*, vol. 5 (1980). Reprinted in C. R. Stimpson and E. Spector (eds.), *Women: Sex and Sexuality* (Chicago: University of Chicago Press, 1980), pp. 81–82.

CHAPTER 17   *Pornography and Fantasy*

1 Helen E. Longino, "Pornography, Oppression, and Freedom: A Closer Look," in L. Lederer (ed.), *Take Back the Night: Women on Pornography* (New York: Morrow, 1980), p. 42.

2 Robin Morgan, "Theory and Practice: Pornography and Rape," in L. Lederer (ed.), *Take Back the Night*, pp. 134–140.

3 Beverly LaBelle, "Snuff—The Ultimate Woman-Hating," in L. Lederer (ed.), *Take Back the Night*, p. 274.

4 Nancy Friday, *My Secret Garden: Women's Sexual Fantasies* (New York: Pocket Books, 1973), p. 109.

5 Matt. 5:28–29, King James version.

6 Herbert Fingarette, "Real Guilt and Neurotic Guilt," in *On Responsibility* (New York: Basic Books, 1967), pp. 91–94.

7 "Excerpts from the Minneapolis Ordinance," in V. Burstyn (ed.), *Women Against Censorship* (Vancouver, British Columbia: Douglas & McIntyre, 1985), pp. 206–207.

PART FIVE   *Caring Relationships and Community*

1 David Hume, *An Enquiry Concerning the Principles of Morals*, J. B. Schneewind (ed.) (Indianapolis, IN: Hackett, 1983), pp. 16–17.

CHAPTER 18 *Parents and Children*

1 Franz Kafka, *Letter to His Father* (New York: Schocken, 1966), p. 7. For an illuminating discussion, see Alice Miller, *Thou Shalt Not Be Aware: Society's Betrayal of the Child*, trans. H. and H. Hannum (New York: New American Library, 1986).

2 Ibid., p. 21.

3 Ibid., p. 89.

4 Kenneth Keniston and The Carnegie Council on Children, *All Our Children: The American Family Under Pressure* (New York: Harcourt Brace Jovanovich, 1977), pp. 17–18.

5 Maya Angelou, *I Know Why the Caged Bird Sings* (New York: Bantam, 1969).

6 Natalie Abrams, "Problems in Defining Child Abuse and Neglect," in O. O'Neill and W. Ruddick (eds.), *Having Children: Philosophical and Legal Reflections on Parenthood* (New York: Oxford University Press, 1979), p. 160.

7 Cf. Claudia Card, "Gratitude and Obligation," *American Philosophical Quarterly*, vol. 25 (1988): 115–127.

8 Jane English, "What Do Grown Children Owe Their Parents?" in O. O'Neill and W. Ruddick (eds.), *Having Children* (New York: Oxford University Press, 1979), p. 351.

CHAPTER 19 *Friendship*

1 Lillian Hellman, *Pentimento* (New York: New American Library, 1974), p. 93.

2 Ibid., p. 96.

3 Ibid., p. 95.

4 Ibid., p. 85.

5 Marilyn Friedman, "Friendship and Moral Growth," *The Journal of Value Inquiry*, vol. 23 (1989): 7.

6 Ibid., p. 8.

7 David B. Annis, "The Meaning, Value, and Duties of Friendship," *American Philosophical Quarterly*, vol. 24 (1987): 352.

8 Ibid., p. 354.

9 Montaigne, "Of Friendship," in *The Complete Essays of Montaigne*, trans. D. M. Frame (Stanford, CA: Stanford University Press, 1971), pp. 141–142.

10 E. M. Forster, "What I Believe," in *Two Cheers for Democracy* (New York: Harcourt, Brace & World, 1951), pp. 68–69. For an illuminating discussion of betrayal of friends, see A. I. Melden, *Rights in Moral Lives* (Berkeley, CA: University of California Press, 1988), pp. 123–135.

11 E. M. Forster, *A Passage to India* (New York: Harcourt, Brace & World, 1924), p. 175.

12 James Rachels, *The Elements of Moral Philosophy*, 2nd ed. (New York: McGraw-Hill, 1993), p. 13.

13 Lawrence A. Blum, *Friendship, Altruism and Morality* (Boston, MA: Routledge & Kegan Paul, 1980), p. 76.

14 Aristotle, *Nicomachean Ethics*, trans. W. D. Ross, in R. McKeon (ed.), *The Basic Works of Aristotle* (New York: Random House, 1941), p. 1093.

15 Lillian B. Rubin, *Just Friends: The Role of Friendship in Our Lives* (New York: Harper and Row, 1985), pp. 60–61. (Italics removed.) Cf. Barry McCarthy, "Adult Friendships," in G. Graham and H. LaFollette (eds.), *Person to Person* (Philadelphia, PA: Temple University Press, 1989), 32–45.

CHAPTER 20 *Meaningful Work*

1 Studs Terkel, *Working* (New York: Avon Books, 1975), p. 1.

2 Ibid., pp. 1–2.

3 Ibid., p. 2.

4 Ibid.

5 Ibid., p. 390.

6 Ibid., p. 393.

7 Karl Marx, *Economic and Philosophical Manuscripts*, in E. Fromm, *Marx's Concept of Man*, trans. T. B. Bottomore (New York: Ungar, 1966), p. 98.

8 Quoted from the writings of the Reverend Richard Baxter by Max Weber, in *The Protestant Ethic and the Spirit of Capitalism*, trans. T. Parsons (New York: Scribner's, 1958), p. 162.

9 Gilbert C. Meilaender, "Friendship and Vocation," in *Friendship* (Notre Dame, IN: University of Notre Dame Press, 1981), p. 97.

10 Craig K. Ihara, "Collegiality as a Professional Virtue," in A. Flores (ed.), *Professional Ideals* (Belmont, CA: Wadsworth, 1988), p. 60.

11 Josiah Royce, *The Philosophy of Loyalty*, excerpted in J. K. Roth (ed.), *The Philosophy of Josiah Royce* (Indianapolis, IN: Hackett, 1982), p. 279.

12 Ibid., p. 281.

13 John Ladd, "Loyalty," in P. Edwards (ed.), *The Encyclopedia of Philosophy*, vol. 5 (New York: Macmillan, 1967), p. 98.

14 Cf. Ronald Duska, *Whistleblowing and Employee Loyalty*, excerpted in J. Halberstam (ed.), *Virtues and Values* (Englewood Cliffs, NJ: Prentice-Hall, 1988), pp. 246–251.

15 From Dan Applegate's memo, quoted by P. Eddy, E. Potter, and B. Page, *Destination Disaster* (New York: New York Times Book Co., 1976), p. 185.

16 Norman S. Care, "Career Choice," *Ethics,* vol. 94 (1984): 298.

17 Hastings Rashdall, "Vocation," in *The Theory of Good and Evil,* vol. 2 (Oxford: Clarendon Press, 1907), pp. 123–124.

18 Cf. Peter A. French, *Ethics in Government* (Englewood Cliffs, NJ: Prentice-Hall, 1983), pp. 5–6.

19 Bernard Williams, "A Critique of Utilitarianism," in J. J. C. Smart and B. Williams, *Utilitarianism For and Against* (Cambridge: Cambridge University Press, 1973), pp. 97–98.

CHAPTER 21   *Community Service*

1 Brian O'Connell, "What Colleges Ought to Do to Instill a Voluntary Spirit in Young Adults," *The Chronicle of Higher Education* (April 15, 1987): 104. Robert L. Payton offers an overview of the importance of philanthropy, including a version of the definition of philanthropy adopted here, in *Philanthropy: Voluntary Action for the Public Good* (New York: Macmillan, 1988).

2 Jane Addams, *Twenty Years at Hull-House* (New York: New American Library, 1981), p. 92.

3 Ibid.

4 Robert N. Bellah, Richard Madsen, William M. Sullivan, Ann Swidler, and Steven M. Tipton, *Habits of the Heart: Individualism and Commitment in American Life* (Berkeley, CA: University of California, 1985), p. 162.

5 Peter Singer, "Famine, Affluence, and Morality," in W. Aiken and H. La Follette (eds.), *World Hunger and Moral Obligation* (Englewood Cliffs, NJ: Prentice-Hall, 1977), p. 24.

6 Ibid., p. 26.

7 Immanuel Kant, *The Doctrine of Virtue,* trans. M. J. Gregor (Philadelphia, PA: University of Pennsylvania Press, 1964), p. 21.

8 David Heyd, *Supererogation* (Cambridge: Cambridge University Press, 1982), p. 115.

9 James D. Wallace, *Virtues and Vices* (Ithaca, NY: Cornell University Press, 1978), p. 135.

10 Mark 12:41–44, King James version.

11 Brian O'Connell, "What Colleges Ought to Do ... ", p. 104.

12 Ralph Waldo Emerson, "Self-Reliance," in R. Bellah et al. (eds.), *Individualism and Commitment in American Life* (New York: Harper & Row, 1987), p. 59.

13 John O'Connor, "Philanthropy and Selfishness," in E. F. Paul et al. (eds.), *Beneficence, Philanthropy, and the Public Good* (New York: Basil Blackwell, 1987), p. 114.

PART SIX   *Animals and the Environment*

1 Victor Hugo, *En Voyage, Alpes et Pyrenees* (Paris: J. Hetzel, 1890), pp. 180–181. Quoted by Holmes Rolston III, as the book epigraph for *Environmental Ethics: Duties to and Values in the Natural World* (Philadelphia, PA: Temple University Press, 1988).

CHAPTER 22   *Animals*

1 John Steinbeck, *Travels with Charley* (New York: Bantam, 1963), p. 8.

2 Ibid., p. 163.

3 Ibid., p. 33.

4 Ibid., p. 9.

5 Mary Midgley, *Animals and Why They Matter* (Athens, GA: University of Georgia Press, 1984), p. 31.

6 René Descartes, *Discourse on Method*, excerpted in T. Regan and P. Singer (eds.), *Animal Rights and Human Obligations* (Englewood Cliffs, NJ: Prentice-Hall, 1976), p. 62.

7 Benedict de Spinoza, *The Ethics*, trans. R. H. M. Elwes (New York: Dover, 1955), Proposition 37, note 1.

8 Immanuel Kant, "Duties Towards Animals and Spirits," in *Lectures on Ethics*, trans. L. Infield (New York: Harper & Row, 1963), pp. 239–240.

9 Jeremy Bentham, *Introduction to the Principles of Morals and Legislation* (New York: Hafner, 1948), p. 311n. First published in 1789.

10 Peter Singer, *Animal Liberation*, rev. ed. (New York: Avon Books, 1990), p. 6.

11 Ibid., p. i.

12 Ibid., pp. 82–83.

13 II Sam. xii:3, King James version. Discussed in Mary Midgley, *Animals*, p. 116.

14 Jeremy Bentham, *Introduction to the Principles of Morals and Legislation*. Quoted in Peter Singer, *Animal Liberation*, p. 210.

15 Peter Singer, *Animal Liberation*, pp. 121–128.

16 Ibid., pp. 47–48.

CHAPTER 23   *The Environment*

1 William T. Blackstone, "Ethics and Ecology," in W. M. Hoffman and J. M. Moore (eds.), *Business Ethics*, 2nd ed. (New York: McGraw-Hill, 1990), p. 473.

2 Cf. Gregory Kavka, "The Futurity Problem," in E. Partridge (ed.), *Responsibilities to Future Generations* (Buffalo, NY: Prometheus, 1980).

3 Thomas E. Hill, Jr., "Ideals of Human Excellence and Preserving Natural Environments," in *Autonomy and Self-Respect* (Cambridge: Cambridge University Press, 1991), p. 104.

4 Ibid., p. 108.

5 Albert Schweitzer, *The Philosophy of Civilization* (Tallahassee, FL: University Presses of Florida, 1981), p. 309. First published 1949.

6 Ibid., p. 310.

7 Kenneth Goodpaster, "On Being Morally Considerable," in S. J. Armstrong and R. G. Botzler (eds.), *Environmental Ethics: Divergence and Convergence* (New York: McGraw-Hill, 1993), p. 352.

8 Aldo Leopold, *A Sand County Almanac* (New York: Ballantine, 1970), p. 239. First published 1949.

9 Ibid., p. 262.

10 J. Baird Callicott, "Environmental Ethics," in L. C. Becker (ed.), *Encyclopedia of Ethics*, Vol. 1 (New York: Garland, 1992), pp. 313–314.

11 Paul W. Taylor, *Respect for Nature: A Theory of Environmental Ethics* (Princeton, NJ: Princeton University Press, 1986), p. 121.

12 Garrett Hardin, "Tragedy of the Commons," *Science*, vol. 162 (13 Dec 1968): 1243–1248.

13 R. Gordon Cummings, *Five Years of a Hunter's Life in the Far Interior of South Africa* (1850). Quoted in R. Carrington, *Elephants* (Chatto & Windus, 1958), p. 154; in M. Midgley, *Animals and Why They Matter* (Athens, GA: University of Georgia Press, 1984), pp. 14–15.

14 Holmes Rolston III, "Challenges in Environmental Ethics," in D. E. Cooper and J. A. Palmer (eds.), *The Environment in Question: Ethics and Global Issues* (London: Routledge, 1992), p. 139.

15 Rosemary Ruether, *New Woman/New Earth: Sexist Ideologies and Human Liberation* (New York: Seabury Press, 1975), p. 204. Quoted by K. J. Warren, "Feminism and Ecology: Making Connections," *Environmental Ethics*, vol. 9 (1987): 3–20.

Index